W9-CNN-530

# World Agriculture: Toward 2000

## An FAO Study

The present volume was originally issued for the 24th Session of the FAO Conference, Rome, 7–26 November 1987, as document C 87/27. The version at hand contains some revisions and updates to reflect the Conference discussions and more recent information.

# World Agriculture: Toward 2000

## An FAO Study

Edited by

Nikos Alexandratos

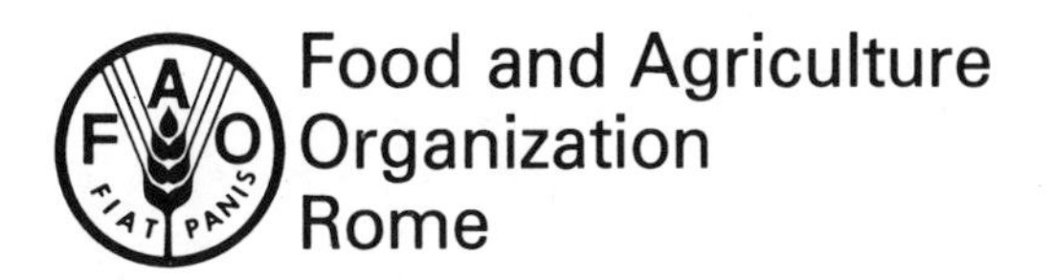

Food and Agriculture
Organization
Rome

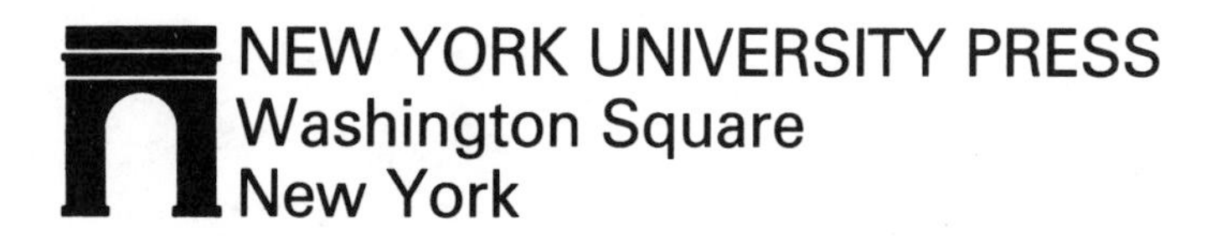

NEW YORK UNIVERSITY PRESS
Washington Square
New York

First published in the U.S.A in 1988 by
New York University Press
Washington Square
New York, NY 10003



The designations 'developed' and 'developing' economies are intended for statistical convenience and do not necessarily express a judgement about the stage reached by a particular country or area in the development process.

The designations employed and the presentation of material in this publication do not imply the expression of any opinion whatsoever on the part of the Food and Agriculture Organization of the United Nations concerning the legal status of any country, territory, city or area or of its authorities, or concerning the delimitation of its frontiers or boundaries.

**Library of Congress Cataloging-in-Publication Data**
World agriculture: towards 2000: an FAO study/edited by Nikos
Alexandratos.
p. cm.
Bibliography: p.
Includes index.
ISBN 0-8147-0592-8
1. Food supply—Forecasting. 2. Agriculture—Economic aspects—
Forecasting. 3. Agriculture—Forecasting. 4. Produce trade—
Forecasting. I. Alexandratos. Nikos. II. Food and Agriculture
Organization of the United Nations.
HD9000.5.W564 1988
338.1—dc19

88-21479
CIP

Typeset by Joshua Associates Ltd, Oxford
Printed in Great Britain

# Contents

# List of tables

# List of figures

# List of boxes

# Preface

*By the Director-General of FAO*

We live in times of rapid change when current policy choices need the framework of a longer term perspective. In agriculture, decisions made today concerning such matters as investment, land use, human resources development, research and technology, or trade and price policies will frequently exert their full effects only much later.

The FAO is in a unique position to view food and agriculture in this longer run and to build up a global assessment which systematically integrates detailed projections for individual countries. The present report is a revision and updating of the study *Agriculture: Toward 2000* submitted to the 1979 FAO Conference session and published in a shorter form in 1981. It analyses and as far as possible quantifies major changes likely to emerge in world agriculture, forestry and fisheries by the end of the century. These global perspectives on production, consumption and trade and the light which they throw on future policy issues are intended to help FAO member governments in making their own choices as well as providing an essential background to international discussions and negotiations concerning agriculture.

The growth rates of agricultural output per caput have improved in the last ten years for the developing countries in the aggregate and for a great many individual nations—although not for most countries in sub-Saharan Africa. This remarkable achievement must be further built on, and where growth rates are still inadequate, their improvement should be sought as a top priority. This is the essential basis for the continuation and strengthening of trends towards better nutrition for a developing world which will be faced with the need to provide food for over 1 billion more people by the year 2000 than in the mid-1980s.

Against a substantial achievement of a more ample diet for the majority of the world's population, food supplies per caput in the low-income countries other than China were not significantly different in 1983/5 from those of 15 years earlier. The estimated numbers of undernourished increased, not fell, over those years. The unnecessary tragedy of widespread hunger remains and for many developing countries it must be faced against an unfavourable international background: real prices of most commodities at their lowest post-war level, slow economic growth of the industrialized countries, agricultural trade in disarray as a consequence of rising protection and export subsidies of industrialized countries, and heavy burdens of debt servicing. For sub-Saharan Africa, recovery from the recent famine and the underlying economic and agricultural deterioration is particularly difficult.

Developing countries vary greatly with respect to their food and agricultural sectors. Both production performance and demands made on their agricultural sector differ widely and may change considerably over time. While production growth in some countries will be constrained predominantly by technological and cost considerations, in others the lack of adequate demand will be the limiting factor. Demand will be greatly influenced by changes in population, in income growth and in the international conditions which affect export markets.

The food and agricultural sector should continue to make a considerable contribution to economic growth and better nutrition. The growth rate of agricultural output per caput in the developing world is projected as being maintained. Three figures alone illustrate the magnitude of the projected changes for the developing countries by the year 2000 as compared with 1983/5: agricultural production would be 60 percent higher; average per caput food availabilities would be 2620 calories a day compared with 2420 calories at present; and net cereal imports would increase by 40 million tonnes to a total of 110 million tonnes. Despite this last increase, the study envisages a virtual halt to the serious decline in the self-sufficiency of the developing countries which has been under way since the early 1970s. The study dispels any idea that increases in production can be achieved cheaply. The cumulative total investment in the agricultural sector from 1982/4 to 2000, estimated conservatively, amounts to nearly $1500 billion (in 1980 prices).

Alleviation of hunger is a matter not only of augmenting food supplies but also of ensuring access to food by the poor, through an increase in their purchasing power. Policies that sustain the momentum of growth in production should therefore go hand in hand with greater efforts to raise the incomes of the small and marginal farmers and to expand employment opportunities for the landless. The study analyses and presents options for policy measures needed to meet the dual challenge of ensuring adequate supply and of improving access to food by all.

While poverty can be significantly lessened by such determined action, the problem cannot be solved exclusively within agriculture. This sector alone cannot provide enough employment and income. Agricultural development and industrialization are complementary and mutually reinforcing. In rural areas, there is great scope for the expansion of agro-industries. But industrialization must not be pursued through policies which depress incentives to farmers and starve the sector of its input requirements. The study points out that the importance of the linkages of agriculture to the economy as a whole have often been seriously underestimated.

The question of the links between technology and ecology is also addressed. A careful assessment concludes that the projected expansion of output, which must now depend increasingly on technological progress in raising yields rather than on expanding cultivated areas, is compatible with safeguarding the environment. For this fundamental requirement to be met, however, more resources must be devoted to conservation and improved farming and forestry methods, particularly in large areas of the developing world where the natural environment is highly vulnerable to damage as production expands.

Developed countries also face severe and complex problems in their farm sectors. The study puts into perspective the likely extent of an adjustment to production trends in developed market-economy countries as a group. A slowing down of their production growth, not its cessation, is the long-term requirement. It is earnestly hoped that measures to curb their overabundant production, combined with the lowering of protectionist barriers, will contribute to greater agricultural price and trade stability as well as to greater export opportunities for developing countries. Such an improvement in trading conditions would greatly reinforce the efforts being made by developing countries to promote economic growth. These efforts must also be underpinned by an adequate flow of financial and technical assistance from developed nations.

The elimination of hunger remains the central challenge facing global policy-makers in food and agriculture. The developing countries themselves bear the primary responsibility for bringing about a further strengthening of their productive capacity while simultaneously generating effective demand among those still short of food. At the same time, their efforts alone cannot meet this challenge. A global problem demands a global solution and the combined efforts of all partners in development. The international community must play a crucial and supporting role in promoting a favourable external environment, which will contribute to an equitable and balanced growth of the world food and agriculture economy.

**Edouard Saouma**
*Director-General of FAO*

# Explanatory notes

## Symbols and units

| | |
|---|---|
| ha | hectare |
| kg | kilogram |
| $ | US dollar |
| tonne | metric ton (1000 kilograms) |
| billion | thousand million |
| p.a. | per annum |
| calories | kilocalories (kcal) |
| $m^3$ | cubic metre |
| fob | free on board |
| cif | cost, insurance, freight |

## Time periods

| | |
|---|---|
| 1985 | calendar year |
| 1983/5 | average for the three years centred on 1984 (1983–5), except if specified otherwise |
| 1961–85 | period from 1961 to 1985 |
| 1983/5–2000 | period from the three year average 1983/5 to 2000 |

## Abbreviations

| | |
|---|---|
| BMR | Basal Metabolic Rate |
| CGIAR | Consultative Group on International Agricultural Research |
| CPEs | Centrally Planned Economies |
| DMEs | Developed Market Economies |
| ECDC | Economic Cooperation among Developing Countries |
| EEC | European Economic Community |
| GDP | Gross Domestic Product |
| GSP | Generalized System of Preferences |
| HYV | High Yielding Varieties |
| ICA | International Commodity Agreement |
| IDS | International Development Strategy of the United Nations |
| IPC | Integrated Programme for Commodities (UNCTAD) |
| OCA | Official Commitments to Agriculture |
| SSR | Self-Sufficiency Ratio |
| WCARRD | World Conference on Agrarian Reform and Rural Development |

(Note: other abbreviations are explained in the text)

## Countries and country groups

See Appendix 1 for a list of countries and the standard country groups used in the report. Note that in Chapter 5 (Forestry), 'Africa' includes sub-Saharan Africa and North Africa, and 'Asia' the Near East and Asia as defined in the Appendix.

## Commodities and commodity groups

See Appendix 1 for a list of the standard commodities and commodity groups used in the report.

## Land definitions

The *arable area* is the physical land area used for growing crops (both annual and perennial). In any given year, part of the arable area may not be cropped (fallow) or may be cropped more than once (double cropping). The area actually cropped and harvested in any given year is the *harvested area*. The harvested area expressed as a percentage of the arable area is the *cropping intensity*. The *potential arable area* consists of all land area which is at present arable or is potentially arable, i.e. is suitable for growing crops when developed.

## Data sources

All data are derived from FAO sources unless specified otherwise.

# Acknowledgements

This study is the product of common work of many units and staff of FAO as well as of persons from outside FAO. It was prepared by a team led by Nikos Alexandratos, Chief, Global Perspective Studies Unit, under the direct supervision of Nurul Islam, then Assistant Director-General, Economic and Social Policy Department. The team received valuable guidance and advice from Milan Trkulja, Special Assistant to the Director-General.

The main contributors, other than the team leader, included: *FAO Staff*: Jelle Bruinsma (full-time member of the team, responsible for modelling and quantitative analysis), David Norse (coordination of agronomic contributions; Chs. 10 and 11), R. J. Perkins (coordination of commodity analysis contributions; Ch. 7), Howard Hjort (contributions to policy analysis aspects of the study, particularly to Ch. 8), Philip Wardle (Ch. 5) and John Naylor (Ch. 6). *External*: J. P. O'Hagan, Janos Hrabovszky, Kutlu Somel, Raghav Gaiha, Trevor Young, Steven Magiera and Alan Piazza. Many other persons both within and outside FAO contributed to the work of the team or provided useful comments and suggestions for improvements. Maria Grazia Ottaviani and Isabel Reyes provided efficient computational and statistical assistance. Monica Brand assisted by Silvia Moroni provided secretarial assistance to the team.

# 1 Introduction and overview

## Scope and nature of the study

This report, a revised and updated version of the 'Agriculture: Toward 2000' (*AT 2000*) study submitted to the 1979 Conference of FAO and the shorter version published in 1981 (FAO 1979, 1981), examines world agricultural perspectives and policy issues for the 15 years between the mid-1980s and 2000, with particular attention to the developing countries. The study examines individually 94 developing countries accounting for all but 1.5 percent of developing country population. The coverage of the study now includes China, although the unavailability as yet of detailed data on land use limits the depth of production analysis for this country. Thirty-four developed countries are included, but their projected production is limited to trend analysis by major groups of countries and to analysis of adjusted output levels required to arrive at approximate world balance of supply and demand. Demand projections for developed countries are in the same detail as for developing countries.

Drawing fully on the economic and technical disciplines and field experience of FAO, the report therefore represents a global assessment of possible future world and country-group production, trade and nutrition. Within this framework of quantification and analysis, selected issues of food and agriculture with which countries must grapple in the years ahead are examined.

The present study, while using the same methodology of the earlier study, has a 15-year in place of 20-year perspective, and its base period of course encompasses more recent years. There is, however, a more fundamental difference. A major purpose of the earlier study had been to explore the implications of a rate of growth of agricultural production in developing countries as close as FAO considered feasible to the overall 4 percent growth target for agriculture of the United Nations International Development Strategy (IDS). A prerequisite for the resultant 3.7 percent agricultural sector growth rate for developing countries (Scenario A of the earlier *AT 2000*) was the assumption of the IDS high 7 percent annual growth in real terms in their gross domestic product (GDP) and a 3.8 percent growth in the GDP of developed countries.

These assumptions of high economic growth rates for the remainder of the century now look overly optimistic. A consensus exists that economic growth in the years ahead is likely to be relatively moderate in most regions and certainly actual growth rates during 1980–6 were low: 3.5 percent in developing countries, or 2.2 percent excluding China, and 2.5 percent in developed countries.

These significant deviations of actual developments from the earlier growth assumptions and revised views as to the future make it necessary to take a fresh look at world food and agriculture prospects to the end of the century. The impact of global recession which has changed conditions significantly since the earlier study was completed in 1979—especially for export-oriented countries in Latin America and Africa—must be taken into account in the assessment of future prospects.

The present study could therefore be limited to the one scenario which, compared with the main scenario of the earlier study, postulates the less rapid overall economic growth which is now generally forecast and hence leads to a slower expansion of demand facing agriculture. The growth rate of population is also forecast to be lower than that used nearly ten years ago. For the 90 developing countries of the earlier study, the year-2000 population is now forecast to be 3485 million compared with 3630 million then projected. Both these factors would lead to a more moderate rate of increase in agricultural output.

Another change from the earlier study is that the main results implied by a continuation of past trends in production and consumption are presented only very summarily. A number of factors which strongly influenced historical trends of agriculture—the rise in incomes, the overall international economic climate and the associated potential for expanded trade, the policy attitude to agriculture in many countries and the pace and patterns of spread of improved technology—are assessed to be very different in the future, particularly as compared with the 1970s. Extrapolations of these past trends are therefore of somewhat limited value as a guide to the future. Nevertheless, they do give a broad indication of adjustments which must be made in order to avoid undesirable or unrealistic outcomes. In addition, the study makes considerable use of the extrapolation of past trends in the examination of complex situations of individual commodities.

## Methodology and main assumptions of the scenario

The scenario is a quantification for agriculture of a moderate growth path of world economic development. The methodology, which is complex and data intensive, is similar to that employed in the earlier study, although experience has enabled a number of detailed improvements to be introduced.

Projections of domestic demand are first made (by country and commodity) on the basis of the GDP and population growth projections (given in Table 3.2). Initial assumptions follow as to national self-sufficiency goals of developing countries. The implied tentative production 'targets' are then evaluated (and modified as required) for their technical and economic feasibility taking into account the full range of relevant factors: agricultural resources, technology, productivity trends, input requirements and required policies. In parallel, assessments are made of possible production trends in each developed country to define possible net trade positions. Implied import requirements and export availabilities of all countries are aggregated to form an initial estimate of world balances. Further iterations ensure that adjusted exports and imports of each commodity are brought into balance at the world level, with related production levels respecting explicit technological and resource constraints in developing countries and taking account of explicit assumptions as to modifications of the trend outcomes in developed countries. In particular, it is assumed that the developed market economies as a group will moderate their import substitution policies so as to avoid further declines of their net imports from the developing countries of competing commodities such as sugar and vegetable oils. This issue is at the heart of the current debate concerning agricultural policy reform in the industrialized countries. Consequently, a very wide range of outcomes is possible ranging from the developed market economies reverting to being large net importers of these commodities to becoming net exporters.

The quantification is in terms of physical units which are aggregated using world average producer prices of 1979/81 to derive total agricultural production, consumption and trade. The analysis covers demand for and production of 33 individual crop and six livestock products (listed in the Appendix). For the 93 developing countries of the study (excluding China) production assessments for these commodities were carried out in terms of six agro-ecological classes of rain-fed and irrigated land and the associated yields and input requirements. A summary account of the methodology is given in the Appendix.

The main findings of the study are given very briefly below. It is stressed that a summary, referring mostly to regions or to large groups of countries, inevitably masks the realities of wide divergences between countries within regions or groups.

## The past 25 years

The past does not determine the future, but it does strongly influence developments and the concerns of policy. The study therefore begins with a glance backwards.

*A better fed world but with exceptions*: The outstanding fact in food and agriculture is that the past 25 years have brought a better-fed world despite an increase of 1.8 billion in world population. Average food availability rose from 2320 calories per caput in 1961/3 to 2660 calories in 1983/5. Earlier fears of chronic food shortages over much of the world proved unfounded. But the exceptions are many and various. In the low-income countries as a group, apart from China and India, per caput food supplies in 1983/5 were no higher than those 15 years earlier. Some 350 millions or 510 millions (alternative estimates) remain seriously undernourished. The problem of hunger was solved only for the majority of the world's population.

*Productivity transformed agriculture*: The world's expanding population could be better fed because agriculture was being transformed into a dynamic productive sector, first in the developed market economies but increasingly in the developing countries also, where the use of biochemical technology starting in the 1960s was the watershed. Rice yields rose by 41 percent in developing countries between 1969/71 and 1983/5, and wheat yields by 77 percent. Labour productivity in those countries rose by a half, although in absolute terms it is still only a fraction of that in developed countries.

Regional production growth rates in the developing world all averaged around 3 percent a year during 1961–85, with the exception of sub-Saharan Africa, where sluggish growth in the 1960s worsened in the 1970s and, aggravated by droughts, became a full-scale crisis in the early 1980s. In 1980–5, only Asia exceeded the long-term growth rate. All regions contained a number of fast- and slow-growing countries. Output in developed countries grew at 2 percent a year, the rate of expansion falling sharply for centrally planned economies in the 1970s and in the first half of the 1980s in the market economies. The latter reduction, however, was not enough to prevent the building-up of large surpluses.

*Increased reliance on imports of food*: This was a feature of the world food system. In 1961/3, world trade was 8 percent of production but had risen to 12 percent by 1983/5. The increase took place in both developed and developing countries, with the latter approximately doubling imports per caput in the 1970s. However, this source of more ample food supplies could, by and large, be exploited only by the middle-income developing countries, including oil-exporting countries. In the low-income countries the increase was negligible, apart from some rise in imports by China.

*Recognition of need for policy change*: For different reasons, most countries began to change their policies bearing on agriculture. In developing countries, most national policies, up to quite recently, gave priority to industrialization. Consequently, widespread bias against agriculture brought serious distortions and checked economic growth. All regions were affected, Africa most and Asia least. The threat of food shortages in the 1970s and balance-of-payments problems and debt crises of the 1980s have led to policy reforms which recognize the essential role of agriculture in economic growth. This has been a fundamental change in policy emphasis.

Developed market economy countries, too, are now being forced into policy reform in order to solve problems of subsidized production growing in excess of demand. The adjustment, long foreseen by FAO (FAO 1972), was postponed by the temporary surge in import demand in the 1970s. Policy change in centrally planned countries is taking the form of some relaxation of detailed central direction and more exposure to market forces.

*Rural poverty persisted*: The long-standing problem of rural poverty in developing countries was rendered more acute by the need to absorb 300 million more workers. Highly unequal land ownership remained a fundamental cause in many countries. The World Conference on Agrarian Reform and Rural Development in 1979 gave agreed signposts, but decisive action is still generally awaited. In a number of developed countries, policies which raised producer prices so as to try to assure farm/non-farm income parity contributed to production imbalances without solving substantially farm income problems within agriculture.

*Agriculture became more closely integrated in the overall economy*: Within countries, a rising share of production became marketed, more off-farm inputs were purchased, more institutional credit was used and more off-farm income was earned by agricultural households. These increased links with the monetary economy and the rising share of output traded internationally made the agricultural sector more open to external economic influence. The full bearing of this increasing interdependence was not always appreciated.

*Consequently, international economic conditions have recently become a powerful influence on agriculture*: Characteristics of the 1970s and early 1980s—instability, debt, recession, fluctuations in exchange rates, good commodity prices and then a slump—inevitably affected agriculture. Heavily indebted countries with high dependence on agricultural exports were worst hit—in regional terms, Latin America and Africa. Government expenditures on agriculture and food subsidies were reduced. In general, however, agriculture emerged relatively unscathed basically because food demand was maintained except in the worst-affected countries, and devaluations and support measures gave some protection to producer incomes.

*Agriculture featured prominently in international cooperation efforts*: Examples of these are the UN International Development Strategy, summit meetings and various forms of technical cooperation. But progress was negligible as regards agricultural trade and inadequate as regards food security, while development assistance never reached agreed targets. Agricultural trade issues remained basically unresolved in GATT chiefly because of the insistence of some developed countries on their right to pursue heavily protectionist policies. Few commodity agreements were negotiated and fewer succeeded.

*Food security*: This became a leading issue following the world food crisis of 1972–4. The World Food Conference of 1974 sought to abolish hunger by a combination of national and international measures, including a commitment on food aid. Some major countries did not find the goal of a formal stock policy at a global level acceptable. Increasing experience with various institutional arrangements has, however, led to a better understanding of food security but meeting any food crisis still depends essentially on effective *ad hoc* action by individual countries. The recent African famines pointed again to the urgent need for effective national and international arrangements for quicker action.

*Agriculture fared well in assistance to developing countries*: The share of the sector in total official commitments rose from 12 percent in 1974/5 to between 18 and 20 percent in the early 1980s. The focus of this assistance has been increasingly on low-income countries. The total flow of assistance has however been approximately unchanged over the 1981–5 period. Food aid has accounted for 9–15 percent of total official development assistance since the mid-1970s and provided 14–24 percent of the cereal imports of low-income, food-deficit countries. It played a critical role in the African famines. The need to prevent food aid from depressing producer prices in recipient countries is still an issue, although the means of doing so are now better understood.

*Agricultural exports became a weaker and more uncertain engine of growth*: Large and unforeseen changes took place in agricultural trade after the early 1970s. A surge in world import demand, particularly by developing and centrally planned countries, was met by an expansion of exports by the developed market economies. Developing country exports grew only sluggishly and their net agricultural trade surplus deteriorated. Then a sudden halt in demand growth after 1980, despite increasingly depressed prices, brought stagnation to world agricultural trade. Products exported by developed countries were increasingly heavily subsidized, and this cut-throat competition drove international prices down to the lowest levels of the postwar period in real terms. Tropical exports not in direct competition with supplies from developed countries tended to be in over-supply and consequently their prices also fell.

*The overall assessment for agriculture in the past 25 years is positive*: A remarkable and sustained improvement in food supplies and the extension to all parts of the world of more productive farming systems was the essence of the achievement. Nevertheless, a number of serious problems were left unsolved: access of the very poor to food, trade and related production adjustments, and the avoidance of environmental damage as production pressure on resources rises, are major issues. The rehabilitation and development of sub-Saharan African agriculture is a critical regional problem with international dimensions.

## World food and agriculture to the year 2000

Following brief consideration of the outcomes of the continuation of past trends, the main future prospects are given below, first for developing and then for developed countries.

*Projections of trends emphasize the need for adjustments*: The continuation into the future of past trends would, in many instances, exacerbate present problems and disparities or imply unrealistic outcomes.

Developing countries' agricultural production would rise by 3.5 percent a year, compared with 3.2 for 1961–85, because of the increasing weight in total production of the fast-growing countries. Mere extrapolation of trends implies that production growth rates of between 4 and 7 percent would continue in a number of countries, including China, for 15 years despite more slowly growing population and demand and constraints of resources and technology. Low-income countries would continue with too sluggish a growth rate of around 2.5 percent. Sub-Saharan African output would grow more slowly than population.

The continuation of consumption trends would bear particularly hard on the group of low-income countries apart from China. By the year 2000, their per caput availability of calories would be only just over 2000, not significantly different from now and only 71 percent of the average level of middle-income countries. The numbers of undernourished would rise by over 100 million.

The existing commodity-surplus problem would worsen. Extrapolated trends in production, including an expansion of output in developed countries at 2 percent a year, would result in cereal surpluses of over 200 million tonnes a year by the year 2000 and export availabilities of other products, including sugar, milk, meat and vegetable oils, far in excess of import requirements. Such projected imbalances are of course quite unrealistic and will not materialize; policy- and price-induced changes will bring supply and demand more nearly into equilibrium. The trend projections, however, do underline the seriousness of the need for orderly adjustment of past production patterns and point to the products involved.

From this point onwards, the study therefore consists of reasoned outcomes of the future which embody significant adjustments in many cases from the outcomes of trend extrapolations.

### Scenario results: developing countries

*Nutrition improves, but not everywhere*: Further increases in food demand and consumption would continue to improve nutrition in the developing countries.

For the 94 developing countries together, average per caput food availability for direct human consumption would rise from 2420 calories in 1983/5 to 2620 calories in the year 2000. The gains registered in the last few years by some major low-income countries (e.g. China and India) can be expected to be consolidated and levels improved further. Increases in food consumption in the middle-income countries (e.g. Near East/North Africa, Latin America) will be much less pronounced than in the 1970s, mostly because of slower growth in incomes and reduced import capacity, but also because in some of these countries food consumption levels are already high. The regional data on food-calorie availability per caput are given in Table 1.1.

**Table 1.1** Food availability: calories per caput per day

| | 1983/5 | 2000 |
|---|---|---|
| Africa (sub-Saharan) | 2050 | 2190 |
| Near East/N. Africa | 2980 | 3100 |
| Asia | 2380 | 2610 |
| Latin America | 2700 | 2910 |
| Low-income countries (excluding China) | 2130 | 2350 |

The slow-down in total demand for all food and agricultural commodities in developing countries from 3.5 percent a year during 1961–85 to 3.1 percent for the period from 1983/5 to 2000 leaves the projected growth in per caput demand virtually unchanged at 1.2 percent.

Some low-income countries with currently very low food availabilities per caput would make little progress, mainly because of unfavourable overall economic growth prospects and continued high and, in some cases, accelerating population growth. In particular, many countries in sub-Saharan Africa can be expected to have in the year 2000 food availability levels not much above those of the pre-drought years. The problem of improving food consumption levels in these countries assumes, therefore, centre stage in any debate on the future of the world food economy, together with that of maintaining the momentum of progress in the other developing countries.

*Hunger persists*: In the Fifth World Food Survey, FAO estimated that between 335 million and 500 million people in the developing countries were undernourished in 1979/81. During the first half of the 1980s, the African drought and the overall economic crisis added to the number of undernourished people. The scenario projections imply that the persistence of very low levels in per caput food supplies in a number of low-income countries, particularly in sub-Saharan Africa is a real possibility and, in combination with their rapid population growth, would result in further increases of the undernourished in the region and in the developing countries as a whole, despite projected modest declines in Asia, the other region with high incidence of undernutrition. Thus, for the developing countries as a whole—outside the Asian centrally planned economies (CPEs)—numbers with per caput calorie levels below the threshold of 1.4 times the basal metabolic rate (BMR)—roughly 1520 calories—could rise somewhat from the present 510 million to 530 million in the year 2000, although their percentage of the total population would decline. Their numbers in sub-Saharan Africa would rise from 140 million to 200 million. Increasingly, the global problem of undernutrition would continue to shift from the traditionally more affected region of Asia to sub-Saharan Africa. Improved distribution of income and of access to available food supplies would help improve the situation, though not by much in the countries with very low food average availabilities per caput.

*Total production increases slightly more slowly but is maintained in per caput terms*: For the 94 developing countries as a whole, agricultural production is projected to rise by 3 percent a year between 1983/5 and the year 2000. This is lower than the 3.3 percent growth rate achieved in the preceding 15-year period, but in per caput terms there is no decline in the growth rate because of parallel declines in population growth. The projected growth rate of per caput production is thus 1.1 percent per annum, the same as for 1970–85 but higher than for the long-term period 1961–85. The production of livestock products would grow the fastest and, amongst cereals, that of coarse grains. Some of the main export commodities and the starchy roots have lower than average growth rates, mainly because of demand constraints.

*Regional production rates diverge from the past*: There would be significant differences among regions compared with the past, as shown by the following annual growth rates given in Table 1.2.

**Table 1.2** Growth rates of total and per caput production (% p.a.)

| | Total production | | Per caput production | |
|---|---|---|---|---|
| | 1970–85 | 1983/5–2000 | 1970–85 | 1983/5–2000 |
| Africa (sub-Saharan) | 1.7 | 3.4 (3.1)* | −1.3 | 0.1 |
| Near East/N. Africa | 2.9 | 3.1 | 0.2 | 0.5 |
| Asia | 3.7 | 3.0 | 1.7 | 1.5 |
| Latin America | 3.1 | 2.7 | 0.7 | 0.6 |

* Growth rate in parentheses is from post-drought 1985 production level.

Asia's growth can be expected to be significantly below that of the recent past, which reflected the high growth rates of China and some other countries in the last ten years or so. The region's population growth rate of 2.0 percent per annum in the last fifteen years is expected to continue declining, to 1.5 percent per annum in the next fifteen years. Because some of the major countries have already made significant gains towards improved self-sufficiency, the room for further production growth to substitute imports will be less than in the past.

Latin America's production growth rate is also expected to be lower than in the past fifteen years. The slow-down in population growth from 2.4 to 2.0 percent per annum will cause demand to expand less rapidly. In parallel, the persistence of unfavourable overall economic conditions in many countries over the medium term, and continued slow growth of the region's agricultural exports, will also restrain the growth of total demand and, hence, of production.

In the Near East/North African countries the slower growth of incomes and foreign-exchange earnings in combination with the fairly high food consumption levels already attained in some major countries, will make for less buoyant demand growth compared with the past. Production growth in the past, however, has been well below that of demand in the region as a whole. Given the significant investments in agriculture, the region's total agricultural growth could be maintained and somewhat improved.

The special FAO study of Africa submitted to the 1986 African Regional Conference (FAO 1986a) concluded that a significant acceleration in production from the disastrous levels of the past is possible if appropriate policy reform and priority to agriculture in resource allocations were implemented. This is reflected in the growth rate projected for sub-Saharan Africa for 1983/5–2000, 3.4 percent per annum compared with 1.7 percent of the period 1970–85. It already includes an element of recovery from the drought years. If measured from the post-drought production of 1985, the projected growth rate is lower. This is certainly not a very encouraging situation, but it arises from the assessment of the constraints to faster production growth and underlines the problems stemming from high population growth in combination with the persistence of unfavourable overall economic conditions, even when agriculture can be made to grow twice as fast as in the past.

*Self-sufficiency falls but only just*: The 1983/5 total agricultural self-sufficiency ratio (SSR) of 101 percent for developing countries falls only fractionally to around 100 percent in 2000. This would be a big improvement in performance compared with the preceding 15 years when the SSR fell by over 5 percent. Most countries are confronted with commodity-specific demand constraints (domestic or external) or production constraints which together are projected to check the aggregate SSR from rising to over 100 percent in the period.

*Continued but much slower growth in cereal deficits*: The net cereals deficits of the developing countries, which have risen by three and a half times in the past 15 years to nearly 70 million tonnes in 1983/5, would continue to grow but at a much slower rate, to approximately 110 million tonnes by 2000. Some of the major importers of the past, including China and India, may not have large deficits in the future, while those of the other major importing country groups (oil-exporting and other middle-income countries) would grow at much slower rates compared with the past. The Near East/North Africa region would continue to account for just over one-half of the total deficit, while Latin America should be fully self-sufficient on the aggregate. Sub-Saharan Africa, with a high and accelerating growth of population, would need to increase further its imports of cereals if nutritional levels are to be maintained at those of the pre-drought period, despite the projected substantial acceleration of production. Since the overall economic and balance-of-payments prospects are unfavourable, food aid would continue to play an important role in meeting the region's deficits.

*Agricultural trade surpluses of developing countries continue to decline*: The import demand for the main agricultural exports of the developing countries would continue to grow but, as in the past, at very low rates. This reflects both the nature of the commodities exported (e.g. tropical beverages) which face nearly saturated and inelastic demand in the main consuming and importing countries, as well as the policies of protection and the associated generation of surpluses and subsidized exports of competing commodities, such as sugar and vegetable oils in many developed countries.

Faster growth in import demand for some products from deficit developing countries would not be enough to offset these constraints. The 1983/5 net balance (exports fob, imports cif) of $US12.7 billion would fall further to $7.8 billion (1983/5 prices) for all agricultural products. Trade liberalization could improve the agricultural trade balance of developing countries by improving market access for the commodities for which they are low-cost producers.

In conclusion, the picture emerging from the scenario projections for the developing countries is one of continuing development of their agricultural sector overall but with some significant black spots: unfavourable overall economic environment constraining growth of demand, export opportunities limited by protectionism and, in terms of large regional aggregates, only minimal improvement in the food situation in sub-Saharan Africa and no decrease in the total number of undernourished people.

## Scenario results: developed countries

*Moderate progress in the European centrally planned countries*: Because of the reconsideration of policy approaches and structures in the economy, including agriculture, now going on in this group of countries, longer-term outcomes are difficult to project. However, the disappointing agricultural sector results, especially in the USSR, of the decade and a half to the mid-1980s need not be a permanent feature of the future. A moderate improvement in agricultural performance, together with a relatively slow growth in food demand (reflecting existing high levels of consumption in terms of calories reported by the countries, the effects of higher food prices following reduction in food subsidies and the slow growth of population, but with continued emphasis on diet diversification and quality improvement) would result in a better balance of production and demand and improved self-sufficiency. A basic prerequisite is a distinct improvement in feed/livestock efficiency. If this and a moderate average growth rate of 1.3 percent a year in cereal production could both be achieved, cereal imports for the region could be held at around 35 million tonnes a year, approximately the average for recent years, and cereal self-sufficiency improved from 87 to 90 percent.

*Slower but continued production and export expansion in developed market economies (DMEs)*: In the 1980s the focus of attention as regards agriculture in the developed market economies has shifted, with much publicity, to their chronic overproduction and to huge and mounting food surpluses. The study puts these developments into perspective. A careful examination of demand prospects, domestic and external, and of production trends confirms the inevitability of a reduction in the rate of growth of agricultural output in developed market economies as a whole. Their domestic demand (as regards quantities of farm produce, although not necessarily consumer expenditures) will grow only very slowly in the future while the growth in their export markets will be considerably below that of the 1970s.

Supply–demand balance implied by the projections of agricultural trade outcomes of developing countries, the projected trade balances of Eastern Europe and the USSR and the growth in their own domestic demand would mean, broadly speaking, agricultural growth rates approximately halved over 1983/5–2000 in the developed market economies compared with the preceding 15 years, to just under 1 percent a year. Retardation of past trends in output growth, not their cessation, is the requirement. Exports would also continue to rise but much more slowly than in the past. For example, the net cereal import requirements of the rest of the world are projected to increase by some 35–40 million tonnes from the average of 1983/5. This is less than half the increase of the last fifteen years. In practice, all major commodity sectors (cereals, livestock, oilseeds, sugar) would need to grow at rates below those that would result from a mere continuation of the historical trends.

Livestock products and cereals accounted for three-quarters of the total gross output of the DMEs, and this proportion would not change significantly by 2000. Meat production trends in developed market economies would need to continue to be reduced from the 2.5 percent a year in the 1970s and 1.2 percent during 1980–5 to approximately 0.9 percent over the projection period. The slower growth projected in production reflects chiefly a slower future growth in consumption in the DMEs. Developing countries are projected to be approximately self-sufficient, except for mutton and lamb, and the net trade of the developed centrally planned countries would remain roughly constant.

For milk and dairy products, however, trade prospects are important. The projections indicate a continued growth in the import requirements of developing countries at a rate much below that of the past 15 years (though some low-income countries would import more only in the form of concessionary sales or food aid), maintenance of small net exports of the European CPEs and very slow growth of demand within the DMEs. Consequently, the net exports of the latter countries would rise by 1.6 percent a year, requiring a retardation in production growth rates from around 1.3 percent a year in the past to 0.8 percent in the future.

The slower growth of livestock production reduces the rate of growth of demand for cereals for feed, while demand for their food use is also projected to rise more slowly. Taking account of the projected future demands for *total cereals* in developing countries (net imports 112 million tonnes) and the European CPEs (net imports 35 million tonnes) as well as the slow-down in demand within DMEs, their cereals production growth rate would need to be reduced from the 2.9 percent of the 1970s and the 2.3 percent during 1980–5 to a future rate of approximately 0.9 percent a year to avoid surplus. This projected situation would, however, still require DME cereal production to be by the year 2000 some 100 million tonnes above the 1983/5 level.

Sugar projections are made difficult by the existence of competing sweeteners and the strong protection regimes. Assuming demand to rise at the same rate as population, continuation of the slowing trend of production in the DMEs and the policy assumptions indicated above (page 2) net import requirements could be around 2 million tonnes in the year 2000, about the same as in 1979/81. Together with projected 5 million tonne net imports of the European CPEs, this would allow developing countries to maintain current net exports of around 6.5 to 7 million tonnes.

Vegetable oils and oilseeds are a complex group. The projections indicate that if the trend of production continues, the DMEs would become a significant net exporter of vegetable oils and oilseeds in place of 1983/5 net imports of just under 1 million tonnes (oil equivalent). If livestock production increases more slowly in the future, as indicated above, these countries would tend to become self-sufficient in oilcakes/meals rather than substantial net importers as at present. Two complicating factors are the pressures for switching some land from cereals into import-substituting oilseeds to reduce cereal surpluses and the possibility of additional demand for imported oilmeals by the European CPEs in the course of improving efficiency in feed use of cereals.

## Factors in production growth in developing countries

Increased agricultural production in the future, involving larger absolute yearly increases than in the past, will be the result of combining multiple inputs. The study makes the assessment that the technologies which will actually be used in the next 15 years are those which are already known and in use, as evolved through adaptive and maintenance research. Any fundamental breakthroughs over this period, would encounter the typical 10–15 year lag between scientific accomplishment and widespread use at the farm level.

*Yield increases the major source of increased crop production*: No less than 63 percent of the growth in crop output of 93 developing countries (information on China was not sufficient to allow its inclusion in the analysis of factors underlying production growth) comes from higher yields, 22 percent from increased arable areas and 15 percent from higher cropping intensities (the number of times an area of land is cropped in one year). Historical and projected yield increases for major crops are shown in Table 1.3.

**Table 1.3** Past and projected yields for major crops (tonnes per ha)

| | 1961/3 | 1982/4 | 2000 |
|---|---|---|---|
| Wheat | 1.0 | 1.7 | 2.3 |
| Rice (paddy) | 1.7 | 2.4 | 3.0 |
| Maize | 1.1 | 1.6 | 2.3 |
| Sugar cane | 46.0 | 57.0 | 69.0 |
| Pulses | 0.5 | 0.5 | 0.7 |
| Groundnuts | 0.8 | 0.9 | 1.0 |

The attainment of projected yields will require an improvement of around 30 percent on average of present yields. Of the major crops, the output of coarse grains is projected to grow the fastest, reflecting both the broadening of research from rice and wheat and strong demand for livestock feed.

*Continued increase in cereals used for livestock feed*: The feed use of cereals in developing countries, including China, is projected to more than double to almost 300 million tonnes in the year 2000. For pigs, poultry and to a lesser extent dairy cattle, the use of supplementary feeds in more intensive commercial production will generate much of the expansion in livestock production. The increase in feed uses of cereals, however, is limited almost entirely to middle-income countries and China. Just over 1 percent of cereals in low-income countries outside China goes to feed use and this proportion is expected not to exceed 2 percent in 2000.

*Area expansion is still a significant source of additional production*: This is projected to expand to 39 percent in Latin America, 26 percent in sub-Saharan Africa, 11 percent in Asia (excluding China) but none in the Near East/North Africa in the period to 2000. The expansion of 80 million hectares of the arable land in agricultural use between 1985 and 2000 in developing countries is equivalent to the current area of arable land in Western Europe. Large areas of land reserves would still exist in 2000 but chiefly in only a few countries, with much of the reserves having soils of comparatively low quality. Their use would also involve further deforestation. Where land reserves are scarce or exhausted, as in India, further expansion or irrigation becomes essential.

*Increasing importance of irrigation*: The share of irrigated crops in the total value of crop production is projected to rise by a fifth to 43 percent by the year 2000. Almost one-fifth of arable land in the 93 developing countries will then be irrigated and two-thirds of all wheat and rice production will be grown under irrigation. India alone will account for almost half of the total. Irrigation of rain-fed and desert lands will be the sole source of expansion of harvested land in Near East/North Africa, while irrigated areas in Latin America and sub-Saharan Africa, while increasing, will remain very limited.

*Fertilizer use is projected to almost double*: Between 1982/4 and 2000, fertilizer use in the 93 developing countries is projected to more than double. Since fertilizer use is much greater now than in earlier decades, its growth rate is consequently projected to fall from 7.1 percent a year from 1975 to 1985 to 4.6 percent for 1982/4–2000. Substantial fertilizer use in Asia and Near East/ North Africa reflect land-substituting technologies that are dependent on fertilizers and irrigation. In the 93 countries, wheat, rice and other cereals will account for 55–60 percent of all fertilizer use.

*Other off-farm inputs also continue to rise*: Mechanization, improved seeds and chemical plant protection materials will all continue to be used in increasing quantities. The total number of tractors is projected to almost double to 6.5 million between 1983 and 2000, reducing the average arable area per tractor from 233 to 131 ha. The annual rate of increase, however, would be only a little over 4 percent a year, less than half the rate of increase during the surge in the tractor park after the early 1970s. This future slow-down in growth rates will reflect, in addition to the effects of the larger starting base, fewer subsidies and less buoyant income growth. The use of improved cereal seeds approximately doubles by 2000, which would raise their share of total cereal seed requirements from 34 percent in 1983 to 57 percent in 2000. The small but rising use of improved seeds in production of coarse grains and pulses contrasts with the much higher and still rising share in rice and wheat production. Indiscriminate and excessive use of plant protection chemicals has stimulated interest in integrated pest control using plant breeding, cultural practices and biological pest control, and the study projects a moderate rate of increase of somewhat less than 3 percent a year in expenditures, including pesticides and herbicides, on plant protection.

*Employment in agriculture is projected to expand*: The agricultural sector in year 2000 would still have half of the total labour force of the developing world excluding China. Between 1982/4 and 2000, this labour force, of which the great majority is concerned with crops, would grow by 128 million people to a total of 663 million. The increase of agricultural production of approaching 60 percent would contribute to increased employment, reflecting the probability that new mechanization, for reasons given in the above paragraph, will be undertaken more selectively than in the past and will take place chiefly where the agricultural labour force will cease to grow and where draught animal numbers are projected to fall or remain stationary. Taking the 93 developing countries as a single group, higher productivity would still enable average per caput income from agricultural production activities to rise by almost one-third. Increased agricultural employment would be located more in sub-Saharan Africa, Central America and part of Asia. In a number of countries in Latin America and Near East/North Africa the agricultural labour force is already declining.

*Agricultural growth demands substantial investments*: The study dispels any idea that the increase in developing-country production can be done at low capital cost. The cumulative gross investment for the whole period, including both primary sector and support investments is almost $1,500 billion (1980 prices). The largest item is irrigation followed by tractors and equipment, 16 and 10 percent respectively. Half of total investment is for the primary sector (i.e. directly concerned with crop and livestock production) and it would account for some 16 percent of agricultural GDP. The balance would be for supporting investment, for example processing, transport, storage and marketing.

## Agricultural policy issues

Chapters 7 and 8 of this study are devoted to key issues facing both developed and developing countries which must be tackled in the course of ensuring an adequate development of food and agriculture.

### International trade

Agricultural trade is in disarray and the concern arising from past failures to agree on an effective and equitable international framework for agricultural trade is reinforced by the study. The adjustments to past trends in production and consumption needed to bring about the approximate balance of world supply and demand as suggested in Chapter 3 would require considerable policy changes. The study therefore examines various approaches and instruments of trade liberalization.

Recent action has been taken by a number of industrialized countries to limit the growth of export surpluses and thereby limit expenditures on support, including mounting export subsidies, while still protecting farm incomes as far as possible. The action has so far not been sufficient to reverse the deteriorating situation of agricultural trade and consequent mounting tensions amongst exporting countries.

Continuing trade conflicts amongst industrialized countries cannot be ruled out. They could lead to most undesirable results. For heavily protected dairy products, the economically absurd consequence could be that international prices would be driven to such low levels that the lowest-cost producers and present exporters would become importers unless they too provided large subsidies. Somewhat similarly in the case of wheat, the United States and some other exporters would suffer substantial loss of markets to the EEC unless they too were willing to increase subsidies substantially. While some developing countries would benefit from lower import prices, it would become increasingly difficult to maintain domestic incentive policies, especially in countries close to self-sufficiency.

Trade liberalization and enhanced access to international markets would, according to a number of studies of individual commodities, offer better outcomes than trade conflicts. They suggest in general that partial or full liberalization of agricultural trade may increase world market prices and would decrease their variability, and that the volume of trade would rise.

The short-term impacts on developing countries would depend largely on their share in the world market of specific products. Considerable gains would result from the liberalization of sugar markets to the benefit mainly of Asian and Latin American exporting countries. The elimination of preferential treatment in certain developed country markets would, however, adversely affect some developing-country exports. The potential considerable benefits from liberalization of meat and dairy products would accrue predominantly to Latin America amongst developing countries. For the developing countries as a whole, however, the short-term impact on trade balances would be negative. Liberalization of cereals is also usually estimated to have a negative short-term effect on trade balances of developing countries as a group, because of the increased world prices they would have to pay for their imports.

The fewer studies with wide commodity coverage suggest that greater access to industrialized country markets could yield important benefits to developing countries. Their balance on agricultural trade would increase substantially despite higher prices for imports of some temperate-zone products. These benefits would have a multiplier effect on their national economies.

GATT trade negotiations currently under way are therefore of great importance for bringing significant, but most probably gradual, progress. The Ministerial Declaration that the negotiations 'shall aim to achieve greater liberalization of trade in agriculture and bring all measures affecting import access and export competition under strengthened and more operationally effective GATT rules and disciplines' points to the essence of what is required. A range of options is open for the achievement of these goals.

Trade liberalization amongst developing countries, of which the principles, rules and timetable have been endorsed at ministerial level, could also generate additional trade in such products as sugar, vegetable oils, tobacco, pulses, tropical beverages, and forestry products.

Policy adjustments bearing on trade required for the projections of the study to be feasible, and hopefully for a further improvement on those outcomes, will involve both developed and developing countries. While they are built around trade measures, trade policies are essentially based on domestic policies bearing on production and consumption. Adjustment at those levels will basically determine whether a trade environment can be created in which greater market orientation will enable comparative advantages to exert more influence on global resource use in the agricultural sector.

### Macro-economic policies

Many governments of developing countries now face the need to bring about structural adjustments in their economies. The thrust of policies as regards agriculture must be to redress disadvantages imposed by past development strategies. The external setting of these policies has been distinctly adverse since the early 1980s, particularly the depressed commodity prices, heavy debt-servicing burdens and slow growth in industrialized countries. Countries also vary widely in their capacity to apply policies effectively.

The importance of macro-economic policies to agriculture has increased as the sector has become more integrated in the economy as a whole. The linkage also works in the opposite direction. Experience shows that macro-policies have often introduced disincentives to agriculture, sometimes inadvertently so. Examples of macro-policies which have often damaged agriculture are patterns of sectoral protection and exchange rates.

The industrial sector is often highly protected as compared with agriculture. This raises the profitability of manufacturing relative to agriculture, thus discouraging investment in agriculture. Prices paid by farmers for inputs to production and for consumer goods, are raised. While some protection to manufacturing is usually essential, its typical differential extent *vis-à-vis* agriculture should be greatly reduced.

Overvalued currencies can directly damage agriculture, being a disincentive to the production of agricultural exports and of import-competing foodstuffs. There are numerous examples of the intent of agricultural policy incentives being reversed by exchange-rate policy. Exchange-rate correction is usually difficult and will not be effective without strong economic administration. Improvement in producer prices through an exchange rate change must be accompanied by attention to other influences on production in order to be effective.

Deficits in government budgets affect agriculture adversely by adding to inflationary pressures while export prices, determined by world market conditions, typically lag. Commodity taxes distort producer prices and decisions as to recourse use.

There is consequently a clear need to reduce inconsistencies which have existed between macro- and agricultural policies and to avoid creating new ones. The economic institutions of the sector should develop the technical competence to monitor authoritatively the implications for it of actual or proposed macro-policies.

The high level of external indebtedness has recently come to pose a major issue in many countries, particularly in Latin America and Africa, and to lenders. Agriculture was not the focus of the wave of borrowing but it did benefit indirectly, and investment in the sector and nutritional standards have both been reduced by the subsequent financial stringencies arising from debt-servicing. There appears only limited scope for agriculture to contribute to the increase required in government revenue, while reductions in government expenditure on food and agriculture may entail high social and economic costs. It is neither desirable nor acceptable that the food consumption of the poorest people should be reduced to secure funds required to service external debts. Agricultural trade could contribute to larger trade surpluses of some indebted countries, but this will be largely dependent on improved commodity prices and market access.

## Agricultural price policies

Many aspects of price policies in food and agriculture remain controversial. Price interventions are almost universal, but effective design and implementation is difficult. Producer prices influence aggregate production, especially over the longer run, and price incentives cannot be replaced by input subsidies. But to be effective they must be accompanied by action to improve the effectiveness of the whole infrastructure of agriculture and the local availability of incentive consumer goods. Producer price policies must also ensure that small farmers are fully catered for by the marketing systems through which the policies are applied. Producer prices should not move too far and for long periods away from long-term international price trends, although allowance must be made for some deviation from this principle in the case of heavily subsidized exports.

Consumer subsidies given on food in many developing countries are now being scaled down, chiefly because of budgetary pressures. Nevertheless, humanitarian as well as political considerations require some form of intervention to be widely employed. Targeting the beneficiaries is essential so as to limit costs and to ensure that subsidy schemes benefit only or chiefly the very poor. Effective targeting is difficult, but widening experience points to a number of options. The rural poor need greater access to such schemes.

## The role of the public sector in agriculture

A smaller role now tends to be given to the public sector, a reversal of earlier emphasis. This change is brought about by financial constraints and by the frequent low cost-effectiveness of public enterprises. Government marketing agencies have been phased out in some cases or have had their role diminished by exposure to competition from the private sector. More prices of agricultural products are being freed from regulation, although basic foods generally remain subject to government interventions.

Governments must, however, keep an appropriate balance between the public and private sectors and enthusiasm for reform must not lead governments to curtail too severely the involvement of the public sector. The focus should be rather on improving efficiency, which will often imply some shift in the composition of the public sector rather than an overall reduction in size, for example more resources devoted to building roads and fewer to commercial marketing of food. Care must be taken to avoid the collapse of a particular service through withdrawal of the public sector when there is no private enterprise ready to take over. Any change-over must be phased and assistance given to the private sector to equip itself to be an effective replacement.

## Financing agricultural development

The growth of external financing, which provides around 10–15 percent of total development resources of agriculture in developing countries (excluding China), has lost momentum in recent years. Official commitments of assistance to agriculture, the bulk of this resource flow, seems unlikely to expand as in the 1970s. Hence, greater effectiveness in its use will be needed, and this is now widely considered to require a more balanced composition as between project and programme or sectoral approaches.

Public-sector spending, approaching one-third of the total, is now encountering some budgetary stringency, which imposes the need for cost-effectiveness. In these circumstances, provisions to meet current expenditures are often more vulnerable than those for investment expenditure, but severe pruning of recurrent expenditures will reduce the effectiveness of past capital investment.

Private investment, including own-labour, typically accounts for over half of total agricultural investment. The issue here is the need to encourage private savings and to channel them into rural investments. Experience shows that even poor people usually save if they have access to suitable savings mechanisms. Institutional development is usually needed. In order to promote the important component of own-labour investment, security of tenure for the farmer is essential.

## Rural poverty, growth and equity

The need to reduce rural poverty and to bring about greater equity is one of the most pressing economic and social issues in developing countries. The circumstances of poverty and hence the detailed nature of measures to combat it vary widely amongst countries as well as within them.

In 1980 some 780 million people in the developing world apart from China and other Asian centrally planned economies were conservatively estimated to live in conditions of absolute poverty. All regions were represented, but two-thirds were in Asia and a sixth in sub-Saharan Africa. Of the total, 90 percent were rural people, dependent wholly or partly on agriculture. Incomes per caput of the bottom decile of the rural population were generally less than a third of average national incomes.

The poor are a heterogeneous group—landless, nomads, fishermen and so on—but they typically have limited assets, environmental vulnerability and lack of access to education, medical facilities and other public services. Landlessness is a major characteristic; in 1979 an estimated 30 million agricultural households were landless and another 138 million near landless. The problem is most widespread in South Asia but is growing in South-East Asia, Africa and Latin America.

Poverty is associated with other disadvantages. Undernourishment is largely concentrated amongst those living in poverty. Seasonality in food production is also often associated with acute undernourishment, especially amongst the landless and near landless. The health of children is particularly at risk when undernourished; mortality increases rapidly as the weight-for-age indicator falls.

Illiteracy is prevalent amongst the rural poor and infant mortality is higher in households where parents have no schooling. Poor households tend to be larger. The poor are at a disadvantage in commercial transactions where, for instance, the benefits of a controlled price can be offset by the weak position of the poor farmer in a related transaction.

Recent economic difficulties have worsened poverty and undernutrition. A study of ten countries representative of most regions for the period between the late 1970s and the early 1980s shows that real wages declined in all but one country. In six countries where GDP per caput fell, unemployment rose. Inflation accelerated in all countries in the early 1980s, with food prices generally rising faster than overall prices. Where expenditures such as on health and education fell, the rural sector was disproportionately affected.

Agricultural growth generally—but not always—lessens rural poverty. Experience in a number of countries and local situations indicates that a better agricultural performance generally results in a lower price of food, higher agricultural wage rates and employment and consequently a lower incidence of rural poverty. Nevertheless, the actual outcome in each specific case will be conditioned by the institutional setting. With very unequal distribution of assets, especially land, and unequal access to other resources, most of the benefits of growth in the agricultural sector as a whole will largely bypass small farmers and agricultural workers.

Land redistribution and tenancy reforms are the most fundamental of anti-poverty measures. The history of land reforms is largely one of failures. Usually only a small fraction of the surplus land has been actually redistributed; often it has been the poor-quality land which has been redistributed and regulatory tenancy measures have frequently been evaded. On the other hand, sufficient examples exist to show that land reform can be made to work. There is now a large measure of agreement that there is no real substitute for a change in the ownership of production assets, particularly land, in order to reduce rural poverty.

Other measures to strengthen the asset base of the rural poor are best combined rather than applied separately and need to be adapted to the requirements of women as well as men working in agriculture.

Experience with improved access of the small farmer and the landless to credit has been mixed, but the initial results of a number of recent schemes are sufficiently promising for substantial longer-term results to be possible. The problem of the lack of collateral must be overcome. Credit should not be unduly limited to single crops or activities. Access to irrigation is also important for raising the productivity of the small farmer and the construction and maintenance of irrigation schemes can create additional employment. In order to ensure the spread of improved technologies, extension and training facilities are essential. Where facilities do exist, they are often underfinanced or poorly maintained, and access to them has favoured larger farmers.

Employment should be added to by rural work programmes which create durable assets. Experience indicates that schemes of these kinds have expanded employment opportunities, although because of typically unequal sharing of power in rural communities, leakage of benefits normally occurred outside the target groups. There is a need to encourage the wider participation of rural people in these and all other approaches to lessening rural poverty. Government policy should also support the trade-union movement in rural areas. Subsidized mechanization will generally affect agricultural employment adversely. Within the constraints of demand, the choice of crop mixes can also influence employment.

Food distribution schemes which, by the use of subsidies, lower the retail price of food for target groups of the very poor, have been of greater benefit to urban rather than rural populations. While there is scope and need for their extension to rural areas, the administrative difficulties and the greater food self-sufficiency of rural populations will remain as limiting factors.

Promoting the non-farm sector to provide non-farm employment to members of agricultural households is essential as a means of preventing an expansion of the agricultural labour force to an extent which would reduce average incomes. An expanding non-farm sector does not, however, lead automatically to a reduction in poverty, and attention must be given to conditions of employment. Experience in a number of countries points to the importance of the non-farm enterprises generating significant linkages with the rural sector. Positive government support in such forms as technical advice, market information, credit and training are needed. Also, as shown by Asian experience, rural people must be given the opportunity to save and invest in local industry.

## Forestry

Forestry makes an important contribution to the world economy which will expand with the growth of population and wealth. As well as its direct economic contribution, the forest is vital for the conservation of soil and water and the security of agricultural production.

The pressure for land resources and the immediate need to cut trees for fuelwood means forests are being cleared and depleted in many developing countries. This is reducing the capability of forests to meet future needs for fuelwood and industrial wood and is severely detrimental to the performance of the forests' environmental role. To offset this deterioration and to secure future supplies, considerable investment in conservation and reafforestation is required, and justified by good economic returns.

High rates of growth in consumption of forest products for housing, education, packaging and other uses are projected for developing countries. There is a danger that due to lack of investment in industry and infrastructure, production may fail to keep pace with the growth of demand, and developing countries may become more dependent on imports for forests products in the production of which they should have comparative advantage. Forest industries should be priority industries in the process of development because they are substantially based on indigenous renewable natural resources and the capability of people.

Through trade, developing countries with plentiful forestry resources have the possibility of improving their own economies as exporters and in supplying their neighbours. The promotion of trade between neighbouring developing countries could foster the development of efficient industrial units that can benefit from larger markets.

## Fisheries

After almost doubling in the 1950s and 1960s, production increases slowed down markedly. Reflecting resource barriers and the continuing pressure of demand, the trend in the real prices of fish has been rising. Around one-third of total fish catches are exported, chiefly to developed countries. Developing countries have become larger exporters in recent years.

The adoption in 1982 of the UN Convention on the Law of the Sea represented a new stage in the ownership and use of marine resources. National jurisdiction by coastal states over fisheries was extended within, typically, seaward zones of 200 miles. The 1984 FAO World Fisheries Conference adopted a Strategy which sets out principles and guidelines for future management and development of fisheries and approved five Programmes of Action to provide assistance in this regard to developing countries.

World demand for fishery products to the end of the century is expected to continue to be strong, with the greater part of additions to food demand arising in developing countries, and in the year 2000 might well exceed 100 million tonnes. This could be met by a combination of better fisheries management, increases in output from aquaculture and improved utilization of the catches. Increased investments in better handling, preserving and distribution facilities will be needed to reduce present substantial post-catch losses. Increased demand will also tend to reduce quantities discarded and encourage exploitation of species little used at present for human consumption, including some now used only for fishmeal. The time of spectacular and sustained increases in fisheries catches is, however, over.

With the resources of traditionally exploited species under mounting pressure, the need for effective management is paramount. Better measures will be required to monitor and control fishery operations. Steps must be taken to reduce costs, to improve the socio-economic position of small-scale fishermen and to enhance productivity in coastal areas under environmental threats.

Aquaculture production could be doubled by year 2000 but only if national organizational requirements—a central agency, adequate supplies of inputs especially of seed fish, marketing channels and an extension service—are met.

## Technological developments of the future

Technological change has been at the heart of the capacity of world agriculture to respond to the challenges arising from the explosion in world population. In the course of the present century, a fundamental transition has taken place from extensive to intensive production systems. While intensification must be taken much further still—by the end of this century there will be comparatively little suitable new land available for agriculture—there is an urgent need to develop and promote technologies that increase or sustain productivity at lower costs and do not harm the environment.

*Genetic potentials of foodcrops have not been exhausted*: Despite the great strides made in the last 50 years in raising the yields of major foodcrops, the potential for further improvement has not been exhausted. The development and use of high-yielding varieties of crops will therefore continue to be a very important part of technological progress. Quality improvements and better resistance to pests and diseases can also be expected as part of this progress.

*New opportunities through biotechnology*: Recent advances in biotechnology sciences, despite some disappointments and exaggerated claims, must now be taken into account in the planning of agriculture. The prospect of being able to transform plants in directed ways opens up new possibilities for plant breeders. In the foreseeable future it will be possible to transfer genes from one species to another, regardless of how unrelated they are, and without taking unwanted genes normally transferred through the use of prevailing techniques. New ways of manipulating genetic variation and extremely precise techniques for evaluation and selection should not, however, justify undue optimism as to the creation of entirely new plant-types. Embryo transfer for the upgrading of livestock could become widely practised in developing countries, especially when further research makes the techniques more reliable and economical.

*Improved rainfall and water conservation*: Water is a binding constraint on production in the approximately 80 percent of arable land in sub-humid or semi-arid and erratic-rainfall areas of developing countries. Irrigation expansion is feasible on only a small fraction of these areas. Soil management systems and cropping practices that both prevent erosion and excessive leaching must therefore be devised. Some already exist, but the problem of creating incentive for their use remains. Plant varieties suitable for these conditions must be developed. More economical forms of minimum tillage than those used in some developed countries are required.

*The addition of nutrients to the soil remains an essential component of production technology*: Attempts to increase productivity without adding nutrients to the soil will ultimately fail. Especially when soils are already on the verge of degradation, technologies that use minimum inputs are unlikely either to increase yields significantly or to prevent further degradation in adverse seasons. The work of plant breeders cannot overcome those conditions. Technologies of the future must therefore continue to use mineral fertilizers or relatively large dressings of organic manure in order to restore soil structures and fertility.

*Prerequisites for the generation of new technologies*: Developing countries need to generate both relatively unsophisticated technologies (e.g. improved farm tools, simple irrigation systems, planting of indigenous crops and trees for soil and water conservation) and high-level technologies, or at least have access to them (e.g. biotechnological methods of gene manipulation). Priority requirements needed to do so include well-trained research workers imbued with the importance of developing technologies appropriate to local conditions; workshops and laboratories adequately funded; strong links and cooperative arrangements with other research centres; attention to socio-economic research and 'second-generation' problems, for example technologies for sustainable agricultures and effects of technological innovations on income distribution.

*Technological developments must be made known to the farmer*: New or modified technologies must not only be targeted to the real needs of the producer but must reach him or her. Effective diffusion is essential. This requires closer cooperation between research and extension personnel than often exists now. Fuller use should be made of approaches which recent experience has shown to be effective. These include on-farm research and demonstration, use of a minikit (commitment by farmers of only a small part of their farm to try out the new technology) and pilot projects (intensified institutional support and extension advice in a particular area).

*Economic incentives are essential for the adoption of improved technologies*: Policies which reduce or eliminate the profitability of a new technology discourage its adoption by farmers and thereby retard desired technical changes and reduce the return to, and probable allocation of, funds to research. Farmers must also be made aware of the true benefits and costs of the innovation. Although the socio-economic content of agricultural research has increased notably in international research centres, it is still too limited in the national agricultural research systems of developing countries. More use should be made of the farming systems research approach which integrates socio-economic analysis with technical research and extension.

*Prospects for technological advances are good*: The fast progress of scientific knowledge in developed countries, added to by increasing numbers of researchers and improved and enlarged facilities in developing countries, is expanding appreciably the stock of research knowledge which has been accumulated internationally. In this process, the contribution of the system of research centres of the Consultative Group on International Agricultural Research continues to be very important. These investments in research, particularly since the 1970s, have led to a substantial pipeline of research results. Some of these results can be applied immediately, but others require further adaptations before they will be ready for use by farmers. Given the typical lag time of up to 15 years for such adaptation, it can be expected that significant 'ready-to-use' technological innovations will become available in the last decade of this century. While developed countries' innovations will be towards viable low-cost and efficient but environment-preserving technologies, those of developing countries will be oriented towards raising production without damaging the natural resources used by agriculture.

## The environmental challenge in agricultural development

The 60 percent increase in agricultural production in developing countries and 20 percent in developed countries projected for the next 15 years will inevitably press more heavily on natural resources already under strain. Some industrial processes add further to this strain. Environmental isues are rightly coming to the fore as fundamental to development strategies.

Some problems cross many frontiers, such as acid rain, or are truly global, most notably the irreversible climatic changes resulting from the increasing concentration of carbon dioxide in the earth's atmosphere. Substantial potential impacts of this latter change on agriculture—such as greater climatic instability and shifts in agro-ecological zones—will be a threat in the next century rather than the present one.

Developing-country environmental issues are fundamentally concerned with the reversal of present degradation and the introduction of production systems that will sustain substantially increased output in the long term. Critical problems include deforestation, desertification and degradation of existing cultivated lands.

The FAO estimates that because of the expansion of agriculture and the need for fuelwood, net deforestation of tropical forests is approaching 10 million ha a year. Increased erosion and flooding follow. The ever-increasing demand for fuelwood together with overgrazing is also causing an accelerating rate of desertification with approximately one-quarter of the earth's land surface now damaged by factors that contribute to desertification. Poor land- and water-management have led to resource degradation in the form of erosion, salinization and alkanization, acidification and the spread of water-borne diseases. While expanded irrigation is essential for larger crop production, some 20 percent of irrigated areas are waterlogged or excessively saline or both.

Developed-country environmental issues related to agriculture stem from the intensification of farming methods. Heavy application of fertilizers and intensive stock-raising operations have led to soil and water contamination with high levels of nitrates also possibly posing health hazards. Practices such as monocultures have encouraged increased use of pesticides with consequent rising concentration of pesticide materials in food chains. At the same time, pesticide-resistant species of pests evolve and natural predators are eliminated. From the wider social viewpoint, modern farming has tended to detract from the visual variety, amenity and wildlife habitats of farmland.

Future strains on the environment from increased agricultural production will be considerably greater in developing than in developed countries. The slower growth of output in developed countries will facilitate a sound management of the natural resources used by agriculture. In developing countries, on the other hand, the large increases in production will increase significantly the strain on natural resources. A continuing modernization of production technology will involve a more intensive use of mineral fertilizers and pesticides and larger areas under monoculture and irrigation. Some 80 million ha of land will be brought newly into cultivation by the year 2000. In broad terms, the environmental problems will be Asia, from increased irrigation and deforestation; Near East/North Africa, from shortage of arable land and increased desertification; sub-Saharan Africa, from livestock and crop pressures on fragile soils; and Latin America, from deforestation and increased monoculture.

Policy action is made much more difficult because of the incomplete understanding of how many environmental systems actually work. Nevertheless, action must be taken, as stressed by many investigators including the recent World Commission on Environment and Development. Enough is known for remedial treatment of most damage and for sound management practices to be formulated. Government intervention is essential; environmental considerations cannot be taken care of by free market mechanisms. The integration of agriculture and environmental policies is also essential.

Specific lines of action include:

- improved agricultural technologies (e.g. more mixed cropping, grazing management with fodder crops and temporary pastures in crop rotations), development of sustainable farming systems for fragile tropical soils;
- preservation of genetic resources (avoiding the loss of genetic diversity in primitive cultivars);
- development and application of tropical forest management systems;
- integrated pest control (e.g. use of pesticides in combination with other methods, introduction of parasites and predators of the target pest species).

Finally, economic and social aspects must be attended to. Environmental treatment and protection is not cheap. The full benefits of allocating scarce funds to this objective come only in the long term, but they are shared by all members of society, not only those directly using the natural recourses for productive purposes. Properly costed, environmental projects generally give a high rate of return. Some community-implemented conservation gives benefits quickly. Farmers in secure possession of their land will try to safeguard its quality but they need advice and sometimes material help.

The FAO believes that agricultural development can continue to the extent projected without seriously damaging the world's natural resources. This assessment, however, carries a proviso: that more weight be given to environmental requirements in development policies and expenditures.

# 2 World food and agriculture to the mid-1980s

The past does not determine the future but it does strongly influence development and the concerns of policy in the years ahead. By reviewing what has happened in world agriculture over approximately the past 25 years, but with emphasis on the more recent years, this chapter sets the scene for the heart of the study, the quantification of forward-looking scenarios and analysis of issues.

## A better-fed world—but with serious exceptions

The past quarter-century has brought extraordinary achievements in food and agriculture. One measure stands above all others: the successful response to the challenge of feeding 1800 million more people in the 25 years to 1985, at levels of average per caput food consumption which have been constantly improving, in terms of both quantity and quality. Fears in the 1960s and early 1970s of chronic food shortages over the larger part of the world have proved unfounded. At the regional level, however, sub-Saharan Africa still faces a critical problem of producing more adequate food supplies.

In the early 1960s only five developing countries with a combined population of 100 million had average per caput calorie supplies exceeding 2500. Progress was modest up to the early 1970s, though many countries (including some of the most populous) had graduated out of the bare minimum level of 1900 calories. The real surge in food consumption levels, however, occurred in the 1970s and, chiefly for China, in the early 1980s. By 1979/81 32 countries with a combined population of nearly 600 million had exceeded the 2500–calorie mark, many of them by a good margin, and by 1983/5 this group comprised—with the addition of China—35 countries and 1.86 billion people (see Table 2.2).

The first five years of the current decade present a mixed picture. The shift of China into the 'high' level of per caput food availability has tripled in five years the population living in countries with over 2500 calories per caput to 1.86 billion, or 53 percent of the total population of the developing countries. At the same time, however, the overall economic crisis of the last few years virtually arrested the rising trend of average calorie consumption in Latin America and, together with the effects of drought and deterioration of agricultural conditions, reduced consumption in sub-Saharan Africa; per caput food availabilities were lower in 1983/5 than in 1979/81 in 37 of the 94 developing countries. Of the 37 countries, 24 were in sub-Saharan Africa.

A good deal of the improvement was the result of two significant developments: the rapid growth of incomes and foreign-exchange availability of the oil-exporting and some other middle income countries in the 1970s, and favourable developments in food production in a number of other countries, including low-income ones. The most spectacular gains in this group came in China from the late 1970s but in many non-African low-income countries gains in food availability, although modest, were solidly based on improved performances of domestic agriculture. The regional data as well as those grouping countries by income levels in Table 2.1 demonstrate the concentration of improvements in the Near East/North Africa region, China and the group of the middle-income countries.

**Table 2.1** Food availabilities for direct human consumption, calories per caput per day

| | 1961/3 | 1969/71 | 1979/81 | 1983/5 |
|---|---|---|---|---|
| *World* | *2320* | *2450* | *2600* | *2660* |
| *Developing countries* | | | | |
| 94 developing countries | *1960* | *2110* | *2320* | *2420* |
| 93 developing countries (excluding China): | *2070* | *2170* | *2330* | *2360* |
| Africa (sub-Saharan) | 2050 | 2100 | 2150 | 2050 |
| Near East/N. Africa | 2220 | 2370 | 2850 | 2980 |
| Asia | 1860 | 2030 | 2240 | 2380 |
| Asia (excluding China) | 1970 | 2070 | 2200 | 2250 |
| Latin America | 2380 | 2520 | 2680 | 2700 |
| Low-income countries | 1870 | 2010 | 2180 | 2310 |
| Low-income countries (excluding China) | 2000 | 2050 | 2100 | 2130 |
| Low-income countries (excluding China and India) | 1950 | 2080 | 2090 | 2090 |
| Middle-income countries | 2160 | 2340 | 2620 | 2660 |
| *Developed countries* | *3090* | *3260* | *3370* | *3370* |
| N. America | 3250 | 3460 | 3590 | 3630 |
| Western Europe | 3110 | 3260 | 3390 | 3380 |
| Other developed market economies | 2590 | 2810 | 2920 | 2890 |
| European centrally planned economies | 3160 | 3330 | 3410 | 3410 |

Improvements took place in the other low-income countries but only slowly and, significantly, the 1970s witnessed a reversal of the trend towards improvement at the lower end of the distribution with a quasi tripling of the population living in countries with average per caput calorie availabilities under 1900. This retrogression to levels of per caput food availabilities below those achieved in earlier years was accentuated in the first half of the 1980s. For most of the drought-affected countries the decline had been reversed in good measure following good harvests in 1985 and 1986. Unfavourable weather, however, reduced harvests again in many countries. Preliminary data for 1987 indicate decline in cereal production of some 15–16 percent in sub-Saharan Africa and some 8 percent in Asia outside China. At the same time, however, the declines due to more fundamental causes of overall economic crisis or unsettled political conditions are not being reversed.

In most of the low-income countries, the numerous very poor people simply did not get enough food to lead a normal life. As shown in Table 2.1, the per caput food supplies in the low-income countries, excluding China and India, were in 1983/5 no higher than 15 years earlier. Consequently, the numbers of undernourished people in the developing countries (outside the Asian CPEs) were conservatively estimated by FAO to have risen slightly over the 1970s.[1] Most of the 350 millions or 510 millions (alternative estimates for 1983/5) still lived in Asia, followed by Africa, although the trend has been for the incidence of undernutrition to rise in Africa and remain nearly stationary in Asia in terms of the absolute numbers affected.

The progressive shift of most countries and their populations to higher levels of food availability is shown in Table 2.2. The bulk of the population of the developing world other than China has now moved into the middle category of 1900–2500 calories per caput and a steadily rising number, substantially enlarged by the population of China in the most recent period, have shifted into the top category of over 2500 calories. Distressingly, however, populations in the under–1900 calories category have also increased. The general rise in consumption levels thus left behind large populations; undernourishment remained a stubborn and multifaceted problem within the distinctly improved global situation.

**Table 2.2** Distribution of developing countries by calories per caput

| | 1961/3 | 1969/71 | 1979/81 | 1983/5 |
|---|---|---|---|---|
| *Under 1900 calories p.c.* | | | | |
| No. of countries | 23 | 7 | 8 | 9 |
| Population (million) | 996 | 65 | 173 | 196 |
| Population excl. China | 311 | 65 | 173 | 196 |
| Population excl. China and India | 311 | 65 | 173 | 196 |
| *1900–2500 calories p.c.* | | | | |
| No. of countries | 66 | 74 | 54 | 50 |
| Population (million) | 1036 | 2345 | 2485 | 1446 |
| Population excl. China | 1036 | 1516 | 1489 | 1446 |
| Population excl. China and India | 573 | 961 | 800 | 702 |
| *Over 2500 calories p.c.* | | | | |
| No. of countries | 5 | 13 | 32 | 35 |
| Population (million) | 100 | 184 | 590 | 1878 |
| Population excl. China | 100 | 184 | 590 | 831 |
| Population excl. China and India | 100 | 184 | 590 | 831 |

[1] Undernourished: persons with estimated calorie intakes below 1.2 and 1.4 times (alternative assumptions as to thresholds) the BMR (energy requirements in a state of fasting at complete rest in a warm environment). These levels are approximately equivalent, for example, to between 1450 and 1610 calories in India or 1550 and 1720 calories in Egypt. For methods of estimation and other details see FAO 1987a.

Some developing countries introduced schemes to improve nutritional conditions through the subsidized sale or distribution of food for the benefit of the very poor. While experience was mixed, often with the better-off and not only the very poor benefiting, it is generally agreed that the measures did achieve at least part of their aim.

In the developed world, consumption per caput continued to rise but ever more slowly as calorie intakes around 3400–500 calories became typical in the last ten years as compared with the 3100–250 of the early 1960s. Concern over the relationship between diet and health became more pronounced in a number of these countries and is beginning to have significant influences on the growth and commodity composition of their demand.

The composition of food consumption continued to change in both developing and developed countries. While the extent of the modifications were fairly small, they represented a firmly rooted trend pointing to future changes in the patterns of output. The share of cereals directly consumed for food declined, together with pulses, roots and tubers while the share of other vegetable products (sugar, vegetables and fruit, oils and fats and alcohol) rose. Animal products, consumed in much larger quantities in developed countries, supplied a rising share of calorie intakes and still more of consumer expenditure on food (Fig. 2.1).

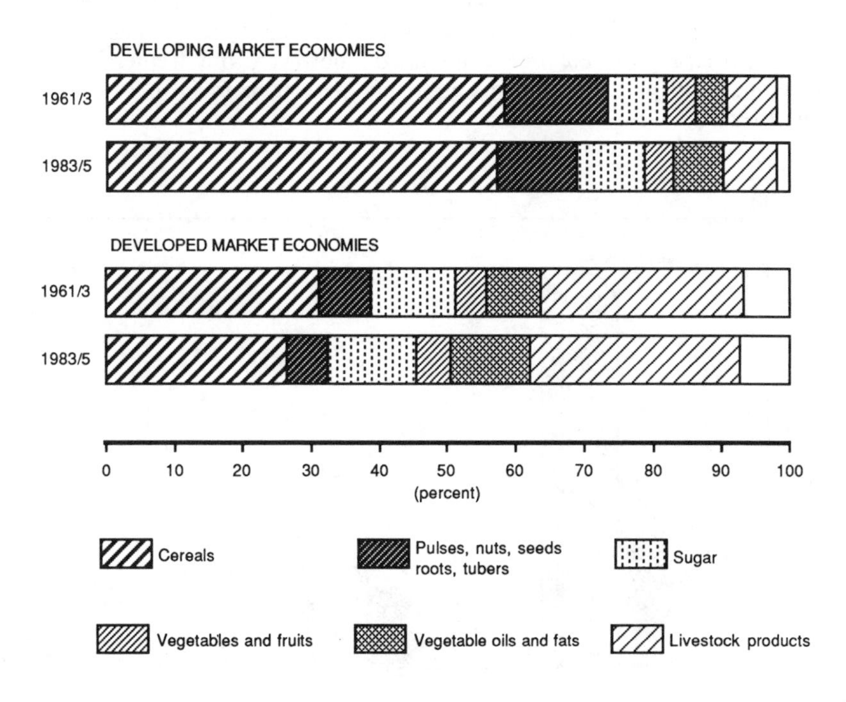


**Figure 2.1** Shares of selected food groups in total energy consumption

While dietary changes in the developing world were somewhat more pronounced in the higher-income countries, the same direction of changes also took place in other developing countries. Two additional and significant changes were the increasing consumption of wheat in developing countries, from an average 31 kg per caput in 1961/3 to 60 kg in 1983/5, and the rising indirect use of cereals, as livestock feed, in both developed and developing countries, as follows (million tonnes):

| | *1961/3* | *1983/5* |
|---|---|---|
| Developed countries | 252 | 474 |
| 94 developing countries | 30 | 126 |

## Sources of gains

*Productivity and increased production*: The expanding world population could be better fed because agriculture was being increasingly transformed into a dynamic productive sector. The developed countries led the way in this, while in the developing world Asia from the later 1960s led in the introduction of high-yielding varieties of wheat and rice. Rice yields rose on average by 41 percent in developing countries between 1969/71 and 1983/5, wheat by 77 percent. Labour productivity in agriculture nearly doubled over the same period in developed countries, and even in developing countries, where the agricultural labour force kept increasing, productivity rose by a quarter during those years. Figure 2.2 does emphasize, however, the tremendous—and widening—gap which exists in output per person in the two categories of countries.

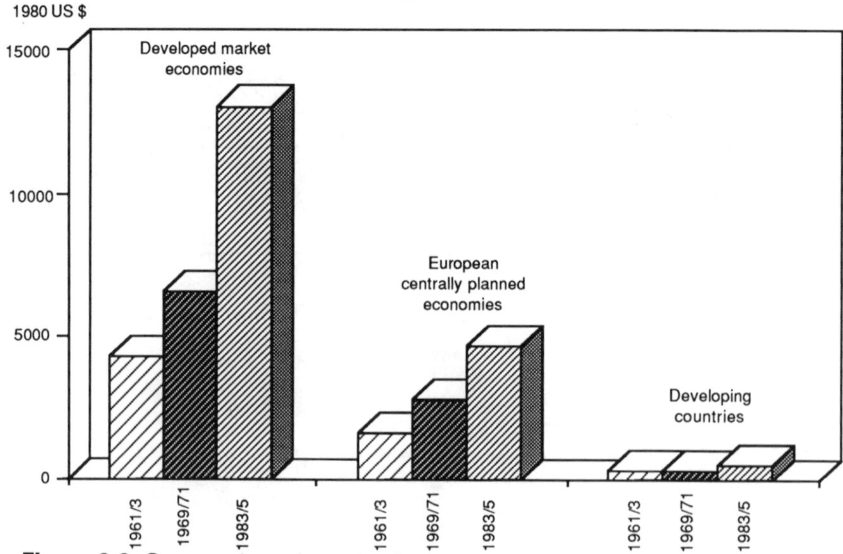


**Figure 2.2** Gross value of production per caput of the agricultural labour force

Technological, economic and managerial factors contributed to the productivity transformation. A tremendous increase in fertilizer usage—a tenfold increase in developing countries and a doubling in developed market economies between 1961/3 and 1983/5—was possibly the most potent single factor in raising productivity, but it could not have had such an impact without a whole range of scientific advances and complementary improvements in the availability or quality of other inputs such as high-yielding varieties or improved livestock breeds, irrigation and in farming know-how. In a long-term context, the 1960s and 1970s will be seen as a turning-point, a period when significant agricultural productivity gains were achieved. The underlying technologies became firmly established in large parts of the world's farming systems, including those of poor countries.

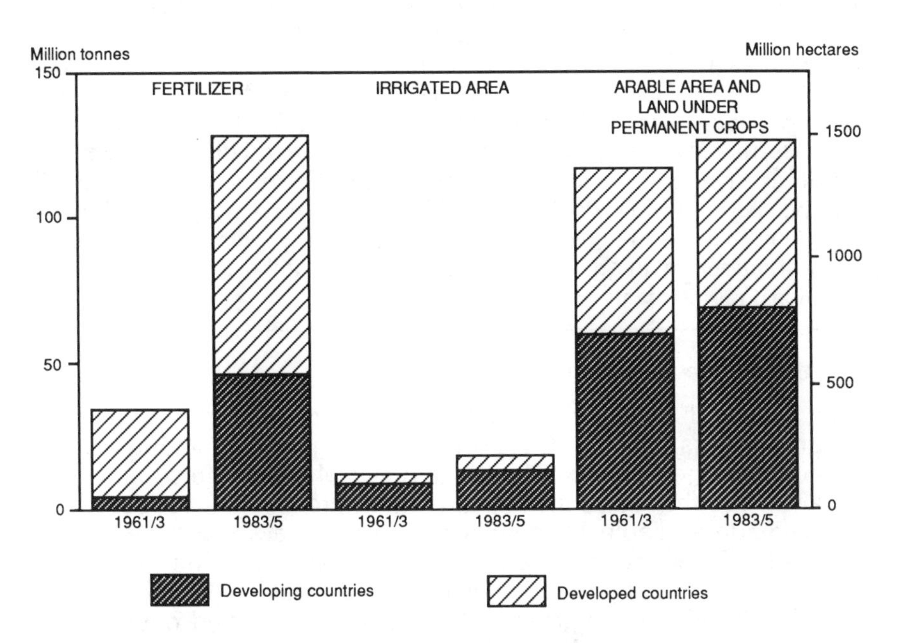


**Figure 2.3** Changes in selected inputs to agricultural production

The strong demand for agricultural products in many countries over most of the 1970s provided favourable conditions for the mobilization of the increased investment necessary to make full use of the new technologies. In developed countries, investment in agriculture was more closely related to temporary conditions of the 1970s and to national policies which added to incentives to expand output. Public expenditure on rural infrastructures was an important element in investment in agriculture in developing countries, a small but significant share of the financing coming from external assistance.

World agricultural production expanded by an average 2.5 percent a year from 1961 to 1985, or 0.6 percent per caput. Contrary to what is widely believed, developing-country agricultural output with a long-term growth rate of 3.2 percent a year grew significantly faster than output in developed countries (2 percent), and although population expansion in developing countries pulled down agricultural growth in per caput terms, the actual trend of 0.8 percent a year increase represented a major achievement.

Agricultural production in *developing countries*, summarized in Table 2.3, differed considerably amongst developing regions and countries. In the 1960s, *Asia*, excluding China, had suffered the lowest of all the regional growth rates in agricultural output, giving rise to grave fears as to the region's ability to meet its rising food needs. The advent of the Green Revolution and then the application of policies which encouraged agriculture, brought about an acceleration of output growth in each of the following periods. Except in the 1970s, the inclusion of China raises the all-Asia growth rate appreciably, reflecting an astonishing 5 percent a year increase in its farm output in the ten years to 1985. Alone amongst the developing regions, Asia maintained its agricultural self-sufficiency over the period as a whole.

Sluggish agricultural production growth in *sub-Saharan Africa* in the 1960s worsened in the 1970s and, aggravated by ravaging droughts, frequently inappropriate policies and unsettled political conditions, became a full-scale and deep-rooted crisis over much of the region in the early 1980s as referred to in the accompanying box. The degree of agricultural self-sufficiency fell precipitously in the 1970s. Recent (1985 and 1986) recovery from drought conditions in most of the region and a number of policy reforms still leaves the trend of output for the first half of the 1980s critically below economic and nutritional requirements.

**Box 2.1** *The famine in Africa*

In 1983 and 1984, sub-Saharan Africa experienced the worst famine in its history. The horrifying images of malnourished and starving people in Ethiopia and elsewhere in the continent galvanized the world into action. International food assistance was made available in a display of international solidarity which saved millions. Yet thousands of people perished. The toll was also great for many of those who survived, but lost their means of livelihood, were uprooted from their homes and could no longer meet their basic needs.

*The dimension of the crisis*: In 1983, Southern Africa experienced a second consecutive year of drought; bush fires swept through West African coastal countries; the cassava belt of West Africa was hit by a major pest infestation; and livestock suffered a serious outbreak of rinderpest. Refugees and internal strife in other parts of Africa caused further strain on domestic food supplies. Unlike the 1968–72 food crisis which was limited to the Sahelian region and Ethiopia, the famine of 1983 and 1984 enveloped North, West, East and Southern Africa, affecting both human and livestock populations. During 1984, almost half of Africa's 51 developing countries experienced abnormal food shortages. It was estimated that at least 30 million people out of a total population of some 240 million in these countries were subject to famine and malnutrition. Of

**Table 2.3** Growth of gross agricultural production and self-sufficiency ratios: 94 developing countries

| | Growth rates (% per year) | | | | SSR* (%) | | | |
|---|---|---|---|---|---|---|---|---|
| | 61–70 | 70–80 | 80–5 | 61–85 | 61/3 | 69/71 | 79/81 | 83/5 |
| 94 developing countries | 3.5 | 3.0 | 3.9 | 3.2 | 106.6 | 105.7 | 100.3 | 101.1 |
| 93 developing countries (excluding China) | 2.7 | 3.0 | 3.0 | 2.9 | 109.8 | 107.5 | 101.2 | 101.4 |
| Africa (sub-Saharan) | 2.8 | 1.5 | 2.0 | 2.0 | 119.8 | 117.0 | 102.9 | 100.8 |
| Near East/N. Africa | 3.0 | 3.1 | 2.4 | 2.9 | 100.9 | 97.4 | 80.1 | 75.6 |
| Asia | 3.8 | 3.2 | 4.9 | 3.5 | 100.9 | 101.9 | 99.5 | 102.0 |
| Asia (excluding China) | 2.5 | 3.1 | 4.0 | 3.0 | 103.7 | 102.8 | 100.8 | 103.5 |
| Latin America | 3.0 | 3.3 | 2.3 | 3.0 | 119.9 | 115.7 | 113.0 | 113.9 |
| Low-income countries | 3.7 | 2.7 | 4.8 | 3.2 | 101.0 | 102.0 | 98.2 | 100.3 |
| Low-income countries (excluding China) | 2.3 | 2.2 | 3.7 | 2.4 | 103.9 | 103.0 | 98.4 | 100.3 |
| Low-income countries (excluding China and India) | 2.7 | 1.9 | 3.0 | 2.3 | 111.0 | 106.0 | 100.8 | 99.5 |
| Middle-income countries | 3.1 | 3.5 | 2.6 | 3.2 | 114.9 | 111.1 | 103.2 | 102.3 |

* Self-Sufficiency Ratio (SSR) = $\frac{\text{Production}}{\text{Domestic use excl. stock changes}}$ percent

these, almost 10 million abandoned their homes and lands in search of food, water and pasture for their herds.

This famine was more than a passing emergency. Many of the causes of the tragedy had been in the making for twenty years or more. It was the result of a combination of factors, both natural and man-made. Prolonged drought served only to trigger events that would probably have happened sooner or later. Before the drought, per caput food production had declined steadily. The fact that African countries were not producing enough food stemmed from serious limitations of the natural environment, an imbalance in the global trade structure, and government policies that had given low priority to food production.

*Countries affected by the African food crisis and the response of donors*

| | Marketing years | | |
|---|---|---|---|
| | 1983/4 | 1984/5 | 1985/6 |
| 1. Countries affected | 24 | 21 | 6 |
| 2. Countries affected by successive bad crops | 14 | 11 | 6 |
| 3. Extent of decline in cereal production—up to 20% | 8 | 9 | 2 |
| —more than 20% | 11 | 11 | 3 |
| 4. Cereal import requirements (million tonnes) | 5.3 | 12.2 | 2.7 |
| 5. Commercial imports (million tonnes) | 2.2 | 5.1 | 0.9 |
| 6. Food aid pledges (million tonnes) | 2.6 | 7.1 | 2.3 |
| (of which delivered) (million tonnes) | (2.3) | (5.9) | (2.0) |

*The response*: The international community initially took time to acknowledge the gravity of the crisis. However, the ultimate response was generous. Food aid pledged to the affected countries during their 1983/4 marketing years of 2.6 million tonnes represented 84 percent of the needs; by the end of the year, 88 percent of these pledges had been delivered. For the 1984/5 marketing year, the donor response in terms of pledges made was even greater with virtually all of the identified food aid requirements covered by pledges of over 7 million tonnes; of these pledges, 5.9 million tonnes were delivered.

Compared with the previous food crisis of the 1970s, the detection of the impending worsening food supply situation in Africa was timely. As early as January 1983, the FAO Global Information and Early Warning System issued its first notice of worsening drought in Southern Africa. In April 1983, a special FAO/WFP Task Force was established to review and monitor the food and crop situation in a number of countries which were affected or threatened by abnormally low production. In the following months, the Director-General launched numerous appeals for assistance for the most seriously affected countries. In October 1983, FAO arranged a meeting of the representatives of the affected countries, bilateral and multilateral donors and non-governmental organizations for a detailed assessment of the food supply situation and food aid requirements.

At the national level, the value of food security measures was confirmed. Tanzania's early warning system, set up with FAO's assistance, kept the authorities well informed of crop conditions, allowing the shortages to be covered by timely imports. Although Niger was among the countries hardest hit by drought, its network of reserve stocks helped it through 1983/4. Only in the following year, when these reserves were exhausted, did Niger request food aid.

After a moderate growth rate of 3 percent in the 1960s, *Latin America* lifted output growth in the following decade. Good export commodity prices and strong domestic economic growth were major factors over much of this period. In the first half of the 1980s, however, production growth deteriorated seriously, reflecting especially the collapse in international agricultural commodity prices, the economic slow-down in the region and the consequences of the external debt crisis for many countries. The highly-skewed distribution of income in many countries of the region continued throughout the 25 years to check the rate of expansion of domestic demand for food and consequently the growth of part of agricultural output. Despite some decline in the 1960s, agricultural self-sufficiency remained consistently higher in Latin America than in the other regions.

Agricultural production within the *Near East and North Africa* increased satisfactorily in the 1960s, rising more rapidly than population. Although an immediate effect of the oil boom and the strong economic growth in the 1970s was to stimulate food and feed imports, production growth was also raised marginally at the regional level but more so for some of the oil exporters. Large-scale investments were undertaken. Livestock output benefited particularly from larger feed imports. The expansion could not be sustained in the first half of the 1980s, partly because of poor seasonal conditions, including drought in the Mahgreb countries. The surge in imports reduced the degree of self-sufficiency of the region drastically in the 1970s and, reflecting the poor agricultural production performance, the fall continued in the first half of the 1980s.

Throughout the period under review there has been a very wide range of agricultural production growth rates amongst developing countries. Not only was the spread wide in each of the periods, but also each category of growth rate accounted for a significant number of countries and share of total population. While a minority of countries recorded impresive production performance, more than one-quarter of the 94 countries expanded output by less than 2 percent a year, a seriously inadequate performance in almost all circumstances (Table 2.4). All regions have had countries with fast- and slow-growing agricultural outputs with growth rates markedly differentiated and the above-average growth of countries in each region recording a distinctly higher

**Table 2.4** Distribution of the 94 developing countries by growth rates of gross agricultural production

| | 1961–70 | 1970–80 | 1975–85 |
|---|---|---|---|
| Over 4% | | | |
| No. countries | 25 (24) | 17 | 16 (15) |
| Population (million)* | 993 (264) | 317 | 1350 (354) |
| 3–4% | | | |
| No. countries | 19 | 17 (16) | 10 |
| Population (million)* | 140 | 1329 (402) | 320 |
| 2–3% | | | |
| No. countries | 26 | 14 | 20 |
| Population (million)* | 432 | 877 | 1133 |
| 0–2% | | | |
| No. countries | 21 | 37 | 37 |
| Population (million)* | 711 | 352 | 389 |
| Negative | | | |
| No. countries | 3 | 9 | 11 |
| Population (million)* | 10 | 49 | 56 |

* Population at mid-point of the period.
(Figures in parentheses exclude China.)

rate of expansion (Table 2.5). Both groups contributed substantially to output in each case.

Agricultural production in the *developed countries* grew at about two-thirds the rate of developing countries so that between 1961/3 and 1983/5 their share in world agricultural output declined from 58 to 51 percent. Developed market economies as a whole raised their farm output fairly steadily by a little over 2 percent a year for most of the past 25 years (Table 2.6). The rate of growth dropped sharply during the first half of the 1980s, reflecting, among other things, the policy-induced declines in the growth rate of the United States compared with the 1970s. European centrally planned economies, after a steep fall in output growth rates in the 1970s, regained during the first half of the 1980s a moderate production growth more in line with longer-term trends. After showing little change in the 1960s, the degree of self-sufficiency rose appreciably in North America and Western Europe in the 1970s, reflecting the expansion of export opportunities or import-replacement policies. A contrary shift occurred in the centrally planned group, the fall in self-sufficiency having only partly recovered in the first half of the 1980s. While Western Europe continued to raise its degree of self-sufficiency in the recent years, the weakening of export opportunities was a major influence in bringing about declining degrees of self-sufficiency elsewhere.

Year-to-year instability of output continued to be a serious problem for many countries. At the world level, however, output failed to increase in only two years, 1972 and 1983. In the former year widespread unfavourable weather coincided with insufficient and declining stocks. There followed sudden increases in imports by some countries, and this setback in output was enough

**Table 2.5** 94 developing countries: comparative country performances in agricultural production, 1961–85

| | Annual growth rate of output | Share of total production | |
|---|---|---|---|
| | 1961–85 (%) | 1969/71 (%) | 1983/5 (%) |
| Africa (sub-Saharan) | | | |
| High growth* | 3.6 | 23 | 28 |
| Others | 1.5 | 77 | 72 |
| Near East/N. Africa | | | |
| High growth* | 4.4 | 21 | 27 |
| Others | 2.5 | 79 | 73 |
| Asia | | | |
| High growth* | 4.1 | 65 | 69 |
| Others | 2.5 | 35 | 31 |
| Asia (excluding China) | | | |
| High growth* | 4.0 | 37 | 41 |
| Others | 2.5 | 63 | 59 |
| Latin America | | | |
| High growth* | 3.6 | 62 | 68 |
| Others | 1.9 | 38 | 32 |

* High-growth countries: those with growth rate of production during 1961–85 above 3 percent per year.

to set off panic reactions. In fact, supplies continued to be available on world markets for all with the money to pay for them, but the crisis atmosphere led to a steep rise in international cereal prices and to widespread reappraisal of food and agricultural policies. The 1983 stagnation in world output was above all due to a 15 percent decline in US production which, although affected by a rather poor season, was in large part the result of deliberate policies following the experience of supplies in excess of effective demand. Unlike the experience of 1972, this decline in output growth had a stabilizing effect on world markets.

*Increased imports*: Increasing reliance on international trade as a source of food supplies and for the disposal of increased output represented a fundamental change in the world food system in the period under review (Fig. 2.4). In 1961/3, world agricultural imports were equivalent to 10 percent of output and by 1983/5 this share had risen to 14 percent (8 and 12 percent, respectively, for food). The increase took place in both developing and developed countries, largely in the 1970s.

Gross imports of food commodities for both food and feed by the 94 developing countries as a whole in terms of calories per caput remained stable during the 1960s, doubled over the 1970s and then increased only very little in the first half of the present decade (Table 2.7). Over the same period the developing countries turned from net exporters to net importers of food in terms of calories.

**Table 2.6** Growth of gross agricultural production and self-sufficiency ratios: developed countries

| | Growth rates (% per year) | | | | SSR* (%) | | | |
|---|---|---|---|---|---|---|---|---|
| | 61–70 | 70–80 | 80–5 | 61–85 | 61/3 | 69/71 | 79/81 | 83/5 |
| Developed countries | 2.7 | 1.9 | 1.6 | 2.0 | 96.7 | 96.7 | 100.0 | 99.9 |
| Market economies | 2.2 | 2.1 | 1.4 | 2.0 | 95.7 | 95.7 | 103.8 | 102.6 |
| North America | 2.1 | 2.3 | 1.2 | 2.0 | 105.5 | 105.2 | 120.1 | 113.5 |
| Western Europe | 2.0 | 1.9 | 1.5 | 1.8 | 86.6 | 87.4 | 92.8 | 95.7 |
| Others | 3.3 | 2.1 | 1.8 | 2.2 | 102.5 | 98.4 | 97.3 | 95.5 |
| European centrally planned economies | 3.7 | 1.5 | 2.1 | 2.0 | 98.9 | 98.7 | 92.8 | 94.8 |

* Self-Sufficiency Ratio (SSR) = $\frac{\text{Production}}{\text{Domestic use excl. stock changes}}$ percent

**Table 2.7** Food imports by developing countries

| | (calories per caput per day)* | | | |
|---|---|---|---|---|
| | 1961/3 | 1969/71 | 1979/81 | 1983/5 |
| 94 developing countries | 160 | 160 | 310 | 330 |
| 93 developing countries | 190 | 220 | 400 | 430 |
| Africa (sub-Saharan) | 130 | 160 | 290 | 300 |
| Near East/N. Africa | 400 | 480 | 1090 | 1490 |
| Asia | 110 | 100 | 160 | 150 |
| Asia (excluding China) | 140 | 150 | 190 | 190 |
| Latin America | 270 | 300 | 690 | 640 |
| Low-income countries | 100 | 90 | 130 | 120 |
| Low-income countries (excluding China) | 120 | 120 | 130 | 140 |
| Low-income countries (excluding China and India) | 150 | 200 | 210 | 210 |
| Middle-income countries | 290 | 330 | 730 | 780 |

* Calorie content of gross imports of food commodities for direct food consumption and for indirect consumption (livestock feeding-stuffs).

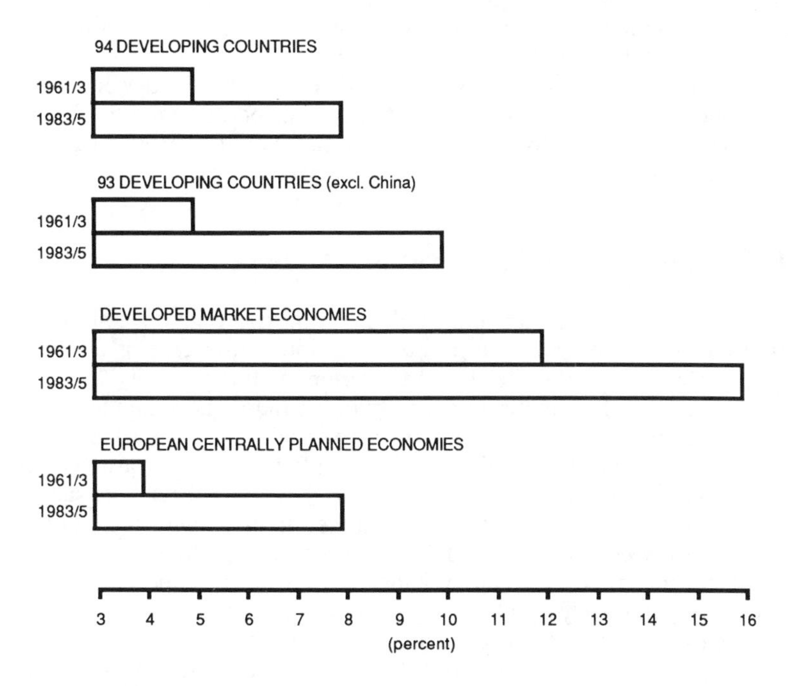


**Figure 2.4** Food imports as share of food supplies

The rise in imports as a source of calories was particularly striking for the Near East/North Africa and the Latin America regions. Asia remained the region least dependent on imports for its food supply. Increased food imports by sub-Saharan Africa included sizeable shipments of food aid which helped to prevent more drastic declines rather than, as elsewhere, in raising consumption levels. Middle-income countries increased their dependence on imports very considerably, the low-income countries, very little.

The Near East/North Africa region was the major exception to the halt in the first half of the 1980s in the increasing dependence on imports as a source of food calories. Latin American imports dropped quite sharply. The period of rapidly expanding food imports was over. These supplies had contributed significantly to the raising of food-consumption levels in a number of developing countries, but chiefly the better-off countries. Their poorer inhabitants probably benefited through the larger food imports moderating the effects on food prices of rising incomes and demand. Apart from food aid supplies, the surge in food imports by developing countries as a whole had little relevance to the serious problems of hunger in many low-income countries.

Some developing countries faced with rising debt-service burdens and a subsequent fall in prices of their export commodities could no longer spare the foreign exchange for expanded food imports. Food imports whose prices became increasingly depressed, partly because of export subsidies of industrialized countries in recent years, led to disincentives for competing domestic producers in developing countries. The low-priced imports also created a growing, strong demand for kinds of food which often could not be economically produced in sufficient quantities in the importing country. Wheat became a major example, gross imports by developing countries increasing from 22 million tonnes in 1961/3 to 60 million tonnes in 1983/5.

As discussed later, the expansion of food/feed exports by developed market economies which made possible the big rise in food imports by developing countries contributed to the creation of production capacity which soon proved excessive but could not be easily removed.

## National policies and their setting

*Evolving national policies*: Economic policies in most developing countries up to quite recently gave priority to industrialization as the core of development strategy, but without sufficient appreciation of the necessity for vigorous agricultural growth as an essential condition for industrialization to firmly take root. The consequences for agriculture were serious. On the one hand, national agricultural policies frequently gave favourable treatment to farmers through such means as support prices, subsidized credit and fertilizers and substantial public expenditures for agricultural infrastructures. On the other hand, however, such policies as high levels of tariff and quota protection to local manufacturing and overvalued exchange rates worked against agriculture and reduced or completely offset the price and profitability incentives to increased production sought as an objective of the agricultural sector policies.

While the situation varied over time as well as amongst countries and commodities, the overall effect of policies in many developing countries was to bring about a pronounced price bias against agriculture. All regions were affected, Africa most and Asia least. This adverse consequence has been analysed in a recent FAO study (FAO 1987b). It was only in the later 1970s, under the threat of critical food shortages, that rectification began to be made of the price bias and other constraints affecting agriculture in a number of countries. The process of policy reform favouring the tradeables sectors, including agriculture, assumed added momentum in recent years under the programmes for macro-economic stabilization and adjustment following balance-of-payments crises and needs for debt-servicing. This recognition of the essential role of agriculture in the economic growth of developing countries represented a fundamental change in the emphasis of policy in many developing countries.

The thrust of agricultural policies in the developed market economies has essentially been to improve farm incomes and raise self-sufficiency or expand exports. These basic objectives have been sought by facilitating productivity growth and by supporting producer incentives in various ways. The extent of price/income support and the insulation of domestic markets from international competition was generally greatest in countries which had not been self-sufficient in food and feed. Traditional large net exporting countries exposed their producers of export commodities much more to international market influences. The food crisis of the 1970s and the rapid growth of food imports, particularly by the developed centrally planned economies and the oil-exporting and middle-income developing countries, encouraged the continuation of these policies of the developed market economy countries towards their agriculture. In importing countries, or those with an earlier tradition of importing, the threat of shortages was widely interpreted as validating the protectionist policies which, through high prices to farmers, were stimulating production growth. In the more open agricultural economies of traditional exporters, high international prices fed through to prices received by farmers and so encouraged expansion of capacity and output in these countries also. A large share of increased agricultural production in developed market economy countries over the 1970s went to expand exports or to replace imports.

Any thoughts of adjusting production and farming systems to a slowing down in long-term demands were thus shelved. Before long agricultural surpluses re-emerged in the 1980s as the demand for imports weakened, giving rise to greatly intensified export competition by industrialized market economies and to unprecedented export subsidies. Economic resources absorbed by farm support programmes became increasingly visible and the subject of political debate as importing countries became more self-sufficient and in a number of cases changed to become net exporters, and the burden of further increases in output started to shift from the consumer (through higher prices) to the taxpayer (for exports subsidies). Well before the mid-1980s it became evident that these policies would have to be modified so as to induce an orderly retardation in production trends, but most governments hesitated to make sufficient changes unilaterally and no agreement was forthcoming multilaterally. Only towards the mid-1980s steps were taken to begin to curb excess production.

Policies in the USSR and Eastern Europe continued to reiterate the long-standing objective of improving food consumption standards and boosting agricultural production, especially of livestock. While significant gains were achieved in food consumption, agricultural efficiency of the group as a whole declined, reflecting developments in the USSR. This country's new readiness as from the early 1970s to compensate shortfalls in cereal production by increasing imports, particularly of cereals for feed rather than by reducing livestock numbers and domestic consumption represented an important change in policy.

Throughout the group of the developed CPEs, and led by Hungary, ways of evolving forms of socialist agriculture more responsive to market-oriented signals, and incentives came to the fore in agricultural policy discussions in the 1980s, leading to some innovations but more importantly raising the prospect of greater changes in the future. In the developing centrally planned economies, China was implementing dramatic policy changes from 1979 with significant success, giving peasant families much more control over production decisions and relaxing marketing controls so that price incentives could become effective. The very success of these policies did, however, lead to the need for further policy modifications by the mid-1980s, notably the perceived need to check the switch which was taking place from cereal production to higher-priced and more profitable crops.

*Structural changes and rural equity*: The agricultural labour force halved in numbers in developed countries between 1960 and 1985 but doubled in developing countries. This fact alone carried important implications for the structure of agriculture and farming systems and policies.

In developed countries the bulk of output, particularly of crop output, came increasingly from a minority of farms which grew steadily bigger. Policies, however, remained largely oriented to the traditional family farm of which large numbers, often relatively small in area, and in the livestock sector, remain in some countries. Producer prices were thought to need government support for the income of these family farms to be brought to parity with non-farm incomes. Owners of larger farms were in practice the main beneficiaries. Policies did not keep in step with these changes, and furthermore they only rarely addressed questions which were becoming more prominent of the desirable future farming systems or the future pattern of land use and its implications for the environment.

The long-standing problems of rural equity in developing countries were rendered ever more acute over the review period by the necessity for agriculture to absorb an additional 300 million workers on a farm land area that could be expanded only very modestly in many countries. Most of the world's poor are rural people; an estimated 700 million rural people lived in developing countries excluding China and other Asian socialist countries in 'absolute poverty', that is deprived of certain basic necessities of life, in 1980 (see Ch. 9). Highly unequal land ownership remained a fundamental cause. Data for the early 1970s for 57 developing countries show that at one extreme farms of 1000 ha and over accounted for only 0.1 percent of all holdings but held more than 35 percent of the total arable land. At the other extreme, almost 50 percent of holdings were less than 1 ha but occupied only 2.9 percent of the total area. Land remained most unequally distributed in Latin America, followed by countries in the Near East and in South-East Asia.

Most governments officially adopted policies of improved rural equity during the review period. Effective implementation, however, has been lacking except in a few countries. Several strategies were tried. Substantial redistribution of land, the most fundamental approach, proved politically and administratively difficult and was achieved only in few countries. A combination of land settlement programmes, tenancy reform and welfare food schemes improved rural equity in a few countries. Others opted for high overall economic growth with dependance chiefly on market forces to enable benefits to trickle down to the very poor. This approach, however, met with mixed success.

Earlier fears that small farmers could not share in the benefits of the Green Revolution proved unfounded and it is now generally agreed that the production technology which uses high-yielding varieties of cereals is scale-neutral. However, in practice, the whole process of modernization and commercialization of agriculture inherently favoured larger farmers because of their much better access to the new inputs and technologies. In some countries, perhaps most of all in Latin America, existing tendencies to dualistic farming systems were thereby continued, with heavy welfare and equity costs.

Despite progress in a few countries, there is consensus that rural poverty and inequality remains a severe problem and that in some countries the situation has probably worsened since the 1960s. These circumstances led to the World Conference on Agrarian Reform and Rural Development (WCARRD) in 1979. The Declaration of Principles and Programme of Action are agreed signposts for policy reorientation. They have markedly influenced the development policies and strategies of FAO, other UN Agencies and bilateral donors, with more weight now placed on equity. At the country level, however, decisive action was still generally being awaited by the middle 1980s (see FAO 1987c).

*Closer integration of agriculture in the overall economy*: A secular change of considerable importance which has gathered pace over the past quarter-century is the increasing integration of agriculture in both domestic economies and the international economy. Sales and purchases by farm families of their food production or requirements steadily encroached on largely subsistence agriculture, although production for home consumption still remains a basic part of developing-country agriculture. The importance of off-farm inputs to production grew steadily in developing countries and reached very high levels in mechanized, capital-intensive farming in developed countries. Institutional credit became more important in the financing of farm operations. Off-farm sources of income provided a rising share of the total income of farm families—some 40–50 percent for very small farmers and landless labourers in developing countries in the early 1980s, more than half in the case of US farm families.

As developing country agriculture became more monetized, its linkage with industry also became more prominent. Rural purchases provided a significant part—and often the largest part—of the market for goods produced by domestic manufacturing industries, while the processing of food and agricultural raw materials has typically been the basis of developing-country industrialization.

At the same time, the food and agricultural sector became more closely integrated in the international economy, following the rising share of output which is traded internationally and the increased links to the monetary economy. Exchange rates, interest rates and the availability of capital are strongly affected by the international environment. The latter, therefore, influences directly or indirectly the cost of finance to the sector, the prices of imported inputs and those of the commodities exported or competing with imports in the domestic market.

Economic and financial developments, especially in recent years, have thus meant that agriculture too became more affected by macro-economic policies and general economic conditions both within the country and internationally. The full bearing of this increasing interdependence was, however, not widely appreciated until recently. Chapter 8 examines some issues in this field.

## The international setting

The 1960s were characterized by comparative stability in overall economic growth, exchange and interest rates and, at least to present-day eyes, in commodity prices also. The 1970s and the first half of the 1980s however, have brought very different international economic conditions.

*Recent international economic environment*: In the early 1970s, exchange rates became unstable as major currencies were floated. The real price of petroleum rose steeply, boosting the economies of oil exporters and international bank liquidity but slowing growth elsewhere. Inflation gathered pace in most countries and low real interest rates in the second half of the decade encouraged expanded borrowing by many developing countries. The world food crisis of 1972–4 sharply but temporarily increased international prices of food commodities while other agricultural prices rose briefly later in the decade.

Industrialized countries slumped into their deepest postwar recession at the end of the 1970s, their growth averaging just over one percent a year between 1980 and 1984. Consequent sluggish demand in these major markets, together with more than ample supplies, led to heavy falls in many international commodity prices. For agricultural products of developing market economies the fall in nominal prices was as follows:

| | 1980 | 1981 | 1982 | 1983 | 1984 | 1985 | 1986 |
|---|---|---|---|---|---|---|---|
| Food | 100 | 82 | 67 | 70 | 70 | 63 | 77 |
| Non-food | 100 | 89 | 76 | 85 | 90 | 73 | 70 |

For capital-importing developing countries the cost of servicing of external debt rose to a quarter of export earnings by 1986. Net capital inflows from private creditors and short-term flows, the largest source of loans for developing countries, collapsed early in the present decade, and by 1986 there was a net outflow on capital account. Rising interest rates, impaired export earnings and the steep fall in capital inflows thus brought about a crisis in the external indebtedness of developing countries, a crisis which up to 1987 has been barely contained, let alone solved.

Agriculture was inevitably affected along with the rest of the economy.

Imports of production prerequisites and raw materials had to be reduced by developing countries faced with balance-of-payments difficulties. Budgetary pressures as well as the views of financing institutions led to subsidies on inputs and on food consumption being reduced, while government expenditures on the infrastructure of agriculture were also reduced in a number of countries. Such changes cut most deeply in countries heavily dependent on agricultural commodity exports and with high external indebtedness. Thus Latin America and Africa were more affected than Asia. The African drought compounded the economic problems of the region which culminated in the full-scale food crisis that engulfed the majority of African countries.

Many developed countries, especially those with large and relatively unprotected agricultural export sectors, experienced serious falls in farm incomes and in export earnings from agriculture. Domestic problems were intensified where farmers, encouraged by good prices in the 1970s, had borrowed heavily.

Despite such adverse effects, however, on a global scale agriculture weathered the economic storms of the late 1970s and early 1980s as regards production growth and had a steadying influence on the overall economy in many countries. Demand facing the sector tended to remain relatively steady in face of moderate income falls and general economic instability, reflecting the essential nature of food. Employment in agriculture was less affected by national recession or difficulties than employment in industry. Furthermore, many governments intervened to limit the impact of international price falls on domestic agricultural prices. Exchange rate devaluations and a halt in the rise of food imports tended to improve the position of producers in a number of developing countries.

*International cooperation*: As noted, trade, monetary and technical developments in recent decades have appreciably accelerated the integration of agriculture into national economies and of national economies into a global economy. The agricultural sector has featured prominently in UN discussions seeking consensus for world development strategies, with the interests of developing countries in the foreground. Summit meetings of leaders of the major industrial countries have also endeavoured to agree on broad lines of policy for dealing with prominent issues, including food and agriculture. Increased technical cooperation amongst countries and their relevant institutions has brought useful results in a number of more technical aspects of agriculture. Progress has been negligible, however, in the area of agricultural trade, and inadequate as regards food security while disquietening trends have emerged in development assistance to developing countries, which overall has never reached agreed targets.

*Trade issues*: These have been almost constantly on international agendas in the past decades, with the three rounds of multilateral trade negotiations under the auspices of GATT, the Generalised System of Preferences (GSP) and commodity agreements in UNCTAD, and with many preferential trade arrangements. Ever since the early 1960s agricultural commodities have, even formally, escaped GATT disciplines. In sharp contrast with manufactures, negligible progress has been achieved in relation to agricultural commodities under GATT negotiations. The stumbling block remains the insistence of some developed countries on the right to pursue agricultural policies that pay little, if any, regard to the consequences of these policies on international trade and hence on the agricultural sectors of other countries. In recent years ample evidence has been gathered of the substantial costs to the protecting countries themselves and to other countries, but experience over this period indicated clearly that progress towards phased reduction of protection would depend on the national economic and international political costs of the continuation of present protection being assessed by top policy-makers in major countries as unacceptably high. Recent ministerial-level Declarations concerning the new round of GATT multilateral negotiations and economic policy cooperation amongst OECD member countries indicate that this stage may now have been reached. The Declarations explicitly recognize the need for increased discipline on measures affecting agricultural trade and on a concerted reform of agricultural policies.

The thrust of UNCTAD's efforts as regards agriculture has been to promote a series of commodity agreements (ICAs) linked to a Common Fund—that is exporter/importer agreements on price stabilization, increased export earnings, and other issues related to trade in a commodity. The principle of ICAs has been widely, although not in all quarters strongly, supported. However, the implementation has encountered numerous difficulties. A number of attempts to negotiate ICAs, on the basis of the original concept, have failed. For various reasons, the agreements concluded mostly failed to achieve basic objectives. Even the Common Fund, with almost symbolic resources, is still awaiting ratification.

While intensive trade negotiations in recent decades have largely failed to bring about any substantial improvement in international agricultural trade, it has, however, become increasingly evident that action to solve the pressing problems of creeping protectionism, structural surpluses, bilateralization of trade, and so on, could not possibly be postponed much longer.

*Food security*: During the quarter-century following the Second World War the faster growth of world food production than of both population and effective demand and the existence of large surplus stocks, although held mostly in North America, kept the subject of global food security in the background. The world food crisis of 1972–4 challenged prevailing complacency. Food suddenly appeared to be in short supply on world markets, cereal prices rose sharply and food aid fell; those on whom the heaviest burden fell were the poor people in poor countries. Impetus was immediately given to proposals for national and international measures for the holding of stocks, for regular intergovernmental consultations and other related actions. The FAO Conference adopted an International Undertaking on World Food Security, and the World Food Conference of 1974 recommended that world food security at national and international levels be achieved by a combination of measures concerning production and access to supplies, together with a commitment to provide at least 10 million tonnes of cereals as food aid each year.

The right of people to a reasonable degree of food security, together with some joint responsibility of the international community, for arrangements to meet shortages became generally accepted in recent years, but the original goal of a formal stock policy at a global level was not attained. The guideline of adequacy of world cereal stocks at 17–18 percent of annual consumption did however gain implicit acceptance.

Experience with various institutional arrangements concerning food security such as a Standing Committee on World Food Security, the FAO Global Information and Early Warning System to monitor continuously the changing food supply situation and a modest-sized International Emergency Food Reserve for quick responses to food emergencies led to a clearer understanding of the three underlying goals of action in regard to food security: ensuring adequacy of production of food supplies, maximizing stability in their flow and securing access to available supplies by those who need them.

These three goals have become accepted as the pillars of a broadened concept of world food security, requiring action at national, regional and global levels, not all of it in the food and agriculture sector alone. In particular, the paradox of food plenty and scarcity, on a local plane within developing countries or sub-regions, is now focusing increasing attention on the need to improve ways of ensuring access to food by the poor. Similarly, on a global plane, the paradox highlights the need for a world trading system which can be relied upon to provide access to food imports through enhanced export earnings.

In the first half of the 1980s, ample global food stocks, excess global production capacity and the readiness of donor countries to provide food aid have apparently lessened the earlier urgency of developing international food security arrangements. Although, as just noted, there were useful institutional innovations, adequate international institutional arrangements were not made. If a world-level crisis should emerge, its resolution would therefore have to depend essentially on effective *ad hoc* action by individual countries although, as noted, institutional machinery was evolved in recent years to facilitate coordination and guidance of their initiatives. Such action could face difficulties should the excess supplies on hand in most of the period since the middle 1950s be gradually eliminated as a result of policy reforms concerning agriculture now being asked of developed market economies.

That no firmer arrangements were agreed in the decade since the World Food Conference for international action in the event of a global or widescale food crisis can be only interpreted as a challenge for efforts to be continued. Even the World Food Security Compact, which simply reaffirmed moral commitments, did not meet with universal acceptance in the form adopted by the twenty-third FAO Conference in 1985 (FAO 1985a). These efforts can now draw on growing experience with the use of such institutional arrangements as have been introduced during the past decade. For instance, the Early Warning System referred to above has been tested and developed in practice as an effective means of ensuring that the international community is alerted in good time of impending food shortages. Experience has also indicated how bilateral action can be better coordinated. Lessons learned from the African crisis are referred to in the accompanying box.

**Box 2.2** *Meeting emergencies: lessons learned from the African crisis*

The hopes of a decade ago that famines and lack of preparedness of the early 1970s would never be repeated, and that the new initiatives and commitments which emerged from the 1974

World Food Conference would meet the challenge of ensuring food for all people, have been realized only in part. This is the lesson of the African famine. Although more food aid than ever before was delivered during 1983–5, it came too late in some cases to prevent deaths from hunger. This tragic outcome, at a time when world cereal supplies were well in excess of requirements, demonstrates the crucial need to be better prepared for an emergency. Preparedness planning is essential at all levels: donors, recipient countries and international organisations alike.

The *assessment of needs* through regular monitoring of the changing food situation is the basic prerequisite for a timely response. In this connection, priority needs to be given to strengthening of collection and dissemination of timely information to give warning of the likelihood of substantial food deficits and/or the occurrence of a clearly abnormal event which leads to the inability of people to meet their minimum food requirements. Monitoring should include socio-economic indicators such as unusual migratory movements in search of food or work, rises in the prices of staple foods, and other indicators of family deprivation, together with projections of food aid and other food imports. Where adequate nutritional data are not available, nutritional surveys should constitute an integral part of the assessment of emergency situations.

The responsibility for collecting timely and accurate information lies primarily with the governments of the emergency-prone countries. Wherever they do not exist, national structures in disaster-prone countries should be established to deal with food management in general; these should include early warning systems, food relief contingency schemes, back-up arrangements for mobilizing supplies and detailed plans for distributing emergency food supplies. Existing units should be strengthened to permit more efficient emergency planning and intervention.

Emergency-prone countries should also set up *permanent coordination arrangements* for all stages of the emergency response. Within such coordination mechanisms, recipient governments, donors, NGOs and multilateral organizations should agree to the extent possible on a jointly planned implementation of emergency programmes. Where there are pockets of surplus food in areas of the affected countries alongside those with a serious deficit, governments, donors and aid agencies must make an attempt to plan delivery and distribution of food aid efficiently, resorting to the maximum extent possible to commodity exchanges to reduce excessive food movements.

As regards *requests for emergency assistance*, recipient countries need to make every effort to ensure that these are submitted as early as possible. In certain circumstances, such as the sudden influx of displaced persons, the donor community may need to act prior to the receipt of an official request, for which administrative arrangements need to be developed.

Most of the supplies pledged to the affected countries in 1983/4 and 1984/5 were timely and made during the early part of the emergency year. In many cases, however, the emergency supplies did not reach the population in need within the period for which they were intended, partly because of the limited handling capacity of the affected countries and partly because of late and often uncoordinated arrivals.

A considerable part of the delay in the total response time, from the time donors decide to act and announce their pledges of emergency aid and the time of arrival of supplies in the affected countries, is attributable to administrative and procurement procedures in donor countries. Delays in procurement and transportation of emergency supplies could be considerably reduced by pre-positioning food stocks in advance of possible emergencies. Other available options to accelerate the delivery of emergency food aid include, *inter alia*, diversion of non-emergency food aid shipments already in transit, triangular transactions and local purchases, borrowing arrangements, advance supply mobilization and pre-shipment of food supplies to an affected country as soon as early signals are received regarding likely food shortages.

Finally, although the substantial achievements in food production made the likelihood of a world-level food crisis seem remote, experiences such as those of the 1972–4 food scare or of the Chernobyl nuclear accident in 1986 were reminders that the unforeseen can indeed happen. The coincidence of poor harvests in major producing and consuming regions would be enough to provoke a world food crisis of which poor people in developing food importing countries would be the first victims.

*Assistance*: Assistance to the economic development of developing countries has been financial, technical and policy advice, and food aid. The provision of continuing assistance has become a significant feature of the postwar economic scene, although agreed targets have been met by very few countries. Since 1981, *capital flows* from all sources to developing countries have declined, at both gross and net levels. The estimate of net external borrowing in 1986 at $37.6 billion is less than one-third of the peak 1981 level. Official development assistance declined in real terms in the early 1980s and by 1985 was only fractionally higher than in 1981.

Within this discouraging overall situation, the agricultural sector has fared relatively well. Its share of official commitments to all sectors rose from 12 percent in 1974/5 to 18–20 percent between 1979/80 and 1983/4. An increase of over a third in the second half of the 1970s, and after the world food crisis, to an annual average of $13.3 billion during 1982/4 (in 1980 prices), mainly reflected the increasing emphasis referred to earlier by governments and lending agencies to more rapid agricultural and rural development.

Concessional assistance has averaged about 60–70 percent of total official assistance to agriculture and grew particularly rapidly in Africa. The focus of official commitments to agriculture (OCA) has been increasingly on low-income countries with, for example, the share of low-income food-deficit countries rising from 59 percent in 1974 to 65 percent in 1984. Since 1981/2, however, the upward trend in OCA has slowed.

External assistance has become indispensable in helping to raise more quickly the production of developing-country agriculture, especially that of the least-developed countries. It is also evident on the basis of experience in many countries that stronger coordination of internally and externally generated resources would improve the effectiveness of assistance.

Cooperation between developing countries and the World Bank and the IMF on national economic policies became a more prominent feature of the international scene in recent years. The two organizations are coordinating their activities more closely in drawing up and supporting programmes concerned with macro-economic policies, including structural and sectoral adjustments. Sector adjustment loans of the Bank are frequently made for agricultural purposes and the two organizations have encouraged removal or reduction of policy distortions adverse to agriculture. The views of the Bank and IMF on the appropriateness of national policies have become influential in determining not only their own lending but also the decisions of other lenders concerning new borrowings or refinancing of existing external debt. While these views are generally accepted, their implementation did not meet with ready acceptance everywhere, particularly in some of the countries concerned.

Since its inception in 1954, *food aid* has become established as a way not only of meeting emergency situations but, with safeguards, as a useful means of augmenting concessional transfers of resources to developing countries. Food aid has thus accounted for a share varying from, in the mid-1970s, 12–15 percent of total official development assistance to, from the late 1970s onwards, 9–11 percent. The great bulk of food aid has always been in cereals and has provided a significant proportion of the cereal imports of low-income food-deficit countries (from 14 to 24 percent in the different years from the mid-1970s to the mid-1980s). Sizeable amounts of dairy products and vegetable oils have also been provided.

Food aid, however, has not been without its share of problems. Since it was originally based on supplies arising from production in excess of current demand and stock requirements, future availability of food aid supplies was inherently uncertain. This problem has been only partly met by the 1980 Food Aid Convention, which raised its guaranteed safety net to 7.6 million tonnes of cereals.

The potential or actual harmful effects of food aid on recipient countries, have been widely analysed and debated. Some negative impacts in the early phase of food aid are well recognized. In the 1960s, when food aid covered a sizeable part of import needs of developing countries, it did encourage the tendency in a number of developing countries to attach low priority to agriculture. When allowed to affect local food prices unduly, it has acted as a disincentive to farmers in recipient countries. Adverse effects of food aid on consumption patterns (e.g. toward imported wheat, especially in sub-Saharan Africa) have also become obvious. Now, however, means of absorbing food aid without adversely affecting the incomes of farmers in recipient countries have become better understood and applied. It is also possible that the disposal of part of surplus production as food aid has helped to delay agricultural adjustment measures in some donor countries.

The broad assessment of 30 years of experience with food aid is favourable. Food aid has featured prominently in responses of the international community to emergencies which have arisen throughout the review period and to the need to accelerate development in poor and food-deficit countries. Apart from providing valuable additional resources to developing countries, food aid arrangements, incomplete and somewhat *ad hoc* as they are, have the capacity to abolish the threat of localized famines on the scale of the past, although in practice, complete success has not yet been achieved. The assumption by the world community of a limited but vital degree of food security in the form of food aid is one of the great accomplishments of recent decades in cooperation amongst countries.

Food aid has played a critical role in limiting the ravages of the famines which have struck much of Africa in recent years. In sub-Saharan Africa, however, the emergency is deeply rooted in a progressive deterioration in the effectiveness of the economic system of countries and, in particular, of their agriculture, further aggravated by unsettled political conditions in some of them.

In these circumstances, the response has now taken the form of a comprehensive and long-term UN Programme of Action for African Economic Recovery and Development (UN/PAAERD). Its contents and emphasis draw on the experience, now lengthy, of assisting developing countries to establish or strengthen the bases of economic growth. In particular, reflecting the importance of food and agriculture in economic development and for African economic recovery, this and agro-based sectors are being given overriding priority. It is already evident that the programme calls for a generosity of support and a level of effectiveness in its application which, if successful, will mark a new stage in international cooperation for development.

*Regional and sub-regional cooperation*: This has become a prominent form of international cooperation, additional to those referred to above. The European Community, with its substantial implications for agriculture, is the outstanding instance in the developed world. Each of the developing regions has economic integration or cooperation schemes. While industry and investment are the chief forms of such schemes, agriculture is too important not to be included. Largely because avoidance of possible decreases in existing degrees of national self-sufficiency in any staple food remains a goal of all governments, however, experience has shown that the full incorporation of agriculture always raises difficult problems.

To sum up, experience with cooperative action amongst countries concerning agriculture presents a mixed picture. Valuable achievements include a rising flow of assistance to the agriculture of developing countries, together with technical and policy advice, comprehensive action programmes such as the UN/PAAERD, innovations aimed at famine prevention and numerous specific and limited cooperative initiatives. Set against these accomplishments, however, are the resounding failures to deal with the critically important issue of reducing protectionist agricultural policies and bringing agricultural trade effectively within GATT disciplines, and the dangerously incomplete state of international cooperative arrangements for food security. Recent changes in the overall capital flow to developing countries and the related burden of debt-servicing imply adverse affects for food and agriculture which need to be redressed.

*Agricultural exports—an uncertain and weakening engine of growth*: Large and unforeseen changes took place in agricultural trade after the early 1970s. A marked rise in import demand by middle-income and oil-exporting developing countries, by the European CPEs and from the intra-trade of developed market economies was the stimulus. The export scene was dominated by the expansion of supplies from developed market economies, an expansion which lasted through most of the 1970s until arrested in recent years. The volume of agricultural exports of developing countries grew very sluggishly, while those of developed market economy countries surged ahead in the 1970s. Both groups of countries experienced a fall in the value of their agricultural exports at current prices in the first half of the 1980s. The outcome is best summed up in terms of movements in net agricultural trade balances, shown in current dollars (exports fob, imports cif) in Figure 2.5.

Figure 2.5 shows the marked deterioration in the net agricultural trade balances of developing and of European centrally planned countries in the later 1970s through to 1981 together with the matching improvement in the position of developed market economies; and between 1981 and 1985 a reversal of the trends of the previous decade, with net agricultural trade flows in 1985 tending broadly towards the patterns typical of the 1960s.

The rapid expansion in agricultural trade in the 1970s will probably be seen in retrospect as an extraordinary and temporary phenomenon. The impetus had come from the side of demand and had met with a ready response from exporters, chiefly developed market economies. Their technical advances, producer price and income supports or good levels of market-determined prices, and substantial agricultural investment had together built up an expansion in production capacity well beyond that dictated by the slowing growth in their domestic demand. This capacity expansion which enabled exports to be increased rapidly is the fundamental cause of current problems of overproduction in many of these countries and of the painful process of retardation of agricultural growth and elimination of excess stocks currently under way.

The surge in demand for imports stopped when previously expansionary influences reversed at more or less the same time at the start of the 1980s. Many developing countries cut back on import growth because of the slow-down in income growth and demand and because of the need to service greatly enlarged external debt at a time when export earnings, including those from oil, had fallen. Other previously food-importing countries, most notably China and India, had succeeded in raising their own food production substantially. Increasing foreign-exchange constraints and occasional better harvests in the European CPEs led to a reversal in their rising trends of imports of food and feed. In addition, the scope for more import replacement in many countries, particularly in the EEC had been greatly reduced.

There were two interrelated consequences: a collapse of international prices of major agricultural commodities, and mounting pressure on exporters either

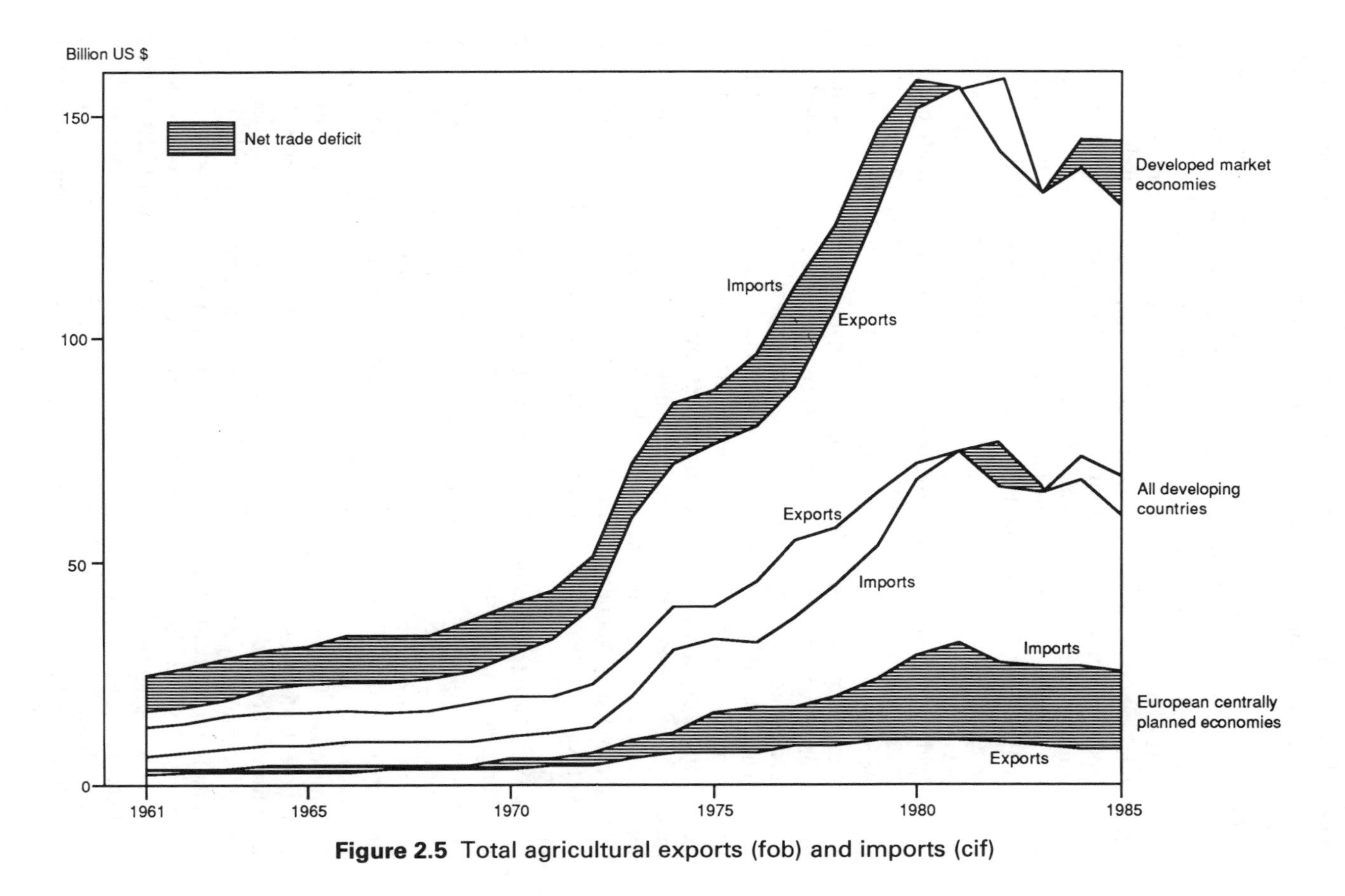


**Figure 2.5** Total agricultural exports (fob) and imports (cif)

to slow down their production growth or to hold existing markets and find new ones at the expense of competitors. A third impact—a marked slowing down in some developing countries of improvements in calorie intakes based on food imports—was noted earlier.

The trend of real prices for exported agricultural commodities had been fairly stable over the 1960s and had fluctuated widely during the 1970s. After 1980 prices fell almost continuously and reached their lowest level, compared with prices of manufactured goods, of the past 40 years. While the volume of agricultural exports of developing countries continued to grow in the first half of the 1980s (except for sub-Saharan Africa) the falling world prices offset most of the volume increase. Apart from the trend level of prices, shorter-term instability of export prices continued to be a major characteristic. For instance, between 1960 and 1984, the highest deflated annual prices in international trade were the following multiples of the lowest annual prices: wheat 2.1, beef 2.2, coffee 3.2, sugar 8.0.

The widespread existence of agricultural protectionism and trade controls conditioned and distorted the response of both exporting and importing countries to the cessation of growth in trade in the first half of the 1980s. In these circumstances, international price falls had little effect on protected production of which both the import-replacement as well as the export and stock-accumulation components continued to expand, and the competition for stagnant, shrinking or controlled external markets became intense. A high level of protection in some developed countries made the maintenance or expansion of exports by other countries that much more difficult, impelling them to match the export subsidies and similar practices of their competitors. Developing countries and the smaller developed exporting countries were at a decided disadvantage in this war of subsidized exports. By the mid-1980s, these practices had brought a large part of agricultural trade into disarray.

This response to a change in world import demand raised the question of whether governments viewed agricultural trade as intrinsically different from other merchandise trade where protection had been lowered in successive GATT rounds. The experience of recent years has shown that while governments are prepared to accept, even if reluctantly, some shrinkage in uncompetitive manufacturing industries as protection is reduced, they have not so far been prepared to contemplate a similar shrinkage in agriculture, at least for major food and feed commodities. Consequently, it seems that most governments do indeed view agricultural trade as different in degree if not in kind from other trade. The objectives of maintaining or raising the degree of food self-sufficiency and improving farm incomes still remained at the heart of most national agricultural policies (with little regard to foreign trade effects in most cases) while there was nothing comparable in industrial sectors. By the 1980s agricultural trade conflicts inherent in the uninhibited pursuit of these objectives by countries which could afford high-cost import replacement and expensively subsidized export sales, had seriously weakened the contribution which agricultural exports could make to orderly economic growth.

## Achievements and problems

Changes in the quarter-century as reviewed above thus include both substantial achievements as regards food and agriculture, but also the persistence of some long-standing problems and the advent of others. On balance, however, developments have been positive, world food and agriculture a success story.

The outstanding achievement has been the rise in food consumption of the majority of people of a substantially enlarged world population. This was made possible only by great progress in farming methods and inputs as well as in the volume of output traded internationally. World agriculture became a dynamic sector over the period. In developing countries, a fundamental shift took place in some countries and is now being given heed to elsewhere towards fuller recognition of the role of agriculture in their economic growth. The implicit acceptance by the international community of a degree of responsibility for food security and for assistance to the agricultural development of poor countries marked a historical change in international affairs.

Against these achievements must be noted a lack of progress in a number of areas and the emergence of other problems which will beset the future. Without trying to rank them or to downplay the importance of other questions, three problems will remain of very great concern to food and agriculture in the remaining 1980s and the 1990s; trade and related production adjustments, access to food and the environment. Disarray in agricultural trade, and its underlying protectionism, is creating tremendous real costs for both developed and developing countries and cries out for a more effective framework and rules. Retardation—not cessation—required in the growth of production of developed market economies will cause severe adjustment difficulties in the medium term. The poor of the world need improved access to food; the increasingly frequent paradox of hunger, still afflicting hundreds of millions of people, and excess supplies has been left to the future to solve. There is a trade as well as a domestic economic growth and income distribution aspect to this problem. Likewise, the world has still left unanswered the question of how best to be prepared for any widespread occurrence of crop failures. The third problem, becoming more serious each year, is the protection of the agricultural resources and environment from pollution and degradation; at present there is more publicity than action (see Ch. 11).

Agriculture is also very much involved in the external debt problem of many developing countries, with their efforts to slow the perilous urban population explosion and with questions of how to locate more of their industrialization outside larger urban centres. Finally, the complex and acute problem of rehabilitating sub-Saharan African agriculture and avoiding the recurrence of famines or minimizing their impacts, faces both the region and the world.

Experience points to the fundamental importance of a vigorous agriculture as one of the prerequisites for an adequate response to these problems in the remaining years of the century. The next chapters analyse the requirements for and prospects of such an agricultural performance.

# 3 World food and agriculture to 2000

## The developing countries

### Continuation of trends

Chapter 2 indicated that the food and agricultural trends in the developing countries have been mixed. At the aggregate level significant progress was achieved in production and consumption accompanied by large increases of food imports from, and slower growth of exports to, the rest of the world. In many countries, including some of the most populous ones, gains in consumption relied mainly on genuine improvements of domestic agriculture. In other countries, such gains depended overwhelmingly on increased imports. A third class of countries, many in the low-income category, experienced only meagre gains in consumption, and some suffered declines, since neither their incomes and production nor their capacity to import grew as much as required to improve consumption.

It is customary to address the issue of what the food and agricultural situation in the developing world would look like if these historical trends were to continue for another 15 years. In many respects, this is only of theoretical interest. There is really no satisfactory method for extrapolating trends of a set of interdependent variables. For example, extrapolation of trends in production and consumption independently of each other results in surpluses or deficits whose behaviour over the projection period does not represent the evolution of trends in the net trade positions. The longer the period of extrapolation, the less credible the results. A mere extrapolation of trends presupposes that the forces that shaped the past will continue to evolve in the same manner in the future, for example the growth of population and incomes, foreign exchange to finance imports, development of land and water resources, spread of technology and yield increasing innovations, export markets, prices and so on. Yet it is precisely these factors that may be different in the future, partly because the overall economic scene has changed radically, as discussed in Chapter 1. Moreover, the initial conditions today are very different from those of 15 or 25 years ago; for example, per caput consumption levels in many countries are higher, some of the available yield increasing technologies have already been adopted, and unused resources that could be brought into agricultural use are less plentiful than in the past. All these factors would make for future gains to be less rapid than in the past. At the same time, other factors would work in the opposite direction—for example the recent policy reforms in favour of agriculture—or the accumulated experience in modern agricultural practices and application of technology would enable some countries to do better in the future compared with the past.

To illustrate the above, some of the implications of trend continuation have been computed and the following results emerge. Concerning aggregate *production*, a straightforward extrapolation of past trends (practically, each country's agricultural production continuing to grow at the same rate as in the period 1961–85) would result in a growth rate of production of the developing countries as a whole of 3.5 percent p.a. which is higher than that of the period 1961–85 (3.2 percent). This is a 'paradox' of aggregation as high-growth countries increase their weight in the total agriculture of the developing countries, and given sufficient time, the aggregate growth rate would tend to rise, even though the growth rate of each country would remain unchanged.

As noted, many of these trend extrapolations do not represent a realistic outcome in the face of a multitude of factors (physical, technological and market) that would tend to make the future course of events deviate from that of the historical period. A few examples will suffice to illustrate this point.

A mere trend extrapolation implies continuation, for another 15 years, of production growth rates of between 4.0 and 7.0 percent p.a. in countries like Libya, Saudi Arabia, Côte d'Ivoire, Malaysia and China.

The growth rate of production in Asia (including China) would continue to rise to an average of 3.7 percent p.a. at a time of slow-down in population growth, near completion of the import-substitution process for some major commodities and countries, expected sluggish growth in export demand and less scope than in the past for further expansion of land and, in some cases, average yields.

The growth of production in sub-Saharan Africa would continue to be well below that of population, implying rapid growth of import requirements beyond what is probably feasible from the financial and infrastructural standpoints. Otherwise per caput consumption levels could not be maintained even at the current very low levels, which implies that famine conditions would become more widespread and endemic.

Net balances of export availabilities, being in most cases a small residual between the much larger quantities of production and consumption, would tend to exhibit totally erratic behaviour and assume values bearing no relationship to possible trade opportunities offered by the rest of the world. For example, the growth of sugar production in the context of the trend extrapolations of overall agriculture, particularly in some major exporting countries, would lead to export availabilities in excess of 20 million tonnes, when, as it will be shown later, the rest of the world may not take more than 7 million tonnes, roughly the same level of 1983/5. The above examples are sufficiently eloquent to demonstrate that projections built around mere extrapolations of trends do not provide an appropriate basis for discussing the future.

Concerning *food consumption and nutrition*, a mere extrapolation of the longer-term trends in per caput calorie levels of the different countries would continue the pattern toward increased polarization among countries.[1] The average in the developing countries as a whole would rise from 2420 to 2750 calories, that is a level above what would appear to be realistic given the probable evolution of per caput incomes. Improvements would be concentrated in the middle-income countries (essentially Near East/North Africa and Latin America)

[1] In the trend extrapolations, the growth rate of per caput calories is constrained to slow down with increasing levels over the projection period as well as not to exceed upper and lower bounds representing rough physiological limits of energy intakes.

while little progress would be made and some deterioration would occur in the low-income countries of Asia and especially in sub-Saharan Africa.

The trend continuation outcome for the middle-income countries appears unrealistic, mainly because economic growth rates are expected to be significantly below those of the historical period. For different reasons, some Asian low-income countries may continue to improve nutritional levels at the rates of their more recent trends rather than at those of the longer term, which were lower. Both these factors would tend to reduce the polarization projected under the trends. The prospects for sub-Saharan Africa doing better than the trends are, however, shrouded with uncertainty. This point is discussed at some length later on in this chapter.

It is worth noting that if these trends in per caput calories were to materialize, the projected numbers of undernourished would rise significantly above current levels, from 512 million to 628 million persons below the 1.4 BMR calorie threshold in the 89 countries for which estimates could be made. This would be the direct result of the above-mentioned accentuation of the inequality of distribution of food availability among the developing countries.

Concerning the evolution of *food deficits*, concretely import requirements of cereals, the trend extrapolation of production and consumption imply that such deficits would continue to increase rapidly in all regions except in Asia (including China). In this latter region, the trend continuation of the rapid growth of production would soon lead to substantial surpluses which would offset the increases in the other regions' deficits. As a consequence, the cereals deficit of the developing countries as a whole would in the year 2000 be approximately the same as in the last three-year average (just over 60 million tonnes). As will be discussed later in this chapter, Asia is highly unlikely to play this role in the future, firstly because it cannot possibly sustain the same high growth rate of cereals production as in the recent past; secondly because its own consumption may grow faster than suggested by the trends; and thirdly because the intense pressure on world markets from the developed exporters of cereals is likely to continue to render it unattractive for Asian countries to produce permanently substantial surpluses for export, even if they could.

The above examples make it clear that many of the results of trend extrapolations are not tenable from the standpoints of economics, resources and technology. In the rest of this chapter the task is precisely to investigate in what ways these trends may evolve, or be modified by policy intervention, taking into account a host of factors that are relevant in charting the course to the year 2000.

## Food consumption and nutrition

As noted in the preceding chapter, the last 25 years witnessed significant improvements in per caput food availabilities of the developing countries as a whole when average per caput food supplies increased from just under 2000 calories in the early 1960s to 2420 in the mid-1980s. These improvements were by no means evenly spread and many low-income developing countries are today no better off, and some are worse off, nutritionally than 10 or 20 years ago. The problem of improving food consumption and nutrition in the countries that have lagged behind assumes therefore centre stage in any analysis of future prospects of the world food and agricultural economy, together with that of maintaining the momentum of progress in the other countries.

Figure 3.1 presents the projections of per caput food demand in terms of calories while Table 3.1 shows the implications of these projections for the distribution of countries and population. These projections are derived from the assumptions concerning projected overall economic growth and per caput incomes presented in Table 3.2, with some important qualifications concerning the evolution of food consumption in countries facing unfavourable prospects in per caput incomes, as discussed in the remainder of this chapter.

It must be noted that the projected calories of Table 3.1 refer to the calorie equivalent of the component of total demand for food commodities which is represented by final direct human consumption. As such, they are only partial indicators of the growth of *total* demand for food products, which also encompasses other uses of such products, principally demand for feedingstuffs. The latter is, of course, indirectly linked to the food demand for livestock products and depends, among other things, on the extent that it is met by domestic livestock production or imports. Hence, the aggregate demand for food and feed would grow faster than that for direct human consumption, particularly in the middle-income countries which may exhibit limited growth of demand expressed in calories per caput but faster growth of 'indirect' demand for feed, given the continuation of structural shifts in diets towards more livestock products.

Returning to the projections of food demand for direct human consumption of Table 3.1, their main characteristics are highlighted as follows. At the one extreme, many countries can be expected to graduate into the top echelon of per caput food availability so that by the year 2000 over 2.7 billion persons (58 percent of the total population of the 94 countries) would live in countries with average levels above 2500 calories.

At the other extreme, not all countries presently at the very bottom of the scale would make the shift into the next echelon of over 1900 calories. Four African countries with 117 million people may be expected to continue to be

**Table 3.1** Distribution of the 94 developing countries by calories per caput per day

| | 1983/5 | 2000 projected |
|---|---|---|
| Under 1900 calories | | |
| No. of countries | 9 | 4 |
| Population (million) | 196 | 117 |
| 1900–2500 calories | | |
| No. countries | 50 | 42 |
| Population (million) | 1446 | 1868 |
| Over 2500 calories | | |
| No. countries | 35 | 48 |
| Population (million) | 1878 | 2760 |

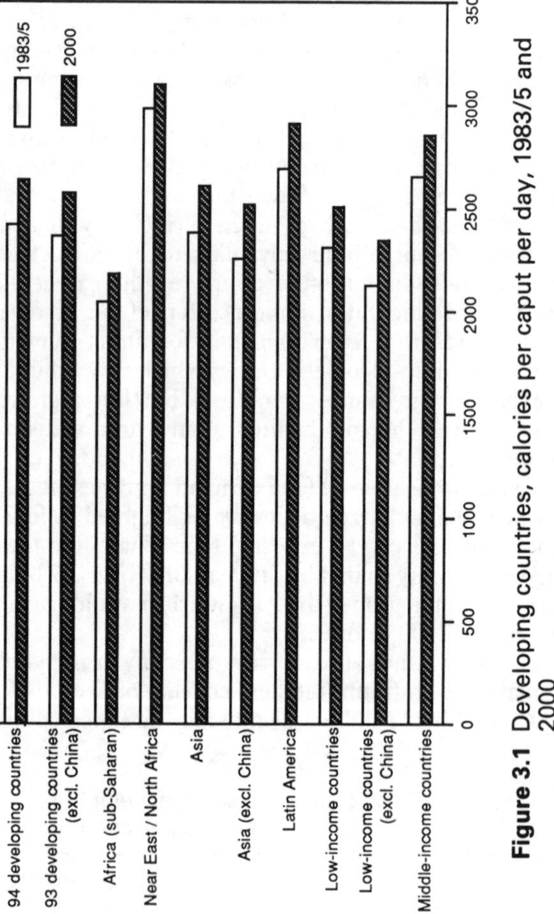


**Figure 3.1** Developing countries, calories per caput per day, 1983/5 and 2000

**Table 3.2** Projections of population and gross domestic product (GDP)

| | Population | | | | | GDP | | |
|---|---|---|---|---|---|---|---|---|
| | million | | Growth rates (% p.a.) | | | Growth rates (% p.a.) | | |
| | 1985 | 2000 | 1970–80 | 1980–5 | 1985–2000 | 1973–80 | 1980–6 | 1986–2000 |
| *World** | 4837 | 6122 | 1.9 | 1.7 | 1.6 | 3.4 | 2.7 | 3.7 |
| *All developing countries* | 3627 | 4793 | 2.3 | 2.0 | 1.9 | | | |
| 94 developing countries | 3591 | 4746 | 2.3 | 2.0 | 1.9 | 5.0 | 3.5 | 4.9 |
| 93 developing countries (excl. China) | 2532 | 3490 | 2.5 | 2.4 | 2.2 | 5.0 | 2.2 | 4.4 |
| Africa (sub-Saharan) | 416 | 675 | 3.0 | 3.1 | 3.3 | 3.1 | −0.5 | 3.5 |
| Near East/N. Africa | 265 | 387 | 2.7 | 2.7 | 2.5 | 4.3 | 2.2 | 4.0 |
| Asia | 2510 | 3144 | 2.1 | 1.8 | 1.5 | 5.7 | 7.0 | 5.7 |
| Asia (excl. China) | 1451 | 1888 | 2.3 | 2.1 | 1.8 | 6.0 | 4.8 | 4.8 |
| Latin America | 399 | 539 | 2.5 | 2.3 | 2.0 | 5.4 | 1.1 | 4.5 |
| Low-income countries | 2457 | 3166 | 2.1 | 1.8 | 1.7 | 4.6 | 7.3 | 5.7 |
| Low-income countries (excl. China) | 1397 | 1910 | 2.4 | 2.3 | 2.1 | 3.8 | 4.2 | 4.4 |
| Low-income countries (excl. China and India) | 638 | 946 | 2.6 | 2.7 | 2.7 | 3.4 | 3.1 | 4.3 |
| Middle-income countries | 1134 | 1580 | 2.6 | 2.4 | 2.2 | 5.2 | 1.9 | 4.4 |
| *Developed countries* | 1210 | 1329 | 0.8 | 0.7 | 0.6 | 3.0 | 2.5 | 3.4 |
| Centrally planned | 392 | 437 | 0.8 | 0.8 | 0.7 | 4.7 | 3.8 | 3.7 |
| Market economies | 818 | 891 | 0.8 | 0.7 | 0.6 | 2.8 | 2.3 | 3.3 |

*Sources*: Population data—UN, *World Population Prospects: Estimates and Projections as Assessed in 1984*, Population Studies, No. 98, New York (the projections are those of the Medium variant). GDP Historical data—World Bank, supplemented by data from UNIDO. Projections—Latest assessments available in different international organizations, supplemented by FAO for countries and periods for which such external assessments were not available. The demand projections of the study are based on the GDP growth rates for the period 1983–2000.

* GDP growth rates for the World are calculated from totals which exclude the smaller developing countries not covered in this study.

under what may be termed 'critical nutritional situations', though more than the 'usual' degree of uncertainty attaches to these projections because initial conditions and the assessment of future economic prospects reflect, among other things, the current difficult situation, often linked to unsettled political conditions.

There should be significant gains in many countries presently in the middle ranges of per caput food availability. In particular, nearly 1.2 billion persons would live in countries with calories in the middle range of 2300–500 calories, compared with only 300 million at present. Significantly, this group could include the second most populous developing country—India—which has had slow long-term growth in per caput food availability (0.3 percent p.a. over the last 25 years), having achieved 2160 calories per caput in 1983/5. It can be expected that the better growth record of the last ten years can be maintained in the future. To the extent, however, that continued economic and agricultural growth does not automatically 'trickle-down' to the poor (see Ch. 9), appropriate policies would be required for this result to be achieved.

The import component of food availability would continue to increase, though at rates significantly below those of the 1970s, which witnessed a real explosion of food imports. In particular, the very rapid growth of per caput import requirements of food commodities in the Near East/North African region could continue. In this region and in some other middle-income countries an increasing proportion of the grain imports would be for use as feed grains in domestic production of livestock products reflecting the rising share of these preferred products in the structure of food consumption (see Table 3.3). The other regions would increase per caput imports of food commodities only modestly compared with the past trends, though total imports would, of course, increase faster than implied in these per caput numbers because of population growth (see also Tables 3.7 and 3.12).

Sub-Saharan Africa's recovery of per caput food availability to the pre-drought levels (2150–200 calories) would also require increased imports per caput, although the projected increase of approximately 20 percent in the next 15 years would be far below the rise of almost 100 percent experienced during the last 15 years. There is, however, significant uncertainty about the ability of countries to raise per caput food availability to the pre-drought levels. Import requirements (much of them possible only on concessional terms), to maintain consumption levels, would have to be more than projected if the unfavourable conditions checking increased food production for the urban populations are not improved. This argument is developed further in the next section.

The historical trends towards diet diversification away from staples in favour of the higher-value commodities such as livestock products, oils, sugar and fruit and vegetables, can be expected to continue. There will, however, be wide variations among countries and regions, and overall change would occur at a slower pace compared with the past (Table 3.3). In the middle-income countries and China all increases in per caput food consumption will be concentrated in the above-mentioned higher-value products. By contrast, many low-income countries (particularly in sub-Saharan Africa) will have to depend for improvements, or even maintenance, of their food consumption levels on increased per caput consumption of cereals (mainly coarse grains) and starchy products (roots, tubers, plantains).

The preceding discussions highlighted the possible changes in the distribution of the developing countries and their population in terms of food (calories) availability or demand per caput. However, an assessment of the incidence of undernutrition can only be made in terms of the number of persons (not countries or their total populations) with per caput calories below given thresholds. This was attempted in the Fifth World Food Survey (WFS) of FAO by taking into account, in addition to average country calories, whatever information could be obtained on the distribution of income within countries and its relation to the distribution of food consumption. The survey concluded that in 1979/81 between 335 million and 495 million people in the developing countries (excluding the Asian CPEs) or between 15 and 23 percent of total population could be classified as undernourished depending on the threshold calorie level considered (1.2 and 1.4 times the BMR). The method and other considerations related to these estimates, including required caution in interpreting them, are discussed fully in the above-mentioned FAO publication (FAO 1987a).

What would happen to the incidence of undernutrition in the year 2000 if the country-level calorie projections presented here were to materialize? It is not really possible to answer this question precisely in the absence of specific assumptions concerning changes in the distribution of income and consumption of food in each country. The only alternative is to estimate a hypothetical outcome on the assumption that the per caput food consumption projected for the year 2000 (see Fig. 3.1) is compatible with the distribution of these two variables within each country in 1979/81, the reference year of the Fifth WFS. Significant changes in the distribution of income are, however, believed to be taking place currently in many countries as a consequence of economic difficulties or crises and debt management and related adjustment policies. Whatever may be the situation as it is actually evolving, and assuming the projected food demand is compatible with the 1979/81 national patterns of distribution, the numbers of undernourished in the year 2000 have been computed and are shown in Table 3.4. and Figure 3.2.

The estimates in Table 3.4 have been brought up to date to 1983/5 by using the latest available data on per caput food supplies. They bring out clearly the reversal of progress that occurred in the early 1980s in Africa and the virtual interruption of progress in Latin America. By contrast, the process of improvement (decline in the share of people below the two calorie thresholds) continued in Asia and also, though less so, in the Near East/North Africa region.

The projections of Table 3.4 indicate that for the developing countries as a whole the pace of progress towards reduction of the share of populations classified as undernourished would continue very much as in the past. There are, however, important differences among regions. Most of further progress would be due to developments in Asia (excluding the region's centrally planned economies, for which data were not available) which implies not only relative reduction of population shares below the calorie thresholds but also reduction in absolute numbers of population, perhaps for the first time in the region's history.

In both the Near East/North Africa and the Latin America regions progress can be expected to be much slower than in the past, and absolute numbers of

**Table 3.3** Developing countries: per caput food demand, major commodities (kg p.a., direct human consumption only)

| | Cereals* | Roots, tubers, plantains | Veg.oil & oilseeds† | Sugar (raw equivalent) | Meat‡ | Milk§ |
|---|---|---|---|---|---|---|
| 94 developing countries | | | | | | |
| 1983/5 | 173 | 63 | 7 | 18 | 14 | 34 |
| 2000 | 173 | 60 | 9 | 22 | 19 | 41 |
| 93 developing countries (excluding China) | | | | | | |
| 1983/5 | 154 | 63 | 8 | 23 | 12 | 46 |
| 2000 | 162 | 67 | 10 | 26 | 15 | 51 |
| Africa (sub-Saharan) | | | | | | |
| 1983/5 | 113 | 192 | 8 | 9 | 10 | 27 |
| 2000 | 121 | 196 | 8 | 11 | 11 | 27 |
| Near East/N. Africa | | | | | | |
| 1983/5 | 212 | 28 | 12 | 33 | 21 | 72 |
| 2000 | 204 | 28 | 14 | 37 | 24 | 77 |
| Asia | | | | | | |
| 1983/5 | 184 | 44 | 6 | 14 | 10 | 21 |
| 2000 | 187 | 32 | 9 | 18 | 15 | 28 |
| Asia (excl. China) | | | | | | |
| 1983/5 | 159 | 30 | 7 | 19 | 5 | 34 |
| 2000 | 173 | 28 | 9 | 23 | 7 | 39 |

| | | | | | | |
|---|---|---|---|---|---|---|
| Latin America | | | | | | |
| 1983/5 | 136 | 73 | 9 | 44 | 37 | 94 |
| 2000 | 141 | 71 | 11 | 49 | 43 | 107 |
| Low-income countries | | | | | | |
| 1983/5 | 179 | 57 | 6 | 13 | 10 | 24 |
| 2000 | 179 | 50 | 8 | 16 | 15 | 30 |
| Low-income countries (excl. China) | | | | | | |
| 1983/5 | 149 | 51 | 7 | 17 | 5 | 40 |
| 2000 | 161 | 57 | 8 | 20 | 6 | 42 |
| Low-income countries (excl. China & India) | | | | | | |
| 1983/5 | 145 | 89 | 6 | 11 | 9 | 32 |
| 2000 | 154 | 96 | 7 | 14 | 11 | 34 |
| Middle-income countries | | | | | | |
| 1983/5 | 160 | 78 | 10 | 30 | 22 | 54 |
| 2000 | 162 | 78 | 12 | 35 | 26 | 62 |

* Rice is included in milled terms.
† Oil equivalent.
‡ Carcass weight, excluding offals.
§ Milk and dairy products, excluding butter, in fresh milk equivalent.

**Table 3.4** Estimates of undernutrition: 89 developing countries*

| | 1969/71 | 1979/81 | 1983/5 | 2000 |
|---|---|---|---|---|
| **I. Below 1.2 BMR** | *% of population* | | | |
| *89 countries* | *18.6* | *14.7* | *14.6* | *10.5* |
| Africa (sub-Saharan) | 23.5 | 21.9 | 26.0 | 20.3 |
| Near East/N. Africa | 15.7 | 6.7 | 5.6 | 4.6 |
| Asia | 19.5 | 15.6 | 14.3 | 8.7 |
| Latin America | 12.7 | 9.8 | 9.5 | 8.0 |
| | *No. of persons (million)* | | | |
| *89 countries* | *316* | *320* | *348* | *353* |
| Africa (sub-Saharan) | 63 | 78 | 105 | 137 |
| Near East/N. Africa | 28 | 16 | 15 | 18 |
| Asia | 190 | 191 | 191 | 155 |
| Latin America | 35 | 35 | 37 | 43 |
| **II. Below 1.4 BMR** | *% of population* | | | |
| *89 countries* | *27.0* | *21.8* | *21.5* | *15.6* |
| Africa (sub-Saharan) | 32.6 | 30.6 | 35.2 | 28.7 |
| Near East/N. Africa | 22.9 | 10.8 | 9.1 | 7.6 |
| Asia | 28.7 | 23.5 | 21.8 | 13.9 |
| Latin America | 18.5 | 14.6 | 14.2 | 11.6 |
| | *No. of persons (million)* | | | |
| *89 countries* | *460* | *475* | *512* | *532* |
| Africa (sub-Saharan) | 86 | 110 | 142 | 194 |
| Near East/N. Africa | 41 | 25 | 24 | 29 |
| Asia | 281 | 288 | 291 | 246 |
| Latin America | 51 | 52 | 55 | 62 |

* The historical estimates for 1969/71 and 1979/81 are somewhat different from those of the Fifth WFS shown earlier, because some smaller countries of the WFS are not included in this study and because revised estimates of per caput food supplies for these years were used to compute them. These differences are not, however, significant.

undernourished could increase a little, though the incidence of undernutrition would remain at fairly low levels (4.6 percent and 8.0 percent in the two regions, respectively) and, at least in the Near East, high population shares would remain in only a few of the poorest countries.

By contrast to the developments in the above three regions, the undernutrition problem would continue to be severe in sub-Saharan Africa, with the share of population below the 1.2 BMR threshold being in the year 2000 little below that of the 1979/81 pre-drought period. Absolute numbers would increase rapidly, by one-third between 1983/5 and 2000.

In conclusion, the global problem of undernutrition in terms of absolute numbers affected would continue to shift from Asia to Africa. This would be due both to the differences in progress in raising per caput food supplies and to the higher population growth rate of Africa. In practice this would be a continuation of the longer-term trend: in 1969/71 for every person below the 1.2 BMR threshold in Africa, there were three persons in Asia. By 1983/5 the

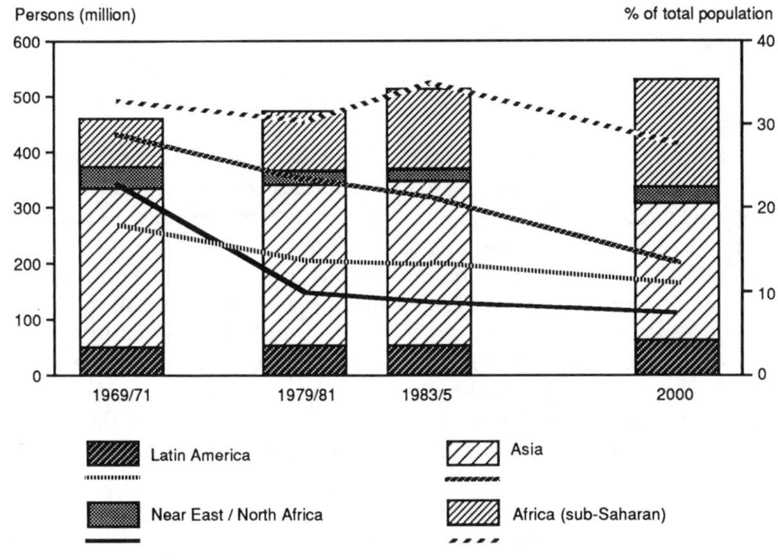


**Figure 3.2** Estimates and projections of undernutrition: number of persons and percent of population (1.4 BMR threshold)

ratio had changed to one (in Africa) to 1.8 (in Asia). In the year 2000 the ratio will be nearer one to one, with 137 million in Africa (20.3 of total population) and 155 in Asia (8.7 percent of total population).

These estimates of future incidence of undernutrition depend crucially on the assumption that the distribution of food consumption within countries is in the year 2000 the same as in 1979/81. It is, however, by no means certain that growth in the national averages indicators—be they per caput calories or incomes—'trickles down' to benefit in equal proportion all population groups, including the poor. If such 'trickle-down' effects do not operate fully, the projections of the incidence of undernutrition in Table 3.4 would be optimistic. This issue is discussed in Chapter 9, where it is argued that specific policy interventions are needed to strengthen the poverty alleviation effects of growth.

## Aggregate demand

The projections of the preceding section were in terms of the calorie content of the part of aggregate demand for direct human consumption. Aggregation of quantities consumed in terms of their calorie content understates the growth of demand because of the general trend for demand to grow faster for the commodities which have lower calorie content in relation to their prices (meat, milk, fruit and vegetables), compared with staples (see also Table 3.3). For example, for the 94 developing countries, meat consumption provided in

1983/5 3.8 percent of total calorie availability while it accounted for 20 percent of the value of consumption. The growth of demand in primary product equivalent expressed in monetary values (using average 1979/81 producer prices) would, therefore, be higher than implied by the growth of calorie availability.

Another factor that will tend to raise the growth rate of demand for the *gross output* of agriculture to above that of demand for direct human consumption is the increasing use of cereals as animal feed, which is projected to account for 24 percent of total cereal use in the developing countries in the year 2000 compared with 15 percent in 1983/5. This factor is entirely insignificant in the low-income countries outside China since just over 1 percent of total cereals use is for feed and it is expected to be around 2 percent in the future. It is the middle-income countries and China, which use a considerable proportion of cereals for feed, 123 million tonnes in 1983/5 (21 percent of their total cereal use) rising to 290 million tonnes in the year 2000 (33 percent of the total; Fig. 3.3). The trend is clearly for these countries to move closer to the patterns observed in the developed countries.

Following the above considerations, the demand for food and agricultural products for all food and non-food uses in the developing countries is projected to grow at 3.1 percent p.a. over the period 1983/5–2000. This is lower than the 3.7 percent growth rate achieved over the last 15 years, 1970–85 (Table 3.5). The difference is *partly* explained by the slow-down in the growth of population which is projected to grow at 1.9 percent p.a. compared with 2.2 percent over the period 1970–85 and 2.5 percent during the 1960s. In per caput terms, the projected slow-down in demand growth is therefore less, from 1.5 percent in 1970–85 to 1.2 percent in the future, which is the same as for the longer period 1961–85. The slow-down in the growth rate is caused by a number of factors.

Many developing countries (e.g. China, some other Asian countries and many of the countries in Latin America and the Near East and North Africa) have already attained fairly high food-consumption levels, and therefore further improvement will be more in the form of qualitative changes in the structure of food consumption and less by way of increases in the volume of primary agricultural products consumed directly (Table 3.3). Therefore, actual expenditure on food may be expected to grow faster than the growth rates indicated above which refer to demand for the primary product equivalent of consumption, particularly in the middle-income countries. Comparisons of the growth rates of private consumption expenditure on food, beverages and tobacco as defined in the National Accounts, with those of food demand in primary product equivalent, indicate that in most countries the former growth rates exceed the latter by a good margin. Increasingly, a higher share of total expenditure on food is accounted for by the distribution and processing margins, a phenomenon which is very pronounced in the industrial countries. For example, in the United States only 30 percent of the retail value of food purchases for home consumption is represented by the farm value of the food products. Ten years earlier the share was 40 percent (USDA 1987a).

If China and the middle-income countries are excluded from the projections, in the remaining countries ('Low Income excluding China' group in Table 3.5), the per caput demand is projected to grow faster than in the past.

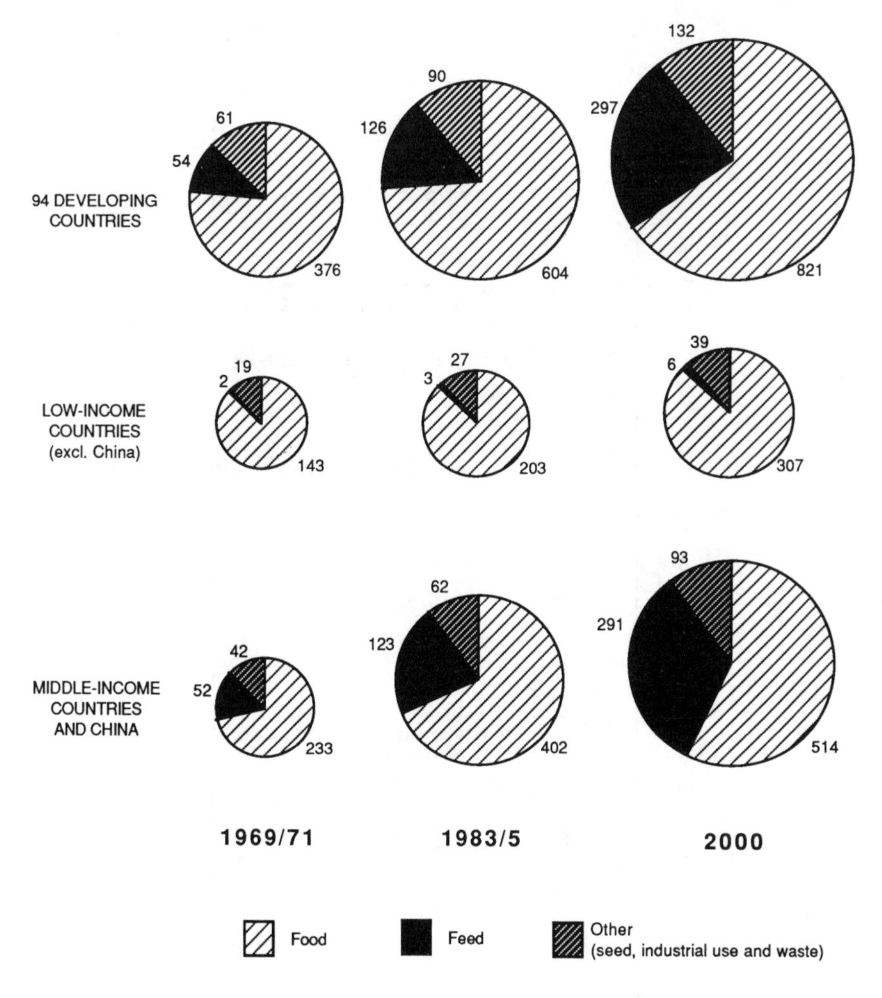


**Figure 3.3** Food and feed uses of cereal (million tonnes)

This reflects the fact that there are still many countries which have very low levels of food consumption, some of them lower today than ten years ago. These low-income countries, many of them in Africa, represent a potential source of rapid growth in per caput food demand if the circumstances are propitious. The projected higher growth rate in their per caput demand compared with the past includes an element of recovery from the drought-depressed levels of 1983/5. It is, however, totally inadequate in relation to their needs and also insufficient to boost total demand growth in the developing countries back to the levels of the 1970s. This is so because it is precisely these countries that face formidable constraints in their prospects of increasing per caput consumption levels. Sub-Saharan Africa, for example, is projected to

**Table 3.5** Developing countries: growth rates of demand for all food and agricultural products, total and per caput

| | Total demand | | | | Per caput demand | | | |
|---|---|---|---|---|---|---|---|---|
| | 61–70 | 70–85 | 61–85 | 83/5–2000 | 61–70 | 70–85 | 61–85 | 83/5–2000 |
| 94 countries | 3.6 | 3.7 | 3.5 | 3.1 | 1.1 | 1.5 | 1.2 | 1.2 |
| 93 countries(excl. China) | 3.0 | 3.5 | 3.3 | 3.0 | 0.5 | 1.0 | 0.8 | 0.8 |
| Africa (sub-Saharan) | 3.1 | 2.9 | 2.9 | 3.5 | 0.5 | −0.2 | 0 | 0.2 |
| Near East/N. Africa | 3.4 | 4.9 | 4.3 | 3.1 | 0.7 | 2.2 | 1.6 | 0.6 |
| Asia | 3.6 | 3.7 | 3.5 | 3.1 | 1.2 | 1.7 | 1.3 | 1.6 |
| Asia (excl. China) | 2.5 | 3.3 | 3.1 | 2.8 | 0.1 | 1.0 | 0.7 | 1.0 |
| Latin America | 3.6 | 3.2 | 3.2 | 2.8 | 0.8 | 0.8 | 0.7 | 0.7 |
| Low income | 3.5 | 3.5 | 3.3 | 3.1 | 1.1 | 1.5 | 1.1 | 1.4 |
| Low income (excl. China) | 2.3 | 2.8 | 2.6 | 2.8 | −0.1 | 0.5 | 0.3 | 0.7 |
| Low income (excl. China, India) | 3.3 | 2.8 | 2.8 | 3.2 | 0.8 | 0.1 | 0.2 | 0.5 |
| Middle income | 3.6 | 3.9 | 3.8 | 3.0 | 0.9 | 1.4 | 1.1 | 0.8 |

have accelerating population growth at 3.3 percent p.a. and per caput incomes which, in some countries and for the region as a whole, would be declining. Under these conditions, even the maintenance of low per caput consumption levels of the pre-drought period becomes problematic.

For the middle-income developing countries as a whole, the growth rate of per caput incomes is expected to be below that of the 1970s, which included the rise of incomes of the oil exporters. The difference is even more pronounced if measured in terms of per caput consumption expenditure which in the oil-exporting countries had been boosted by terms-of-trade gains following the increases in oil prices. However, the projected growth rate of per caput demand for the middle-income countries (0.8 percent) is well above that of the recent crisis years (0.3 percent in 1980–5).

These projections of total demand can be better appreciated if examined at the level of the individual regions. Much of the slowdown in total demand growth is due to possible developments in Asia (including China), where demand is projected at 3.1 percent compared with 3.7 percent in 1970–85. A significant decline in the growth rate of population from 2.0 percent p.a. in 1970–85 to 1.5 percent p.a. over the projection period already accounts for two-thirds of the decline in the growth rate of total demand. Indeed, in per caput terms, the growth of demand slows down only from 1.7 to 1.6 percent p.a. Moreover, China's spectacular growth during the period starting from the late 1970s in both production and consumption of agricultural products cannot be expected to continue at that pace for much longer, given, in particular, the relatively high levels of per caput consumption already attained (2560 calories in 1985). If China is excluded from the projections of Asia, per caput demand in the rest of the region is projected to grow at 1.0 percent p.a., the same rate as for 1970–85. If anything, this may be considered optimistic given the less favourable economic growth prospects in some of the countries of the region compared with the 1970s.

In the Near East and North Africa, per caput demand is projected at 0.6 percent p.a. compared with 2.2 percent in 1970–85. This deceleration reflects essentially the high consumption levels already attained in many countries during and following the years of the oil boom. In addition, the same kind of growth in consumption expenditures and foreign-exchange earnings of the 1970s may not be repeated in the next 15 years.

In Latin America, per caput demand is projected to grow at 0.7 percent p.a., a rate equal to that of the longer-term historical period (1961–85). This growth in demand is comparatively low given the many people with inadequate nutritional standards (see Table 3.4), for the average income of the region, and the significant resource potential of the region for increasing agricultural production. However, overall economic growth and, in particular, the growth of disposable incomes may be lower than in the past, in part because of the debt-servicing obligations of many countries in the region. The maintenance of the growth of demand and consumption could be somewhat encouraged by the continuation of the recently observed countercyclical behaviour of basic food production, particularly in the smallholder sector in some countries. This reflects the tendency for the sector to retain more, or to lose less, labour in times of overall crisis, thus easing seasonal labour constraints.

In sub-Saharan Africa, the growth of total demand is projected at 3.5 percent p.a., a growth rate only slightly above that for total population. This already includes a recovery from the depressed levels of the drought years. The growth rate is 3.4 percent p.a. if measured from the first post-drought year 1985. In practice, per caput consumption levels by 2000, although above those of 1983/5, may be no higher than those of the pre-drought years 1979/81. The macro-economic projections (Table 3.2) imply very little growth in the per caput incomes of the region between 1986 and 2000, and this after a fall of 15–20 percent during 1980–6. In such conditions of quasi-perennial crisis, the relationships between average per caput incomes and food consumption tend to become erratic and unstable, and consumption depends more on subsistence food production and access to low-priced food imports, including food aid. Therefore, per caput consumption levels could be maintained at their pre-drought levels if production could grow at a rate approximately equal to that of population growth. The difficulties that may be encountered in the effort to reverse the trends for per caput production to decline are discussed below. If these difficulties are not overcome, the maintenance of per caput consumption levels will continue to depend on ever-increasing imports of food, a large part of which on concessional terms; in many countries the room for further decline in per caput consumption is really minimal.

In conclusion, the slow-down in economic growth in many countries, compared especially with the 1970s, along with the lower growth rates of population and the comparatively high consumption levels already attained in some middle-income countries, would all contribute to the slow-down in the growth of total demand. Increasingly, the continuation of the economic crisis conditions and foreign-exchange shortages in many countries will make the growth of consumption depend more than in the past on developments in their agricultural sector, which will have to provide both the food and contribute to the generation of incomes.

**Box 3.1** *Population and agricultural development*

World population is projected to grow at 1.6 percent p.a. between 1985 and 2000 to nearly 6.1 billion, of which 4.8 billion will be in the developing countries. This is the 'medium' projection variant of the United Nations and it is used throughout this study. Alternative low and high projection variants imply growth rates of 1.4 and 1.8 percent p.a. and year 2000 world populations of 5.9 billion and 6.3 billion, respectively. Population projections are subject to uncertainty, though the forecasting performance of demographers is now better than in earlier times. Moreover, aggregate world projections are subject to a smaller degree of uncertainty than those for individual countries.

Concern has often been expressed about the capacity of agriculture to feed ever-increasing populations. On a global scale agriculture has proven its potential to increase food supplies faster than the growth of population and, as this study demonstrates, it can be expected to continue to do so in the foreseeable future, particularly in the face of the projected decline in the growth rate of world population. The countries and regions with population growth rates well above the average and with inadequate agricultural and overall economic growth rates face the continuing challenge of providing adequate per capita food supply. The physical potential for expanded food production exists in most countries. The growth of population and agricultural or overall economic development are interrelated. At issue is how population growth affects that of food demand and supply.

It is often believed that population growth contributes to aggregate food demand in the same proportion. This is a reasonably good assumption in high-income countries with levels of per caput food consumption close to saturation and low income and price elasticities of demand. In such cases, even if population growth affected the other variables determining the growth of aggregate consumption (per caput incomes, income distribution, prices) the effects would be insignificant. It is therefore legitimate to ignore such 'second order' effects of population growth and to consider that it contributes to the growth of total demand a part equal to its growth rate.

The situation may be different in the developing countries, if population growth influences—and in most cases does affect—other variables. Population growth *per se* may cause food demand to grow by an amount higher or lower than its growth rate, more often the latter, though conditions vary widely among countries and the net effect may be in either direction. High population growth may cause average per caput incomes to be lower than otherwise, either because it increases the dependency ratio and lowers directly productive investment per person or because the lower income groups have higher fertility and, therefore, the proportion of the poor in total population may increase, thus accentuating inequalities in distribution. In many countries high population growth rates coexist with insufficient effective demand and compound the problem of maintaining per capita food consumption levels.

On the production side, if agricultural land resources do not expand and technology does not progress, a growing agricultural labour force would cause production per caput to decline. Historically, however, a growing population/land ratio has normally led to intensification of production. Technological change and modern inputs (fertilizer, improved seeds, irrigation) more than made up for the unfavourable changes in land/man ratios. As a result, in global terms, the rapid population growth of the last decades has been matched by more than commensurate increases in agricultural production.

The situation, however, is not so comforting in all countries and regions. Over the last two decades, per caput agricultural production did decline in many countries, particularly in Africa, including in countries in which there was scope for maintaining or increasing the land/man ratios. Inadequate infrastructure and economic incentives, including insufficient effective demand, impeded the advent of technological change which underpinned growth in other countries and regions.

In some areas, population growth can contribute to depletion of land resources through the cultivation of marginal lands, soil erosion, deforestation and overgrazing. This aggravates the instability of food supplies as fragile soils accentuate weather-induced variations in production. However, the social institutions, agrarian systems and economic policy in countries do determine the magnitude and nature of the adverse consequences of population growth. Institutional and agrarian systems and structures are in turn affected by the high rate of population in relation to the land and natural resource base. Under the impact of heavy pressure of population, the size of family holdings declines, and frequently small, uneconomic holdings are absorbed into larger farms. As a result, inequality and landlessness increase.

## Production and self-sufficiency

The production projections presented below are derived on the assumption that each developing country would pursue the objective of improving self-sufficiency and also produce for export to the extent that this is feasible from the standpoint of resources, technology and cost effectiveness. The methodology is presented in the Appendix. The agronomic and technological aspects of these projections are discussed in Chapter 4, while the policy aspects are discussed in Chapter 8. Naturally, not all countries can make progress towards this objective for all commodities since constraints of ecology, resources and technology prevent the growth of production of some commodities, while demand constraints (domestic and external) limit the growth of output of other commodities for which production potential exists.

These differences in the growth rates of demand and in production possibilities influence the commodity pattern of projected production (Fig. 3.4). Production of livestock products would grow the fastest and, among cereals, that of coarse grains, reflecting both increased demand for feed and the need to increase domestic production as much as possible in countries in which coarse grains are the main food cereals. Commodities with lower-than-average growth rates, mainly, though not exclusively, because of demand constraints include the starchy products (roots, tubers, plantains) and some of the main export commodities.

The resource and technological parameters underpinning these production projections indicate that for the developing countries as a whole (excluding China[2]) arable land would to expand at 0.6 percent p.a. Harvested area would,

[2] The data on present land use and still unused land reserves by agro-ecological class were not available for China as for the other countries.

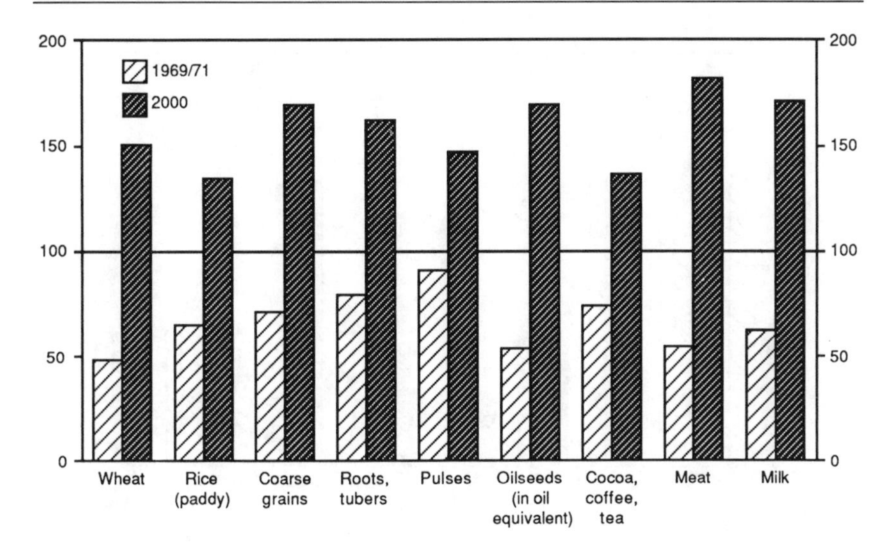


**Figure 3.4** Production increases, main products: 94 developing countries (1983/5 = 100)

however, grow faster (at 1.0 percent p.a.) due to increases in cropping intensity (the ratio of land cropped in any one year on the average, to that of physical area in agricultural use), which is projected to increase from 78 to 84 percent (for more details, in particular the sharp country and regional differences in the potential for land expansion, see Ch. 4).

Much of the production growth would, however, come from increases in yields. The potential for this also differs significantly among products and countries, depending on the agro-ecological environment in which they are grown, the relative importance of irrigation (projected to increase from 22 percent of total harvested area to 29 percent by the year 2000), the yield levels already achieved, and the scope for further growth in the use of improved seed varieties and the intensity of input use. In general, as shown in Figure 3.5, average yields for wheat and rice may be expected to improve at a somewhat slower pace than in the past 15 years, which included the period of rapid expansion of the high-yielding varieties (HYVs) in the major producing areas. By contrast, maize yields could continue to grow at rates somewhat above those of the historical period of growth.

The projected growth rate of gross aggregate production is 3.0 percent p.a. (Table 3.6) which is just below the long-term growth rate (3.2 percent p.a. in 1961–85) and that of the last 15 years (3.3 percent). In per caput terms, however, the growth rate of projected production would be higher than in the past, 1.1 percent p.a. in 1983/5–2000 compared with 0.9 percent p.a. in 1961–85. A major reason why agricultural output in the developing countries (including China) may grow in the next 15 years at a rate lower than that of the last 15 years is the slowing down of demand growth (Table 3.5) which reflects, in turn, slower growth of population and of per caput incomes in many countries. It is to be noted, however, that the divergence between the projected

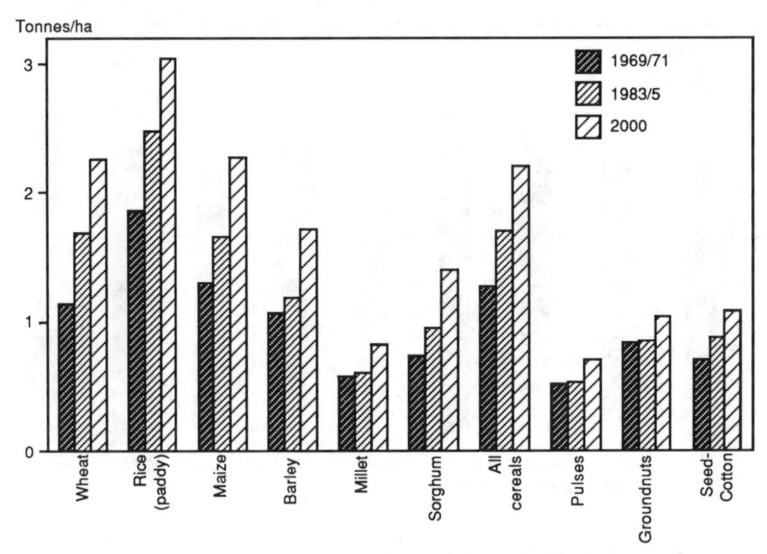


**Figure 3.5** Yields of main crops: 93 developing countries

growth rates of production and demand (3.0 percent production, 3.1 percent demand) is much smaller than in the period 1970–85 (3.3 and 3.7 percent, respectively). Under these conditions the declining trend of the overall agricultural self-sufficiency ratio (which fell from 106 percent in 1969/71 to 101 percent in 1983/5) would be greatly attenuated and the ratio could be around 100 percent in 2000 (Fig. 3.6).

In this context, it may be asked why the declines in self-sufficiency may not be arrested or actually reversed? This would be possible if agricultural production were to grow faster than domestic demand, with the increased output going to reduce import requirements from, or increase exports to, the rest of the world. This question can only be answered in the context of a closer examination of the individual country and commodity situations. Putting it succinctly, most countries have some commodity sectors with excess production potential which cannot, however, be utilized for lack of demand, at least not at prices that producers would find remunerative. In parallel, most countries face production constraints in certain commodity sectors and they therefore cannot increase production to meet their demand fully. This interplay of demand and production constraints at the country level is at the root of the trend for the agricultural self-sufficiency of the developing countries to decline. The situation varies widely amongst commodities and countries, in some instances demand and in others production conditions being the major source of constraints to faster growth in output.

*Demand constraints* originate in both the export and the domestic markets. Many countries could produce more of some commodities and not necessarily at the expense of the medium and longer term output of other commodities, if demand were there. For example, in the roots/plantains sector, which for the 94 countries accounts for 7.2 percent of total output by value, demand is projected to grow at 2.7 percent a year, following continuation of declines on

**Table 3.6** Developing countries: growth rates of total and per caput agricultural production

| | Production (% p.a.) | | | | | |
|---|---|---|---|---|---|---|
| | Total | | | | Per caput | |
| | 1961–70 | 1970–85 | 1961–85 | 1983/5–2000 | 1961–85 | 1983/5–2000 |
| 94 countries | 3.5 | 3.3 | 3.2 | 3.0 | 0.9 | 1.1 |
| 93 countries (excl.China) | 2.7 | 3.0 | 2.9 | 2.8 | 0.4 | 0.6 |
| Africa (sub-Saharan) | 2.8 | 1.7 | 2.0 | 3.4* | −0.9 | 0.1 |
| Near East/N. Africa | 3.0 | 2.9 | 2.9 | 3.1 | 0.2 | 0.5 |
| Asia | 3.8 | 3.7 | 3.5 | 3.0 | 1.3 | 1.5 |
| Asia, excl. China | 2.5 | 3.4 | 3.0 | 2.6 | 0.7 | 0.8 |
| Latin America | 3.0 | 3.1 | 3.0 | 2.7 | 0.5 | 0.6 |
| Low-income countries | 3.7 | 3.3 | 3.2 | 3.1 | 1.0 | 1.3 |
| Low-income countries (excl. China) | 2.3 | 2.6 | 2.4 | 2.7 | 0.1 | 0.6 |
| Low-income countries (excl. China & India) | 2.7 | 2.3 | 2.3 | 3.0 | −0.3 | 0.4 |
| Middle-income countries | 3.1 | 3.3 | 3.2 | 2.9 | 0.6 | 0.6 |

* Africa's projected growth rate is 3.1 percent if measured from the post-drought level of 1985.

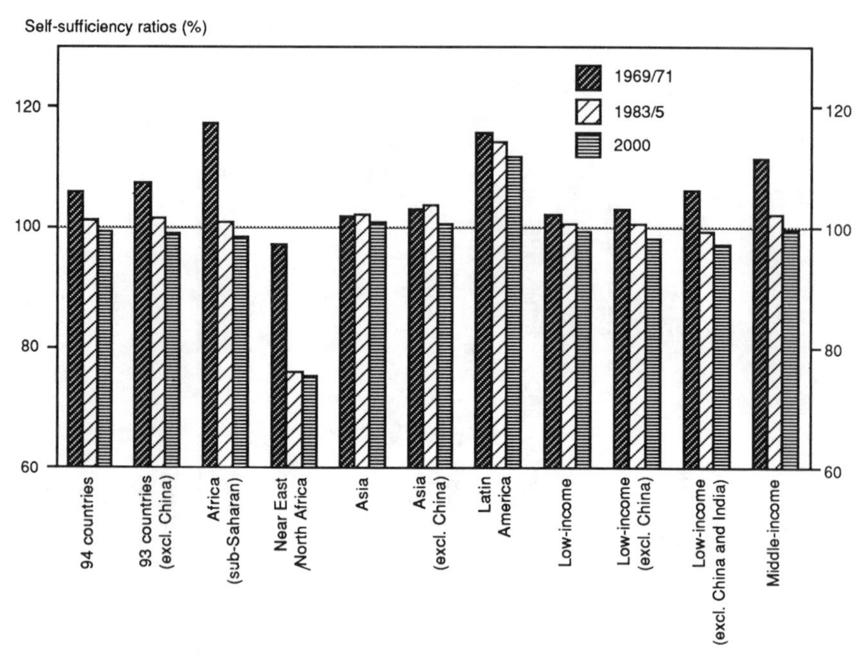


**Figure 3.6** Self-sufficiency ratios, total agriculture, 1969/71, 1983/5 and 2000

per caput consumption in all regions except in sub-Saharan Africa (see Table 3.3), and exports (comparatively small quantities of cassava) at less than 2.0 percent. By implication, production cannot grow by more than 2.6 percent, though the potential for faster growth exists. Likewise, the non-food crop sub-sector, which includes the tropical beverages and raw materials and accounts for approximately 8 percent of agricultural output (nearly 40 percent exported), faces constraints on the export demand side. Similarly, sugar (4 percent of agricultural output by value) is another example of a product facing significant demand constraints in the export markets, mostly due to protectionist policies in the developed countries.

*Production constraints* arise more often for commodities in which the country is in deficit. For example, since the self-sufficiency ratio in 1983/5 for wheat (6 percent of total agricultural output by value in the 94 countries) was 80 percent, there is ample potential scope for import substitution at the level of the developing countries as a whole, while transition to 100 percent self-sufficiency by the year 2000 could provide room for production growth at nearly 4.0 percent p.a. for the period 1983/5–2000. The production projections of this study nevertheless assume a growth rate of only 2.6 percent, slightly above that of domestic demand, with the self-sufficiency ratio rising to 83 percent by 2000. This is because of the assessesment of the study that the deficit countries cannot increase wheat production fast enough to reduce their deficits or in a number of cases to prevent them from increasing further. The net wheat deficit of the developing countries (including the smaller ones not covered in this study) is projected at around 67 million tonnes by the year 2000 compared with nearly 50 million tonnes in 1983/5 and 25 million tonnes in 1969/71. It may, however, be noted that the net deficit in 1983/5 was significantly below that of the immediately preceding years because of drastic reduction in the imports of some countries and regions in 1985, including China, India and Latin America.

While growth is impeded by production constraints in the deficit countries, countries, such as Argentina, with surplus capacity could expand production to fill a good part of the deficits of other developing countries if prices were sufficiently remunerative. Yet Argentina's wheat production and exports are not projected in this study to grow at rates anywhere near those that would be possible if, in addition to the country's traditional exports to the developed countries, they were to also meet even a modest part of the import requirements of the deficit developing countries. This is because the exploitation of Argentina's export potential is limited by the competition of other wheat exporters, including those who export at subsidized prices in order to retain or expand their shares of the world market.

The divergence between the growth rates of domestic demand and of production for the developing countries as a whole can therefore be explained in terms of the interplay of demand and production constraints operating at the different country/commodity situations, given international prices which are artificially depressed as a result of domestic support policies in many of the major trading countries. Analysis along these lines substantiates the projection that the collective agricultural self-sufficiency of the developing countries may decline somewhat by 2000, although at a greatly attenuated pace compared with the past.

## Regional profiles of production and demand

Regions will continue to differ in their production and demand developments. While the developing countries as a whole and the two major agricultural regions (Asia, Latin America) can be expected to have in the future production growth rates lower than those of the last 15 years, *sub-Saharan Africa* is the stark exception. Its production growth is projected to accelerate from the average 2.0 percent p.a. of the last 25 years to 3.4 percent p.a. The latter is just above the growth rate of total population and includes an element of recovery from the drought period. Already, 1985 production of cereals was 24 percent above the average of 1983 and 1984, and in 1986 it had increased by another 6.6 percent. If the projected production growth of total agriculture is measured from the level of 1986, rather than from the depressed three-year average 1983/5, it would be 3.2 percent p.a. This would still represent a radical reversal of trends and as such it deserves special scrutiny.

As in the FAO Africa Study (FAO 1986a) both demand and production are projected to grow at rates approximately equal to that of population after the recovery from the drought. At the same time, the macro-economic assessments indicate only slight growth in per caput GDP for the period 1986–2000, and this after a decline of 15–20 percent over the first six years of the decade (Table 3.2). As shown in Figure 3.1, in the year 2000 per caput food consumption in terms of calories would be only slightly above that of the pre-drought years, and the gains from the depressed levels of 1983/5 are mostly explained by the recovery from the drought. As already noted, under conditions of nearly permanent economic crisis the relationship between average levels of food consumption and of income tend to become erratic and unstable. In such circumstances it is not uncommon for average per caput consumption of food to be maintained even when average incomes decline, particularly when consumption has already fallen to very low levels, as is the case in many African countries.

The problem, of course, is that historically this maintenance of per caput consumption at times of crisis depended more on food imports (much on concessional terms) and less on production, which declined in per caput terms. The key question is whether future conditions in Africa would permit maintenance of per caput consumption based on growing food production rather than on ever-increasing low-priced and concessional imports. Raising the growth rate of production to at least match population growth is considered feasible from the standpoint of the required land and water resources, inputs and technology (Ch. 4). One can also be optimistic that recent trends towards agricultural policy reform (Ch. 8) would be consolidated and further strengthened. However, the macro-economic consistency requirements may not be fulfilled if the total economy is to grow at only 3.5 percent p.a., a rate close to that of agriculture, unless the rate of rural–urban migration were to be less than projected. In the demographic projections, the agricultural population, which accounts for 74 percent of total population, is projected to grow at 2.5 percent p.a. The projected growth rate of the non-agricultural population is 5.1 percent. The implications of this configuration of the growth rates is that the GDP of the non-agricultural sector would grow at rates only slightly above those of agriculture, and its per caput incomes would fall. Evidence is accumulating that this is already happening and that the gap in per caput incomes between the rural population and the bulk of the urban population is narrowing.

Under these circumstances, per caput food consumption levels of the non-agricultural population (35 percent of the total in the year 2000) could only be maintained if food prices declined and would probably have to be met by food aid, at least in part. These are certainly not encouraging circumstances for accelerated agricultural growth, and serious efforts would be essential if the reversal in production trends were to be achieved. Some of the variables in the system would need to adjust. There is some evidence (e.g. in Nigeria) that the rate of urbanization may be slowing. Therefore, the growth rate of the agricultural population in Africa could turn out to be nearer 3.0 percent. However, under these circumstances, agricultural growth would hardly be defined as dynamic, since per caput production would grow only very slowly and would be less oriented towards the production of a marketed surplus.

In conclusion, the assessment that Africa's agricultural growth can be accelerated to around the growth rate of population depends, in addition to appropriate agriculture-specific policies, also on the adoption of economy-wide policies aimed at revitalizing the non-agricultural sector so as to create the necessary effective demand at remunerative prices. There is a *prima facie* case that if overall economic growth is not more than the projected 3.5 percent p.a., the chances of achieving nearly equal agricultural growth will be in serious jeopardy. The accumulation of surpluses of coarse grains in some countries for lack of effective demand following two successive good crops in the post-drought years, is a telling example of how this factor operates.

Agricultural production in the *Near East/North African* region is projected to grow at 3.1 percent p.a., which is slightly above that of the past 15- and 25-year periods. This assessment might be optimistic since past growth, particularly over the last decade and a half, was fuelled in a number of countries in the region by significant investments and generous incentives to the producers. While these investments, if properly maintained, would continue to underpin the production momentum in the future, the region may be expected to run increasingly into resource constraints, the relaxation of which will require continuous investment activity, more than in other regions in relation to the size of the agricultural sector (see Ch. 4). Overall investment resources may, however, be less plentiful than in the past, and therefore the maintenance of growth will depend more on increased efficiency in the use of the investments already in place. Another significant factor that may be less favourable in the future than in the past is the greatly reduced stimulus provided by demand, projected to grow at rates significantly below those of the last 15 years.

In *Latin America* growth is projected at 2.7 percent p.a., lower than the 3.0 percent p.a. achieved in the past, and slightly below that of projected demand. With the exception of some countries, this region, contrary to the Near East and to some extent Africa, faces less significant production constraints, and therefore agricultural growth may be considered as being essentially demand constrained. For the countries specializing in production for export, the constraints mainly arise from conditions on international markets, while both foreign and domestic demand factors play a role in holding down agricultural growth in many other countries, particularly in the Southern cone.

Unlike Africa, where a very weak commercial infrastructure reinforces the constraints due to stagnant purchasing power of the consumers, in Latin America it is predominantly the latter factor that dominates the food production system of the region and prevents the matching of production potential to the effective nutritional needs of large population groups. What is more important, the inadequacy of purchasing power as a factor retarding agricultural growth, seems to be in significant part embedded in the rural sector itself. Very pronounced dualism means that a highly commercialized sector catering to the needs of the relatively affluent high and upper middle classes and the export markets coexists side-by-side with large segments of the rural population in the class of minifundistas and landless peasants. Without some significant changes in these structural characteristics of the rural sector, the substantial production potential of Latin America will not be utilized as fully as required to meet the consumption needs of these segments of the population.

The abundance and the agro-ecological diversity of the resources of Latin America suggest that agricultural growth may also be constrained by the inadequate development of trade within the region. Given the potential for increasing production, it appears that the exporters could meet a greater part of the importers' deficits without jeopardizing their exports to other parts of the world. For example, the region's net wheat-importing countries import around

12 million tonnes p.a. while net exporters export approximately 9 million tonnes (annual averages for the period 1983/5), much of it to destinations other than the deficit countries of the region. For coarse grains, gross imports and exports nearly balance out at 11 million tonnes, though again the origins of imports and the destination of exports are dominated by suppliers and markets outside the region.

Agricultural production growth in *Asia* can be expected to decelerate to 3.0 percent for the period 1983/5–2000. This contrasts with growth rates of 3.5 percent p.a. in 1961–85 and 4.6 percent p.a. in the six years to 1986. This deceleration can be explained in terms of both demand and production constraints. On the demand side, the deceleration of population growth and the relatively high consumption levels already achieved in some countries (e.g. China) would lead to domestic demand growing less fast than in the past, as discussed in the preceding section. On the export side, it may be noted that the period 1980–6 was the heyday of fast-growing cereal exports from some countries, when regional exports grew at 12.8 percent p.a. (4.2 percent if China is excluded). The 1970s witnessed the fast expansion of cassava exports (Thailand, and to a smaller extent Indonesia and China) mostly to the EEC to substitute for grains in feed. They also witnessed the rapid increase of export availabilities of vegetable oils, mostly from Malaysia.

For a number of countries in Asia, therefore, agricultural growth in the future would be significantly influenced by developments in their export prospects. As discussed in the next section, countries which in the 1980s have tended to become fully self-sufficient in cereals (before the 1987 Asian drought which reduced regional cereal production by some 2.5 percent, or 8.0 percent if China is excluded) may not find it profitable to become permanent substantial exporters of cereals in the context of slowly growing and highly competitive export markets. This category includes some of the largest cereal-producing countries of the region (China, India, Pakistan, Indonesia). As the scope for import substitution becomes more limited, particularly for rice, further growth in production will be largely determined by the growth in domestic demand which, following the slow-down in population growth, is not expected to be as buoyant as in the past. In parallel, it may be some time before some of these countries raise their consumption of livestock products to levels high enough to require radical shifts of livestock production towards a feedgrain-based system as is happening in the middle-income developing countries and China, where feed use of cereals accounts for 21 percent of total consumption and is growing fast (see Fig. 3.3). In Asia as a whole (excluding China) this use accounts for only 5 percent of the total, and although the proportion may grow by 50 percent by the year 2000, it would still account for under 8 percent of total cereals demand. Feed use would, therefore, generally provide only a weak stimulus to total domestic demand in the low-income countries of the region outside China.

It may be noted, however, that the tendency for cereals surpluses to emerge in some countries reflects essentially the inadequate purchasing power of large population groups. It was shown in Table 3.4 that between 190 million and 290 million people in Asia (excluding the Asian CPEs) are estimated to be undernourished, and given the growth of incomes, there may still be between 150 million and 250 million people in this class by 2000. The scope and need for further increases in food consumption is therefore substantial, and the tendency towards surpluses would disappear if demand could be stimulated.

On the other hand, the traditional exporters of rice may find it increasingly difficult to expand exports at the past rates (4.2 percent p.a. for 1970–80, but only 2.4 percent p.a. in 1980–6). In parallel, the EEC has negotiated voluntary export restraints on cassava, thus curbing the possibility of maintaining the rapid growth rate of the 1970s. The installed capacity for vegetable oil would continue to increase rather rapidly the supplies available for export, and therefore the volume of exports may continue to increase at relatively fast rates.

On the side of production, in many Asian countries much of the area suitable for the existing HYV has already been put under such varieties, and therefore further production increases from this source cannot be expected to be as fast as in the past.

## The cereals sector: self-sufficiency and deficits

The net cereal imports of the developing countries, including those few not included in this study, increased rapidly during the 1970s and early 1980s from 20 million tonnes in 1969/71 to a peak of 76 million tonnes in 1984 before falling back to 62 million tonnes in 1985. This recent significant development reflects above all the upsurge of production in India and China in the first half of the 1980s so that by 1985 the net exports of the two countries together amounted to some 3 million tonnes compared with net imports of 10 million tonnes in 1984.

The estimation of the possible net import requirements in the year 2000 has therefore to be based on a careful assessment of the possible positions of the large producers and consumers of cereals in the developing countries in the context of possible export supplies of the traditional and new exporters in international markets as well as the probable slow growth of these markets. India and China account for 55 percent of production and 52 percent of consumption of cereals of the developing countries, so that even small variations in their self-sufficiency would tend to cause wide swings in the aggregate net trade position of the developing countries. It is clear that if the production trends of the years up to 1985 in these two countries continued, they would tend to become major net exporters. This study assumes that both India and China will not find it economically attractive to be permanent and growing net surplus producers of cereals for the export market, particularly if the depressed world market prices of recent years continue to prevail, though they could continue to export some cereals and import others. It is considered that they would instead increase their per caput domestic consumption (of which an increasing proportion will be for feed, particularly in China), India at rates roughly equal to those of the last ten years and China at a rate below the very rapid (2.9 percent p.a. per caput) one of the last 15 years. Consumption per caput in China of both food and feed is already 290 kg p.a., which is above the average of the middle-income developing countries. In addition, it is reasonable to expect that China's production growth in cereals would decelerate to rates well below the spectacular 5.4 percent p.a. achieved in the first half of the 1980s, as a shift has taken place recently in favour of other crops which are more remunerative for farmers. The future points to a significant slow-down in population growth in India and China, 1.6 percent and 1.1 percent p.a., respectively. Moreover, there is the likelihood that, at least in India, part of the potential for rapid improvement from the introduction of new HYV technology has already been achieved. The conclusion may therefore be drawn that growth of cereal production in Asia as a whole, where these two countries account for three-quarters of the region's cereals output, would be slower in the future (2.4 percent p.a. in 1983/5–2000, but 2.6 percent p.a. if measured from 1986 production) compared with that of the last 15 years (3.7 percent).

Gross exports of cereals of the developing countries as a whole were 39 million tonnes in 1983/5 of which 27 million tonnes came from the two major exporters, Argentina and Thailand. As discussed in the remainder of this chapter, the world export market for cereals is expected to grow at rates significantly below those of the past 15 years (6.2 percent p.a. in the 1970s followed by declines in 1980–6). In this context, the major developing exporters will face difficulties in retaining and even more in expanding their market share in an environment of cut-throat competition by the developed-country exporters. Even assuming that together they would be able to retain their present (1983/5) share in world exports, the relatively high growth rate of 5.4 percent p.a. achieved in the 15 years to 1986 seems unlikely to be repeated in the next 15 years. The basic reason is that world exports would also be growing at rates which are only a fraction of those achieved in the past 15 years.

There is, however, a potentially important factor not considered explicitly in this study, namely the possibility that developing countries with surplus production potential in cereals could cover more of the import requirements of the deficit developing countries under an ECDC arrangement or through triangular transactions and barter trade. This matter was discussed briefly in the earlier section on the projection of aggregate agricultural production, and the factors referred to there apply *a fortiori* to the cereals sector: if oversupply conditions and weak world market prices persist over the medium term, actual and potential developing-country exporters would probably not find it profitable to increase production further if they had to compete against subsidized exports from the developed countries. In parallel, the deficit developing countries would find it increasingly less attractive economically to enter into ECDC arrangements and import preferentially from developing-country exporters if the latter cannot match the prices and conditions offered by the developed-country competitors.

This latter factor may, in practice, also influence decisions of the deficit countries concerning the relative priority they would give to domestic production in the face of weak world market prices. The production projections for each commodity and country assume that deficit countries would want to increase production to cover as high a share of domestic demand as would be technically and economically feasible. Clearly, the point at which domestic production is, or continues to be, economic has to be evaluated in relation to the cost of imported supplies and export returns. Although this study did not employ a formal model to determine the level beyond which the pursuit of self-sufficiency becomes uneconomic, it is thought that for a number of reasons the objective of raising cereal self-sufficiency would continue to be valid even under continuing weakness in world market prices. These reasons include:

(1) A high level of self-sufficiency in basic foods is widely held to be an objective transcending purely economic considerations and many countries would wish to pursue it even if it would be more economic (at the prevailing nominal rates of exchange and structure of protection, see below) to resort to food imports. After all, many developing countries, particularly those which did not discriminate against agriculture in their policies, increased their cereals self-sufficiency rate during the last 10 years or so irrespectively of trends and cycles in world market prices.
(2) It is widely considered that prices of cereals in world markets will generally remain weak over the medium term. These prices are closely linked, however, to the domestic policies of the main developed-country exporters which are subject to change, particularly in the light of global structural disequilibrium between supply and demand. Consideration of the alternative of producing or of importing additional cereals must incorporate assessments of risk and uncertainty.
(3) Finally there is an overwhelming economic reason why pursuit of domestic production even at nominal costs which, at the prevailing rate of exchange and structure of protection, are above those of world market prices, may be a sensible course of action. This is because in many developing countries protection from imports is much higher for industrial than for agricultural goods, often implying negative real rates of protection for agriculture. This situation favours imports of food and discourages production. If this discrimination against agriculture were attenuated, the economic advantage of importing would shift from food towards industrial products, thus favouring domestic food production and increased self-sufficiency. In countries with overvalued currencies, incentives to agriculture would be further strengthened by policies aimed at correcting overvaluation.

In brief, low world prices of cereals are more likely to moderate the cereal production growth of the developing-country exporters and of those which are nearly 100 percent self-sufficient and tend to become exporters (by discouraging them from becoming constant exporters) rather than those of the deficit countries.

The above discussion is reflected in the cereals sector projections presented in Figure 3.7 and, in more detail, in Table 3.7 and later on in Table 3.12. The total deficit of the 94 developing countries of the study would continue to increase to around 95 million tonnes by the year 2000 (or to between 110 million and 115 million tonnes if the residual developing countries are included), though the trend for their collective self-sufficiency to decline could be virtually arrested. The great bulk of the increment in the total deficit would originate, even more than in the past, in the middle-income countries, particularly those in the Near East/North Africa. By contrast, sub-Saharan Africa's contribution to the increase in the total deficit would be modest, as in the past. This outcome depends, however, on the materialization of the projected radical reversal in Africa's cereals production growth to attain 4.2 percent p.a., or the more representative 3.3 percent as measured from the post-drought levels. The projected increase in the region's net imports would still

**Table 3.7** Cereals in the developing countries: production, demand,* net balances and self-sufficiency

| | Demand | | | | | Growth rates | | |
|---|---|---|---|---|---|---|---|---|
| | Per caput (kg.) | Total (mill.tn) | Production (mill.tn) | Net balance† (mill.tn) | SSR (%) | Period | Demand (% p.a.) | Production (% p.a.) |
| 94 Developing countries | | | | | | | | |
| 69/71 | 190 | 491 | 480 | −17 | 98 | 61–70 | 3.6 | 4.0 |
| 83/5 | 234 | 820 | 762 | −61 | 93 | 70–85 | 3.8 | 3.4 |
| 1986 | | | 794 | −55 | | 61–85 | 3.7 | 3.5 |
| 2000 | 264 | 1247 | 1152 | −95 | 92 | 84′–2000 | 2.7 | 2.6 |
| Africa (sub-Saharan) | | | | | | | | |
| 69/71 | 142 | 38 | 36 | −2 | 97 | 61–70 | 2.1 | 1.7 |
| 83/5 | 135 | 54 | 43 | −9 | 79 | 70–85 | 2.9 | 1.5 |
| 1986 | | | 53 | −9 | | 61–85 | 2.7 | 1.7 |
| 2000 | 148 | 100 | 83 | −17 | 83 | 84′–2000 | 3.9 | 4.2§ |
| Near East/N. Africa | | | | | | | | |
| 69/71 | 294 | 53 | 46 | −6 | 87 | 61–70 | 2.9 | 2.5 |
| 83/5 | 372 | 96 | 60 | −35 | 63 | 70–85 | 4.6 | 2.1 |
| 1986 | | | 67 | −35 | | 61–85 | 3.9 | 2.2 |
| 2000 | 395 | 153 | 93 | −60 | 61 | 84′–2000 | 3.0 | 2.7 |
| Asia | | | | | | | | |
| 69/71 | 182 | 338 | 332 | −11 | 98 | 61–70 | 3.8 | 4.4 |
| 83/5 | 231 | 565 | 559 | −15 | 99 | 70–85 | 3.7 | 3.7 |
| 1986 | | | 568 | −6 | | 61–85 | 3.8 | 3.8 |
| 2000 | 266 | 830 | 811 | −19 | 98 | 84′–2000 | 2.4 | 2.4 |
| Asia (excl. China) | | | | | | | | |
| 69/71 | 172 | 179 | 174 | −9 | 97 | 61–70 | 3.0 | 3.1 |
| 83/5 | 190 | 269 | 269 | −9 | 100 | 70–85 | 2.9 | 3.3 |
| 1986 | | | 278 | −6 | | 61–85 | 3.1 | 3.2 |
| 2000 | 211 | 398 | 380 | −18 | 96 | 84′–2000 | 2.5 | 2.2 |

| | | | | | | | | |
|---|---|---|---|---|---|---|---|---|
| Latin America | | | | | | | | |
| 69/71 | 224 | 63 | 66 | 3 | 105 | 61–70 | 4.3 | 4.2 |
| 83/5 | 269 | 105 | 100 | −2 | 96 | 70–85 | 3.8 | 3.2 |
| 1986 | | | 101 | −5 | | 61–85 | 4.0 | 3.4 |
| 2000 | 304 | 164 | 165 | 1 | 101 | 84′–2000 | 2.8 | 3.2 |
| Low-income countries | | | | | | | | |
| 69/71 | 180 | 324 | 317 | −11 | 98 | 61–70 | 3.6 | 4.3 |
| 83/5 | 221 | 529 | 520 | −15 | 98 | 70–85 | 3.6 | 3.5 |
| 1986 | | | 532 | −8 | | 61–85 | 3.6 | 3.7 |
| 2000 | 250 | 784 | 770 | −14 | 98 | 84′–2000 | 2.5 | 2.5 |
| Low income (excluding China and India) | | | | | | | | |
| 69/71 | 168 | 73 | 69 | −5 | 95 | 61–70 | 3.1 | 2.5 |
| 83/5 | 165 | 102 | 95 | −7 | 92 | 70–85 | 2.6 | 2.6 |
| 1986 | | | 106 | −8 | | 61–85 | 2.7 | 2.4 |
| 2000 | 176 | 167 | 153 | −13 | 92 | 84′–2000 | 3.1 | 3.1 |
| Middle-income countries | | | | | | | | |
| 69/71 | 215 | 168 | 163 | −6 | 98 | 61–70 | 3.7 | 3.4 |
| 83/5 | 263 | 291 | 242 | −46 | 83 | 70–85 | 4.1 | 3.0 |
| 1986 | | | 262 | −47 | | 61–85 | 4.0 | 3.1 |
| 2000 | 293 | 463 | 382 | −81 | 83 | 84′–2000 | 2.9 | 2.9 |

84′ = average for 1983/5; rice is included in terms of milled.

* Demand is for all food and non-food uses, e.g. feed, seed etc., but excludes stock changes. For this reason, the sum-total of production and net trade in the historical data is not identical to domestic demand.

† Net cereal deficits for *all* the developing countries including the smaller ones not covered in the group of 94 are 20 million, 69 million and 64 million tonnes for 69/71, 83/5 and 1986, respectively. The projected deficit should, therefore, be increased by some 15 million tonnes to cover all the developing countries.

§ Africa's growth rate of cereals production would be 3.3 percent p.a. if measured from the post-drought production achieved in 1985 or 1986.

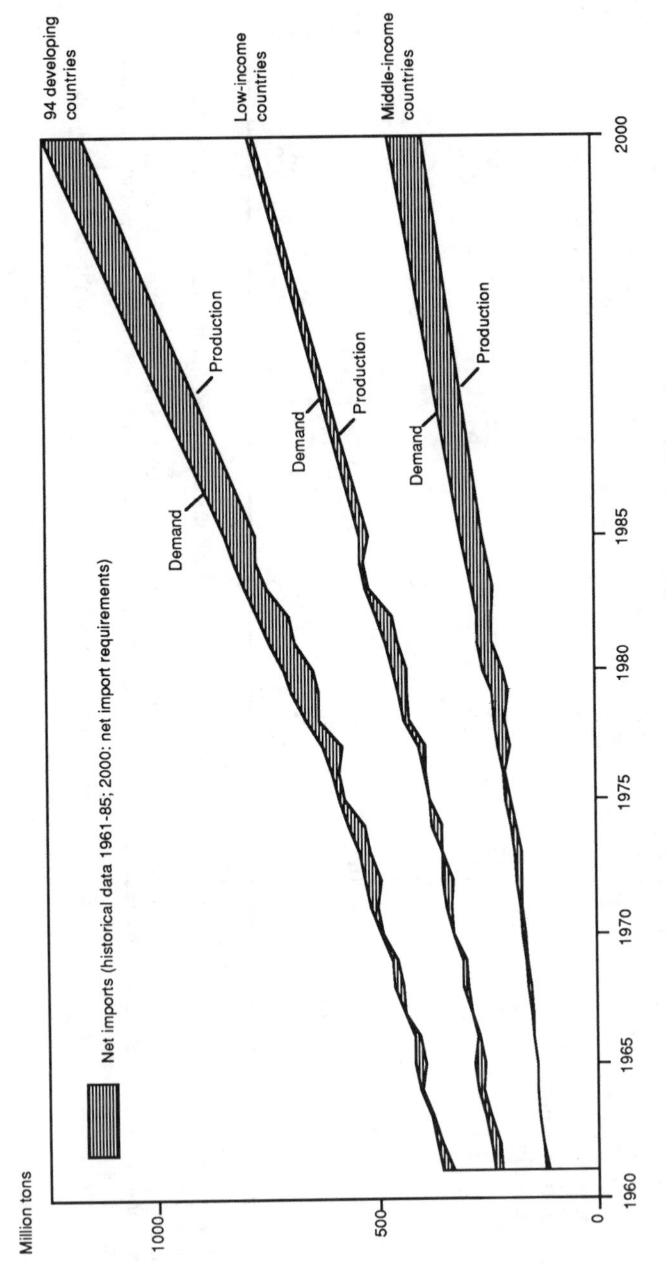


**Figure 3.7** Cereal production, total demand and net imports

be necessary if the per caput consumption levels are to be in 2000 only slightly above those of 15 years ago.

The decisive influence of the projected maintenance of nearly full self-sufficiency of India, China and Latin America in the containment of the developing countries' cereal deficit must be underlined. As noted, the former two countries accounted for 10 million tonnes, or 13 percent of the 76 million tonnes total deficit in 1984. In Latin America, the net exports of the exporting countries (overwhelmingly Argentina) could balance out the deficits of the many other net importing countries so that the region could be just over 100 percent self-sufficient and thus regain the small net exporter status it had up to 1971 and in occasional years over the last decade and a half. Naturally, there is no implication in these numbers for the direction of cereals trade, that is the origin of imports of the deficit countries and the destination of exports of the exporters. Full self-sufficiency for the region as a whole only means that the exports of the surplus countries (to any destination) are equal to the imports (from any origin) of the deficit countries. From this latter standpoint, below are shown the gross cereals imports and exports of the 94 developing countries implied by the net deficits indicated in Table 3.7:

| | *Gross imports* | *Gross exports* | *Net deficit* |
|---|---|---|---|
| 1969/71 | 37 | 20 | −17 |
| 1979/81 | 86 | 27 | −59 |
| 1983/5 | 98 | 37 | −61 |
| 2000 | 156 | 61 | −95 |

## Main export commodities and the agricultural trade balance

As already discussed in the preceding sections, inadequate growth in the demand of the rest of the world for many of the major export commodities of the developing countries is a key constraint in the growth of their production. Consequently, the growth prospects of total agriculture tend to be depressed in the countries in which these commodities have a significant weight in the agricultural sector.

The reason why the growth of exports to the rest of the world is, and may continue to be, sluggish vary among commodities, ranging from inelastic demand to substitution by synthetics to import substitution policies in the importing countries. At the one extreme, commodities like *coffee* and *cocoa* (19 percent of total agricultural exports of the developing countries; Table 3.8) are constrained primarily by the near saturation of consumption levels in their main markets, overwhelmingly the developed market economies, which account for 80–90 percent of world consumption of these two commodities. Future demand growth in these main consumption areas and, hence, of net exports of the developing countries, is projected to be around 1 percent p.a., which is somewhat below that of the last decade and a half.

Consumption growth of both cocoa and coffee in the developing countries and the European centrally planned economies (CPEs) should continue to be higher than in their traditional markets, in the former because of the higher population growth rates and in both because of the comparatively low

**Table 3.8** Main agricultural exports, aggregates for 94 developing countries

| | | Thousand tonnes | | | | Growth rates, % p.a. | | | Value of exports, average 1983/5 | |
|---|---|---|---|---|---|---|---|---|---|---|
| | | 1961/3 | 1969/71 | 1983/5 | 2000 | 1961–70 | 1970–85 | 1983/5–2000 | $ mill. | % of total ag. exports |
| Sugar | Exports | 11 590 | 13 310 | 17 700 | 26 300 | 1.3 | 1.7 | 2.5 | 7 238 | 11.3 |
| (raw equivalent) | Imports | 4 230 | 4 850 | 11 340 | 19 400 | 1.1 | 7.5 | 3.4 | 2 708 | |
| | Net exports | 7 360 | 8 460 | 6 360 | 6 900 | 1.4 | −3.8 | 0.5 | 4 530 | |
| Oilseeds & veg. oils | Exports | 3 870 | 3 920 | 9 950 | 18 920 | 0.1 | 6.8 | 4.1 | 9 668 | 15.1 |
| (oil equivalent) | Imports | 1 010 | 1 530 | 7 510 | 16 720 | 4.9 | 13.3 | 5.1 | 6 790 | |
| | Net exports | 2 860 | 2 390 | 2 440 | 2 200 | −2.0 | −2.4 | −0.6 | 2 978 | |
| Coffee & products | Exports | 2 790 | 3 240 | 4 100 | 4 870 | 2.4 | 1.5 | 1.1 | 9 555 | 15.0 |
| (beans equivalent) | Imports | 140 | 150 | 280 | 500 | 1.4 | 3.9 | 3.7 | 475 | |
| | Net exports | 2 650 | 3 090 | 3 820 | 4 370 | 2.4 | 1.4 | 0.8 | 9 080 | |
| Cocoa & products | Exports | 1 040 | 1 220 | 1 560 | 1 990 | 1.6 | 1.4 | 1.5 | 2 738 | 4.3 |
| (beans equivalent) | Imports | 40 | 60 | 90 | 200 | 5.2 | 4.1 | 5.1 | 241 | |
| | Net exports | 1 000 | 1 160 | 1 470 | 1 790 | 1.6 | 1.3 | 1.2 | 2 914 | |
| Tea | Exports | 620 | 680 | 950 | 1 320 | 1.1 | 2.4 | 2.1 | 2 035 | 3.2 |
| | Imports | 200 | 220 | 390 | 670 | 1.4 | 4.6 | 3.4 | 960 | |
| | Net exports | 420 | 460 | 560 | 650 | 0.9 | 1.1 | 0.9 | 1 075 | |

| | | | | | | | | | | |
|---|---|---|---|---|---|---|---|---|---|---|
| Tobacco & products (unmanufactured equivalent) | Exports | 440 | 530 | 770 | 1 010 | 1.5 | 2.2 | 1.7 | 1 956 | 3.1 |
| | Imports | 110 | 160 | 320 | 520 | 4.8 | 6.4 | 3.1 | 1 434 | |
| | Net exports | 330 | 370 | 450 | 490 | 0.2 | 0.1 | 0.5 | 522 | |
| Cotton (lint) | Exports | 2 100 | 2 580 | 1 990 | 2 300 | 3.0 | −2.0 | 0.9 | 2 982 | 4.7 |
| | Imports | 470 | 640 | 1 110 | 1 600 | 3.3 | 4.3 | 2.3 | 1 748 | |
| | Net exports | 1 630 | 1 940 | 880 | 700 | 2.9 | −8.6 | −1.4 | 1 224 | |
| Rubber | Exports | 2 120 | 2 840 | 3 530 | 4 700 | 3.5 | 1.4 | 1.8 | 3 184 | 5.0 |
| | Imports | 330 | 500 | 740 | 1 080 | 5.4 | 2.9 | 2.4 | 766 | |
| | Net exports | 1 790 | 2 340 | 2 790 | 3 620 | 3.2 | 1.0 | 1.6 | 2 418 | |
| Bananas | Exports | 3 410 | 5 000 | 5 900 | 7 350 | 4.7 | 0.9 | 1.4 | 1 135 | 1.8 |
| | Imports | 300 | 370 | 380 | 470 | 2.3 | 1.5 | 1.4 | 115 | |
| | Net exports | 3 110 | 4 630 | 5 520 | 6 880 | 4.9 | 0.9 | 1.4 | 1 020 | |
| Citrus & products (fresh equivalent) | Exports | 1 210 | 2 280 | 10 330 | 15 960 | 7.2 | 11.3 | 2.8 | 1 638 | 2.6 |
| | Imports | 110 | 210 | 740 | 1 380 | 7.1 | 8.8 | 3.9 | 290 | |
| | Net exports | 1 100 | 2 070 | 9 590 | 14 580 | 7.3 | 11.6 | 2.7 | 902 | |
| All above ($ mill.current prices) | Exports | 8 861 | 1 108 | 42 129 | | | | | 42 129 | 66.0 |
| | Imports | 1 736 | 2 413 | 15 526 | | | | | 15 526 | |
| | Net | 7 125 | 8 695 | 26 603 | | | | | 26 603 | |
| Total agriculture ($ mill.current prices, growth rates from values at constant 1979/81 prices) | Exports | 13 062 | 17 423 | 63 884 | | 2.1 | 2.2 | | 63 884 | |
| | Imports | 6 032 | 8 420 | 51 151 | | 5.7 | 7.4 | | 51 151 | |
| | Net | 7 030 | 9 003 | 12 733 | | −3.8 | −7.3 | | 12 733 | |

consumption levels prevailing at present, particularly in the CPEs in relation to their per caput incomes. It is not, however, expected that the growth of consumption and imports in the importing developing countries will be as buoyant as in the 1970s, which reflected the rapid growth of incomes in the middle-income countries.

Thus the slow increase of consumption and imports of the developed market economies will continue to dominate the growth prospects of aggregate exports, notwithstanding the faster growth in the developing importing countries and in the CPEs. By the year 2000, however, the shares of the faster-growing markets (developing importers, CPEs) should have increased sufficiently (to approximately 17 percent and 28 percent for coffee and cocoa, respectively) to become a more important determinant than at present of the prospects of world exports. Developments in the next 15 years may therefore set the stage for an arrest and perhaps a modest reversal in the years beyond 2000 of the declining growth of world exports of these commodities in recent years.

World exports of both coffee and cocoa would then repeat the experience of *tea* during the 1970s. In 1969/71 the developing countries and the CPEs accounted for 39 percent of world imports of tea. Accordingly rapid growth of demand in these two markets was sufficient to counteract the stagnation of imports of the developed market economies and to impart an acceleration in the growth of world exports from 1.1 percent p.a. in the 1960s, to 2.4 percent in 1970–85. By 1983/5 the share of these two markets had increased to 56 percent of world imports, and therefore in the future their influence will be even more decisive for world exports. Naturally, this does not mean repetition of the high growth rates of the 1970s which reflected favourable economic conditions in the major developing importing countries, particularly in the Near East/North Africa region (23 percent of world tea imports in 1983/5). But even if their growth of consumption and imports should be lower than in the 1970s, it would still be sufficiently high to counteract the near stagnation of imports into the developed market economies and enable world exports to continue to grow at just over 2 percent p.a.

Nearly all other major export commodities of the developing countries compete with production and exports of the developed countries: rubber, jute and cotton from synthetics, sugar, vegetable oils, citrus, cotton, tobacco and fruits from domestic production. While, compared with the developed countries, the developing countries are often low-cost producers for most of these products, their export prospects are decisively influenced by policies of the latter countries related to farm support, agricultural protection, import substitution and export promotion.

*Sugar* exemplifies developments in this area. In 1969/71 the net imports of the developed market economies were 8.5 million tonnes but by 1983/5 they were only 0.2 million tonnes. Country after country turned, over this period, either from small to large exporter (France, the Netherlands, Denmark, Belgium) or from large to small importer (the UK, most non-EEC European countries) or from net importer to net exporter (FRG, the EEC-10 and W. Europe as a whole). The only sizeable net import markets in the developed countries remained those of North America, Japan (both at lower levels today than in earlier years) and the USSR. The decline of net sugar imports into

North America accelerated in the 1980s under the impact of reduced import quotas into the USA which favoured import substitution, including by alternative sweeteners, mainly corn syrup.

Under these circumstances, the share of imports of the developing countries in world imports has risen so that now these countries are major import markets for commodities exported by both the developed and developing countries. For example, the developing countries' share in world imports of sugar increased from 25 percent in 1969/71 to over 40 percent in 1983/5, vegetable oils and oilseeds from 16 percent to 36 percent, tobacco and tobacco manufactures from 15 percent to 18 percent, natural rubber from 17 percent to 21 percent, cotton (lint) from 18 percent to 28 percent. For this latter product the increased share in world imports reflects also the increased importance of the developing countries in world exports of textiles.

Future exports of these commodities from the developing countries depend, therefore, not only on their own production and marketing performance but also, and to a large extent, on the evolution of import requirements of the importing developing countries and on production and trade policies of the developed countries, both importing and exporting.

As regards the developed countries, their import requirements of the non-competing products will continue to evolve following the slow growth in their consumption. For the competing products for which the developing countries are net exporters, however, much will depend on the evolution of policies for farm protection and import substitution. The assumption underlying the projections of Table 3.8 is that the current efforts to contain protection and to move towards a more liberal trading environment (discussed in Ch. 7) will be a slow process so that attenuation of unfavourable trends towards increased self-sufficiency in the developed market economies, rather than radical reversal, can be expected over the medium term.

The following two sections of this chapter discuss the production trends of the developed countries in relation to the evolution of their demand. They highlight the need for rather drastic policy adjustments in the developed market economies to avoid further production of surpluses of their export commodities (cereals, livestock products) and to attenuate the negative trends in their imports from the developing countries for the main competing products (e.g. sugar, vegetable oil and oilseeds). The general assumption underlying the export projections of these competing commodities in Table 3.8 is that current efforts at policy reform will at least succeed in halting the trend towards decline of the net exports of the developing countries. Given, however, the great uncertainties surrounding the prospects for policy reform, a wide range of alternative outcomes is possible.

As regards the importing developing countries, their import requirements are derived directly as difference between their projected demand and their assessed production possibilities taking into account the objective of improving self-sufficiency. The projections of Table 3.8 show that the growth of import requirements of the deficit developing countries should continue to be strong, though less so than that of the 1970s. This would provide the appropriate environment for trade among the developing countries assuming, as noted, that the developed countries do not continue at the same rate as in the past their drive towards import substitution under heavy protection and eventually unloading surpluses on the export market at heavily subsidized prices.

**Box 3.2** *Developing countries: self-sufficiency and ECDC in the traditional agricultural exports*

The pursuit of improved self-sufficiency (in the deficit countries) as postulated in this study is compatible with expanded trade in general as well as among the developing countries. The possible size of the import market of the developing countries is determined by the technical and economic potential of the deficit countries to improve their self-sufficiency. For many of the traditional commodities, the deficit countries either are not producers or face production constraints. Therefore, as their total domestic demand rises over time, their import requirements would continue to expand, as shown in Table 3.8. The market growth conditions for expanded intra-trade therefore exist for many of the traditional commodities. The issue therefore becomes one of the existence of economic, or other, interests of importing and exporting developing countries for trading preferentially with one another, as well as of other conditions (infrastructure, finance) necessary for expansion of intra-trade.

The economics of such arrangements would, however, be radically different, at least for the exporting countries, depending on whether they implied trade creation for them or merely trade diversion. The former case would only be possible under changed policies of the developed exporters of the same commodity, since it would involve reduction (or lower growth than otherwise) of their own production and exports.

For example, the EEC-10 in 1983/5 exported net 3.2 million tonnes of sugar, much of it to the developing countries. At the same time it imported 2.5 million tonnes, mostly from the developing countries, included under the Lomé Protocol. If it were to lose its exports to the deficit developing countries it would have three possible courses of action (or a combination): reduce its production, reduce its imports, including those from the exporting developing countries, or increase its exports to other third markets. In both the last two cases, the exporting developing countries would not find it economically advantageous to enter ECDC arrangements if this would lead to a reduction in their exports to, or increased competition in, their higher priced and therefore more profitable markets in the developed countries (case of ACP/EEC, Caribbean/USA).

These constraints on trade creation by means of increased intra-trade stem directly from the assumption that the total import requirements of the deficit (developing and developed) countries are given and therefore any increased exports from some developing exporter must be offset by a combination of

(i) decreased production and exports in some other surplus country, (ii) decreased production and increased imports in some deficit country and (iii) increased consumption in any country through more trade leading to increased efficiency and lower prices. Despite these constraints intra-trade did expand and will continue to do so. But this was the result of the rapid expansion of imports into the deficit developing countries (7.5 percent p.a. in 1970–85 for sugar, 13.7 percent for vegetable oils/oilseeds) part of which was satisfied by exports from other developing countries.

The last question to be addressed in this section concerns possible developments in the agricultural trade balance of the developing countries. The data in Table 3.8 demonstrate that this balance has been shrinking rapidly in real terms (note the negative growth rates). By 1983/5 60 percent of the net trade balance of the commodities shown in Table 3.9 of $26.6 billion at current prices augmented by the net balance ($4.5 billion) of agricultural commodities other than cereals and livestock products was offset by the net trade deficit for the last two commodity groups as shown in Table 3.9. An attempt is made in this table to project roughly a hypothetical agricultural trade balance at average dollar prices of 1983/5 and assuming that the net trade balance of each commodity in terms of value will grow at the same rate as the net trade balance in terms of volume (shown for cereals and selected export commodities in Tables 3.7 and 3.8).

**Table 3.9** Projected net agricultural trade balance, 94 developing countries ($ billion at 1983/5 prices)

| | 1983/5 | | | 2000 |
|---|---|---|---|---|
| | Exports (fob) | Imports (cif) | Net balance | Net balance |
| 1. 10 commodities of Table 3.8 | 42.1 | 15.5 | 26.6 | 30.1 |
| 2. Other commodities (excl. cereals/livestock) | 10.1 | 5.6 | 4.5 | 5.1 |
| 3. Sub-total | 52.2 | 21.1 | 31.1 | 36.2 |
| 4. Cereals | 5.8 | 18.8 | −13 | −20.2 |
| 5. Livestock and products | 5.9 | 11.3 | −5.4 | −8.2 |
| 6. Grand total | 63.9 | 51.2 | 12.7 | 7.8 |

*Note*: The study's data and projections of net trade balances are in terms of quantities in primary product equivalent. The trade statistics from which the dollar values shown here are taken refer to the commodities in the form actually traded and, moreover, they include commodities not covered in the study, e.g. spices, wool, hides/skins, animal fats, etc. *Projection Assumptions*: Row 1, net dollar surplus of each commodity in Table 3.7 assumed to change at the rate of net exports in volume; Row 2: net surplus assumed to grow at the rate of the total in Row 1; Row 4: net cereal deficit in dollars to grow at the same rate as the cereals deficit in tons of Table 3.7; Row 5: net dollar deficit of livestock products assumed to grow at the rate of the deficit in terms of volume.

The results show that, under these assumptions, the 94 countries as a whole would still remain net exporters of agricultural products though their net surplus would decline at a rate of 3.0 percent p.a. This is a somewhat smaller rate of decline compared with the historical trends when, as shown in Table 3.8, the net balance (at constant prices of 1979/81) declined at 3.8 percent p.a. in the 1960s and at 7.3 percent p.a. during 1970–85.

## The European centrally planned economies (CPEs)

This group includes the seven countries of Eastern Europe (Albania, Bulgaria, Czechoslovakia, German Democratic Republic, Hungary, Poland and Romania) and the USSR. As a group they are net importers of agricultural products, though this reflects above all the position of the USSR, which from the early 1970s onwards, turned from being on average agriculturally self-sufficient, despite large year-to-year production fluctuations, to a sizeable and persistent net importer, mainly of cereals, sugar, butter and meat. By contrast, the other countries collectively are net exporters of some agricultural products (fruit, vegetables, livestock products), but they remain net importers of cereals and in terms of the value of total agricultural trade.

The food balance sheet data indicate rather high levels of food consumption, now around 3400 calories and somewhat above the average of Western Europe. Notwithstanding the relatively high apparent average levels of consumption, shortages of specific food items, particularly the better-quality ones, are not uncommon in a number of countries. In general, the evolution of food consumption reflects the strong policy emphasis in many of these countries up to quite recently on the maintenance of low and stable food prices for basic foodstuffs (cereals and livestock products), often at substantial expense to government budgets. For example, in the GDR for every 100 marks spent on food in 1985 the state provided around 78 marks in subsidies. In the USSR the subsidy element is even higher, particularly for livestock products with, for example, state expenditure on beef amounting to 5.42 rubles per kg when the retail price is only 1.75 rubles per kg (Semenov 1987). The cost of such policies to government budgets increased as farm prices were raised to provide incentives to producers. In recent years a number of countries also increased consumer food prices, sometimes quite substantially (Bulgaria, Hungary, Poland, Romania). In all countries the transition towards a system of relative prices reflecting more closely production costs has assumed centre stage in the current debate on policy reforms. Maintenance of artificially low food prices has meant that the consumers paid directly only a small fraction of the total cost of food and paid for the balance through higher prices and shortages of other goods. This policy tended to favour food consumption at the expense of other goods and services. It had some justification when food consumption levels were low, but it may be counter-productive at the current high consumption levels since it encourages wasteful use of food and maintenance of poor quality. The related argument that low food prices benefit the poor more than the rich is correct by itself but has probably little relevance in societies considered to have fairly egalitarian income distribution. In the end little or no welfare gains, and more likely losses, may result from such policies if benefits and costs of food subsidization are widely spread. In the USSR, it is thought that the concentration of subsidies on the livestock products tends to accentuate social inequalities since the economically better-off families consume more of these 'luxury' products, and hence benefit more from the subsidies, than the lower income families (Aganbeguian 1987: 200).

Diet diversification has been considerable over the last decade and a half when per caput consumption of staples declined and that of other commodities increased (Table 3.10). Compared with West European patterns, however, the dependence of diets on staples continues to be high, while per caput consumption of the more 'exotic' foods (citrus, bananas, tropical beverages) remains at comparatively very low levels. There is undoubtedly room for expansion of consumption of these products, and they could be an important factor for the exporting developing countries.

Food continues to account for a large share of total household expenditure, 30–40 percent in most countries, despite the prevalence of generally low food prices. In Western Europe the comparable shares are typically in the range of 20–5 percent. Lower per caput incomes explain in part this difference, though lower household expenditures on other important items (rent, education, medical services) are perhaps more important factors.

**Table 3.10** Eastern Europe and USSR: food consumption per caput

| | Eastern Europe | | USSR | |
|---|---|---|---|---|
| | 1969/71 | 1983/5 | 1969/71 | 1983/5 |
| *kg per caput* | | | | |
| Cereals and products (grain equivalent) | 185 | 172 | 197 | 182 |
| Potatoes | 108 | 90 | 130 | 108 |
| Sugar (raw equivalent) | 36 | 40 | 42 | 47 |
| Meat (excl. offals) | 57 | 76 | 48 | 63 |
| Milk and dairy products, excl. butter (fresh milk equiv.) | 184 | 209 | 192 | 162* |
| Butter | 5.7 | 7.1 | 4.8 | 6.5* |
| Veg. oils and products (oil equivalent) | 9 | 10 | 7 | 10 |
| (Calories from above) | (2740) | (2790) | (2880) | (2880) |
| Fish | 10 | 8 | 23 | 18 |
| Fruit | 54 | 62 | 36 | 48 |
| (Citrus) | (4.2) | (4.5) | (1.4) | (2.7) |
| Vegetables | 84 | 110 | 78 | 101 |
| Coffee/cocoa (beans equivalent) | 1.9 | 2.7 | 0.7 | 0.9 |
| Tea | 0.1 | 0.3 | 0.4 | 0.8 |
| Alcoholic beverages (calories) | 157 | 204 | 165 | 170 |
| Total calories | 3290 | 3430 | 3350 | 3400 |

* In 1983/5 the USSR imported 0.8 kg of butter per caput. Adding the milk equivalent of these imports to milk would raise the per caput consumption of the product by some 20 kg. The domestically produced butter is not so converted to avoid double counting since it is a joint product with skimmed milk.

The CPEs as a whole, and particularly the USSR, experienced a sharp decline in the growth rate of agricultural production from the early 1970s. This is clearly seen in the gradual slowdown of the growth rates measured over successive 15-year periods (a time length equal to the projection period of this study) from the mid-1960s to 1986, as follows:

| | 63–78 | 64–79 | 65–80 | 66–81 | 67–82 | 68–83 | 69–84 | 70–85 | 71–86 |
|---|---|---|---|---|---|---|---|---|---|
| USSR | 2.8 | 2.3 | 1.9 | 1.4 | 1.2 | 1.1 | 1.0 | 0.9 | 0.9 |
| E.Europe | 2.5 | 2.4 | 2.1 | 1.9 | 1.8 | 1.7 | 1.8 | 1.6 | 1.5 |
| Total | 2.7 | 2.3 | 2.0 | 1.5 | 1.4 | 1.3 | 1.3 | 1.1 | 1.1 |

The same picture emerges from the indices of agricultural production in the USSR which indicate the following increases in successive 5-year periods (Narodnoe Khozyaistvo SSSR 1987: 213):

| | |
|---|---|
| 1961–5 to 1966–70 | 21 percent |
| 1966–70 to 1971–5 | 13 percent |
| 1971–5 to 1976–80 | 9 percent |
| 1976–80 to 1981–5 | 5 percent |

As a result, the maintenance and improvement of consumption levels, particularly in the USSR, especially of livestock products, came to be increasingly dependent on imports of food and feeding-stuffs. Thus, net cereal imports of the USSR rose to nearly 38 million tonnes (18 percent of total domestic use) by 1983/5, compared with net exports of some 5 million tonnes in 1969/71. Near-record harvests in both 1986 and 1987 have led to lower net imports in more recent years. Net imports of cereals of the Eastern European countries also increased rapidly during the 1970s, to a peak of nearly 14 million tonnes in 1979, before declining significantly to around 1 million tonnes in the crop year 1984/5, though they rose in subsequent years to 4–5 million tonnes. Developments in the last few years reflected both a slow-down in livestock production and feed consumption as well as increasing foreign-exchange constraints in many countries of the region.

These developments in the net cereals deficits of the CPEs were a significant factor in the evolution of cereals production and exports of the rest of the world, particularly of the cereals-exporting developed market economies. It is therefore important to assess carefully the possible future levels of production and consumption in the USSR before a possible picture of the world grain balances can be sketched. In this context there is one single factor that stands out as having an overwhelming influence in these developments. It has to do with the importance attached during the 1970s to increasing production and consumption (and for some East European countries also of exports) of livestock products and the degree of efficiency with which this was pursued.

Between 1969/71 and 1979/81, feed use of cereals in the region increased by 56 million tonnes or 46 percent while livestock production increased by 24 percent. In the subsequent years, the feed use of cereals levelled off at approximately 175 million tonnes while livestock production continued to expand slowly. By 1983/5 the region was using 60 percent more cereals feed than Western Europe per unit of livestock production, though this was still 15 percent below the amounts used in North America. Use of oilcakes in feed rations, however, continued to be very low, only one-third the amounts used per unit of livestock output in both Western Europe and North America. It is widely held that the resulting low protein content of feed rations, particularly in the USSR, is largely responsible for the apparently low efficiency in the conversion of grains into livestock output (UN/ECE 1987: 194–6; Aganbeguian 1987: 160).

Given the above considerations, one of the major avenues to be explored in the future to contain the cereals deficits is the more efficient use of feed grains. It must be noted, however, that smaller grain deficits may imply increased import requirements of oilseeds and oil cakes/meals. Production of oilseeds in the CPEs as a whole (mainly cottonseed and sunflowerseed in the USSR, rapeseed and sunflowerseed in Eastern Europe) increased little over the last 15 years and the net imports of oilseeds, oils and oilcakes/meals increased rapidly, though foreign-exchange constraints halted import growth during the last few years.

Before examining this factor in the context of the projections, another aspect of CPE agricultural policy needs to be examined since it has important implications in the prospects for agricultural growth. This concerns the apparently excessive reliance of many countries on one single policy instrument: investment allocations to agriculture. These appear excessive in relation to both the share of the sector in the total economy and to its performance. The relevant data are shown below (Table 3.11). Having shares of agriculture in total investment well above those of the sector in total net material product (except in Bulgaria and Hungary) could imply less than fully efficient use of the countries' capital resources, given the generally lower growth rate of agriculture compared with the rest of the economy. This is demonstrated by the data in the last two columns of Table 3.11, which show that in all countries except Poland output per unit of capital (fixed assets) declined much faster in agriculture than in the economy as a whole. Increasing amounts of capital went to substitute for agricultural labour, which has been declining steadily, though this decline was temporarily halted or reversed in some countries in recent years. This process should have resulted in output per worker growing faster, or declining less, in agriculture than in the rest of the economy. Yet in the CPEs also this indicator has been unfavourable to agriculture; that is output per worker increased less (or declined faster) than in other sectors, with the exception of Poland in the early 1980s and Romania in the 1970s (UN/ECE 1986: 212).

These developments were accentuated from the second half of the 1970s onwards. Unfavourable weather played a role in these developments, particularly in the USSR, where, during the late 1970s and early 1980s perennial problems like drought seemed to impinge with above-average frequency. Still, there is a *prima facie* case that some essential agricultural policy elements were not adequately represented in the total package of interventions which, as noted, relied heavily on investment allocations. Current debate in many of the CPEs, particularly the USSR, emphasizes the role of the institutional and economic structures within which agriculture operates as one important avenue to be explored in the pursuit of necessary policy reform. So long as

**Table 3.11** Gross fixed investment in agriculture and productivity in the CPEs

| | Share of agriculture in total gross investment in the material sphere | Share of agriculture in total net material product | Average annual changes of output per unit of fixed asset | |
|---|---|---|---|---|
| | 1981–5 (%) | 1981–5 (%) | 1975–83 (%) | |
| | | | Agriculture | Total material sphere |
| | (1) | (2) | (3) | (4) |
| Bulgaria | 11.0 | 14.6 | −9.0 | −3.0 |
| Czechoslovakia | 20.0 | 7.9 | −5.9 | −3.2 |
| GDR | 11.6 | 8.0 | −4.1 | −1.3 |
| Hungary | 19.3 | 19.5 | −4.2 | −2.5 |
| Poland | 28.2 | 17.6 | −5.0 | −6.6 |
| Romania | 20.4 | 15.7 | −6.3 | −4.2 |
| USSR | 25.8 | 10.2 | −5.6 | −2.8 |

*Sources*: Columns 1,2 UN/ECE 1987: 184; Columns 3,4 UN/ECE 1986: 210.

uncertainty persists as to how this important policy debate will be resolved, any projections, particularly of production, can only be taken as a broad indication of a possible outcome.

Concerning the projections of food consumption, the trend towards diversification and qualitative improvements can be expected to continue. This would lead to continued moderate growth of consumption of livestock products and substantial growth in that of fruits and vegetables, including imported fruit like citrus. As a result, diets would be more balanced and diversified, though the total calorie content may increase little. For example, per caput consumption in the region of meat (67 kg in 1983/5) and fruit and vegetables (183 kg, fresh equivalent) may increase by 10 percent and 22 percent respectively, while that of staples (cereals, potatoes, pulses, 290 kg in 1983/5) may decline by some 10 percent. Given a population growth rate of 0.7 percent p.a., total food demand in terms of *value of primary products* in constant prices is projected to grow at around 1.2 percent p.a. or 0.5 percent p.a. in per caput terms. This is lower than the 0.9 percent growth rate of the past 15 years, which is to be expected given the high consumption levels already achieved. Another reason why growth in per caput consumption may be lower than in the past has to do with policy reform and consequent increases in consumer prices currently under way or being contemplated in many countries of the region.

By implication, the growth of gross output would also need to be in the area of 1.2 percent p.a. if overall agricultural self-sufficiency (currently 95 percent) and cereals feed/livestock output ratio were to remain unchanged. Both these variables may, however, be changing. Starting with the livestock sector, it is assumed that the countries of Eastern Europe would continue to be net exporters of livestock products at levels 20–30 percent above the current ones, that the USSR would maintain 100 percent self-sufficiency in milk and dairy products (not counting butter) and that it would continue to be a net importer of meat at around current levels. Under these assumptions total livestock production in the CPEs would need to grow at 1.3 percent p.a., which is approximately equal to the growth rate of the last ten years. At present, the feed use of cereals accounts for some 60 percent of total use, and during the period 1975–85 it increased at 1.7 percent p.a., that is faster than the output of the livestock sector. Comparative developments in these two variables are therefore of decisive importance for the cereals sector and the eventual evolution of the cereals deficits of the region. The trend has been for the growth rate of cereals feed to approach that of livestock production, as follows:

| | Growth rates (% p.a.) | | | | | |
|---|---|---|---|---|---|---|
| | 1970–80 | 1971–81 | 1972–82 | 1973–83 | 1974–84 | 1975–85 |
| Cereal feed | 3.9 | 3.3 | 2.6 | 2.0 | 1.8 | 1.7 |
| Livestock production | 2.3 | 1.8 | 1.3 | 1.1 | 1.2 | 1.2 |
| Ratio (elasticity) | 1.7 | 1.8 | 2.0 | 1.8 | 1.6 | 1.4 |

For the purpose of this study, it is assumed that the trend for the growth rate of feed use of cereals to approach that of livestock production would continue, so that for the period 1983/5–2000 feed demand for cereals could grow at a rate just above that of the livestock sector. In this case, feed demand in the year 2000 would be 220 million tonnes, compared with 176 million tonnes in 1983/5. The efficiency increases in the use of cereals as feed implicit in these projections would depend greatly on continued emphasis on the development of alternative sources of feed (grassland, roughages), including increased supplies of protein feeds, both from domestic sources and from imports. If certain problems of transport, storage and processing which currently favour the importation of cereals rather than oilseeds in the USSR, are solved, the economic advantage of importing feeding-stuffs may shift in favour of oilseeds, and this may be a significant factor in containing the growth of feed use and imports of cereals (UN/ECE 1987: 196). Increasing productivity of feed resources (using less feed per unit of output) would be facilitated by prospective developments in animal production technology. Productivity gains of 2.0 percent p.a. in the poultrymeat sector, 0.6 percent p.a. in that of pork but only 0.2 percent p.a. in the beef and dairy sectors are thought to be likely up to the year 2000 (US Congress, Office of Technology Assessment 1986: 10).

To the above estimates of feed demand for cereals are added those for food and other uses (industrial, seed) to obtain an estimate of total cereal requirements of around 365 million tonnes by the year 2000, compared with

305 million tonnes in 1983/5. The implied growth rate is 1.1 percent p.a. This is below that of the 1970s, though it is equal to the average of the last ten years (1975–85) which includes the slow growth period of 1980–5. Continuation of this relatively slow growth of total cereals demand over the next 15 years depends crucially on the above-discussed assumption of increased productivity in the livestock sector. If this assumption were not to materialize, demand could be higher in the year 2000. Indeed, other projection studies have invariably higher levels of projected demand ranging from 379 million tonnes in a study by the International Wheat Council (1983, 1987; their projection includes Cuba, though) and in the reference scenario of a study by the International Institute for Applied Systems Analysis, IIASA (Parikh *et al.* 1988) to 421 million tons (World Bank 1986). The underlying assumptions of these studies as to the growth and efficiency of the livestock sector are not always explicit. Therefore it is not possible to analyse in detail the reasons for the deviations, though it would appear that in all cases the feed demand is projected to be above that used in this study. These differences underline the extent to which the demand projections of this study depend crucially on policy reforms and efforts to increase the productivity of the livestock sector.

The cereals production trends of the last ten years for the region as a whole were dominated by very pronounced production instability and declining trends in the USSR, which accounts for two-thirds of regional production. This was only partly counterbalanced by continued production growth in the East European countries. In the end, regional self-sufficiency declined from 98 percent in 1969/71 to 82 percent in 1979/81 before recovering to 87 percent in 1983/5. The recent recovery in self-sufficiency reflected both better production growth in Eastern Europe and slow-down in the feed use of cereals everywhere. The region certainly has the natural and other resources to continue to raise self-sufficiency through increased production. Yet experience suggests caution concerning the extent to which the policy problems associated with slow growth will be resolved successfully.

For the purpose of deriving world cereal balances this study assumes that the efforts at policy reform will meet with some degree of success making it possible for cereals self-sufficiency to continue to rise to reach an average level of around 90 percent by the year 2000. This implies production levels of 330 million tonnes and a growth rate of 1.3 percent p.a. measured from the average 1983/5 production of 267 million tonnes or 1.2 percent p.a. if measured from the higher three-year average of 1984/6. This growth rate is well above those achieved over any recent 15-year period (1972–87, 1971–86, 1970–85, 1969–84) which were characterized by wide production fluctuations in the USSR and growth rates for the region as a whole not significantly different from zero. These production projections can be better understood if account is taken of the fact that the highest cereals harvest on record was 312 million tonnes in 1978. This was an exceptional event and in the subsequent eight years to 1986 production fluctuated between 233 million tonnes (1981) and 296 million tonnes (1986). Preliminary data indicate that the good harvest of 1986 was repeated in 1987.

Given the wide instability of production in the USSR, achieving an output level of 330 million tonnes in an average year can be quite demanding but feasible, given the impetus towards policy reform. One study estimates that only one half of cereal yield variability can be explained by weather variation while the other half can be attributed to fluctuations in input supplies, a problem that can be remedied by policy action (Desai 1986). The other studies cited earlier have production projections which are either nearly equal to the projection of this study (World Bank, 333 million tonnes) or 5–8 percent above it at 348 million tonnes (IIASA) or 359 million tonnes (IWC, including Cuba). These projections can be better understood if the implications of production of 330 million tonnes are analysed in terms of area and yield requirements of the cereal sector. Between 1969/71 and 1984/6 they evolved as follows:

| | USSR | | Eastern Europe | | Total | |
|---|---|---|---|---|---|---|
| | 1969/71 | 1984/6 | 1969/71 | 1984/6 | 1969/71 | 1984/6 |
| Area (m. ha.) | 114.8 | 111.3 | 25.3 | 24.8 | 140.1 | 136.1 |
| Yield (tonnes/ha) | 1.5 | 1.6 | 2.5 | 3.9 | 1.7 | 2.0 |

If the area under cereals were to continue declining like in the past to around 132 million ha, then production of 330 million tonnes would require an average yield of 2.5 tonnes/ha for the region as a whole. This is 25 percent above current (1984/6) levels. In the preceding 15 years (1969/71–1984/6) average yield increased by 18 percent. Overall, therefore, the projection of production of 330 million tonnes by 2000 is moderately optimistic if judged by the historical trends of any 15-year period from the mid-1960s to the present. It is, however, decidedly optimistic if the implied yield increases are examined separately for Eastern Europe and the USSR. In the former group of countries 100 percent self-sufficiency can be achieved through a combination of land area under cereals of around present levels and a 10–12 percent rise in average yields, an increase which is well below those achieved in the past. Assuming the balance of around 225 million tonnes is to be produced in the USSR, the average yield must rise by 25–30 percent in the next 15 years, depending on whether area would continue to decline or not. As shown above, it increased by only 7 percent in the last 15 years.

If the production of 330 million tonnes were to be achieved, net import requirements of the region would be 35 million tonnes. This would mean stabilizing the net imports of the region at around current levels. Estimated net imports were 32 million tonnes in the the 1986/7 crop year and are forecast to be around 34 million tonnes in the 1987/8 crop year. It must be noted that both 1986 and 1987 were near-record harvest years for the region. The projected net imports of the other studies (derived as difference between the production and consumption projections given above) range from 20 million tonnes (IWC, including Cuba) to 31 million tonnes (IIASA) to 88 million tonnes (World Bank).

## The developed market economies

The group of the developed market economies (DMEs) includes the industrial countries of North America, Western Europe, Japan, Oceania and, conventionally, some other countries as listed in the Appendix.

The basic tendency at the aggregate level has been for agricultural production growth to outstrip that of demand (domestic and foreign). This problem reached crisis proportions in recent years with, for example, carry-over stocks of cereals in North America reached at the end of the 1986/7 crop year some 220 million tonnes or 65 percent of combined domestic consumption and exports compared with only 105 million tonnes (31 percent) for the average of the three marketing years 1979/80 to 1981/2. Likewise, dairy surpluses were most pronounced in the EEC. Butter stocks were around 1.5 million tonnes at the end of 1986 and those of skimmed milk powder approximately 1 million tonnes. These stocks correspond to around 75 percent and 50 percent of combined domestic consumption (both of food and feed) and extra-EEC exports, respectively. The ratios would have been significantly higher if it were not for the increased exports promoted with subsidies.

In attempting to sketch out a possible course of events in the future, it is important to understand how and why the above-mentioned trends developed over the last 25 years. In the early 1960s per caput consumption of food had not yet reached the near saturation levels of recent years. Per caput calorie levels were 3100 in Western Europe and 3250 in North America, compared with current levels of 3380 and 3630, respectively. Therefore there was still room for expansion of per caput food demand. Population growth was also higher than in more recent years, 1.3 percent in North America and 0.8 percent p.a. in Western Europe in the 1960s, compared with 1.0 percent and 0.3 percent p.a. in 1980–5, respectively. These two factors combined with fairly buoyant economic growth to sustain the growth rate of food demand during the 1960s at 2.4 percent p.a. in North America and at 2.1 percent p.a. in Western Europe.

Another significant factor in the expansion of the markets was the increasing intensity of cereal feeding in livestock production. The amount of cereals feed used per unit of livestock output increased by around 10–15 percent in both Western Europe and North America during the 1960s. This factor proved to be of paramount importance in the expansion of both the domestic and export markets for cereals, since in the early 1960s feed accounted for over three-quarters of total domestic use of cereals in the North America and for over one-half in Western Europe. Domestic demand and production (gross output) grew therefore in unison during the 1960s so that the overall rates of agricultural self-sufficiency were maintained nearly stable, though there were significant changes for individual commodities.

In the 1970s the situation changed drastically. All factors which underpinned the growth of domestic demand in the 1960s weakened considerably, particularly in the second half of the decade. Overall economic growth was slower, reflecting among other things the increases in the cost of energy. Food consumption levels were higher, thus affording less room for further expansion. Population growth was also slower. Then the trend for increasing amounts of cereals to be used per unit of livestock output was reversed, reflecting both gains in feeding efficiency and, mostly in the EEC, the displacement of cereals by cheaper imported cereal substitutes such as manioc with oilmeal supplements, corn gluten feed and citrus pulp.

As a consequence of the above developments the growth rate of domestic demand for agricultural products as a whole compared with the 1960s was nearly halved in the EEC-10 and Japan and more than halved in North

America, though it was maintained in the rest of Western Europe. Yet only in Japan did the growth of production decline to the same extent reflecting the country's policy to adjust rice production to demand, while it accelerated in North America and fell only marginally in the EEC-10. Developments in the foreign trade sector compensated for the deceleration of growth in domestic demand in these two regions.

The role of trade in cereals was particularly important. The combined cereal output of the three major exporting regions (North America, EEC-10, Australia) increased between 1969/71 and 1983/5 by 147 million tonnes of which 110 million tonnes, or 75 percent, were absorbed by increases in exports and, in the case of the EEC-10, also by elimination of net imports. In 1969/71 the EEC-10 was a net importer of 16 million tonnes of cereals, and by 1983/5 it had turned into a net exporter of 17 million tonnes. At the same time, however, the EEC-10 increased the import of cereal substitute feeds (mostly manioc, corn gluten feed and other by-products) nearly four-fold to some 15 million tonnes (Schmidt and Gardiner 1988:18). This was largely the results of the maintenance of high internal prices of cereals and liberal import policies for cereal substitutes. In the 1960s the pattern was radically different: only 16 percent of the increment in the combined cereals production in these regions was absorbed through the foreign trade sector (exports and import substitution). The contributions of the different cereal importing countries or country groups to these radical shifts in the sources of market expansion are shown in Table 3.12. The major single contributor to the expansion of cereal imports between 1969/71 and 1983/5 was the group of the CPEs (mostly the USSR) with an increase in net imports of 42 million tonnes. Next came the group of the developing oil-exporting countries with a net contribution of 31 million tonnes. The net imports of China (including Taiwan Province) rose by 7 million tonnes and those of Japan by another 12 million tonnes. Other major net importers included Egypt, Brazil, the Republic of Korea, Morocco, Spain and Portugal.

Future DME production of cereals, therefore, will be significantly influenced by possible developments in these major import markets as well as by the prospect that other countries may become large net importers of cereals. The projections of the combined net import requirements of the developing countries and the CPEs are shown in Table 3.12. They imply that the net export market growth from these sources (36 million tonnes between 1983/5 and 2000) will be less than one-half of that observed during the period 1969/71 to 1983/5 (91 million tonnes). The key element in this slow-down in market expansion is the assumption that the CPEs will at best not increase their net import requirements and will probably reduce them. Among the developing countries, China's position is a major factor since its net import requirements are assumed to decline to well below the average of 6.2 million tonnes of 1983/5, though the country would continue to import some cereals and export others, and moreover, if Taiwan Province is included, net imports may increase somewhat from the 1983/5 level of 10.8 million tonnes (combined China and Taiwan Province).

Overall, therefore, the developed market economies would need to produce around 150 million tonnes of cereals by the year 2000 above their own requirements compared with 120 million tonnes in 1983/5. If their production trends continued, however, their net export availabilities, particularly of wheat,

**Table 3.12** Net cereals balances by major importers and exporters (million tonnes)*

| | 1969/71 | 1979/81 | 1983/5 | 1986 | 2000 |
|---|---|---|---|---|---|
| *Developing net importers* | *−33.8* | *−87.3* | *−98.4* | *−87.8* | *−157* |
| *Oil exporters*† | *−5.8* | *−28.3* | *−37.3* | *−30.6* | *−61* |
| Mexico | 0.2 | −5.9 | −6.2 | −2.6 | |
| Saudi Arabia | −0.5 | −3.1 | −5.7 | −4.7 | |
| Algeria | −0.5 | −3.0 | −4.3 | −4.6 | |
| Iran | −0.5 | −2.7 | −4.9 | −4.1 | |
| Iraq | −0.4 | −2.7 | −3.8 | −3.3 | |
| Indonesia | −0.9 | −2.6 | −1.9 | −1.6 | |
| Venezuela | −1.0 | −2.5 | −2.9 | −1.9 | |
| Nigeria | −0.4 | −2.1 | −1.9 | −1.8 | |
| Others§ | −1.8 | −3.7 | −5.7 | −6.0 | |
| *Other net importers* | *−28.0* | *−59.0* | *−61.1* | *−57.2* | *−96* |
| China (incl. Taiwan Province) | −3.8 | −15.8 | −10.8 | −4.8 | |
| Brazil | −1.0 | −6.3 | −4.8 | −6.0 | |
| Egypt | −1.1 | −5.9 | −8.2 | −8.5 | |
| Korea, Rep. | −2.5 | −5.7 | −6.4 | −7.4 | |
| Cuba | −1.2 | −2.1 | −2.2 | −2.2 | |
| Morocco | −0.3 | −2.0 | −2.3 | −1.6 | |
| Malaysia | −0.9 | −1.7 | −2.4 | −2.1 | |
| Bangladesh | −1.3 | −1.3 | −1.7 | −1.2 | |
| Vietnam | −1.8 | −1.3 | −0.3 | −0.6 | |
| Peru | −0.7 | −1.3 | −1.2 | −1.8 | |
| Chile | −0.5 | −1.1 | −0.9 | −0.2 | |
| India | −3.6 | 0.4 | −1.7 | 0.3 | |
| Others§ | −9.4 | −14.9 | −18.2 | −21.1 | |
| *Developing net exporters* | *14.1* | *21.5* | *29.5* | *24.1* | *45* |
| Argentina | 9.4 | 14.4 | 20.2 | 13.6 | |
| Thailand | 2.9 | 5.2 | 7.1 | 8.7 | |
| Others§ | 1.8 | 1.9 | 2.2 | 1.8 | |
| *All developing countries§* | *−19.8* | *−65.8* | *−68.9* | *−63.7* | *−112* |
| *E. Europe and USSR* | *−0.1* | *−43.9* | *−41.7* | *−27.4* | *−35* |
| *Net balance, all above* | *−19.9* | *−109.7* | *−110.6* | *−91.1* | *−147* |
| *Developed market economies* | *22.6* | *113.1* | *117.4* | *98.0* | |
| North America | 49.6 | 129.4 | 118.5 | 83.2 | |
| EEC-10 | −16.2 | 3.1 | 17.2 | 22.4 | |
| Other W. Europe | −5.1 | −11.1 | −5.6 | −1.7 | |
| Oceania | 8.9 | 14.6 | 16.8 | 22.7 | |
| Japan | −14.4 | −24.5 | −26.6 | −27.4 | |
| Others | −0.2 | 1.6 | −2.9 | −1.1 | |

* A minus sign denotes net imports. All quantities include rice in milled terms.

† IMF classification of countries (20) in which fuel exports accounted for more than 50 percent of total exports in 1980 (IMF, *World Economic Outlook*, 1986).

§ Including developing countries not included in the 94 study countries. Countries listed separately had net imports of the 1 million tonnes or more in 1979/81, except for India.

would exceed the above-indicated requirements by a large margin. Before an examination of possible outcomes in the cereals sector can be attempted, however, the *livestock* sector prospects, and the associated demand for feed use of cereals, must be evaluated.

Concerning *meat*, the developed market economies as a whole are net exporters to the rest of the world, though their net exports of around 1 million tonnes account for only 1.5 percent of their combined output. This is not to imply that export trade is unimportant since a large part of meat production in a number of countries is directed to the export markets, for example Oceania, the Netherlands, Denmark, Ireland and so on. Much of this trade is, however, intra-DME, although exports of mutton/lamb, beef and poultry to the developing countries are considerable.

By and large, therefore, the meat sector prospects depend on consumption trends within the DME group. The growth rate of per caput consumption of meat has been slowing down and it is projected to continue to do so, as follows:

| | *1961/3* | *1969/71* | *1983/5* | *2000* |
|---|---|---|---|---|
| kg/caput | 57 | 69 | 79 | 83 |

The developing countries and the developed CPEs were net exporters of meat (1.2 million tonnes) in 1969/71 (self-sufficiency 104 percent) and had turned into small net importers (600 000 tonnes) by 1983/5 (self-sufficiency 99 percent). In many of the middle-income developing countries where consumption expanded the fastest, the general policy has been to import feedgrains rather than meat. In the projections it is assumed that this general approach will continue and therefore their combined self-sufficiency in meat will remain at around 100 percent. To some extent, exports of coarse grains as such rather than in their processed form (meat) are alternative trade flows for the developed countries also, particularly those which could export meat and/or coarse grains.

The DMEs as a whole will thus find it difficult to maintain the historical growth rates of meat production. A straightforward extrapolation of production trends at the level of the individual meats (beef, mutton, pork, poultry) and DME countries/country groups[3] results in a growth rate of 1.5 percent p.a. for 1983/5–2000 and a net surplus of close to 10 million tonnes by 2000, consisting mostly of pork and poultry, given their relatively high growth rates in the historical period. Assuming the net surplus should not exceed 1.5 millions tonnes, the projected production growth rate must be brought in line with the growth of demand, that is 0.9 percent p.a., as shown below:

| Growth rates | 61–70 | 70–80 | 80–5 | 83/5–2000 |
|---|---|---|---|---|
| Per caput demand | 2.4 | 1.2 | 0.5 | 0.3 |
| Total demand | 3.5 | 2.1 | 1.2 | 0.9 |
| Production | 3.4 | 2.5 | 1.2 | 1.5 trend<br>0.9 adjusted |

[3] All trend projections were estimated separately for each of the following countries or country groups. USA, Canada, EC-10, Spain and Portugal, other Western Europe, Japan, Oceania, RSA, Israel. The historical time series data used for this purpose were those of 1970–85 or 1975–85.

For *milk and dairy products* the DMEs are substantial and growing net exporters, with net exports of some 20 million tonnes (fresh milk equivalent)[4] in 1983/5, double the level of 1969/71. One half of it comes from the EC-10 and another 35–40 percent from Oceania, while the USA has recently become the third largest exporter of milk products. The only major net importing DMEs are Italy (by far the largest), and other southern Mediterranean countries (Spain, Portugal, Greece) and Japan. Expansion of exports played a key role in maintaining production growth since one-fifth of the increased production (30 percent for the EC-10) was absorbed through increased net exports and significant quantities were accumulated as stocks which, as noted, have reached very large levels in the EEC-10 in terms of skimmed milk powder and butter. In the future, therefore, like cereals but unlike meat, domestic production will be strongly influenced by prospects for continued growth of exports.

The projections indicate continued growth of net import requirements in the developing countries to around 27 million tonnes, fresh milk equivalent, an increase of 7 million tonnes over current levels.[5] In parallel, food consumption in the DMEs should continue to expand, though at slower rates than in the past, given that present average consumption levels per caput are just over 200 kg and may grow only marginally over the next 15 years. Total production growth in the DMEs is therefore conditioned by these two variables (demand and net exports), which, following the above discussion are projected as follows (growth rates, percent p.a.):

| | 1961–70 | 1970–80 | 1980–5 | 1983/5–2000 |
|---|---|---|---|---|
| Demand (all uses) | 0.6 | 1.2 | 1.8 | 0.7 |
| Net exports | 3.1 | 6.8 | −0.3 | 2.4 |
| Production | 0.6 | 1.3 | 1.4 | 1.2 trend<br>0.8 adjusted |

[4] To obtain the fresh milk equivalent of consumption and trade, all milk and products are converted to fresh whole milk equivalent using appropriate coefficients. Butter is not so converted to avoid double counting since it is a joint product with skimmed milk.

[5] The growing net deficit of the 93 developing countries (outside China) of 23.7 million tonnes in year 2000 (of which 19 million tonnes in the middle-income countries) is based on projected per caput consumption growing to 51 kg by 2000 compared with 46 kg in 1983/5 and 38 kg in 1969/71 (Table 3.3). In parallel their production is projected to grow at 3.1 percent p.a., roughly the same rate as for 1970–85. Their net imports grew very fast in the past 15 years, 7.8 percent p.a. The above projected deficit means that they would grow at only 1.9 percent p.a. in the future. The projected import requirements rise to around 27 million tonnes if an allowance is made for China and the other developing countries which currently import 2.2 million tonnes. These projections are subject to more than the 'usual' degree of uncertainty since a good proportion of developing country imports in the past were concessional, including food aid, which in 1983/5 accounted for 28 percent of all imports of skimmed milk powder, the main dairy commodity imported. Food aid volumes and prices of commercial imports are likely to be affected by policies to curtail growth in milk production in Western Europe and the USA. Some other studies also project milk import requirements of the developing countries. The IIASA study cited earlier (Parikh *et al.* 1988) projects such imports at 23.5 million tonnes (reference scenario) while a trend projections study of the International Food Policy Research Institute (IFPRI, Sarma and Yeung 1985) has much higher net import requirements, 61.9 million tons for the 90 developing countries of the 1981 edition of *Agriculture: Toward 2000*.

The adjusted growth rate of 0.8 percent p.a is the implied growth rate required to balance production with total demand (domestic plus export) facing the DMEs.

With the above adjusted production growth of meat and milk, the cereals demand for feed grains would grow at around 0.9 percent p.a., half the growth rate of the past ten years. The main reason for this deceleration is the slower growth projected for livestock production. The comparative growth rates of these two variables are shown below (percent p.a.):

| | Livestock production | Cereals feed |
|---|---|---|
| 1961–70 | 2.2 | 3.6 |
| 1970–80 | 1.9 | 0.4 |
| 1980–85 | 1.2 | 1.8 |
| 1983/5–2000 | 0.9 | 0.9 |

The pronounced fall in the growth rate of feed demand for cereals in the 1970s reflects the extent of substitution and the gains in feeding efficiency of this period. This was above all the result of increased prices of cereals for a period in the mid-1970s combined with the penetration of the feed markets by cheaper cereal substitutes, particularly in the EEC. In the EEC-9 the share of cereals in total concentrates in terms of metabolizable energy declined from 60 percent in 1973/5 to 52 percent in 1979/81. They were substituted mainly by oilmeals, manioc and brewing/distilling/starch by-products. The equality between the two projected growth rates reflects mostly the slower growth compared with the past of the pig and poultry sectors (which are more intensive in the use of concentrates) in relation to the rest of the livestock economy. This may still be on the high side in view of technological developments which tend to reduce the amount of feed per unit of livestock output (US Congress, Office of Technology Assessment 1986: 10). In addition, demand for concentrate feeds may be adversely affected by the shift of arable land to livestock production following the imposition of production controls on cereals, oilseeds and so on in Western Europe (Douw *et al.* 1987).

Following these considerations of livestock production, aggregate domestic demand for cereals in the DMEs (excluding stock changes) may be projected at some 520 million tonnes in the year 2000, compared with 457 million tonnes in 1983/5. This projection is best seen in the context of the historical evolution of demand, as shown in the following:

| Million tonnes | 1961/3 | 1969/71 | 1983/5 | 2000 |
|---|---|---|---|---|
| Food | 89 | 93 | 103 | 110 |
| (kg per caput) | (133) | (128) | (127) | (124) |
| Feed | 196 | 264 | 297 | 341 |
| Other | 29 | 33 | 57 | 71 |
| Total | 314 | 390 | 457 | 522 |

| Growth rates | 1961–70 | 1970–85 | 1983/5–2000 |
|---|---|---|---|
| Food | 0.6 | 0.8 | 0.4 |
| Feed | 3.6 | 0.9 | 0.9 |
| Total | 2.6 | 1.2 | 0.8 |

To this projected aggregate domestic demand for cereals of around 520 million tonnes the net import requirements of the rest of the world (Table 3.12) may be added in order to define the approximate total market size faced by the DMEs. This is done in terms of the main groups of cereals (Table 3.13).

The total demand for cereals projected as in Table 3.13 is confronted in Table 3.13 with production assuming continuation of trends. Overall, production of cereals, even if projected conservatively, would grow at 2.0 percent p.a. and tend to exceed projected demand by some 120 million to 130 million tonnes annually in the year 2000, mostly in wheat. This is because over the last ten years (1975–85) the area under wheat in the main producing countries has been increasing and that under rice and coarse grains has been on the decline, while average yields of wheat and coarse grains grew faster than those of rice (Fig. 3.8).

As a result of the above trends, wheat production grew rapidly at 3.8 percent p.a. compared with that of coarse grains (1.8 percent p.a.) and with absolute declines of rice (−0.7 percent p.a.). Therefore any projections of trends, being essentially some form of an extrapolation of the historical patterns of change in the relevant variables per unit of time, is bound to reproduce these differentials in production performance in the different crops, though not in exactly the same manner as in the historical period. The resulting trend growth rate is, as noted, 2.0 percent p.a. for 1983/5–2000, compared with 2.9 percent in the 1970s and 2.3 percent in 1980–5. To avoid the projected surpluses a fall in this aggregate growth rate of cereal production to around 0.9 percent p.a. would be required.

The possibilities and policy adjustments required for modifying downwards the production growth rates are discussed later in the context of efforts to bring about orderly change in world agriculture (Ch. 7). This policy discussion will, however, be better appreciated if the method of projecting production trends in

**Table 3.13** DMEs: total domestic and net export demand for cereals

| | Domestic demand | | Net exports | | Total demand | | Production |
|---|---|---|---|---|---|---|---|
| | 1983/5 | 2000 | 1983/5 | 2000 | 1983/5 | 2000 | 2000 trend* |
| Rice (milled) | 13.5 | 13.8 | 1.4 | 2.0 | 14.9 | 15.8 | 16 |
| Wheat | 113.5 | 122 | 77.3 | 81.0 | 190.8 | 203 | 303 |
| Coarse grains | 329.8 | 386 | 38.7 | 64.0 | 368.4 | 450 | 477 |
| Total cereals | 456.8 | 522 | 117.4 | 147.0 | 574.1 | 669 | 796 |

* Trend production before adjustments for world balance.

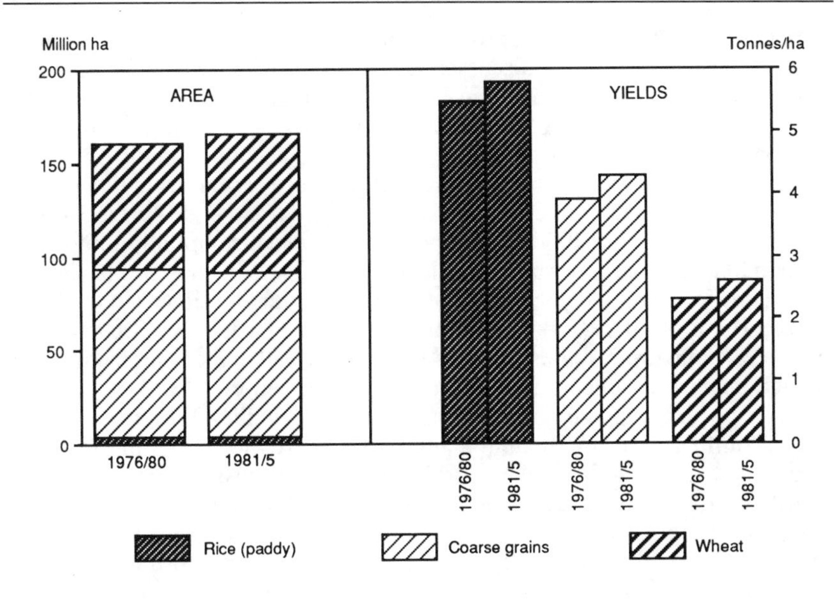


**Figure 3.8** Developed market economies: area and yields of cereals

the different country groups is described in some detail. In the last ten years total harvested area (all crops) was changing slowly, if at all, except in Canada, Oceania (increasing) and Japan (declining). The trend projections assume that the five-year average area of 1981/5 will not change much in each of the regions/countries for which the analysis has been conducted separately, except for Canada, Oceania and Japan, for which somewhat slower rates of change than in the past ten years are assumed to prevail in the future. This projected total harvested area is then allocated to different crops assuming cropping patterns will continue to evolve as they have been doing in the past.

Subsequently, yields are projected on the assumption that their past growth rates will continue in the future in somewhat attenuated form.[6] Constraints based on agronomic considerations on upper limits of projected yields to avoid results which may verge on the technically unfeasible have been applied only in very exceptional cases. The projected average yields of, for example, 8.0 tonnes of wheat and 10 tonnes of maize in the EEC-10 are therefore considered agronomically feasible. Reported record yields for these two crops are 14.5 and 19.3 tonnes/ha, respectively (Coffman 1983: 11). Current average yields in the EEC-10 are 5.2 tonnes/ha for wheat and 6.7 tonnes/ha for maize, and among the major producing countries they are 7.0 tonnes for wheat in the UK and 6.3 tonnes for maize in France. The results of these projections of production trends are as shown in Table 3.13. It is, however, emphasized that these trend extrapolations result in production levels which will not materialize if they are not compatible with market balance and/or policies.

[6] Positive growth in the past is projected on a linear trend, negative growth on an exponential trend; this tends to dampen the rates of change in the future compared with the past.

Some adjustments are made to these projections before the policy implications of these trends can be discussed. On rice, the reduction of area in the last ten years reflects developments in the largest rice-producing DME country, Japan, which has allowed production to decline more or less in line with domestic consumption. Its per caput consumption declined rapidly up to 1980 (2.3 percent p.a.) but at a much slower rate in more recent years (0.8 percent p.a. in 1980–5). In the projections, the more recent trend of decline is assumed to continue to the year 2000, so that per caput food consumption should reach some 62 kg, compared with current levels of 70 kg. With this result, the past rate of decline of total demand (0.9 percent p.a.) would be slowed in the future to only 0.2 percent p.a. The assumption is made that Japan will continue to produce as much rice as it is required to maintain 100 percent self-sufficiency, though much will depend on the results of current efforts at the international level for reducing agricultural protection. Therefore, the DME trend projection of (milled) rice production is adjusted upwards to 16 million tonnes, a level which is compatible with the projected net trade position of the rest of the world. Another adjustment is made to the projected trend production of coarse grains in South Africa, whose trends were strongly biased downwards due to the drought of the early 1980s. Correcting for this distortion results in projected DME production of coarse grains of 477 million tonnes. The trend projections of Table 3.13 already incorporate these two adjustments.

The projected trend production of wheat and coarse grains are shown by region of origin in Table 3.14. Wheat and coarse grains are best discussed together since there exists a significant degree of substitutability in production (e.g. barley for wheat in Europe) and in consumption (a quarter of all cereals feed in the EC-12 consists of wheat—23 million tonnes in 1986/7). The DMEs as a whole would tend to produce a net surplus of 272 million tonnes, if their production trends continued, while the net import requirements of the rest of the world are projected to be between 140 million and 150 million tonnes. The adjustment problem may therefore be defined as requiring curbing of the growth in the combined production of wheat and coarse grains in the DMEs to avoid the generation of surpluses of some 120 million to 130 million tonnes.

It is to be noted that this projected situation would still allow DME cereal production to be by year 2000 some 100 million tonnes above the level of 1983/5, though rather drastic declines would be needed in the short term to bring the stock situation to 'normal' levels. In absolute terms, this increase of 100 million tonnes is lower than that of the last 15 years (160 million tonnes between 1969/71 to 1983/5) but only by about one-third. Therefore, alarm about impending catastrophy in the DME agriculture due to required permanent declines in output does not seem to be justified. The required short-term declines may, however, prove quite painful and will require serious efforts in multilateral cooperation to ensure orderly transition to a new situation. For the longer term, however, what is required is lower growth than in the last 15 years, which, as noted, included the period of the 1970s, which in retrospect may be considered as exceptional from the standpoint of the growth of the world cereals market.

**Table 3.14** Wheat and coarse grains by DME country group (million tonnes)

| | 1983/5 | | | 2000 | | |
|---|---|---|---|---|---|---|
| | Production | Dom. demand | Difference | Production (trend) | Dom. demand | Difference |
| North America | 331 | 215 | 116 | 436 | 241 | 195 |
| EEC-10 | 138 | 117 | 21 | 211 | 131 | 80 |
| Other W. Europe | 54 | 62 | −8 | 68 | 71 | −3 |
| Oceania | 29 | 9 | 20 | 44 | 11 | 33 |
| Others | 10 | 40 | −30 | 21 | 54 | −33 |
| Total | 562 | 443 | 119 | 780 | 508 | 272 |
| Rest-of-the-world balances | | | 117 | | | 140–50 |

**Box 3.3** *Factors in the growth of cereals deficits of the developing countries*

The argument of the required adjustment in the growth rate of the DME cereals sector assumes as given the projected net import requirements of the rest of the world presented in Table 3.12. These projections may appear to be on the conservative side in the light of past experience. They are more so if viewed in the context of the widely held belief that the developing countries are embarked firmly on a path of increasing consumption of livestock products which will continue to fuel import demand for feedgrains even if their own cereal sector were to grow reasonably fast. Empirical evidence to support this argument is mixed. It is true that in countries with rapidly rising incomes the demand for livestock products is strong and imports of feedgrains grow rapidly. It is, however, equally true that in many developing countries the rapid growth in cereal imports was caused by the slow growth in their production rather than by acceleration in their (food and feed) consumption of cereals. In these countries there is a strong import replacement effect when production growth improves. There are major cereal importers in both classes of countries. On balance, therefore, what will happen to the growth rate of net import requirements of the developing countries will depend on whether the income effect or the import displacement effect will dominate in the future. Given the less favourable income growth prospects in many middle-income countries and the increasing foreign-exchange constraints compared with the past, it is reasonable to expect that acceleration of consumption spilling over into rapid growth of imports will be less of a factor in the future compared with the past. The import scene may, therefore, be determined more by the extent to which importing countries are successful in maintaining or improving their production performance.

Other projection studies indicate cereal deficits of the developing countries which, in most cases, are above those projected here, as follows (million tonnes, deficits derived as difference between projected production and consumption):

Developing countries, cereal deficits in the year 2000

| | Total | China and India | Latin America | All others |
|---|---|---|---|---|
| This study | −112 | −11 | 1 | −102 |
| World Bank (1986b) | −163 | −61 | − 8 | −110 |
| International Wheat Council (1987) | −211 | −31 | −31 | −149 |
| International Institute for Applied Systems Analysis—IIASA (Parikh *et al.* 1988)* | −146 | −15 | | |
| International Food Policy Research Institute—IFPRI (Paulino 1986)† | −80 | | | |

* Deficit shown is for the study's reference scenario.

† Deficit shown is for the 90 countries of the 1981 edition of Agriculture: Toward 2000 (comparable deficit from this study: 93 million tonnes).

The above numbers are not fully comparable with each other because of some differences in the countries classified as developing. These differences in country coverage are not, however, very significant for explaining the discrepancies in projected deficits. A full explanation of differences cannot be made without a detailed comparative study of country-level results as well as of the methodology and assumptions, a task which is not possible from the published material. The regional differences that could be identified are shown above. The deficits, even when not very different from each other, are the results of projected production and consumption which can differ widely among studies, including in commodity composition (wheat, rice, coarse grains) and in the distribution of cereal consumption between food and feed.

Cereals and livestock account for three-quarters of total gross agricultural output of the DMEs. Among the other major traded commodities, oilcrops account for another 6.5 percent of gross production and sugar crops for just under 2 percent. For *sugar*, trend projections of DME production derived with the methodology described above, indicate an annual growth rate of 0.6 percent during 1983/5–2000. This reflects a continuation of the trend for production growth to slow down, from 4.0 percent in the 1960s to 2.6 percent in the 1970s to 1.5 percent in the period 1975–85. The deceleration in production reflected by similar developments in consumption which grew slowly during the 1960s and has been declining ever since, to the current level of 36 kg per caput. A key factor has been the substitution in consumption by other sweeteners, particularly high fructose corn syrup (HFCS) in the USA, where the share of sugar in total caloric sweetener consumption declined from 76 percent in 1975 to 49 percent in 1985.

The difference between the continuous, though decelerating, growth in production and declining consumption was absorbed through drastic substitution of imports from the developing countries, resulting in rapid increases in overall self-sufficiency ratio (SSR) of the DMEs until they turned into net exporters in most years after 1981, as the following data indicate:

| | 1961/3 | 1969/71 | 1979/81 | 1983/5 | 1986 |
|---|---|---|---|---|---|
| Net imports (mill. tonnes, raw equivalent) | 8.0 | 8.5 | 1.8 | 0.2 | −1.3 (net exports) |
| SSR (%) | 65 | 73 | 96 | 98 | |

The direction of trends were similar in almost all DME country groups, but the major impact on the decline in net imports originated in the EEC-10, which turned from net importer of 1.6 million tonnes in 1969/71 to a net exporter of 3.1 million tonnes in 1983/5, followed by the USA, which reduced net imports from 4.6 million to 2.5 million tonnes over the same period. The situation was further aggravated recently following further reduction in the US import quotas of sugar, so that 1987 imports are estimated not to exceed 1 million tonnes.

The projections of sugar consumption indicate consumption would nearly stabilize at around 35 kg, reflecting essentially a slow-down in the pace of substitution in consumption of sugar by HFCs, though there is great uncertainty about these projections, given the tendency for other sweeteners to penetrate the market. Total demand is therefore projected to increase at the same rate as population (around 0.7 percent p.a.), and if the trend projections of production were to materialize, they may lead to a modest reversal in the declining trend of net import requirements, which could increase to some 2 million tonnes, implying a decline in the aggregate DME self-sufficiency to 94 percent by the year 2000. Under these conditions, the developing countries would be able to arrest the decline of their net exports to the rest of the world and maintain them at around current levels of 6.5 million to 7.0 million tonnes. This would cover the net deficit of around 5 million tonnes of the developed CPEs and the above trend-projected 2 million tonnes deficit of the DMEs, provided the latter do not continue to strengthen their import-substitution policies.

It is recalled that the 2-million-tonne sugar deficit of the DMEs results from the specific assumptions used, that is a per caput consumption level of 35 kg and continued slow-down in the growth of production to 0.6 percent p.a. over the period 1983/5–2000. This latter outcome results from the assumption of continuation of the slow decline in the area under sugarbeet (-1.1 percent p.a.) while yields would continue to grow, also slowly (at 1.4 percent p.a.). Developments in the area and yields of sugarcane over the last ten years have been in the opposite direction (area increasing slowly, yields declining slowly) and the trend projection implies continuation of these developments to 2000. The final outcome will depend, however, on policy decisions of the different DMEs concerning their sugar sectors. Current attitudes are not encouraging: the EEC is continuously examining the possibilities of shifting cereals area to other crops, and in the USA pressures are mounting to reduce further sugar import quotas. These issues are scheduled to be examined in the context of the new round of GATT negotiations in which agriculture will be given more prominence than in earlier rounds. If they are even moderately successful, it can be expected that the developing countries which are low-cost producers of cane sugar will be able to expand their net exports to the DMEs substantially.

The *oilseeds* sector in the DME countries expanded very rapidly during the 1970s when area increased at 4.6 percent p.a. before stabilizing at around 37 million ha, or 16 percent of total area under crops (1983/5). More than 75 percent of the area is in the United States which account for almost all production (97 percent) of by far the most important oilcrop of the DME countries, soyabeans. The USA also accounts for the major part of production of some of the other main oilseeds (groundnuts, cottonseed) while the production of the other major oilseeds (sunflowerseed, rapeseed and linseed) is more evenly spread among the different regions. Both the North American and the European regions participated in the rapid expansion of oilseed production.

On the demand side, the major impetus came from the feed use of oilcakes/meals, particularly in Europe, where consumption almost doubled in the 1970s. Food consumption of vegetable oils grew at much slower rates. As a consequence, oil production tended to grow faster than consumption and it had a strong import-substitution effect. For the DME countries together, net imports of vegetable oils and fats (actual product weight), which were 1.2 million tonnes in 1969/71, had almost disappeared by the end of the 1970s before rising again to around 0.5 million tonnes in 1983/5. The net imports of oilcakes/meals, however, kept increasing rapidly, from 3.4 million tonnes in 1969/71 to 5.8 million tonnes in 1979/81 to 9.5 million tonnes in 1983/5.

The balance sheet of the sector is rather difficult to draw up because of the joint-product nature of the oils and oilcakes/meals and the different markets (food, industrial uses, feed) to which these products are directed. The matter is further complicated by the existence of vegetable oils of origin other than the oilcrops proper, for example cottonseed and maize and rice bran oils. An attempt at drawing a balance sheet is presented in Table 3.15, which shows in section B the indigenous production of all oilseeds and oils expressed in oil equivalents. The trade and food consumption data of oilseeds, oils and fats, always in oil equivalents, are then compared with production to derive the net trade balances and provide a basis for the evaluation of production trends.

The production projections of Table 3.15 are computed with the same method described above for the other crops, that is assuming their share in total area continuing to develop as in the past ten years, keeping aggregate cropped area constant in the major regions while yields would continue to grow as per past trends. The projections of demand for oils assume slow growth in per caput consumption. They indicate that the trend for indigenous oil production to displace imports from the developing countries would continue with the DME region eventually turning into a net exporter if the growth of production is not restrained. On the oilcakes/meals side, the assumption of a slow-down in livestock production (discussed earlier) would inevitably imply a slow-down in the growth of the demand for feed, and the DME region would tend to become self-sufficient in these products. The more detailed FAO projections to 1990 indicate that feed demand for oilmeals might be weak and it may grow less rapidly than the livestock sector.

The above implications for the net trade positions of this group of countries depend crucially on the continuation of production trends in the oilseeds sector—even if at a slower rate than in the historical period—and derived demand in the livestock sector. In the past the rapid growth of oilseed

**Table 3.15** Oilseeds, vegetable oils and cakes/meals: trends in the developed market economies (million tonnes)

| | 1969/71 | 1983/5 | 2000 trend |
|---|---|---|---|
| (A) *PRODUCTION* (product weight) | | | |
| Soybeans | 31.6 | 52.4 | |
| Groundnuts in shell | 1.9 | 2.0 | |
| Sunflowerseed | 0.8 | 4.4 | |
| Rapeseed | 2.7 | 7.1 | |
| Linseed | 1.6 | 0.9 | |
| Cottonseed | 4.2 | 5.0 | |
| Total above (seed weight) | 42.8 | 71.8 | 108 |
| Olive oil | 1.1 | 1.4 | 2.5 |
| Maize & rice bran oil | 0.8 | 0.9 | |
| (B) *OILSEEDS, OILS & FATS IN OIL EQUIVALENTS* | | | |
| Production (oil equivalent of section A) | 11.0 | 18.5 | 26.7 |
| Food consumption | 10.2 | 14.6 | 23–5 |
| Other uses | 3.4 | 5.1 | |
| Net imports | 2.8 | 0.9 | |
| (C) *OILCAKES/MEALS* | | | |
| Production | 29.7 | 48.4 | 73* |
| Feed consumption | 33.0 | 56.9 | |
| Net imports | 3.4 | 9.5 | |

* Oilcake/meal equivalent of trend oilseed production (section A) reduced by 6 percent to reflect current relationships between the cake equivalent of oilseed production and actual cake/meal production.

production was underpinned by that of livestock, which provided growing markets for both indigenous oilseeds and imports. If livestock production growth were to slow down as assumed here (after the adjustment of the production trends), it can be expected to have a restraining influence on the growth rate of the oilseeds sector, which would also face increasing competition in the international markets from some major developing-country exporters. It seems likely, however, that pressures for continuing the rapid growth of oilseeds production will intensify in the light of the need to contain the growth of the cereals sector. In the policy debate on possible uses of land released from cereals production, the idea of diverting it into import-substituting oilseeds, particularly in the EEC, is not new. It must be noted, however, that this would result in reallocation of DME production from the surplus to the deficit regions (aggravating in the process the policy conflict) and would not, by itself, solve the problem of aggregate market constraints.

## Aggregate agricultural growth adjusted for world balance and implications

The preceding commodity-specific analyses covered over 80 percent of the agricultural sector of the DMEs. The picture that emerges suggests that their aggregate agricultural growth in terms of gross output should be constrained to approximately 0.9 percent p.a. over the next 15 years. This would still be slightly above that of their own aggregate domestic demand for the primary products of the sector, the difference being accounted for by continuing expansion of demand for cereals on the part of the rest of the world, as shown in Table 3.12. Aggregate self-sufficiency of the DMEs as a whole may therefore improve only marginally from the current level of 102.5 percent, given that the scope for further import substitution in some of the major DME country groups has been virtually exhausted.

In conclusion, after the short-run adjustments required to bring stocks back to normal, agricultural growth in the DMEs may be resumed at rates about one-half those of the past 15 years. In parallel, the medium-term outlook is for international prices to continue to be under downward pressure for some major commodity sectors (cereals, oilseeds). These two factors will therefore continue to affect unfavourably the evolution of farm incomes, particularly in the export-oriented countries. The pressure for farm income support will continue to be strong. The major policy issue is, therefore, how to meet the opposing objectives of farm income support, avoidance of accumulation of unwanted surpluses and the related potential for trade conflicts, containment of budget expenditures and infusion of more economic rationality in the system viewed at the economy-wide level.

For agriculture, this would mean greater efforts to achieve structural change by creating units which are economically viable without excessive support. This process may be aided by the projected continuation of declines of the population economically active in agriculture. It is estimated that the latter declined in the DMEs at 3.1 percent p.a. between 1970 and 1985, so that now it represents only 6.7 percent of the total economically active population. The outlook is for this trend to accelerate further to a rate of decline of 3.6 percent p.a. for 1985–2000. By the year 2000 the share of agriculture in the total labour force of the DME countries as a whole may be only 3.5 percent.

These estimates and projections refer to the farm production sector and do not include employment in the related sectors of the entire food system, which is considerable. For example, US data show that farming accounts for only 11.5 percent of total employment in the country's 'food and fiber' system (USDA 1987b). Unfavourable conditions in primary farming would therefore have wider repercussions, for example in the input supplying and processing and transport sectors. The need to seek solutions at the economy-wide level through more rational use of resources becomes all the more imperative. Farm policy reform aimed at reducing the overall economic-efficiency losses inherent in many of the existing farm support programmes, could therefore make an important contribution to this objective. The objective should be a restructured farm sector composed of units which can be economically viable in the context of the total sector-expansion possibilities subject to the absorptive capacity of domestic and foreign markets. In the meantime, the general orientation of policy reform should be to achieve the income-support objectives by means other than those which encourage increased production of commodities which are in, or tend toward, surplus, including at the global level.

# 4 Sustainable growth in production

The annual growth rates for agricultural production projected in Chapter 3 present mankind with serious but surmountable challenges. This is true both for the developed countries which have to slow down production growth without undermining the economic and social welfare of rural communities, and for the developing countries, many of which will have to accelerate production substantially.

In the developing countries this requires first and foremost a conducive policy environment as discussed in Chapters 3 and 8. Second, it needs substantial investment in infrastructural and manpower development. Third, existing technologies and the inputs they require must be made more widely available. Fourth, these technologies and inputs must be used in the context of a strategy of conservation-based resource development. Current modes of development are, in many instances, unsustainable—cropland is being over-exploited, rangelands overstocked and forests cut down.

As noted in Chapter 3, the situation in the developed countries, particularly those of the developed market economies (DMEs) is in stark contrast to that in many developing countries. Their problem is one of success, which they are finding great difficulty in managing. The issue of sustainable growth in production, and hence sustainable development, has to be addressed in both developed and developing countries, albeit their priority actions may differ as discussed in Chapter 11. Priority actions in the developed countries need to be increasingly centred on environmental protection measures. Whilst those in most developing countries (to which the rest of this chapter is devoted) must focus on resource conservation and the adoption of farming systems that reverse current degradation (particularly soil erosion and salination) and allow sustainable increases in production.

## Crop production

Growth in crop production may be ascribed to changes in three factors: arable land, cropping intensity and yields. Historically, expansion of arable area has been the main source of growth. However, starting around 1900 in some developed countries, and since 1950 in a number of developing countries, higher yields have increasingly become the only or the major source of output growth.

The overall sources of crop production growth in the developing countries[1] over the next 15 years is very similar to past trends: nearly two-thirds would

[1] In this chapter the term 'developing countries' is used to designate the 93 countries excluding China, unless otherwise stated. This is because data on land use and inputs were not available for China in the same detail as for the other developing countries.

come from increases in average yields, which would grow at an annual rate of 1.6 percent, which is similar to that of the past 25 years. Over a fifth arises through increases in arable land, projected to grow at 0.6 percent a year. The balance would be due to increases in cropping intensity, which is projected to increase from an average level of 78 percent in 1982/4 to 84 percent in the year 2000 (Fig. 4.1).

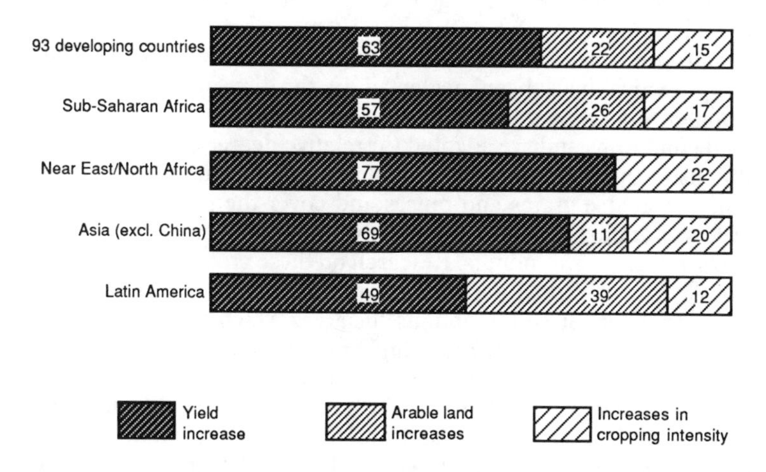


**Figure 4.1** Contributions to crop production increases (1982/4–2000; percent)

Countries and regions differ substantially as to the relative importance of these factors in the growth of production. For example, the Near East/North Africa region and many countries in other regions, particularly in Asia, have reached the limits of land expansion barring major investments or new technologies for marginal rainfall areas and soils. Arable land expansion is to take place mostly in Latin America and, to a lesser extent, Africa (Fig. 4.2).

Area increases for agricultural use must be well planned to avoid uncontrolled expansion in tropical rain forests and rangelands which are only marginally suitable for annual crop production, in order to avoid adverse ecological effects. Part of area expansion will be for irrigation purposes. However, much of the increase in harvested land will stem from reduced fallow periods in areas of sedentary agriculture and of shifting cultivation. In both cases reduction of fallow periods without compensating measures in soil management, particularly in Africa, will have grave consequences, notably the degradation of the natural resource base, soil erosion and desertification.

The 1960s and 1970s saw major technological breakthroughs in biochemical technology now known as the Green Revolution. The nature of these developments and their spillovers to other commodities and other regions will influence crop production in the foreseeable future. The implications of these developments in technological relations for crop production are twofold.

First, in the two main commodities which have benefited from technological developments within the past two decades, namely wheat and rice, there will be a slow-down in the growth of production. Modern varieties now cover around

50 percent of the area for these crops, so the diffusion process is slowing down and quantum increases in yields are not anticipated. Further diffusion will depend largely on the expansion of irrigation and the amount of competition they receive from other crops which can also be profitably grown under irrigation. There will also be need for a constant flow of 'maintenance' research results to sustain what has been achieved. As a consequence, growth rates of both crops will decline as the growth rates of both area and yields decline (Table 4.1).

Second, efforts need to be focused to increase the production growth rates of the crops which have been neglected in the first round of technological developments in the past two decades. These crops are grown primarily under rain-fed conditions and are adapted (in relative degrees) to the environmental conditions of the drier areas of agricultural production. They can be broadly classified as coarse grains and pulses and cover the principal grain crops of maize, barley, millet and sorghum, and pulses such as lentils, chick-peas, beans and peas as well as groundnuts. Research on these crops which has been in the pipeline for the past two decades has produced and is producing technical options. However, these are options for areas which depend on rainfall to a large extent and therefore have the higher degrees of risk. This risk factor has made the diffusion of new technical options produced by research more difficult, and their wider adoption will require special policy measures. The production projections assume appropriate policies to induce expansion of area for these crops—some of which, like barley and millet, have had historically declining areas. The significant increases in production growth rates will be contingent on these factors.

The increasing demand for coarse grains for both food (in some countries) and feed (in others) will require appropriate policies to stimulate their production. As noted (Ch. 3 and Fig. 3.3) and will be discussed later in connection with livestock production, feed demand for cereals would continue to grow rapidly in the middle-income countries and China. This increase in feed demand must be managed so as to stimulate increased production without lowering the availability of these grains for food, particularly in Africa, where these commodities are grown primarily for human consumption. Such competition between food and feed requirements seems unlikely. In fact, provided maize and rice yields continue to improve, the expansion of crops such as sorghum and millet appear likely to depend to a large extent on the expansion of feed demand.

Roots and tubers (cassava, potatoes, yams, taro, sweet potatoes, etc.) are of particular importance as staples in rural areas of sub-Saharan Africa and Latin America, but have commonly become less important in urban areas because of the competition from cereals, including imported cereals, at subsidized prices. They also tend to suffer from high marketing costs due to their bulkiness and perishability. Consequently future growth in production is dependent on removal of the distorted competition from imported cereals, better price incentives, smallholder storage, and marketing arrangements, together with improvements in processing technologies.

There are regional divergences from these global patterns of crop production. In the Near East and North Africa, the area of wheat in rain-fed areas and particularly in marginal areas is expected to decline and be taken over by barley

**Table 4.1** Area and yields for major crops: 93 developing countries

| | Production (P) (million tonnes) | | | Harvested area (A) (million ha) | | | Yield (Y) (tonnes/ha) | | | Growth rates (% p.a.) | | | | | |
|---|---|---|---|---|---|---|---|---|---|---|---|---|---|---|---|
| | | | | | | | | | | 1961–84 | | | 1982/4–2000 | | |
| | 1961/3 | 1982/4 | 2000 | 1961/3 | 1982/4 | 2000 | 1961/3 | 1982/4 | 2000 | P | A | Y | P | A | Y |
| Wheat | 48 | 114 | 177 | 50 | 69 | 78 | 1.0 | 1.7 | 2.3 | 4.3 | 1.7 | 2.6 | 2.6 | 0.8 | 1.9 |
| Rice (paddy) | 142 | 251 | 367 | 86 | 105 | 120 | 1.7 | 2.4 | 3.0 | 2.8 | 1.0 | 1.8 | 2.3 | 0.8 | 1.4 |
| Maize | 51 | 94 | 165 | 45 | 58 | 73 | 1.1 | 1.6 | 2.3 | 2.8 | 1.0 | 1.8 | 3.4 | 1.3 | 2.0 |
| Barley | 15 | 18 | 34 | 16 | 16 | 20 | 1.0 | 1.2 | 1.7 | 1.0 | −0.1 | 1.1 | 3.8 | 1.4 | 2.4 |
| Millet | 18 | 20 | 32 | 34 | 34 | 39 | 0.5 | 0.6 | 0.8 | 0.8 | −0.0 | 0.8 | 2.7 | 0.8 | 1.9 |
| Sorghum | 21 | 36 | 64 | 33 | 39 | 46 | 0.7 | 0.9 | 1.4 | 3.2 | 0.8 | 2.4 | 3.3 | 0.8 | 2.4 |
| Cassava | 73 | 124 | 185 | 10 | 13 | 18 | 7.7 | 9.2 | 10.3 | 2.5 | 1.8 | 0.8 | 2.4 | 1.7 | 0.7 |
| Sugar cane | 363 | 776 | 1146 | 8 | 14 | 17 | 45.7 | 57.4 | 69.4 | 3.6 | 2.6 | 1.0 | 2.3 | 1.2 | 1.1 |
| Pulses | 22 | 27 | 39 | 43 | 51 | 55 | 0.5 | 0.5 | 0.7 | 0.9 | 0.7 | 0.1 | 2.1 | 0.5 | 1.6 |
| Soybeans | 1 | 24 | 45 | 2 | 15 | 22 | 0.7 | 1.6 | 2.0 | 18.1 | 12.9 | 4.7 | 3.8 | 2.5 | 1.3 |
| Groundnuts | 12 | 13 | 23 | 15 | 15 | 22 | 0.8 | 0.9 | 1.0 | 0.2 | −0.2 | 0.3 | 3.4 | 2.2 | 1.2 |
| Coffee | 4 | 5 | 7 | 10 | 10 | 11 | 0.4 | 0.5 | 0.7 | 1.1 | 0.1 | 0.9 | 1.9 | 0.6 | 1.3 |
| Cotton (seed) | 13 | 16 | 22 | 19 | 20 | 21 | 0.7 | 0.8 | 1.1 | 0.8 | 0.1 | 0.7 | 1.9 | 0.3 | 1.6 |

**Table 4.2** Meat production in the developing countries

| | Meat production | | | | | Livestock numbers | | | | |
|---|---|---|---|---|---|---|---|---|---|---|
| | Million tonnes | | | Growth rate | | Million | | | Growth rate | |
| | 1961/3 | 1983/5 | 2000 | 1961–85 | 1983/5–2000 | 1961/3 | 1983/5 | 2000 | 1961–85 | 1983/5–2000 |
| 93 developing countries | | | | | | | | | | |
| Cattle and buffaloes | 8.9 | 13.3 | 20.4 | 2.1 | 2.7 | 637 | 884 | 1033 | 1.5 | 1.0 |
| Sheep and goats | 2.4 | 3.7 | 6.2 | 1.9 | 3.3 | 647 | 854 | 1077 | 1.2 | 1.5 |
| Pigs | 2.6 | 5.9 | 9.9 | 3.8 | 3.3 | 85 | 134 | 201 | 2.0 | 2.6 |
| Poultry | 1.5 | 7.7 | 16.5 | 7.9 | 4.9 | 1233 | 3130 | 4873 | 4.3 | 2.8 |
| Africa (sub-Saharan) | | | | | | | | | | |
| Cattle and buffaloes | 1.3 | 2.1 | 3.5 | 2.1 | 3.2 | 107 | 154 | 186 | 1.6 | 1.2 |
| Sheep and goats | 0.6 | 0.9 | 1.5 | 1.8 | 3.3 | 172 | 245 | 309 | 1.6 | 1.5 |
| Pigs | 0.1 | 0.3 | 0.6 | 4.0 | 4.8 | 4 | 9 | 12 | 4.0 | 2.1 |
| Poultry | 0.2 | 0.7 | 1.8 | 5.8 | 5.5 | 244 | 561 | 968 | 3.8 | 3.5 |

| | | | | | | | | | | |
|---|---|---|---|---|---|---|---|---|---|---|
| Near East/N. Africa | | | | | | | | | | |
| Cattle and buffaloes | 0.6 | 1.1 | 1.8 | 2.5 | 3.3 | 35 | 44 | 54 | 1.2 | 1.3 |
| Sheep and goats | 0.9 | 1.4 | 2.2 | 2.3 | 2.9 | 175 | 227 | 291 | 1.1 | 1.6 |
| Pigs* | 0.0 | 0.0 | 0.0 | 4.8 | 1.6 | 0 | 0 | 0 | 2.6 | 0.5 |
| Poultry | 0.3 | 1.5 | 3.7 | 8.4 | 5.9 | 134 | 477 | 856 | 5.6 | 3.7 |
| Asia (excl. China) | | | | | | | | | | |
| Cattle and buffaloes | 1.1 | 1.9 | 3.2 | 2.5 | 3.2 | 317 | 382 | 432 | 0.8 | 0.8 |
| Sheep and goats | 0.5 | 1.0 | 1.9 | 2.9 | 4.1 | 149 | 239 | 311 | 2.2 | 1.7 |
| Pigs | 0.9 | 2.3 | 4.1 | 3.6 | 3.8 | 30 | 49 | 81 | 1.9 | 3.2 |
| Poultry | 0.4 | 1.7 | 3.9 | 6.2 | 5.6 | 486 | 1027 | 1622 | 3.2 | 2.9 |
| Latin America | | | | | | | | | | |
| Cattle and buffaloes | 5.8 | 8.3 | 11.9 | 1.9 | 2.3 | 178 | 303 | 360 | 2.6 | 1.1 |
| Sheep and goats | 0.4 | 0.4 | 0.5 | −0.7 | 2.2 | 152 | 143 | 165 | −0.5 | 0.9 |
| Pigs | 1.5 | 3.3 | 5.1 | 3.9 | 2.8 | 51 | 76 | 108 | 1.9 | 2.2 |
| Poultry | 0.6 | 3.8 | 7.0 | 9.3 | 4.0 | 370 | 1065 | 1427 | 5.1 | 1.8 |

* 0 or 0.0 implies negligible numbers.

which is more adapted to such areas. Simultaneously the area and production of wheat under irrigation would increase, resulting in an increase in yields. In Latin America, land expansion will in general continue to be an important source of the growth in production, though at reduced rates. This is also the case for cassava in sub-Saharan Africa. The production of other important commodities, particularly industrial or tropical crops grown for export such as sugar cane and beverages will be constrained primarily by the growth in demand in the export markets. Production growth of oilseeds and vegetable oils will continue to be strong, reflecting both areas already planted and increasing demand.

It should be noted that due to the drought conditions which influenced production levels in sub-Saharan Africa in 1982/4 historical growth rates appear low and projected growth rates appear high for this region. The past and the future are more in line than they actually appear (see also Tables 3.6 and 3.7).

## Livestock production

As with crops, three primary sources of production growth can be distinguished: expansion in livestock numbers; increased intensity of range and pasture utilization and better use of feed concentrates and agricultural by-products; and higher output of meat, milk or eggs per animal through improved management, breeds and technologies.

Increases in livestock numbers and the off-take rates are the dominant sources of growth in the developing countries, and this situation is projected to prevail in the future (Table 4.2). However, there are many countries where the lack of potential to either increase the area of grazing land or to raise its productivity will result in higher yields being an increasingly important source of growth. For pigs, poultry and to a lesser extent dairy cattle, much of the increased output will come from intensive or semi-intensive commercial production and the use of supplementary feeds. The overall pattern projected is for some 46 percent of meat production to arise from higher yields per animal, about 20 percent from greater numbers, and the remainder from increased off-takes rates through improvements in pasture carrying capacity, health and feed.

The slow evolution from extensive to intensive production points to consequential increases in environmental degradation. Because in many countries livestock numbers are already in excess of the carrying capacity of unimproved natural grassland, the greatest danger lies in overgrazing. Moreover, there are considerable institutional and economic problems to be overcome in bringing livestock numbers into balance with forage and feed availabilities, problems which will be difficult to overcome in the short to medium term. The limited opportunities to increase livestock production from natural grasslands focuses attention on the need to develop the other components of total feed supplies which are more amenable to increases. Expansion of crop production will increase the availability of crop residues and crop-processing by-products, which already represent a large share of total feed supplies in the more densely populated countries. Wider adoption of

**Table 4.3** Milk production in the developing countries

| | Production (million tonnes) | | | Growth rate (% p.a.) | |
|---|---|---|---|---|---|
| | 1961/3 | 1983/5 | 2000 | 1961–85 | 1983/5–2000 |
| 93 developing countries | 62 | 115 | 188 | 3.0 | 3.1 |
| Africa (sub-Saharan) | 5 | 9 | 15 | 2.4 | 3.2 |
| Near East/N. Africa | 10 | 16 | 26 | 2.4 | 3.2 |
| Asia (excl. China) | 28 | 54 | 84 | 3.1 | 2.8 |
| Latin America | 19 | 37 | 63 | 3.2 | 3.4 |

simple treatment methods of many of the low-quality crop residues can help increase the value of this source of feed supplies in the overall diet of animals.

The projections of this study indicate that for growing demand to be met, livestock production will have to maintain high growth rates, higher than in the past, in both low- and middle-income countries. Even with such a performance, per capita consumption levels will remain low (Table 3.3). Given the inequitable distribution of consumption of livestock products, large segments of populations will continue to depend on alternative sources of protein such as pulses and cereals.

Livestock production takes place under very diverse conditions in the different developing countries. However, the direction of change, even if gradual, is towards more intensive production with less dependence on open-range feeding, which imposes excessive burdens on the environment, and with improved and balanced feeding practices and improved breeds. The improved practices will enable more of the feed to go to increase output rather to inefficient maintenance.

## Expansion of agricultural land

Agricultural production currently takes place on around 770 million ha with a cropping intensity of 78 percent implying an annual harvested area of some 600 million ha. Further expansion depends on the quality of the land reserves available, their costs of development and appropriate incentives to utilize them.

By the year 2000, arable land expansion and cropping intensity increases are projected to account for around two-fifths of the growth in production. This means that if the production projected for 2000 is to be achieved, arable land has to increase by 83 million ha, cropping intensity would rise to 84 percent, and therefore harvested land by 115 million ha. The magnitudes involved are quite large.

Furthermore, this expansion of agricultural land is a *net* process: virgin lands are opened to agriculture while some degraded land is withdrawn either temporarily or in the worst cases permanently; land is lost in the construction of dams and reservoirs, though this may be fully compensated when the water is used for irrigation; and population growth, urbanization and industrial development all remove significant areas of land.

Although some of the land lost is of marginal quality, inadequate land use planning commonly results in high-quality land being lost unnecessarily. Despite these losses, there are generally net additions to the arable area, though some developing countries may find it difficult to maintain this positive balance. Few, if any, developing countries over the next 15 years will join the ranks of some developed countries where the combination of slow growth in demand and continuing technological progress tend to reduce the arable area in farming and allow marginal land to be taken out of agriculture.

The increases in agricultural land will involve expansion into tropical forest areas which are examples of an efficient yet delicate ecological balance. The soils are quite poor in structure and in plant nutrients. It is the vegetative cover that maintains the integrity of these lands by being the primary source of nutrients. In shifting cultivation and bush-fallow systems used by farmers in such tropical forests, the accumulated residues and the vegetative cover provide sufficient nutrients for a limited period of crop production. Production must then be shifted to permit a sufficiently long 'fallow' period during which natural vegetation can be re-established. The danger here is that the pressure on land is causing the fallow periods to be shortened and natural vegetation is not being re-established for long enough to replace the nutrients removed during the cropping cycle. Subsequent crop production on these lands without the application of organic manures and/or mineral fertilizers to compensate for the loss of nutrients leads to declining yields and increasing soil erosion. The expansion of land and the increase in cropping intensity must therefore involve simultaneous increases in complementary input use as part of technology packages.

At first glance the large reserves still remaining in the year 2000 in most regions suggest the existence of substantial production potential (Fig. 4.2). Such is not the case, first because the reserves are heavily concentrated in a few countries, for example Brazil and Zaire. Second, most of the reserves have soils of marginal quality. Some are suited to perennial tree crops, other have very unreliable rainfall, and almost all are dependent on the introduction of existing technologies or the development of new ones before they can be cultivated on a sustainable basis. As discussed below, relative land scarcity, determined both by the magnitude and the quality of the land reserves, will play a role in the future in fertilizer use and irrigation development.

Almost a third of the increase in arable land, including for irrigation expansion, would take place in good rainfall areas.[2] Areas in problem lands

[2] The land classes used in this study are defined using suitability classes from the FAO Agro-Ecological Zone study (FAO 1978–81). The four suitability classes—very suitable, suitable, marginally suitable and not suitable—are related to the anticipated yield as a percentage of the maximum attainable under optimum agro-climatic and soil conditions.

The definition of the six land-water classes is as follows:

1 *Low-rainfall rain-fed land*: Rainfall providing 1–119 growing days, soil quality very suitable, suitable or marginally suitable.
2 *Uncertain rainfall rain-fed land*: Rainfall providing 120–79 growing days, soil quality very suitable or suitable.
3 *Good rainfall rain-fed land*: Rainfall providing 180–269 growing days, soil quality very suitable or suitable.
4 *Problem lands*: The term is used to designate areas with excessive moisture and/or unsuitable

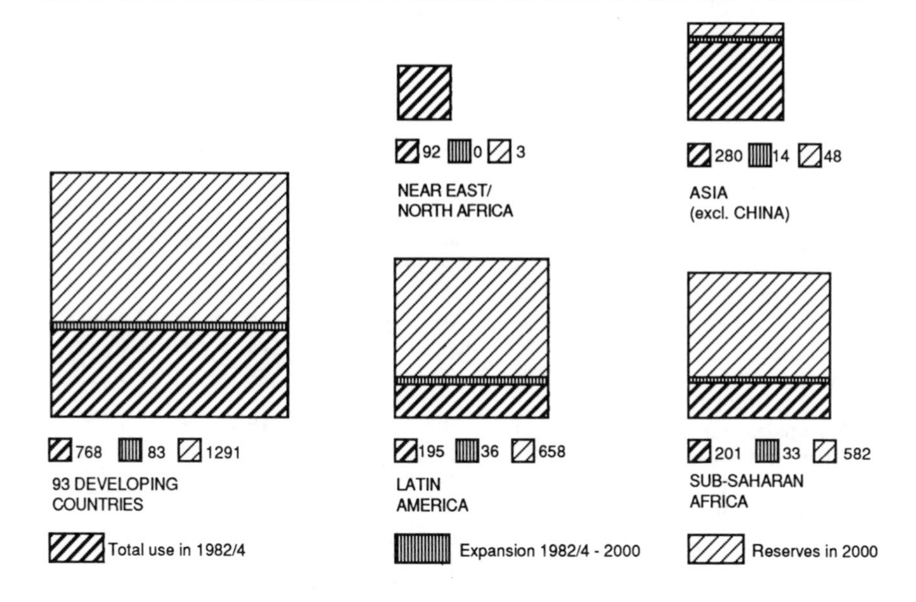


**Figure 4.2** Land use and reserves (million ha, arable land)

would also increase, accounting for one-fourth of the increases in arable land. Naturally flooded lands would decline as controlled irrigation and drainage expands to these areas. Except in sub-Saharan Africa, arable lands in low-rainfall and uncertain rainfall areas would decrease slightly, as marginal lands are removed from agricultural activity. Again, slight improvements in cropping intensity will more than make up for this loss of land.

Between 1982/4 and 2000, about two-thirds of the increase in arable lands will be accounted for by expansion of irrigation (Table 4.4). This implies slightly higher growth rates in irrigated land than has been observed in the recent past on the assumption that unit construction costs can be reduced and water use efficiency raised. As a consequence the share of irrigated land should increase to 20 percent in total arable and 29 percent in total harvested land, from 14 percent and 22 percent, respectively.

Irrigated agriculture is concentrated in Asia and 85 percent of the expansion in irrigated arable and harvested lands is projected to take place there (Fig.

soils. In these areas rainfall provides more than 269 growing days, soil quality is very suitable, suitable, or marginally suitable. Also included in this class is that part of the 120–269 growing days zones where soil rating is only marginally suitable.

5 *Naturally flooded land*: Land under water for part of the year and lowland non-irrigated paddy-fields (gleysols).

6 *Irrigated lands*: These comprise both fully irrigated lands which are equipped for irrigation and suitable drainage and not suffering from water shortages, and of partially irrigated lands which are equipped for irrigation but lacking drainage or reliable water supplies or with low quality and reliability of distribution.

Another land class is desert lands which are not suitable for agriculture except under irrigation. The four rain-fed land classes are alternatively called arid and semi-arid, dry sub-humid, moist sub-humid and humid in the order above.

**Table 4.4** Ninety-three developing countries: land use by agro-ecological category,* 1982/4 and 2000 (million ha)

| | Rain-fed use | | | | | | |
|---|---|---|---|---|---|---|---|
| | Total | LR | UR | GR | PR | NF | IR |
| *1982/4* | | | | | | | |
| 93 developing countries | | | | | | | |
| Harvested land | 598 | 49 | 76 | 144 | 134 | 63 | 132 |
| Cropping intensity (%) | 78 | 48 | 70 | 75 | 72 | 94 | 118 |
| Arable land | 768 | 102 | 108 | 192 | 187 | 67 | 111 |
| Africa (sub-Saharan) | | | | | | | |
| Harvested land | 109 | 19 | 22 | 34 | 29 | 3 | 3 |
| Cropping intensity (%) | 54 | 45 | 53 | 61 | 52 | 67 | 84 |
| Arable land | 201 | 42 | 41 | 55 | 55 | 5 | 4 |
| Near East/North Africa | | | | | | | |
| Harvested land | 63 | 9 | 7 | 12 | 10 | 7 | 18 |
| Cropping intensity (%) | 68 | 44 | 72 | 77 | 73 | 54 | 98 |
| Arable land | 92 | 21 | 10 | 16 | 13 | 13 | 19 |
| Asia (excl. China) | | | | | | | |
| Harvested land | 303 | 19 | 36 | 37 | 66 | 49 | 96 |
| Cropping intensity (%) | 108 | 59 | 100 | 101 | 112 | 118 | 129 |
| Arable land | 280 | 32 | 36 | 37 | 59 | 42 | 74 |
| Latin America | | | | | | | |
| Harvested land | 122 | 2 | 11 | 61 | 29 | 4 | 15 |
| Cropping intensity (%) | 63 | 30 | 51 | 72 | 50 | 50 | 102 |
| Arable land | 195 | 8 | 22 | 85 | 59 | 7 | 14 |
| *2000* | | | | | | | |
| 93 developing countries | | | | | | | |
| Harvested land | 713 | 53 | 78 | 166 | 154 | 58 | 204 |
| Cropping intensity (%) | 84 | 53 | 74 | 79 | 74 | 99 | 123 |
| Arable land | 851 | 100 | 106 | 212 | 208 | 59 | 166 |
| Africa (sub-Saharan) | | | | | | | |
| Harvested land | 140 | 22 | 27 | 42 | 39 | 5 | 5 |
| Cropping intensity (%) | 60 | 49 | 57 | 65 | 59 | 84 | 89 |
| Arable land | 234 | 45 | 57 | 64 | 67 | 6 | 5 |
| Near East/North Africa | | | | | | | |
| Harvested land | 71 | 8 | 8 | 14 | 11 | 7 | 23 |
| Cropping intensity (%) | 77 | 45 | 86 | 88 | 77 | 55 | 109 |
| Arable land | 92 | 19 | 10 | 16 | 14 | 13 | 21 |
| Asia (excl. China) | | | | | | | |
| Harvested land | 349 | 19 | 30 | 33 | 69 | 42 | 157 |
| Cropping intensity (%) | 119 | 70 | 112 | 107 | 121 | 133 | 129 |
| Arable land | 294 | 28 | 26 | 31 | 57 | 32 | 121 |
| Latin America | | | | | | | |
| Harvested land | 154 | 3 | 13 | 78 | 35 | 5 | 20 |
| Cropping intensity (%) | 66 | 36 | 56 | 77 | 49 | 52 | 106 |
| Arable land | 231 | 8 | 23 | 102 | 71 | 9 | 19 |

* Due to rounding, numbers may not add up to total, and cropping intensities may appear to be different than the ratio of harvested to arable land.

LR = low-rainfall rain-fed land, UR = uncertain rainfall rain-fed land, GR = good rainfall rain-fed land, PR = problem lands, NF = naturally flooded land, IR = irrigated land.

4.3), notably in India. Increased irrigation in this country would account for over 80 percent of the increase in irrigated areas in Asia (excluding China) and 70 percent of the increase in irrigated areas in the 93 developing countries. India's arable land reserves are exhausted, and therefore irrigated lands will expand into rain-fed and naturally flooded areas.

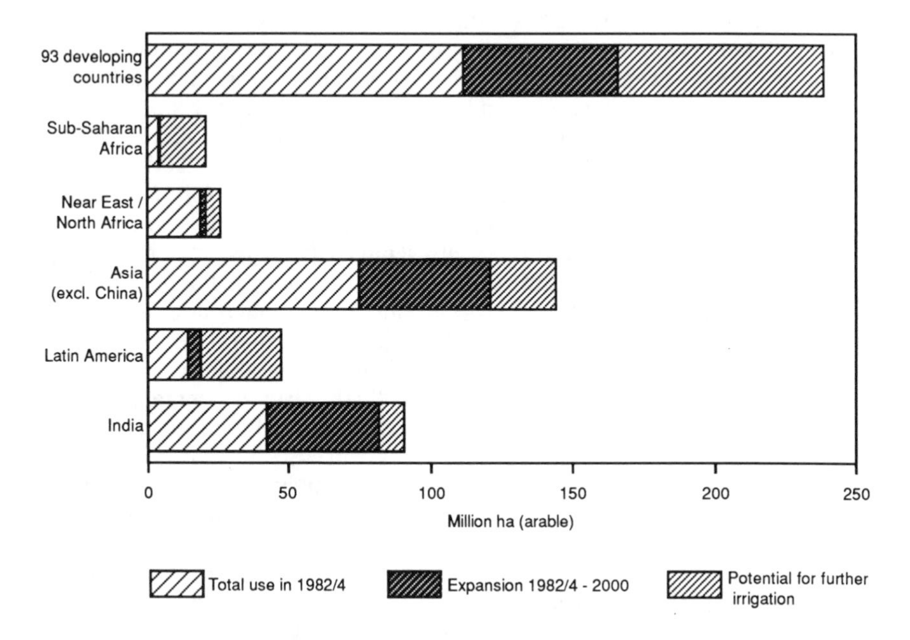


**Figure 4.3** Irrigated land use and potential

Two other regions will have to go through a similar process in expanding irrigated areas. In the Near East/North Africa, potential rain-fed agricultural land is utilized almost fully. Therefore, rain-fed and desert lands must be drawn on for irrigation. With the higher cropping intensity associated with irrigated areas, this will actually be the sole source of expansion of harvested land in this region. Elsewhere, particularly in sub-Saharan Africa, irrigated-land expansion will be a minor part of land expansion, because of the relatively larger reserves of rain-fed land, higher costs of irrigation development and shortage of technical manpower. Hence, the expansion of land in the higher rainfall regions of good rainfall land and problem land takes place mostly in Latin America and sub-Saharan Africa, where a small number of countries have vast land reserves, though these reserves commonly have soils that are only marginally suitable for annual crop production. Moreover, land tenure problems, particularly in Latin America, may make these lands inaccessible to many small farmers. Hence, the recourse may be to expand into tropical forests and marginal areas with serious consequences (see Ch. 11).

## Water: irrigated and rain-fed agriculture

Notwithstanding the fact that land is indispensable for agricultural production, it is water rather than land which is the binding constraint for almost 600 million ha of potentially suitable arable land. It is only when this water constraint is released that other technical constraints such as nutrients and pests become important. Thus irrigation (and drainage) allow the potential (technical or economic) of a crop to be expressed. Hence, substantial resources have historically been allocated to irrigation, and to a lesser extent, to drainage. Higher rates of fertilizer use and, consequently, higher yields prevail in irrigated agriculture. To illustrate this, three groups of countries may be distinguished in terms of the share of irrigated land in arable land in 1982/4.[3]

Figure 4.4 shows how average fertilizer use per hectare (of total area) and average yields tend to increase with the share of irrigated land in total arable land. This is a pattern that was well established in the past, and which is expected to continue in the future. The importance of irrigation is emphasized by its 36 percent share of total crop production, although not more than 15 percent of total arable land in agricultural use is irrigated. Both higher yields and higher cropping intensities explain this difference. Figure 4.5 shows the relevant data for major crops. By the year 2000 the share of production coming from irrigated land will increase further. Crops adapted to drier conditions or grown primarily under rain-fed conditions will also be grown increasingly under irrigation but, of course, the bulk of the production of these crops will be rain-fed. Overall, more than half of the increment in crop production will come from irrigated areas.

Irrigation management can be quite complex. Particularly in large-scale irrigation projects, high technical and managerial skills are required to assure proper drainage to prevent salinity, to maintain irrigation canal networks and pumping stations, to take measures against silting and to use the precious water efficiently. Water wastage in irrigation is a serious problem arising partly because water charges, particularly in major irrigation facilities rarely reflect costs and lead to wastage of water. However, with the relatively high costs of irrigation investment, greater emphasis will have to be placed on water use efficiency.

In areas of rain-fed agriculture, better use must be made of the limited amount of water available in order both to increase yields and to reduce the instability due to weather variability. Appropriate technologies need to be

[3] The country groups are as follows:

Group *IR1* (less than 10 percent of arable land under irrigation): Algeria, Tunisia, Guatemala, Honduras, Nicaragua, Panama, Haiti, Argentina, Bolivia, Brazil, Colombia, Paraguay, Uruguay, Venezuela, Libya, Jordan, Syria, Turkey, Yemen Arab Rep., Kampuchea DM, plus all sub-Saharan Africa except Madagascar, Mauritius, Swaziland, Sudan.

Group *IR2* (10–30 percent under irrigation): Morocco, Madagascar, Mauritius, Swaziland, Costa Rica, El Salvador, Mexico, Dominican Rep., Jamaica, Trinidad and Tobago, Chile, Ecuador, Sudan, Afghanistan, Cyprus, Lebanon, plus all Asia—excluding China—except Pakistan, Korea Rep., Kampuchea DM, and Korea DPR.

Group *IR3* (over 30 percent under irrigation): Cuba, Guyana, Peru, Suriname, Iran, Iraq, Saudi Arabia, Yemen PDR, Korea DPR, Egypt, Pakistan, Korea Rep.

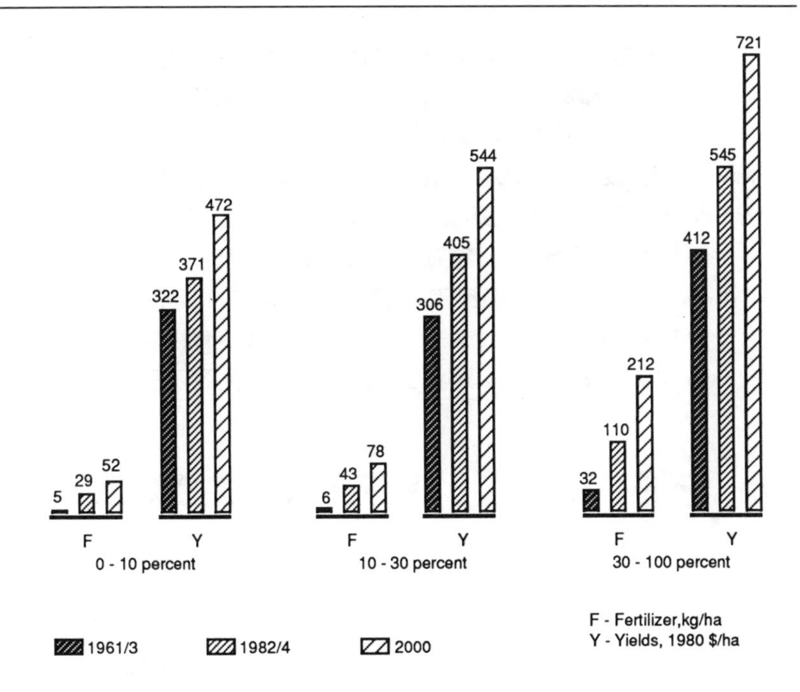


**Figure 4.4** Fertilizer use and yields according to the share of irrigation in arable land (percent in 1983)

identified such that the limited water provided by rainfall is adequately stored in the soil and directed to optimum use by crops.

## Off-farm inputs

As the agricultural sector in the developing countries moves in degrees from subsistence to commercial production, the use of purchased or off-farm inputs increases along with the use of improved technologies and better management. There is no viable alternative to, nor foreseeable break in, this general trend for increasing dependence on off-farm inputs. Most regions will depend on yield increases to meet the bulk of future demand for food and agricultural products. This in turn means that they will become increasingly dependent on off-farm production inputs, notably fertilizer, improved seeds, pesticides, irrigation, agricultural implements and machinery, vaccines, veterinary medicines and feed grains. This will require major investments to establish or expand local production of inputs, and new initiatives by donors and the international community to assist those developing countries whose limited foreign-exchange earnings prevent them importing most of their input needs. One possible initiative is to expand aid-in-kind (FAO 1987e).

The use of off-farm inputs will vary according to the level of agricultural modernization and agro-ecological conditions. The relationship between the

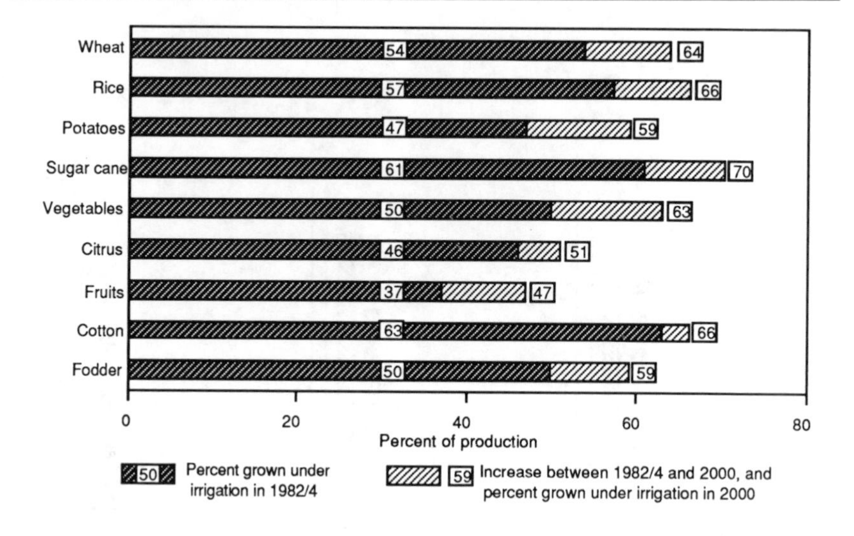


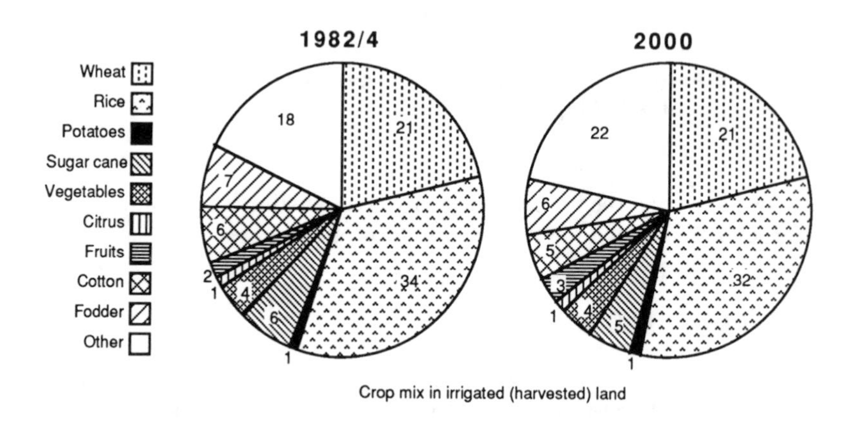


**Figure 4.5** Shares of irrigated production in total production

level of development and input use can be observed in the variation of the share of the value of inputs to that of gross output. For most developed countries this is around 50 percent. For the developing countries, on the other hand, the shares of inputs average less than a quarter of the value of gross output. However, there is substantial variation with quite low values in sub-Saharan Africa to over a third for the Near East/North Africa region. These shares are expected to increase with production intensification, though regional differences will continue to be wide (Table 4.5).

In dryland areas where rain-fed agriculture is dominant, the primary factor in increasing yields may be associated with moisture conservation practices,

**Table 4.5** Share of the value of inputs in the value of gross output (%)*

| | 1982/4 | 2000 |
|---|---|---|
| 93 developing countries | 24 | 27 |
| Africa (sub-Saharan) | 10 | 11 |
| Near East/N. Africa | 36 | 40 |
| Asia (excl. China) | 24 | 28 |
| Latin America | 25 | 29 |
| Low-income countries (excl. China) | 22 | 25 |
| Middle-income countries | 25 | 29 |

* The value of inputs used to compute these shares include feed, seed, fertilizer, pesticides, fuel and other agricultural mechanization operating costs, and irrigation operating costs.

fallow management and other practices to optimize water use by crops. To a lesser degree, but interacting with practices to optimize water use, herbicide and fertilizer use and improved or high-yielding varieties contribute to yield increases. This synergistic effect is more pronounced in irrigated farming. For example, a study at IRRI (Herdt and Capule 1983) of eight major rice-producing countries estimated that the rice production increases achieved between 1965 and 1980 can be disaggregated as follows (the complementarity between HYVs, fertilizers and irrigation makes it difficult to isolate the contribution of and therefore the precise degree of dependence on the different inputs but the broad picture is clear):

| | |
|---|---|
| Total increase in output of paddy rice (million tonnes) | 117.4 |
| Effect of improved varieties (HYV) | 27.4 (23 percent) |
| Fertilizer effect | 28.6 (24 percent) |
| Irrigation effect | 33.8 (29 percent) |
| Residual (other factors) | 27.6 (24 percent) |

The increased use of off-farm inputs reduces dependence on land resources, that is they have an important land-substituting role. This role is most apparent for fertilizer, HYVs and irrigation, but it also exists for herbicides. Irrigation has a similar effect by increasing the productivity of fertilizers and HYVs, and has an even greater effect in some areas because of the double or even triple cropping it makes possible.

Thus inputs can reduce appreciably the pressure to cultivate marginal lands or may even, as in the developed countries, permit its use for more environmentally suitable purposes, notably pasture and forest. Moreover, it follows that dependence on inputs can reduce the competition for land between annual crop production, forestry and livestock production. In many developing countries the viability of forestry and livestock production is already significantly threatened by the loss of land to crop production, and this problem will increase in the future unless production inputs are allowed to substitute for land.

## Fertilizer

Fertilizers have become a *sine qua non* of agricultural production over much of the developing countries and will become so in most other areas before the end of this century. They are no longer used exclusively for those few cash crops grown historically for exports, though this situation still predominates in some African countries.

Since 1967 the share of the developing countries in global fertilizer use has more than doubled from under 10 percent to over 20 percent, with particularly high growth rates in Asia. However, in some countries, and particularly in Africa, growth was insufficient to compensate for the nutrients removed by crops, resulting in declining yields and land degradation. Some developing countries are also high users of organic fertilizers (farmyard manure, night soil, etc.) which are not reflected in statistics of fertilizer consumption, but they are not always sufficient to compensate for low levels of mineral fertilizer. In the other countries, moreover, the lack of alternative energy sources in many rural areas causes manure to be used as fuel for heating and cooking.

The growth rate of fertilizer use (in nutrient weight) in the 93 countries is projected to be 4.6 percent p.a. in 1982/4–2000 (Table 4.6). This is lower than the longer-term historical growth rate of 10.3 percent during 1961–85 but in line with the slow-down to 5.7 percent during the most recent five years 1980–5. The declining growth rate reflects above all the higher levels already achieved but also unfavourable overall economic conditions limiting the possibilities to import and provide subsidies. However, the projected quantity of fertilizer more than doubles between 1982/4 and 2000. The highest growth rates are projected for sub-Saharan Africa, and they reflect the low fertilizer use in the base period.

A small number of countries will continue to dominate fertilizer use in each region: Egypt in North Africa, Nigeria and Zimbabwe in sub-Saharan Africa, Turkey and Iran in the Near East, Mexico and Brazil in Latin America and India in Asia (excl. China).

The intensity of fertilizer use (kg/ha) presents a different picture with Near East/North Africa currently having the highest average fertilizer application rates, followed by Latin America and Asia. Sub-Saharan Africa uses very low amounts of fertilizer per hectare (9 kg/ha) though this is largely a reflection of the small proportion of the arable land which actually receives fertilizer. None the less, average application rates are projected to more than double by the year 2000.

In terms of land classes, irrigated areas will increase their dominant share in total fertilizer from over half to nearly 60 percent and from half of nitrogen to nearly two-thirds. In phosphorus the share of irrigated areas would also increase to slightly more than half, but for potassium rain-fed areas would continue to command more than half. While this is the general picture for most areas in sub-Saharan Africa, the dominance of rain-fed lands imply that they will receive the greatest share of the fertilizer.

The increasing share of fertilizer used in irrigated farming reflects the profitability of its use while irrigated areas are also relatively free of environmental constraints and associated risks. Rain-fed areas receiving high and

**Table 4.6** Fertilizer use in the developing countries*

| | Total (million tonnes) | | kg/ha | | Growth rate, Total fertilizer (% p.a.) | | | |
|---|---|---|---|---|---|---|---|---|
| | 1982/4 | 2000 | 1982/4 | 2000 | 1961–75 | 1975–85 | 1980–5 | 1982/4–2000 |
| 93 developing countries | 25.8 | 55.7 | 43 | 78 | 12.4 | 7.1 | 5.7 | 4.6 |
| Africa (sub-Saharan) | 1.0 | 2.8 | 9 | 20 | 11.9 | 5.8 | 3.1 | 6.4 |
| Near East/N. Africa | 4.6 | 11.1 | 72 | 156 | 12.5 | 7.8 | 6.8 | 5.4 |
| Asia (excl. China) | 13.8 | 28.2 | 46 | 81 | 12.7 | 9.3 | 8.4 | 4.3 |
| Latin America | 6.5 | 13.6 | 53 | 88 | 12.1 | 3.2 | 0.6 | 4.4 |
| Low-income countries (excl. China) | 9.9 | 21.4 | 32 | 59 | 14.7 | 9.9 | 9.5 | 4.6 |
| Middle-income countries | 15.9 | 34.6 | 56 | 98 | 11.6 | 5.6 | 3.5 | 4.6 |

* Nutrient weight of N, $P_2O_5$ and $K_2O$.

stable rainfall also benefit from fertilizer but generally not by as much as irrigated areas. However, if economic considerations are the motivating force behind the allocation of fertilizer, it is the *marginal* rates of return that matter. Currently, the use of fertilizer in rain-fed areas gives marginal rates of return equal to or higher than irrigated areas. This is expected to be the case, in the future as well on large parts of the rain-fed areas.

In the past, economic considerations, notably the need to raise foreign-exchange earnings and favourable producer prices, have biased fertilizer allocation in favour of the few crops grown for export. However, raising staple food production has been given greater priority in the 1970s and 1980s, and currently more than half of all fertilizer is being used for cereals (Table 4.7), with wheat and rice (largely irrigated) accounting for the bulk of it. Other cereals and staples like cassava, which are important in the farming systems of other rain-fed areas and in the diets of the poor in these areas, command only a small portion of total developing countries fertilizer use. The second largest consumer offertilizer is sugar cane. Other major crops with high shares of fertilizer usage are fruits and vegetables, cotton, soya beans (high fertilizer use in Latin America) and fodder.

The expansion of fertilizer use requires considerable investments in infrastructure for storage, transport and marketing. The figures of Table 4.6 are in terms of pure nutrients (N, $P_2O_5$ and $K_2O$). Actual fertilizer volumes and weights will depend on type and composition. However, by the year 2000, facilities (storage, transportation, distribution, credit, etc.) must be available in the developing countries to handle around 150 million tonnes of processed fertilizer (product weight) if farmers are to receive timely and adequate amounts.

## Plant protection

The higher productivity brought about by more intensive cropping, irrigation and fertilizer use is also conducive to the propagation of pests, diseases and weeds that all affect production adversely. Mono-culture and irrigation are major culprits in this respect.

In the case of diseases, use of healthy seeds and planting materials, resistant varieties with or without fungicides are the main control options. Crop rotations and frequent rejuvenation of seed material are also important. For insects, again, resistant varieties and insecticides may provide protection, when used either singly or as part of an integrated pest management (IPM, see Ch. 11) system. Using fertilizers without herbicides invariably implies that weeds will also be fertilized and claim a share of the scarce water and nutrients that are targeted at crops. In some areas, however, weeds can be an important source of human food and livestock feed.

Care must be exercised in associating higher technologies and their implicit high yields with high levels of plant protection, particularly chemical plant protection. The highly beneficial effect of plant protection is that it allows yields achieved by employing advanced technologies to be maintained. It is thus an insurance against the risks of losing not only the crops but the additional expenditures for the many inputs necessary to

**Table 4.7** Fertilizer allocation to principal groups of crops (%), estimates for 1982/4 and projections for 2000

| | 93 developing countries | | Africa (sub-Saharan) | | Near East/N. Africa | | Asia (excl. China) | | Latin America | |
|---|---|---|---|---|---|---|---|---|---|---|
| | 1982/4 | 2000 | 1982/4 | 2000 | 1982/4 | 2000 | 1982/4 | 2000 | 1982/4 | 2000 |
| Wheat and rice | 42.3 | 42.3 | 9.8 | 13.2 | 37.7 | 38.4 | 58.9 | 59.9 | 14.9 | 14.5 |
| Coarse grains* | 11.6 | 15.1 | 24.3 | 37.3 | 14.7 | 22.7 | 7.0 | 6.1 | 17.3 | 23.4 |
| Sugar cane | 10.6 | 8.2 | 12.9 | 9.6 | 1.4 | 1.1 | 7.1 | 6.3 | 24.3 | 17.8 |
| Soybeans | 3.9 | 5.1 | 1.3 | 0.8 | 0.6 | 0.8 | 0.3 | 0.5 | 14.4 | 19.1 |
| Fruits, vegetables and pulses | 11.6 | 10.2 | 8.3 | 8.0 | 18.8 | 16.0 | 8.8 | 7.9 | 12.7 | 10.8 |
| Cotton | 2.9 | 2.2 | 7.4 | 4.5 | 6.3 | 3.6 | 1.6 | 1.5 | 2.6 | 1.8 |
| Fodder crops | 4.3 | 4.4 | 0.5 | 0.4 | 7.9 | 6.8 | 4.0 | 4.6 | 2.9 | 2.6 |

*Note*: The base-year allocation of total fertilizer use to different crops are FAO estimates.
* Maize, barley, millet, sorghum and other cereals.

implement advanced technologies. However, indiscriminate, excessive and uninformed use of plant protection chemicals can bring about vicious circles of pest resistance, elimination of natural predators, and ever more increased use of and dependence on chemicals. The pollution and health problems caused by residues of such chemicals are also of concern. Proper utilization of plant protection material will require adequate farmer training and extension.

The production projections must be taken with the caveat that there will be substantial associated training and extension costs involved to minimize the adverse effects of chemical plant protection and optimize its beneficial effects. Plant protection requirements are estimated to increase over the projection period by some 60 percent, implying an approximate annual cost of over $6 billion by the year 2000, compared with $4 billion currently (constant 1980 dollars). Three-fourths of these expenditures will be concentrated in Asia and Latin America.

It is estimated that cereals, particularly the three main cereals, wheat, rice and maize, account for around 20 percent of total plant protection expenditures, and this share is expected to remain almost constant. The single crop which uses the most plant protection is cotton, and its share should remain around 40 percent, particularly with enhanced implementation of integrated pest management. Other high users will also maintain their shares; coffee and sugarcane (5 percent), fruits and vegetables (around 20 percent).

Plant protection expenditures, principally on chemicals, are a relatively small portion of total production costs. As such they can be interpreted as insurance costs to minimize what can be ravaging effects of pests and diseases. It must however be recognized that beyond a critical level, additional plant protection chemicals do nothing to reduce the risks of damage and, in fact, at high rates of application they themselves can inflict damage through toxicity.

## Seeds for increased production

Improved seeds have always been a central component of man's strategy to increase crop production. For thousands of years he has selected seeds from both wild and cultivated species on the basis of their yield, pest resistance and so on. Modern science has accelerated this process, and in the recent past, High-yielding varieties (HYV) in conjunction with mineral fertilizers and irrigation have been the principal source of yield and production increases. The challenge is to sustain these improvements and to produce similar results in other cereals and important crops such as cassava, pulses and oilseeds, and in areas where irrigation is not possible, particularly where rainfall is both low and erratic.

The focus on HYV should not imply that non-HYV seeds have no potential for yield increases. In the first instance, these seeds have the potential of responding to improved management techniques and fertilizer use but generally not as much as HYV. Except through field surveys, it is quite difficult to assess the coverage of improved varieties. The projections are that total cereal seed requirements are estimated to increase by 17 percent between

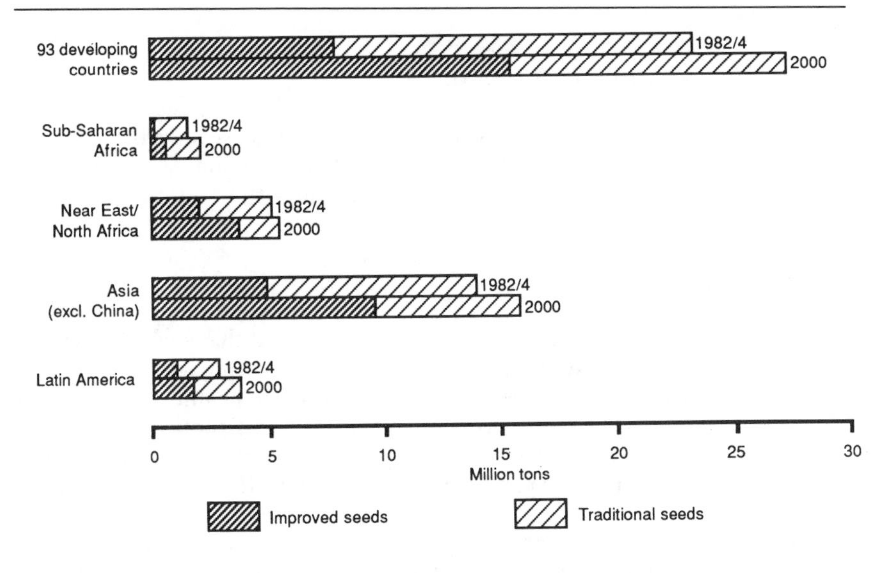


**Figure 4.6** Total cereal seed requirements

1982/4 and 2000. Improved seeds, which currently are estimated to be 34 percent of the total, may account for 57 percent in the year 2000 (Fig. 4.6).

In other crops, substantial growth in seed and planting material requirements will be necessary in soybeans, groundnuts, sweet potatoes, pulses and sunflower. It is estimated that the current improved seed production capacities will have to increase by some 50–100 percent to meet the requirements of improved technologies for the major crops (cereals, oilseeds, pulses).

Consequently there must be a major expansion of seed industries if these requirements are to be met. However, improved seed production capabilities do not exist in all developing countries, in part because seed production is an expensive process and its technical requirements for skilled labour are high. Sometimes it may be feasible to import seeds from a neighbouring country with similar agro-ecological conditions. However, in general imported seeds are not as good as those of local varieties or land races adapted to local conditions. It may be necessary to develop targeted breeding strategies for these areas to improve local varieties. Another problem with importing seed is the need for seed health control and quarantine facilities as, otherwise, there will be increased risk of diseases spreading and epidemics occurring.

In the case of non-cereal crops such as cotton and tobacco, seed production activities are quite developed and should be able to meet future needs. One area with substantial room for development is the improvement of cassava stem stock. Another is the expansion of true potato seed. This could reduce the requirements for seed potato and together with increased adoption of diffused light storage, should reduce the waste in seed potatoes.

## Inputs for livestock production

In the main there are three inputs whose availability and use must be increased appreciably if the growth targets of livestock production are to be met: veterinary health supplies, roughages and feed concentrates.

### Veterinary health supplies

The earlier discussion on sources of growth concluded that some 46 percent would come from yield increases and 34 percent from higher off-take rates (remainder arising from greater numbers). Veterinary health measures and particular preventive medicine to control the major epizootics and various disease vectors, such as ticks and tse-tse fly, together with improved management, will play an important part in increasing both yields and off-take rates.

Meat, milk and egg production are currently reduced by a number of pests and diseases. As the currently major diseases are brought under control, progress towards more intensive production systems will in turn result in a shift in the disease spectrum. Thus, in the cattle sector, as rinderpest and pleuropneumonia decline, diseases such as brucellosis, leptospirosis and mastitis are likely to assume increased importance. Similarly, in the poultry sector, the transition from extensive village poultry keeping to commercial intensive systems is accompanied by shift of importance from, for example, Newcastle disease towards chronic respiratory disease, Marek's disease and Gumboro disease.

In Africa, the existing and planned production capacity should make the continent largely self-sufficient in certain key vaccines and pave the way for significant improvements in livestock health. Some of the requirements are substantial. The Pan-African Rinderpest Campaign will require about 200 million doses per year. Prevention of the cattle population at risk from bovine pleuropneumonia would require some 120 million doses per year. The expansion of intensive pig and poultry production, will, as in other developing regions, depend on regular measures to control diseases like avian encephalitis and infectious bronchitis. The pattern in Latin America will be different because the region is fortunately free from a number of serious African problems—bovine pleuropneumonia, rinderpest and *peste de petits ruminants*. But, in common with other regions, one of the preconditions for improved veterinary health will be investment and training for the expansion of diagnostic facilities.

In Asia, a major emphasis is on improving preparedness to deal with emergency animal diseases as the region is free of major problems. An expanded programme for control of rinderpest is planned, which will give rise to substantive vaccine requirements. Other demands will arise from country programmes to increase livestock trade and to improve dairy cattle. Improved control of foot and mouth disease is of particular concern to them.

In many countries of the region, namely the Philippines, Thailand, Indonesia and Bangladesh, poultry production is a major component of the livestock industry and Newcastle disease is of particular importance. In

Bangladesh the estimated annual loss to poultry diseases is $240 million of which $120 million is attributable to Newcastle disease alone. The country's total annual requirements of Newcastle disease vaccines is about 160 million doses and at most the national production provides only 50 percent of this quantity. Providing the vaccines is not in itself enough. An efficient cold chain network is essential for effective distribution.

In those countries which have built up intensive pig industries the threat of classical swine fever is now recognized as one of the main hazards to production and trade in pigs and pig products. Diagnosis involves sophisticated laboratory tests and trained personnel, and suitable facilities are vital for effective control and eventual eradication of this disease. Strict vigilance must be maintained in Asia to prevent African swine fever from entering into the region as it would have devastating effects on the large pig population.

## Roughages

In the past, grazing, crop by-products and to a lesser extent, fodder crops, have provided the bulk of animal feed requirements. In the future this will be increasingly difficult to sustain.

In the first place this is because over much of Africa and Asia and in certain parts of Latin America, overgrazing is already widespread, and the institutional changes required to prevent it will take many years.

Secondly, pasture improvement and the growing of forage legumes have yet to be widely accepted by pastoralists or settled farmers, except in parts of North Africa, the Near East and China. Forage legumes, in particular, would warrant greater policy attention because of the potential macro-economic and environmental benefits associated with the agricultural benefits. For example, when introduced into the rotation of principal crops like cereals, they may break disease cycles and provide additional nitrogen through bacterial fixation and raise soil organic matter levels. They also tend to reduce soil erosion by providing more effective ground cover, and add to the flexibility of the farming system by giving the option of harvesting for hay or grazing. Imports of nitrogen fertilizer and feed concentrates can be reduced.

Thirdly, the projected crop production in a number of countries will not provide sufficient by-products to meet the required protein and in some cases, the metabolizable energy, needed to fulfil meat, milk and egg production targets. Some of these deficits can and will be met by the use of additives, notably urea and molasses, but greater attention will have to be paid to the production and use of concentrates.

## Concentrates

These will consist largely of cereals, milling by-products, feed pulses, oil meals and cakes. Qualitative and quantitative requirements will be influenced to a large extent by the composition of livestock with higher proportions of intensive dairying, poultry and pigs increasing the use of cereals as feed.

The major part (almost 90 percent) of the cereal demand for feed consists of coarse grains. Currently, almost 98 percent of the feed use of cereals in the developing countries is in the middle-income countries and China. This, of course, is associated with the higher demand for livestock products in the middle-income countries and with the more intensive production systems prevailing in these countries and China, particularly for poultry, eggs and dairy. This pattern can be expected to continue in the future, with the middle-income countries and China accounting for 98 percent of total cereal feed use by the year 2000. In the low-income countries feedgrain use will remain low (Fig. 3.3).

The quantity of feed grain used depends both on the feeding rate and the output of livestock products. Between 1969/71 and 1983/5, the amount of cereals used per unit of livestock output in the developing countries (including China) increased by 35 percent and total feed use of cereals grew by 6.5 percent p.a. (to 126 million tonnes) while livestock production grew at 4.1 percent p.a. Lower overall economic growth and foreign exchange constraints in many middle-income countries should dampen the growth rate of feed demand for cereals to 5.5 percent p.a. over the projection period 1983/5–2000.

## Employment and mechanization

This section discusses requirements of labour, agricultural machinery and draught animals for increasing agricultural production in the 93 developing countries. Only the requirements of the crop sector could be analysed using whatever data could be obtained on the use of these inputs in the different crops. Similar data for the livestock sector are almost entirely lacking. Even for crop production, the analysis is beset with difficulties and shortcomings: data on past trends for inputs from these three sources of power into the production of various crops in distinct agro-climatic and socio-economic environments are scarce, uneven in quality and coverage, and very often are completely lacking. The discussion below, which is based on a crop-by-crop analysis in the different agro-ecological environments in the 93 countries, therefore indicates only broad orders of magnitude and direction of changes.

The current availabilities of agricultural labour force and stocks of tractors and draught animals are given in Table 4.8. Using approximate rates of utilization in man-day equivalents (MDEs) per person, per tractor and per animal, it is estimated that they provide a total power input into crop production of some 90 billion MDEs annually.

Labour is by far the major source of power into crop production followed by draught animals. Tractors are relatively important only in Latin America and the Near East/North Africa regions. In the projections, the first step is to use crop, agro-ecological zone and yield specific power input coefficients in man-day equivalents (MDEs) per hectare to estimate aggregate requirements for each country. The aggregate requirements are subsequently decomposed into the parts to be provided by draught animals, labour and agricultural machinery.

The numbers of draught animals in 2000 are projected independently on the basis of expert judgement. The remainder of power requirements is then shared out between the parts to be supplied by labour and machinery taking

**Table 4.8** Agricultural labour force, tractors and draught animals in 1982/4

| | Labour force | Tractors | Animals |
|---|---|---|---|
| | *(millions)* | *(thousands)* | *(millions)* |
| 93 developing countries | 535 | 3292 | 168 |
| Africa (sub-Saharan) | 124 | 127 | 14 |
| Near East/N. Africa | 33 | 879 | 8 |
| Asia (excluding China) | 338 | 946 | 129 |
| Latin America | 40 | 1340 | 17 |
| | *% contribution to total power use** | | |
| 93 developing countries | 71 | 6 | 23 |
| Africa (sub-Saharan) | 89 | 1 | 10 |
| Near East/N. Africa | 69 | 14 | 17 |
| Asia (excluding China) | 68 | 4 | 28 |
| Latin America | 59 | 22 | 19 |

* Total power use in man-day equivalents is derived by converting the estimated tractor hours and the work days of draught animals into labour day equivalents.

into account existing levels of these two inputs and projecting them on the basis of empirically estimated relationships. The latter indicate that the shares of the two inputs vary among countries with (a) the level of economic development as measured by per caput incomes and (b) the relative abundance or scarcity of labour in relation to cultivated land (ha per person). In general, the higher the per caput incomes and the more land cultivated per person, the higher the share supplied by machinery and the smaller the part contributed by labour. This is largely because the agricultural labour force grows less rapidly in the higher-income countries and relative costs change in favour of machinery. In the past, this process was often reinforced by policies favouring mechanization, for example through subsidies. In the future, this factor may be expected to be less important given the budgetary retrenchment policies and increasing scarcity of foreign exchange in many developing countries as well as the need to promote agricultural employment in the face of slow overall economic growth.

Total power requirements are estimated to increase by some 30 percent between 1982/4 and the year 2000 following the projected 56 percent increase in aggregate crop production. As discussed earlier, harvested area is projected to increased by 19 percent and, other things being equal—in particular the crop mix and yields—it would cause total power inputs to increase by the same proportion. However, both the crop mix and yields would change and they, particularly yield growth, would cause total power inputs to grow by more than in proportion to the growth of harvested area, 30 percent rather than 19 percent between 1982/4 and the year 2000. Thus, harvested area expansion would account for some two-thirds of the increase in total power inputs in the 93 developing countries, while higher yields would account for most of the balance. Crop mix effects would be very small, mainly because overall cropping patterns would not change in favour of the crops which require comparatively more inputs of this type per ha, for example tea, tobacco, cotton, sugarcane, rice.

As noted, yield growth would contribute 63 percent of total increase in crop output (Fig. 4.1). Power requirements per ha increase with yields but much less than proportionally, while other inputs (e.g. fertilizer) increase more than in proportion over certain yield ranges. This is the main reason why growth in output is not accompanied by equal growth in power requirements and, eventually, employment, as will be discussed below.

Regional differences in the sources of output growth (yields, land) result in differences in the growth of power requirements for any given increase in production. For example, each 1 percent increase in crop production would require power inputs to increase comparatively by more in the regions which depend more on land expansion (sub-Saharan Africa, Latin America) than in those with higher contributions from yields (Near East/North Africa, Asia).

In the projections the future size of the agricultural labour force is taken from the FAO projections (FAO 1986c). The share of women in this agricultural labour force is estimated to be 29 percent in the year 2000. Therefore, the special role of women in food production needs to be given increasing emphasis in policy discussions (see Box 4.1). These projections of the agricultural labour force are used together with the projections of per caput incomes and of production, including land and yield contributions, and the above-mentioned empirical relationships to estimate the projected mechanization requirements and employment implications of crop production (Table 4.9). These projections indicate that labour would continue to be the overwhelming source of power input while mechanization would increase its share moderately overall, though rather more significantly in Latin America.

**Box 4.1** *Women and food production*

Food production, distribution and nutrition could be improved through more support for rural women's on-going activities in agriculture as well as in the home. In many societies, women already contribute labour for cash crop production—from which they do not necessarily derive income themselves. In addition they are expected to grow food for daily consumption or to earn money for its purchase from marketing activities or from off-farm enterprises.

Most of the agricultural labour force in Africa is female as is an important but often unrecognized part elsewhere. In addition, for the production of some crops, for small animals and for marketing, women are often the decision-makers. This is more and more the case as the number of female-headed households increases due to male out-migration to find work, or because of separation or divorce. It is rare, however, for women to be recognized as farmers in their own right or to have access to the resources, inputs and services needed to strengthen their skills and to increase their efficiency.

Their situation can be worsened by the development process, in fact. Improvements in technology are making it

**Table 4.3** Agricultural labour force, tractors and draught animals in the year 2000

| | Labour (million) | Tractor (thousand) | Animals (million) | Growth rates 1982/4–2000 (%p.a.) | | |
|---|---|---|---|---|---|---|
| | | | | Labour | Tractors | Animals |
| 93 developing countries | 663 | 6484 | 185 | 1.3 | 4.1 | 0.6 |
| Africa (sub-Saharan) | 168 | 230 | 17 | 1.8 | 3.6 | 1.0 |
| Near East/N. Africa | 37 | 1322 | 7 | 0.6 | 2.4 | −0.9 |
| Asia (excl. China) | 416 | 2246 | 145 | 1.2 | 5.2 | 0.7 |
| Latin America | 42 | 2686 | 16 | 0.3 | 4.2 | −0.2 |
| *% contribution to total power use* | | | | | | |
| 93 developing countries | 73 | 7 | 20 | | | |
| Africa (sub-Saharan) | 90 | 2 | 8 | | | |
| Near East/N. Africa | 74 | 15 | 11 | | | |
| Asia (excluding China) | 71 | 4 | 25 | | | |
| Latin America | 58 | 28 | 14 | | | |

possible for men to increase their farm operations. As a consequence, women may face more demands for their labour but lack the up-to-date mechanical aids for their own tasks. At the same time their responsibilities in the home are not usually reduced by appropriate technology either. Women may want larger rather than smaller families so that there are more hands to help them in the house and in the field when they lack technology.

Women's work, child labour, and population growth could well be diminished—with an improvement of the quality of rural life—through greater attention by research and development programmes to technology appropriate to women's as well as men's responsibilities in agriculture. It would be important also to introduce modern methods and technology to reduce the time constraints imposed on women by the myriad tasks needed for food preparation: fuel gathering, water collection, food processing and cooking.

The number of women's groups and units to represent their interest at national and international levels is growing. The potential of these groups as targets for agricultural extension programmes, for credit and marketing advice, as well as the more traditional home economics is too often overlooked. Extension workers are usually men and tend to aim their advice at men, their activities and crops. This bias can depress production of subsistence food crops (often women's crops) in favour of increased production of cash crops (often men's crops), so that household food security and family nutrition suffer. Efforts are being made to reorient extension services to the importance and feasibility of male agents working directly with women farmers, particularly in groups and under well thought-out conditions in keeping with cultural values.

Although there are many barriers to reaching rural women more directly, the positive response of women and their communities makes it well worthwhile. Although the domestic value of women's economic activities has too often gone unrecognized, rural men usually welcome their wives receiving assistance which will increase production and improve family welfare. Women themselves feel proud and increase their efforts when they know they are being reached in development assistance programmes as food producers for the first time.

The World Conference on Agrarian Reform in Rural Development (WCARRD) identified key principles to promote more equitable development, including greater recognition of and support to women farmers. These principles and the importance of supporting women's contribution to food security have been reaffirmed by the World Conference to Review and Appraise the Women's Decade held in Kenya in 1985, which is now the basis for urgent follow-up at all levels.

The implied growth rate of the tractor park in the developing countries is to be slower in the future compared with the past (4.1 percent p.a. in 1982/4–2000 compared with 8.5 percent p.a. in 1970–84). This is because in the regions with the higher incomes which accounted for much of the increase in the past, tractorization is already well advanced. Thus in the Near East/North Africa region there is already one tractor per 104 ha of arable land and by the year 2000 there will be one per 69 ha. In Latin America the comparable numbers are 145 and 86, respectively. These developments mean that replacement investments in agricultural machinery will grow as a proportion of total gross investment (see following section).

In parallel, the agricultural labour force will continue to grow rather rapidly in Asia and, particularly, in sub-Saharan Africa, the two regions with the lowest incomes and the smallest densities of machines in relation to land (296 and 1588 ha/tractor in 1982/4, respectively). Therefore, the conditions for shifting relative prices in favour of mechanization are not likely to be very strong in the next 15 years, particularly in sub-Saharan Africa. The agro-ecological conditions in some tropical countries of the region are also unfavourable to mechanized cultivation, for example in the humid tropics where mixed cropping (trees and annual crops) are appropriate modes of crop production (Pingali *et al*. 1987).

The preceding discussion assumes that budgetary and balance-of-payment difficulties and also concern with rural unemployment will induce governments not to influence relative prices of machinery *vis-à-vis* wages in favour of the former, for example through subsidization or preferential allocation of foreign exchange, a practice not uncommon in some countries in the past.

The employment implications of the above discussion can be deduced from the projected total increase of power requirements for crop production by 30 percent, and the projected share of labour of 73 percent. This implies that labour input requirements (in MDEs) will increase by 1.8 percent p.a. in 1982/4–2000. Over the same period the agricultural labour force is projected to grow at 1.3 percent p.a. By implication, the average crop-production work time per worker should increase by some 9 percent to an estimated 130 days per year.

These employment effects of crop production growth and of its modalities in combination with projected labour force growth will differ among countries and regions. The most important differences are those due to differential rates of labour force growth and by implication of the relative prices of labour *vis-à-vis* machines. They are best seen in terms of the implicit labour use (demand) elasticities for country groupings according to the growth rate of their agricultural labour force (estimates of labour demand elasticities for selected countries are given in Tyagi 1981 and Singh *et al*. 1986).

As noted, the average days per month in crop production may increase a little, to an estimated average of 130 days per year. Although this is low compared with days available, seasonal labour shortages will continue to exist and act as a limiting factor in production growth and avoidance of labour losses in specific cases.

In addition, labour requirements in livestock production will also increase. Few data are available on labour use in the livestock sector, but requirements can be considerable. One study of five countries (India, Indonesia, Philippines, Thailand and Sudan) estimated that animal husbandry accounts for between

**Table 4.10** Elasticities of labour demand 1982/4–2000*

| | |
|---|---|
| 93 developing countries | 0.62 |
| Countries with projected agricultural labour force growth rates: | |
| —negative or under 0.25% p.a. | 0.40 |
| —0.25–1.5% p.a. | 0.57 |
| —over 1.5% p.a. | 0.78 |

* (% growth in labour demand caused by a 1% growth in crop production)

25 and 30 percent of total employment in the livestock and crop sectors (Vaidyanathan 1983). Labour intensity in commercial livestock production tends to be lower than in traditional enterprises. As growth of livestock production will in part be based on an increasing share of commercial operations, this would imply that labour requirements would grow at a rate lower than that of production.

## Agricultural investment requirements

### Estimates of agricultural investment

This section presents the estimates of investments required to increase agricultural production to the levels projected for 2000. They are specified in terms of the capital inputs required to produce the increased output, for example hectares of land to be developed, to be irrigated, to be put under permanent crops, numbers of tractors, increases in the livestock herds, and so on. Some of the investment activities may not be entirely in the form of monetary expenditures, such as a farmer building a storage bin or an enclosure for animals, but these invisible activities absorb resources with positive opportunity costs, often shifted away from consumption into investment.

The estimated requirements are shown in Table 4.11. They are given in both physical units of the capital inputs and in values derived by applying appropriate average unit costs. The investment requirements in terms of physical units are, in general, sounder than those in monetary values as it proved impossible to account fully for the country- and region-specific conditions making for variation in unit costs of the different investment activities.

Agricultural investment is considered under two main headings: investment in primary agriculture and support investment. Primary investment covers all items contributing directly to crop and livestock production, as described in Table 4.11. Support investment, on the other hand, covers investments for storage, transport, processing and marketing of agricultural products. They are given here for the sake of completeness, though they belong properly to the economic sectors of distribution, transport, and so on.

**Table 4.11** Agricultural investment requirements, cumulative for 1982/4–2000 (93 developing countries)

| | Physical units | | | Agricultural investment 1982/4–2000 US$ billion | |
|---|---|---|---|---|---|
| | Units | Net additions 1982/4–2000 | Average unit cost (1980 US$) | Net | Gross |
| 1. Investment in crop production | | | | | |
| Land development | '000 ha | 77 000 | 746/ha | 57 | 57 |
| Irrigation | '000 ha | 54 900 | 2 254/ha | 124 | 236 |
| Soil and water conservation | '000 ha | 171 200 | 176/ha | 30 | 30 |
| Flood control | '000 ha | 5 100 | 880/ha | 12 | 15 |
| Establishment of permanent crops | '000 ha | 11 600 | 1 760/ha | 21 | 75 |
| Tractors and equipment | '000 units | 3 200 | 13 530/tr | 43 | 156 |
| Draught animals | '000 pairs | 9 900 | 704/pair | 7 | 7 |
| Equipment for draught animals | '000 set | 9 900 | 325/set | 3 | 51 |
| Handtools | '000 set | 131 400 | 18/set | 2 | 37 |
| Increases in working capital | — | — | — | 31 | 31 |
| TOTAL CROP INVESTMENT | | | | 332 | 696 |
| 2. Investment in livestock production | | | | | |
| Increases in livestock numbers | — | — | — | 91 | 91 |
| Dairy production (on farm equipment) | '000 tonnes milk | 51 700 | 53/tonne | 3 | 3 |
| Commercial pig and poultry production (structures and equipment) | | | 1000/sow, 8/bird | 35 | 44 |
| Grazing land development | '000 ha | 79 700 | 264/ha | 21 | 21 |
| TOTAL LIVESTOCK INVESTMENT | | | | 149 | 159 |
| TOTAL PRIMARY INVESTMENT | | | | 477 | 854 |
| SUPPORT INVESTMENT | — | — | — | 437 | 641 |
| GRAND TOTAL | — | — | — | 918 | 1 495 |

All investments related to the industrial production and distribution of agricultural inputs (e.g. fertilizer plants) are excluded from the agricultural investment requirements. These are investments in other economic sectors, for example the chemical and engineering industries. Likewise, requirements for expenditure in agricultural research could not be estimated as part of the investment requirements. Nevertheless, investment in agricultural research produces high returns and should have the highest priority.

The estimates shown in Table 4.11 comprise both the investments necessary to increase the total capital stock (net investments) as well as those required each year for replacement purposes. In fact, replacement investment accounts for nearly two-fifths of the total investment requirements estimated for the period 1982/4–2000.

As noted, some of the investment estimates may not involve monetary transactions, for example growth of the livestock herds, parts of land expansion and so on, and therefore they are often not counted in the national accounts. For this reason, the estimates given here may appear higher than the historical data would suggest, though the latter are often very inadequate, as will be discussed below.

There are other reasons why the estimates presented here may overstate the capital needs of primary agriculture. For example, the irrigation investments may overstate the extent of agricultural investment since large irrigation schemes are often multipurpose and the total costs should not normally be charged fully to agriculture. Indeed, many such schemes would not be economically sound if they were to depend for their returns exclusively on agriculture. Likewise, tractors, primarily power sources for tillage, are also used extensively for transportation in the developing countries. Not all this use for transportation pertains to agricultural production, and in the estimates presented here, transportation is not included under primary agricultural investment. Yet, while as much as half of tractor use can be outside primary production activities, all of the investment in tractors is considered under primary agriculture. This is due to the impossibility of taking into account the high variability of non-farming related uses of tractors in the developing countries. It is thus necessary to view the results, particularly the incremental capital/output ratios (ICORs) with this caveat because gross irrigation and mechanization investment requirements account for nearly half of total gross investment in primary agriculture in the 93 developing countries.

The estimates of Table 4.11 also include some allowance for the costs of environmental protection and conservation of the land and water resources which, again, may not be counted as agricultural investment in normal accounting practice. These investments are necessary to sustain agricultural production in the long term. They indicate the need for increased commitment to protecting the environment, given the serious consequences of the loss of resources through environmental degradation (Ch. 11).

For the production levels projected in this study a cumulative gross total of nearly \$850 billion at prices of 1980 will need to be invested in primary agriculture and \$635 billion in supporting activities between 1982/4 and 2000. This total of nearly \$1500 billion does not include investment in forestry and fisheries. As is indicated in the discussion of forestry (Ch. 5), in the developing countries this sector will require a cumulative total of approximately \$200 billion ($300 billion including China), split almost equally between forestry and forest industries.

The unit costs used to obtain these values are approximately in 1980 US dollars. The dollar exchange rate has been fluctuating widely while the prices of the investment goods have also been changing. Therefore, if these investment estimates were to be expressed in dollars of a more recent year, they could be quite different. Because of the revaluation of the dollar up to 1985, the dollar unit cost of manufactured exports from the industrial to the developing countries actually fell by 5 percent between 1980 and 1985. If this is taken as a rough indicator of the dollar prices of the agricultural investment goods, the estimates of investment shown in Table 4.10 would not be very different if expressed in 1985 dollars. The subsequent fall in the dollar exchange rate would mean that if the investment estimates were revalued in 1987 dollars, the result would probably be some 10–15 percent higher since the dollar price index of manufactured exports to the developing countries is forecast to be in 1987 15 percent higher than in 1985.

Since these investments are an input into agricultural production, they can be better understood if they are examined in relation to agricultural production, level and growth rate. The first indicator useful for this purpose is the agricultural investment rate, that is the average percentage share of gross primary investment to agricultural GDP. The latter is derived by valuing the gross agricultural output at the standard producer prices of the study for 1979/81 and deducting the value of all current inputs (fertilizer, feed, fuel, etc.). The growth rate of the resulting GDP for the 93 countries and 1982/4–2000 is 2.5 percent p.a., that is lower than the 2.8 percent growth rate of gross output because, as discussed earlier, an increasing share of the value of output is accounted for by inputs as farming becomes more intensive.

It is estimated that, for the 93 countries over the period 1982/4–2000, average gross primary investment requirements would account for some 16.0 percent of agricultural GDP. Is this a reasonable investment rate for agriculture? The agricultural investment data of the developing countries are scarce, incomplete and of uneven quality. Therefore, there is no empirical basis for evaluating the estimates of this study. An indirect evaluation may, however, be attempted using related data from the national accounts. They indicate for the developing countries a total (economy-wide) investment rate of 24–5 percent and a share of agriculture in total GDP of 16–17 percent.

These data can be combined with the projected growth rates of total and agricultural GDP (4.2 percent and 2.5 percent p.a., respectively) to yield some useful information concerning investment rates. Assuming the total investment rate of the developing countries would be maintained at 24–5 percent, then the agricultural investment requirements of this study would represent some 9 percent of the total investment bill on the average over the projection period. This is less than the share of the sector in total GDP (it would fall to an average of 13 percent over the period 1982/4–2000) which is as it should be, given the lower growth of the sector compared with the rest of the economy.

It is, of course, by no means certain that the total investment rate of the developing countries will remain at the 24–5 percent level of the last ten years. Investment rates have been falling in sub-Saharan Africa and Latin America, and resources for investment are likely to be less plentiful than in the past in the oil-exporting countries. The overall projected GDP growth rate of 4.2 percent p.a. is less than that of the 1970s. In practice, overall investment rates may be lower in the future, and this raises the problem of securing adequate finance for the estimated investment requirements for agriculture. As noted, these estimates are very comprehensive and the part that would need to be financed through monetary savings may be less than the $850 billion estimated here. The policy aspects of financing agricultural development are discussed in Chapter 8.

A second indicator, related to the investment rate, useful for evaluating the estimated investment requirements, is the incremental capital/output ratio (ICOR—dollars of gross primary investment per dollar increase in agricultural GDP). The resulting average ICOR is 6.3, which is higher than other studies generally indicate. The paucity of comprehensive agricultural investment data makes it impossible to derive empirical estimates of what the ICOR really is. A survey of returns to the FAO questionnaires on the economic accounts of agriculture indicates that only 19 developing countries provided agricultural investment data, which in most cases were less than comprehensive (FAO 1986d). For example only five countries included in agricultural investment the livestock herd increases; only nine, land development and irrigation; only seven, permanent crop establishment, and so on. Most countries reported investments in agricultural machinery. It is obvious that if these data are used to measure the agricultural ICOR, they are bound to understate it by a significant margin. As indicated above, the estimates presented here are comprehensive and they may impart an upward bias because they include investments which are often non-monetary and also those which are primarily but not exclusively directed to farming, for example large irrigation schemes. Overall, however, these estimates, particularly in their physical dimensions (hectares of land, numbers of animals, machines, etc.) are sufficiently robust to bring home the lesson that agricultural growth cannot be achieved cheaply and to dispel the belief held in earlier development thinking that agriculture is not very demanding in terms of capital.

## Structure and regional distribution of agricultural investments

Table 4.12 presents a breakdown of investment requirements by major component and region. In this table, the investment requirements are in terms of *average* annual levels over the period 1982/4–2000. The annual levels are simply the cumulative investments divided by 17—the number of years. Normally, it can be expected that annual requirements will be lower than the overall average in the early years of the period and higher in later years. However, because of the lumpy nature of many agricultural investments, it is not possible to be more precise as to the distribution over time.

The table shows clearly the regional differences in the structure of investment requirements. Irrigation dominates in Asia and Near East/North Africa region. This is a reflection of both potentials and needs. Growth of production will increasingly depend on more irrigated land, particularly in the Near East/North Africa as explained in earlier sections of this chapter. Land expansion investment is concentrated in Latin America and sub-Saharan

**Table 4.12** Annual gross investment requirements by region and major items, averages for 1982/4–2000 (1980 US$ billions)

| | Land expansion | Irrigation | Conservation | Perm. crops | Machinery | Draft animals, handtools | Working capital | Livestock | Total primary | Support investment | Grand total | Primary investment % of Agr. | |
|---|---|---|---|---|---|---|---|---|---|---|---|---|---|
| | | | | | | | | | | | | GDP | ICOR |
| 93 developing countries | *3.4* | *13.9* | *2.6* | *4.4* | *9.2* | *5.6* | *1.8* | *9.1* | *50* | *37* | *87* | *16.0* | *6.3* |
| Africa (sub-Saharan) | 1.3 | 1.1 | 0.6 | 0.9 | 0.5 | 0.9 | 0.1 | 1.5 | 7 | 5 | 12 | 14.2 | 4.5 |
| Near East/N. Africa | 0.0 | 3.6 | 0.4 | 0.4 | 1.7 | 0.3 | 0.3 | 0.9 | 8 | 4 | 12 | 23.8 | 9.1 |
| Asia (excl. China) | 0.6 | 7.3 | 0.9 | 2.2 | 2.6 | 4.0 | 0.8 | 3.0 | 21 | 17 | 38 | 15.0 | 6.2 |
| Latin America | 1.5 | 2.0 | 0.7 | 1.0 | 4.3 | 0.5 | 0.6 | 3.8 | 14 | 11 | 25 | 15.9 | 6.6 |
| Low-income (excl. China) | 1.0 | 7.2 | 1.2 | 1.0 | 2.4 | 4.1 | 0.7 | 2.9 | 20 | 15 | 35 | 15.8 | 6.3 |
| Middle income | 2.4 | 6.8 | 1.4 | 3.4 | 6.8 | 1.5 | 1.2 | 6.2 | 30 | 22 | 52 | 16.2 | 6.3 |

Africa, while mechanization is in the middle-income countries, primarily Near East/North Africa and Latin America. Again, these differences reflect differences in factor endowments and needs: land is comparatively more plentiful in Latin America and sub-Saharan Africa, while the agricultural labour force grows less and per caput incomes are higher in the Near East/North Africa and Latin America compared with the other regions. This leads to comparatively higher rates of mechanization in these two regions.

Requirements for mechanization investments are projected here to be generally lower than suggested by past trends, because the economic crisis and debt problems facing many countries have increased the cost of imported machinery and reduced subsidies for this type of agricultural inputs.

The agricultural investment rates and ICORs shown in the table reflect the significant regional differentials in the capital costs of agricultural growth. The Near East/North Africa region would continue to need substantial investments in irrigation and mechanization, with the overall agricultural investment rate being very high, 24 percent. This must be seen in the context of the high overall (economy-wide) investment rates maintained by many countries in the region, financed from oil-sector resources. The national accounts data indicate that such investment rates over the period 1975–83 have been 30–4 percent in North Africa and 23–31 percent in West Asia.

At the other extreme, sub-Saharan Africa will need less of both these types of investment, with an overall agricultural investment rate of 14 percent. This is not equivalent to saying that agricultural growth in the region is less costly in terms of capital requirements. It only means that investments in support of agriculture will have to be made mostly in infrastructure, which is multipurpose investment and therefore not included in the estimates of requirements of primary agriculture.

## Agricultural research

The production and demand projections described in Chapter 3, and its implications for land development and input use as outlined earlier in this chapter, underline the growing dependence of the agriculture of the developing countries on research. There is no alternative. A large share of incremental production must come from higher yields per unit of land or labour. Yet, in all developing regions there are areas where present agricultural production cannot be sustained with prevailing farming practices. Moreover, this problem will intensify in the future as population pressures force the further development of marginal land. So expanded research is required even to maintain existing yields.

At present the world resources allocated to agricultural research are in the order of between \$4 billion and \$5 billion. This is equivalent to less than 1 percent of an estimated global value of gross agricultural production of over \$1000 billion. The percentage is even lower in some countries in spite of the fact that the returns to research make up for expenditures in multiples. There are no reasons to expect these high benefit/cost ratios to decline in the coming decades. Therefore there is a strong case for increasing resources devoted to agricultural research.

The distribution of research resources are biased towards the developed countries, but much of the basic and some of the applied research in developed country research institutions are also relevant to agricultural issues of the developing countries. Research organizations in the developing countries are, in relative terms, somewhat bureaucratized, underfunded and understaffed. In particular, extension, perhaps the most important link in the research process, is a relatively overlooked and neglected field, with excessive dependence on approaches modelled on developed-country practices, and only limited efforts at formulating approaches more appropriate to the economic and human resources, and social systems of developing countries. Again in developing countries there is some bias towards disciplinary basic research, whereas it is mostly interdisciplinary/multidisciplinary applied research that will provide answers to immediate problems of agriculture. Substantial emphasis will have to be placed on investment and training for agricultural research and extension in the developing countries.

The production projections of this study are based on the application of existing and known technology, and no new major technological breakthroughs were considered when making these projections, although they assume high levels of adaptive research. This does not imply that no such breakthroughs are expected. Thus the critical research for the projections of the study are first 'maintenance' research, and second, adaptive research. Adaptive research is essentially producing or adapting research results to recommendations that are appropriate to farmer conditions, which would be more readily adopted, diffused and translated into production increases.

This type of research is critical for the coming decades because the projected increases in production will involve crops grown under more limiting environments in terms of moisture availability, soils, and so on, as opposed to the high productivity, irrigated environments. As such, more information will be needed on production constraints, and this can be achieved by incorporating into research a systematic effort to gain a better understanding of farmer conditions.

Another important dimension in research and extension is to eliminate the male farmer bias. Women in developing countries are active participants in agricultural production as workers and as decision-makers. As such their perceptions of the issues and constraints should be incorporated into the research process, and research should be targeted at their needs. The need to eliminate the male farmer bias also exists in other institutions that are complementary to agricultural production such as credit mechanisms.

One particular area of research that merits mention is research on livestock health, especially in sub-Saharan Africa. Expanded control of trypanosomiasis will have a tremendous impact on livestock production in Africa. Again in Africa, a recommendation that would be valid for most developing countries, has more urgency and relevance. This is the need to establish and/or develop effective research organizations. This requires funding, staffing and training. More than that, it requires a long-term commitment.

# 5 Forestry

## World forestry in the mid-1980s

The global value of the production of forestry and primary forest industries in 1985 (in 1980 prices) amounted to $300 billion (Table 5.1), around 2.5 percent of world GDP. Exports of forest products in 1985 of $50 billion represented 2 percent of world merchandise exports. Developing-country exports of $6.6 billion were 1.4 percent of their total exports (including oil).

Many non-wood forest products, both plant and animal, add directly to food production, and some are of considerable local nutritional importance. Thus the contribution of forest products may be divided between the contribution to energy supply, to industrial production and to food supply.

### Forestry resources

The world's forests and woods vegetation cover some 4300 million ha, 1800 million in developed countries and 2500 million in developing, of which some 2000 million ha are tropical forest (FAO 1985b). This total encompasses extreme diversity of climate, species, ecological types and condition of the forest. In general the forest area in the developed countries is now relatively stable with a slight tendency to increase in some countries. An element of uncertainty is posed by the impact of atmospheric pollution, which may affect the supply potential in some countries. The forests of many tropical countries on the other hand are subject to severe pressure from conversion of forest to permanent agriculture or shifting cultivation, and to degradation by over-cutting for fuelwood and timber and through grazing and repeated burning. The annual net reduction in the tropical forest area is estimated to be some 11.5 million ha or about 0.6 percent of its total area. The annual rate of reforestation is some 14.5 million ha, but most of this—about 9 million ha—is in the developed countries. China is reforesting about 4 million ha. Tropical developing countries achieve only 1.5 million ha per annum, only one-tenth of their annual deforestation.

### Forest and the environment

Increasing attention is being given to the conservation of the forest resources and to environmental aspects of forestry by governments and by the international community, in view of the current magnitude of deforestation and the resulting degradation of the natural resource base, particularly in fragile ecological situations. This is discussed further in Chapter 12. Only a summary

**Table 5.1** Contribution of wood products to the world economy, 1985

| | Developing countries | Developed countries | World |
|---|---|---|---|
| Volume of production | *million units* | | |
| Fuelwood m$^3$ | 1408 | 255 | 1663 |
| Sawnwood m$^3$ | 107 | 360 | 467 |
| Panels m$^3$ | 19 | 90 | 109 |
| Paper (tonnes) | 27 | 166 | 193 |
| Value of production | *$ billion (1980 prices)* | | |
| Fuelwood* | 70 | 28 | 98 |
| Sawnwood | 14 | 46 | 60 |
| Panels | 6 | 29 | 35 |
| Paper | 16 | 94 | 110 |
| Total | 106 | 197 | 303 |

*Source*: All data on production consumption and trade in this chapter are from FAO, *Yearbook of Forestry Products 1985*, Rome 1987.

* Includes value of wood residues recycled in energy production.

of aspects which will need to be particularly examined in connection with forestry is made here.

In the developing countries, key issues in humid areas include the need for development of appropriate production systems ensuring sustainable use of forest land encroached by squatters and shifting cultivators, the management of wildlife—including game farming, the prevention and control of forest fires, conservation of mountain watersheds and the protection of mangroves and other wetlands and 'in situ' and 'ex situ' protection of genetic resources. In the arid and semi-arid lands, sand dune stabilization, shelterbelts, greenbelts around urban areas, silvo-pasture management, the integration of multi-purpose trees and shrubs in agro-silvo-pastoral systems and the control of bush fires require particular attention.

In the developed countries there are several major environmental issues. Of basic concern are the implications of acid rain and atmospheric pollution on the condition of water and soil and forest health and survival. A second issue is the incidence of forest fires, which constitute a serious hazard particularly in Mediterranean climates. Another issue is the radioactive downfall and its effects on the forest ecosystem, the soil, water, plant and wildlife resources.

## Fuelwood and energy supply

Wood and tree biomass is a major source of energy for developing countries. Wood contributes to world energy supply some 630 million tonnes of coal equivalent, or about 6.5 percent of the total. The developed world consumption of wood as fuel, 185 million tonnes of coal equivalent including recycling, provides 3 percent of its total energy consumption, while the developing country consumption, 460 million tonnes of coal equivalent, amounts to about 19 percent of their total energy (Table 5.2).

With economic development, wood as a source of energy tends to be replaced by fossil fuels and electricity. In developed countries during the 1970s this tendency to substitution was slowed and in some instances reversed. Fuelwood and charcoal gained competitivity, particularly where low-cost supplies were available. Industry invested in equipment for recovery and conversion of wood residues.

In developing countries, the most important role of wood is in providing the energy supply for rural communities, but it is also important for a large number of people in cities. The fuel is local to people with no access to modern infrastructure to transport and with little income to purchase alternative fuel. Thus while on average developing countries depend on fuelwood for some 19 percent of total energy supplies, the dependence is much higher among countries most severely affected by energy supply problems; for example, it averages 62 percent in the African, and 34 percent in the Asian countries in this category.

Until other cheap sources of energy become available, fuelwood and other woody biomass will remain indispensable, especially for the rural poor. Its acute and growing scarcity is already causing severe hardship for vast numbers of people. In many rural areas people (usually the women) have to walk very long distances to collect and haul fuelwood. Often the frequency of cooked meals has had to be reduced because of the shortage of fuelwood, so that it has become a contributory cause of malnutrition and disease.

While in general among the local populations of developing countries the consumption of fuelwood has continued to increase with population, in the deprived regions the diminishing supply is resulting in decreasing levels of consumption and the failure to meet basic energy needs. Rural people are then forced to depend on crop residues and animal dung. The diversion of dung and crop wastes to fuel has detrimental effects on agriculture and food supply (FAO 1983).

During the late 1970s and early 1980s, the awareness of governments and development agencies of the urgent need to increase fuelwood supplies to rural communities within economic distance, was greatly enhanced, and programmes were reorientated to community forestry and forest conservation. The rate of afforestation in the most severely affected countries remains, however, a small fraction of the rate of depletion.

**Box 5.1** *Fuelwood: profiles of African deficits*

FAO recently carried out in-depth analysis of supply/demand of fuelwood in seven Sahelian countries, and six countries each in East and Southern Africa. In 1980, of the 139 million people living in the 19 countries, 78 percent were in areas with overall deficits. On present trends, this ratio will have grown to 97 percent by the year 2000, when population will be 74 percent greater. In the Sahel the proportion of people living in areas of deficit was 43 percent (1980) and will reach 94 percent in 2000.

**Table 5.2** Fuelwood in world energy supply, 1984*

| | Fuelwood† (million $m^3$) | Energy equivalent of fuelwood | Commercial energy | Total | Fuelwood % of total energy supply |
|---|---|---|---|---|---|
| | million gigajoules | | | | |
| Africa | 398 | 3.7 | 3.5 | 7.2 | 51 |
| Asia | 745 | 7.0 | 40.8 | 47.8 | 15 |
| Latin America | 265 | 2.5 | 12.7 | 15.2 | 16 |
| Developing countries | 1408 | 13.2 | 57.0 | 70.2 | 19 |
| Developed countries | 255 | 2.4 | 202.0 | 204.0 | 1 |
| World | 1663 | 15.6 | 259.0 | 275.0 | 6 |

* Fuelwood production refers to 1985.
† Excludes recycling of residues.

in this sub-region, the fuelwood comes from considerable distances: towns of under 50 000 inhabitants are supplied by cart and camels from 10–50 km. In larger cities, an increasing proportion of fuelwood travels from forests which are not less than 50–60 km away and very often over 200 km distant. In Eastern Africa 90 percent of people live in areas of overall deficit and this ratio will reach 98 percent in 2000 on present trends. In Southern Africa, corresponding ratios are 83 and 95 percent.

The most severe current deficits are not in the semiarid areas but in more moist but heavily populated regions such as the Ethiopian, Kenyan and Malawian highlands of East Africa. The existence in many of these areas of fuel-demanding industries worsens the pressures. In 1980, East African fuelwood consumption by rural industries amounted to about 10.5 million cubic metres, of which nearly 10 million went to tobacco processing. Industrial demand was particularly great in Malawi, where it accounted for about 45 percent of total fuelwood usage.

Attempts to reduce household consumption of fuelwood and charcoal have met with limited success, and it is clear that extension methods as well as technology and cost of fuel-saving devices all need further improvement. Kenya has perhaps made most progress in promoting fuel-saving wood stoves through a combination of technology development and extension systems that have encouraged active involvement of the private sector and NGOs, including womens' groups. In the Sahel, promotion of fuel-saving stoves is actively supported by all governments as an integral part of fuel demand management. Attempts are also in progress in all the countries to improve efficiency in industrial fuelwood use.

Natural forests and woodlands provided 76, 61 and 60 percent respectively of accessible fuelwood in Sahelian, East and Southern Africa in 1980. Corresponding ratios projected for 2000 are 67, 52 and 66 percent respectively. The second most important source is trees on agricultural land plus forest fallows close to human settlements. Between them, these highly accessible resources accounted in 1980 for 23, 34 and 18 percent of accessible supply in Sahelian, East and Southern Africa. Their contribution in 2000 will have risen to 28, 40 and 23 percent respectively due to expansion of agricultural land.

In the year 2000, plantations in all sub-regions will supply at best only around 10 percent of fuelwood needs. They are not being established fast enough because of high cost. It therefore seems essential to emphasize the management of improved natural forests and that of trees on farmlands and their surrounding fallows for higher wood yield. Unfortunately, this approach has so far received little attention and investment is directed almost exclusively to forest plantations. In many cases these are the only practical solutions for meeting concentrated commercial or urban demand. In Kenya, for example, the tobacco industry makes tree planting a precondition for granting a licence to grow tobacco; similar legislation exists in Malawi while the tea industry in all the East African countries has in recent years planted trees for fuelwood self-sufficiency. Urban centres are also planting or planning peri-urban fuelwood forests.

Accessibility of fuelwood is a key determinant of supply/demand balance. For example, in East Africa it was calculated that if all forest increment were accessible, then the 1980 estimated volume shortfall of 53 percent would be a surplus instead.

The assessment of likely changes in forest accessibility should be an essential part of planning for solving fuelwood problems. Such planning should ensure that newly-created accessibility does not lead to destruction of fuelwood sources near roads, as is currently the case, but becomes the basis for sustained supplies.

## Food from the forest

Naturally occurring foods from the forest are much more important than was previously realized in the food supplies of rural people. Some wild forest plants, such as the sago palm, provide staple foods, but more generally they furnish nutritionally valuable supplements in diets based on one or a few staple crops and are particularly important seasonally, as they may be available at times such as the pre-harvest period when other foods are short. Forest trees and shrubs also provide fodder for livestock.

Wildlife is probably the biggest source of food directly available from the forest. Including small rodents, reptiles and birds as well as larger species, it makes up a very large part of animal protein supplies in many areas. Attempts are being made to exploit them more effectively by such methods as game cropping and ranching.

One type of indirect forestry contribution to food production and distribution is through farm inputs made from forest raw materials. Wood, bamboo and other forest products are often the cheapest and preferred materials for the construction or manufacture of a wide range of equipment and implements for farming and fishing.

By providing the habitat for the wild relatives of cultivated crop species and conserving other plant species, forest ecosystems—properly managed—contribute to food security by safeguarding genetic resources for future agriculture.

## Non-wood forest products

In several countries, non-wood forest products are of great economic significance. World trade in gum arabic exceeds $50 million. Fifty percent is exported by the Sudan, where the product accounts for 10 percent of total exports. Minor forest products contribute around $100 million to Indonesian export income and generate employment for some 150,000 people. In India employment generated in these activities exceeds 1 million employee years. The contribution of wildlife in African countries has been estimated at $3.5 billion.

## Employment and forestry

Forestry and forest industries generate employment, particularly in rural areas and thereby facilitate the entry of rural people into the monetary economy. The contribution of formal-sector forestry valued at some $30 billion in the mid-1980s, may be associated with the employment of some 35 million people in developing countries.

Forest management operations lend themselves to the use of labour-intensive technologies. Modern industrial plants, such as sawmills and pulp mills, also provide some employment. An important area of employment in the whole forestry sector is informal, small-scale, artisanal activities at the household and workshop level. These include carpentry, furniture making, handicrafts, and the production of simple inputs for farming and fishing.

## Consumption and production of wood products

World consumption of wood products (Table 5.4) is made up of 467 million $m^3$ of sawnwood, 109 million $m^3$ of wood based panels, and 193 million tonnes of paper. While the 1985 world average consumption of sawnwood and wood based panels was 0.1 $m^3$ per caput, the average in developing countries was only 0.03 $m^3$ per caput. The world average consumption of paper was 40 kg per caput, 132 kg in the developed countries and 9 kg in the developing countries. Although developing country consumption is low, growth in consumption of forest products in the last decade has been much more rapid than in developed countries.

The developing countries account for some 20 percent of world production of mechanical wood products—sawnwood and panels, and for 14 percent of world production of paper. However, production growth varied between regions and countries with growth concentrated in wood-rich and larger economies. This concentration is particularly significant in paper, where most small developing economies remain entirely dependent on imports for their consumption.

The largest producers of sawnwood among developing countries (China, Brazil and India) produce mainly for the domestic market. The next largest developing country producers (Indonesia, Malaysia and Chile) export up to 50 percent of their production. Plywood is the principal wood-based panel manufactured in developing countries. Indonesia, starting from the level of 10 thousand $m^3$ in 1973, reached 4.6 million $m^3$ in 1985 and is now the third largest producer in the world, after the USA and Japan. Other large producers are China, Brazil, Korea and Malaysia. The largest producer of paper in the developing world is China and is currently the sixth largest in the world. Half of this production is based on wheat and rice straw as raw material. Other large producers are Brazil, Korea, India, Mexico and Argentina. Expansion in the period 1970–85 in the developing world has doubled the production of sawnwood and paper, and trebled that of wood based panels (Table 5.5). The largest volume growth has been in Asia and the Far East region and in Latin America.

Faster growth of consumption in the developing countries has mainly been met by growth in domestic production. Production for export has expanded considerably. In Asia it has been mainly in sawnwood and wood-based panels, predominant countries being Indonesia and Malaysia. In Latin America the growth in production for export has been in pulp and paper, mainly in Brazil and Chile.

## Trade in forest products

The volume of world trade in forest products grew at 2.7 percent p.a. between 1970 and 1985, while in current dollar terms it increased from $12.5 billion to $50 billion over this period. Developing-country exports in 1985 amounted to $6.6 billion, or some 13 percent of total world exports of forest products.

**Table 5.3** Trade in forest products 1985

| | Developing countries | Developed countries | Total |
|---|---|---|---|
| | *Exports (million units)* | | |
| Roundwood $m^3$ | 30.4 | 77.3 | 107.7 |
| Sawnwood $m^3$ | 9.5 | 76.4 | 85.9 |
| Wood based panels $m^3$ | 7.2 | 11.7 | 18.9 |
| Paper (tonnes) | 1.4 | 38.9 | 40.3 |
| | *Imports (million units)* | | |
| Roundwood $m^3$ | 23.0 | 90.3 | 113.3 |
| Sawnwood $m^3$ | 11.8 | 73.9 | 85.7 |
| Wood based panels $m^3$ | 3.3 | 15.5 | 18.8 |
| Paper (tonnes) | 6.5 | 33.3 | 39.8 |
| | *Total value ($ billion, current prices)* | | |
| Exports (fob) | 6.6 | 43.3 | 49.9 |
| Imports (cif) | 10.1 | 45.1 | 55.2 |

Developing countries are net exporters of unprocessed roundwood but net importers of processed products. Processed product exports have grown faster than those of roundwood so that they now account for two-thirds of export value compared with half in 1970. A factor in this development has been the policy, particularly in countries of South-East Asia, to restrict roundwood exports and encourage development of processing industries.

In 1984, three countries (Malaysia, Indonesia and Brazil) accounted for 56 percent of total exports from the developing countries. Exports of tropical logs from Africa go almost exclusively to developed countries, while 33 percent of Asian tropical-log exports go to other developing countries, mainly within the region.

Some 40 developing countries are largely dependent on imports for their supplies of sawnwood. Most of these are small or arid countries with little opportunity to develop wood industries. Seventy developing countries are largely dependent on imports for their supplies of paper. Again these are predominantly countries with small markets.

International prices of forest products in real terms have been stable overall, the index for all forest products in 1984 being virtually equal to that in 1970. The developing countries have benefited from rising real prices of tropical logs and sawnwood but have suffered from the decline of plywood prices. At the same time, many countries benefited from the downward trend in the real price of pulp and paper, which account for half their total imports of wood products.

The forest products exports generally face tariff barriers and quota restrictions. The favoured treatment of developed-country imports from the developing countries under the Generalized System of Preferences (GSP), applies also to wood products, though quota restrictions exist for some processed products. Manufacturing of forest products is strongly protected in some developing countries, either by high tariffs or by restrictions on imports. In addition, restrictions are often placed on the export of unprocessed roundwood in many developing (and developed) countries to favour development of a domestic industry and to encourage exports of processed products.

## Forestry prospects to the year 2000

### The outlook for wood for energy

It is estimated that world consumption of fuelwood in the year 2000 would be 2235 million m$^3$. In developing countries, consumption growth is constrained by that of supplies, and therefore consumption cannot grow by more than 2.0 percent per annum, to 1900 million m$^3$ in the year 2000. This is inadequate to meet projected needs and it is estimated that as many as 2400 million people would be in areas of acute scarcity or in areas where current levels of use are not sustainable.

It is to be expected that the trend toward greater use of coal, kerosene, gas and electricity will be fastest among urban populations. Among rural populations, with higher cost of distribution of commercial energy where the infrastructure exists, and less disposable income, the growth of substitute energy supplies will be slower.

As noted, the growth of fuelwood consumption in developing countries reaching 1900 million m$^3$ in the year 2000, is constrained by supply. Actual needs for fuelwood in the year 2000 could exceed projected supply by as much as 500 million m$^3$ in Asia, 300 million m$^3$ in Africa and 100 million m$^3$ in Latin America. A tree planting rate of some 7 million ha per year in developing market economies would be required to meet these needs.

With continually high energy prices such as those of the late 1970s and early 1980s, the use of wood as a source of energy would increase further in

**Table 5.4** Consumption of forest products, 1985 and projected 2000

| | 1985 | | | 2000 | | |
|---|---|---|---|---|---|---|
| | Developing countries | Developed countries | World | Developing countries | Developed countries | World |
| | million m$^3$ | | | | | |
| Total roundwood | 1759 | 1417 | 3176 | 2415 | 1830 | 4245 |
| Fuelwood | 1408 | 255 | 1663 | 1900 | 335 | 2235 |
| Industrial roundwood | 351 | 1166 | 1513 | 515 | 1495 | 2010 |
| Sawnwood | 110 | 357 | 467 | 190 | 423 | 613 |
| Wood-based panels | 15 | 94 | 109 | 51 | 181 | 232 |
| | million tonnes | | | | | |
| Paper and paperboard | 33 | 160 | 193 | 71 | 233 | 304 |
| | Growth rates (% p.a.) | | | | | |
| Total roundwood | 2.5 | 0.8 | 1.7 | 2.1 | 1.9 | 2.0 |
| Fuelwood | 2.3 | 2.1 | 2.3 | 2.0 | 1.8 | 1.9 |
| Industrial roundwood | 4.7 | 0.4 | 1.2 | 2.6 | 1.6 | 1.9 |
| Sawnwood | 5.0 | −0.1 | 0.8 | 3.7 | 1.1 | 1.8 |
| Wood-based panels | 9.2 | 2.4 | 3.0 | 8.5 | 1.1 | 5.2 |
| Paper and paperboard | 6.4 | 2.4 | 2.9 | 5.3 | 2.4 | 3.1 |

developed countries at a rate of 1.7 percent per year. However, the high labour and transport components in total cost, as well as the inconvenience and inefficiency in utilization in small volumes, leads to fuelwood being favoured only in situations where the relative cost of other energy sources is very high. Should low energy prices prevail in the period to the year 2000, a return is likely to the declining trends in consumption of wood as fuel which characterized the period before 1973 in the developed world.

## The outlook for industrial forestry products[1]

World consumption of sawnwood is projected to increase at an average rate of 1.8 percent p.a. and that of wood-based panels at 5.2 percent p.a. (Table 5.4). Consumption growth will be the fastest in the developing countries. These products are used in construction, housing and furniture, and the high growth in consumption in developing countries reflects high rates of growth of total and urban populations.

World consumption of paper is projected to increase at an annual rate of 3.1 percent. Again, growth will be faster in the developing countries, which are expected to increase their share in world consumption from 17 to 23 percent. The higher income elasticity of demand in developing countries is associated with the expansion of literacy, generating demand for paper in communications, and the rising standards of packaging, with substitution of traditional packaging materials such as wood, cotton and jute by paper.

Forecasts of capital formation in the wood products industry of the developing countries indicate that production may increase less than demand, while the reverse is the case for developed countries. Projection A in Table 5.5 does recognize the difficulties of many developing countries in mobilizing investment, preventing them from fully exploiting their comparative advantage in domestic production of wood products. The higher alternative B assumes that at least part of these difficulties can be solved. In this alternative, the volume of production in the year 2000 follows the trend in self-sufficiency since 1970 in the case of sawnwood and panels, and retains the 1984 level of self-sufficiency for paper.

Production for the export market may also be expanded. Countries in East and South-East Asia have demonstrated their capability of penetrating world markets for tropical sawnwood and plywood, while Brazil, Chile and Swaziland have developed export pulp industries, and Brazil has expanded paper exports. These developments have been on the basis of a reasonably developed infrastructure and comparative advantage in wood raw material and labour supply. This trend is likely to continue and extend to other countries in the developing world.

The volume of industrial forestry production entering international trade is around 10 percent of developing country production, and approaches 20 percent of developed-country production. In developed countries an increasing proportion of total production is being traded, while in the developing countries the proportion of production traded is decreasing. This is partly

[1] All projections in this section come from FAO 1987d.

**Table 5.5** Consumption and production in the developing countries

| | 1970 | 1985 | 2000 A | 2000 B |
|---|---|---|---|---|
| Sawnwood | | *million m³* | | |
| Consumption | 53 | 110 | 190 | 190 |
| Production | 53 | 107 | 164 | 180 |
| Wood-based panels | | | | |
| Consumption | 4 | 15 | 51 | 51 |
| Production | 6 | 19 | 44 | 51 |
| Paper | | *million tonnes* | | |
| Consumption | 13 | 33 | 71 | 71 |
| Production | 9 | 27 | 46 | 60 |

attributable to the rapid increase in domestic consumption, which absorbs a greater proportion of production of the main developing exporters. The absolute volume and value of developing-country exports have, however, increased at a faster rate than those of the developed countries.

On the assumption of continuation of basic trends in the expansion of trade in forest products, the world value of exports in the year 2000 would be $80 billion (1980 prices), and the developing-country component about $14 billion (Table 5.6). In line with recent trends, it may be expected that an increasing proportion of developing-country exports will go to other developing countries. Expansion of the participation of developing countries in international trade in forest products is dependent on the efficient development of their national industries and the development of marketing infrastructure, including the formation of national and international timber trade institutions.

**Table 5.6** Developing countries' exports of forest products

| | 1970 | 1985 | 2000 |
|---|---|---|---|
| | *million m³ or tonnes* | | |
| Industrial roundwood | 40 | 30 | 20 |
| Sawnwood | 6 | 10 | 17 |
| Wood based panels | 3 | 7 | 16 |
| Paper | 0.3 | 1.4 | 6 |
| | *$ billion (1980 prices)* | | |
| Total exports (FOB) | 5.5 | 6.6 | 14.0 |

### The outlook for forest resources

The continuation of current rates of deforestation and degradation of the tropical forest will result in many countries in a situation in which the forest fails to meet requirements for wood for fuel and industrial uses and at the same time there will be harmful consequences to the environment through soil erosion and deterioration of the water regime. The current rate of reafforestation in tropical countries is around 1.5 million ha p.a. To offset the deficiency in the supply of wood for fuel to rural communities which would continue to depend on biomass for energy, it is estimated that the equivalent of an additional 100 million ha of tree planting, well located and of high-yielding species, would be necessary by the year 2000—that is some 7 million ha p.a. on average.

The expansion of fuelwood supplies must be pursued on a very wide front. Existing forests have to be managed more effectively, with much greater emphasis on fuelwood as an important product. The fuelwood used by poor rural people comes much less from the forest proper than from the diminishing stock of trees in agricultural areas. The principal methods of increasing the supplies available to them are therefore the promotion of village-level community wood-lots and of the increased incorporation of trees in farming systems. Given adequate price incentives, fuelwood becomes a valuable cash crop for the farmer.

## Wood for industrial production

The projected world increase in consumption of industrial roundwood is some 500 million $m^3$ to a total of around 2 billion $m^3$. The projected consumption in developed countries is 1.5 billion $m^3$, with just over 500 million $m^3$ in developing countries. The total includes some 200 million of roundwood utilized in unprocessed form.

The increases in production to meet these demands in developed countries are regarded as broadly feasible within the context of the existing forest resource base and trends in renewal and new investment. There may be some increase in the net dependence on imports of countries such as Japan and countries of the European region. Many developed countries have programmes to support afforestation, reforestation and forest management through direct subsidy or fiscal incentives. Consideration is being given currently to the diversion of land from agriculture to forestry in countries of the European Economic Community. On the negative side, the flow and future potential of forest products from some regions in Europe and North America may be affected by damage to the forest from atmospheric pollution.

Consumption increases in the developing countries are within the capacity of existing forest resources in terms of gross volume. However, the expansion may be expected to be based to an appreciable degree on investment in plantations producing uniform raw material well located for the utilizing industry. In general the rate of new afforestation in the tropical developing countries of 1.5 million ha p.a. would be expected to generate an additional productive capacity of 200 million to 300 million $m^3$ p.a. by the year 2000. The investment in China, estimated at 4 million ha p.a. but in less favourable climatic conditions, may increase its productive capacity by some 200 million $m^3$ p.a. Thus, if plantation production were exclusively available for industrial wood products, the additional capacity would appear ample to meet the increase in requirements to the year 2000. There are, however, many regions where the investment in plantations is at a much lower rate than that needed to meet demand for industrial timber, and there are others where the intense demand for wood for domestic energy will compete for the available wood raw material and restrict the supply to industrial production.

Several countries, including Brazil and the Congo, have developed plantations with very high yields benefiting from modern genetics. Thus certain Eucalyptus plantations in Brazil are achieving yields exceeding 40 m³ per ha per annum—double that of the unimproved varieties. The spread of fast-growing species such as, for example, Eucalyptus, Leucaena and Gmelina, makes the prospect of new afforestation much more favourable.

## Investment and finance for forestry development

World gross total investment in forestry and forest industry in the period 1970–84 was around $400 billion (1980 prices), about $28 billion annually. Developing countries invested about one-third of this total, $130 billion, and half of this was in China, $60 billion. Tropical developing countries invested a total of $70 billion, the bulk of which was in industry, and only $15 billion in forest resources.

The projected expansion of industrial production indicates gross world investment of $475 billion between 1984 and 2000 (Table 5.7). Projections of supply for 1984–2000 suggest additions to production capacity in developing countries of 68 million m³ for sawnwood, 26 million m³ for wood-based panels, and 24 million tonnes for paper. This is estimated to require gross investment of around $150 billion, or $10 billion p.a. (1980 prices). Should the alternative of maintaining higher levels of self-sufficiency in developing countries be achieved (alternative B, Table 5.5), the industry investment in developing countries would need to be increased by another $20 billion.

The investment equivalent to build up forest resources in developing countries in line with expected demands would be of the order of US$145 billion over 15 years, or about $9.5 billion p.a. Domestic and external financing needs in this annual total are estimated to be between $3.5 and $4.5 billion.

Table 5.7 Cumulative gross investment in forestry and forest industries ($ billion in 1980 prices)

| | 1970–84 | | 1985–2000 | |
|---|---|---|---|---|
| | Forestry | Industry | Forestry | Industry |
| Developing countries | 60 | 69 | 145 | 150 |
| Africa | 2 | 4 | 30 | 5 |
| Latin America | 7 | 25 | 20 | 55 |
| Asia | 51 | 40 | 95 | 90 |
| (of which China) | (45) | (15) | (45) | (40) |
| Developed countries | 125 | 145 | 125 | 325 |
| World | 185 | 214 | 270 | 475 |

The remainder of the annual investment estimate not covered by such financing ($5 billion to $6 billion) represents the value at market prices of farmer work in forest resource development. The benefit of this forestry investment may, for example, be assessed in terms of the cost of alternative energy supplies. The annual cost of meeting the fuelwood deficit with imported fuels involving about 90 million tonnes of oil equivalent would be of the order of $20 billion at prices prevailing up to 1985, or $10 billion at prices current at the end of 1986.

Most of the required finance for investment is generated within national economies. In many countries the rate of investment is by no means sufficient. External assistance directed to the forestry sector has aimed to build up the rate of investment. International aid to forestry is a very recent phenomenon and has grown rapidly over the past few years. In the early 1980s the total assistance from external sources amounted to some $460 million annually. The international community has come together to promote greatly increased investment in the sector through the FAO's Tropical Forestry Action Plan. This plan identifies essential programmes of technical assistance amounting to $160 million p.a., but recognizes the vastly greater investment requirements.

Effective mobilization of resources for this considerable expansion of investment represents a major issue in the forestry sector. It will require appropriate policies, development of a legal framework and of institutions and, above all, the growth of people's involvement and commitment to the plans and action programmes for forestry and forest industries, their products and services to the community.

# 6 Fisheries

## World fisheries in the mid-1980s

Fishing, like other hunting activities of men, has been a major source of food for mankind from the beginning. Today, although fisheries may be only a small section of the economy in most countries, in many parts of the world it continues to contribute significantly to supplies of food, to the employment of people in coastal, riverine and lake-side areas and to foreign-exchange earnings. Fish accounts for approximately one-fifth of the world's total supplies of animal protein. It is, moreover, a highly nutritious food and an ideal supplement to the cereal or tuber-based diets typically consumed in many parts of the developing world.

Despite these important nutritional, economic and social contributions by the fisheries sector, its full potential was long neglected by many governments and, as an industry or socio-economic activity, often given low priority in overall national development plans. However, the successive United Nations Conference on the Law of the Sea, which resulted in 1982 in the adoption of a new Convention on the ownership and use of marine resources, focused the attention of governments of both developed and developing countries upon the potentials of the resources off their shores.

Through extended national jurisdiction there is now an opportunity for coastal states to take greater advantage of their resources and to increase the contribution they make to national economic, social and nutritional objectives. At the same time renewed attention has been drawn to the roles of inland water fisheries and aquaculture both as food suppliers and within the overall context of rural development.

These new opportunities, and the considerable challenges they present, have called for a reappraisal of national policies for fisheries management and development.

### Fish production

World fish production in 1985 totalled some 85 million tonnes, an increase of 2.2 percent above that of the preceding year. This, following an increase of almost 7.5 percent in 1984, represents the eighth consecutive year of growth in terms of physical output.

These increases result, almost entirely, from increases in catches of shoaling pelagics, which are notoriously subject to fluctuations in abundance. The recent (1984–5) surge in production is attributable to increased catches in the south-east Pacific (west coast of South America). Elsewhere, for the most part, production has been either relatively stable or marginal increases in some areas have been offset by marginal declines in others.

The explosive growth in world fish production during the two decades after 1950 ceased in the early 1970s (Table 6.1). Underlying the early expansion in fish production was the growth in the world economy, restricted largely to the developed countries in the 1950s but extending to developing countries in the 1960s and 1970s, based mainly on increased income levels and, consequently, on expansion of demand for food products of the fisheries. Concomitantly, an increase in the demand for fish meal (and thus for shoaling pelagics) stemmed from a shift to intensive raising of livestock in North America and Western Europe, which entailed feeding with nutritionally balanced rations.

**Table 6.1** World fish production, by origin, 1950–85 (million tonnes)

| Year | Marine | Freshwater | Total |
|---|---|---|---|
| 1950 | 17.6 | 3.2 | 20.8 |
| 1960 | 32.8 | 6.6 | 39.4 |
| 1970 | 59.5 | 6.1 | 65.6 |
| 1975 | 59.2 | 7.2 | 66.4 |
| 1980 | 64.5 | 7.6 | 72.1 |
| 1985 | 74.8 | 10.1 | 84.9 |

Expansion of the world's fish harvest, in response to the growth in demand, was assisted by two technological innovations of this period, namely the introduction of synthetic fibres in the manufacture of nets and the introduction of freezing at sea. These innovations, in association respectively with mechanical net hauling and stern trawling (both introduced more or less simultaneously) as well as electronic aids, permitted widespread use of large nets and a dramatic increase in the size, versatility and operational range of fishing craft. Purse seining had an important role in the development of the pelagic fisheries of Northern Europe, of the South American anchoveta fishery and of some tuna fisheries, while freezing at sea facilitated the maintenance of Japan's foremost position in the commercial fisheries and the spectacular expansion of the distant-water fisheries of Eastern European countries in the 1960s and 1970s.

Information on investment in the fisheries of the world is quite fragmentary. There is some evidence however, that it has been increasing (at a greater rate, probably, than the harvest) throughout the developed and developing worlds. FAO surveys of external aid to the fisheries sector of developing countries indicate a growth of about 100 percent, in real terms, between 1974 and 1984; the evidence available for 1985 and 1986 suggests, however, a recent decline in such aid. The earlier increase in the flow of aid was almost entirely due to the growth of capital aid, as opposed to technical assistance.

## Utilization of the catch

Since 1970, the total increase in world catches, about 20 million tonnes, has been used for direct human consumption. The reduction of fish for meal and oil, which reached a peak of 40 percent of total catches in 1970, has declined to about 30 percent (Table 6.2). Over the period 1950 to 1985, the proportion frozen increased from about 10 percent to almost 25 percent and the proportion canned from 10 percent to somewhat less than 15 percent. These changes took place mostly in the early part of the period; there has been little change during the last ten years. The proportion of production cured has remained relatively constant at 15 percent.

Table 6.2 World fish production, by end-use, 1950–85 (million tonnes)

| Year | Food | Feed | Total |
|---|---|---|---|
| 1950 | 17.8 | 3.0 | 20.8 |
| 1955 | 23.9 | 4.6 | 28.5 |
| 1960 | 30.8 | 8.6 | 39.4 |
| 1965 | 36.3 | 16.3 | 52.6 |
| 1970 | 39.1 | 26.5 | 65.6 |
| 1975 | 46.0 | 20.4 | 66.4 |
| 1980 | 52.9 | 19.2 | 72.1 |
| 1985 | 59.6 | 25.3 | 84.9 |

## Fish trade

Expansion of the international trade in fish products has paralleled the growth in world production over the past 25 years, the quantity traded having grown from 4.5 million tonnes in 1960 to 12.5 million tonnes in 1985. Converted from product weight to live weight, the latter figure represents approximately one-third of total catch; this ratio has been quite stable throughout the period. The value of fish trade increased steadily from $1300 million in 1960 to $16 900 million in 1985, a threefold increase in real terms.

As currently structured, three trade flows may be distinguished, namely (a) from developing to developed countries (consisting in the main of relatively high-valued products), (b) from developed to developing countries (chiefly low-valued products) and (c) between developed countries. Trade in fish products among developing countries is on a minor scale. Three-quarters of all imports in value terms are divided about equally among Japan, the USA and the EEC (about one-third in the last case being supplied by intra-community trade). Japan's share of the global fish trade is growing, that of the EEC has declined, although it showed an increase in 1985, and that of the USA remains stable.

The fish trade is characterized by extreme heterogeneity of product form and by market specialization. Generalization as to trends and developments therefore tends to be subject to qualification and uncertainty. The trade composition has shifted substantially since 1960. In terms of value (to the nearest 5 percent), the share of fresh and frozen finfish products has increased from 25 percent to 35 percent of the total and that of fresh and frozen crustacean products from 15 percent to 35 percent, while the share of canned fishery products has dropped from 25 percent to 15 percent and that of cured fishery products from 15 percent to 5 percent.

In recent years, developing countries have become net exporters of fishery products, accounting for almost 45 percent of total exports in 1985 as compared with about one-third ten years earlier. Over the same period, their surplus in foreign-exchange earnings from the fish trade increased from $1800 million to $5000 million.

A further phenomenon of the past decade is the upward trend of fish prices in real terms, that is at a faster rate than prices in general: by an average of 6.5 percent annually in Japan, for example, and similar rates are observable elsewhere in both developed and developing countries. This trend reflects contraction of overall supply, in that of preferred species in particular, in relation to rising demand. It has provided the basis in recent years for growth in aquaculture production of certain freshwater and marine (anadromous and demersal) finfish as well as crustaceans and molluscs.

The rising trend in the real price of fish products is in fact one of the two most significant developments in the fisheries during the later years of the period under review, the other being the adoption of the United Nations Convention on the Law of the Sea and the concomitant extension of national jurisdiction by coastal states over fisheries within, typically, seaward zones of 200 miles.

## Exclusive Economic Zones (EEZs) and trade

Prior to the extensions of national jurisdiction, the total value of the fishing harvest by distant-water fleets operating off the shores of other countries approximated $7300 million (1978 prices). Excluding oceanic pelagics, however, two-thirds of this harvest was taken off the coasts of developed countries and most of the remaining third off north-west Africa, leaving little more than 5 percent off developing countries elsewhere. Besides gaining twice the amount of fishery resources, the developed countries possessed an industrial organization and infrastructure that enabled them readily to expand their harvest, and trade in the products, of those resources.

For the distant-water fishing countries, the effects of establishing Exclusive Economic Zones (EEZ) included the need for (a) a reduction in fleet size and a rationalization of craft mix and deployment, (b) a search for alternative resources and fishing grounds on the high seas and within EEZs and (c) negotiation of fishing agreements with coastal states. The result for some of these countries is a reduction in harvests and/or a switch to the harvesting of lower-value species.

The impact of coastal state extensions of jurisdiction in the later 1970s, which was expected to bring about a major realignment of the international fish trade, has been masked by the 30 percent increase in overall production during the subsequent period. It had been expected that countries previously having large foreign fleets operating off their coasts would benefit most from the establishment of EEZs, the areas identified being the north-east Pacific and north-west Atlantic (for developed counties) and the south-west, east central and south-east Atlantic (for developing countries). Some of the countries involved have increased their exports. Several countries which have lost access to fishing grounds have also increased their exports.

## Prospects to the end of the century

### Demand

The demand for fish products in the aggregate depends on three factors, namely population, income and price, the latter incorporating a number of factors such as consumer preferences. Of these, population is the most important since, with stable prices, it normally accounts for about two-thirds of change in total demand (see, however, Box 3.1).

World population is expected to continue increasing, at a declining rate, through the year 2000, when it is estimated it will reach 6100 million. At 1980 levels of consumption (50 million tonnes), and assuming no change in relative prices of fish to other food products, that number of people would require an additional 20 million tonnes of fish, that is a total of about 70 million tonnes simply to maintain present levels of consumption. It should be noted, however, that consumption has already increased by about 7 million tonnes in the period between 1980 and 1985 (Table 6.2). Added to this direct demand for fish as a food, there is likely to be a requirement for at least 20 million tonnes for reduction to fish meal, bringing the total requirement to 90 million tonnes.

In this respect, account has to be taken of the divergent growth trends in various regions. The developing countries already contain almost 75 percent of the world's population and, by the year 2000, this will have increased to 78 percent. It is in these countries that the impact of population growth on the demand for fish is the greatest. In Asia, for example, where there are a number of countries in which fish represents half or more of animal protein supplies, an extra 5 million tonnes per year would be required by the end of the century to maintain present levels of consumption. Fish also is important in the African diet, especially in the western half of the continent.

Projections of income change, being subject to special uncertainty, are more hazardous than are those of demographic trends. The effect of the relatively modest increases in incomes projected to year 2000 (Table 3.2) would be to raise per caput consumption by 1 kg. in each decade in the developing countries and by slightly more in the developed ones. As a result, total world demand for fish as food would be raised by a further 10 million tonnes, that is over and above what would be required to maintain constant per caput consumption in the face of increasing population. This would imply, assuming no change in the use of fish for fish meal, a prospective total demand for fish by the year 2000 exceeding 100 million tonnes, on the basis of stable relative prices.

## Supply

The slow-down in the growth of fish production after 1970 reflects the encounter, at that time, of fishing industries around the world with a resource barrier to further rapid expansion. Although, with the surge in 1984–5, annual production overall has increased by 30 percent since 1970, it appears unlikely that this can be sustained in the long run.

Almost all important stocks of demersal species are either fully exploited or overfished. Many of the stocks of more highly valued species are depleted. Reef stocks and those of estuarine/littoral zones are under special threat, from illegal fishing and environmental pollution. Year-class (recruitment) variations may have a marked effect on catches, and there is evidence that some species may be subject to long-run changes in abundance due to climatological or other factors.

There is little prospect, therefore, of increasing the catch of demersal species. It is necessary to distinguish between landings and catch, however, since quantities of these species are taken, for example in shrimping operations, and then discarded, and this is likely to continue until incentives are provided to encourage the landing and marketing of these fish. Scattered stocks of unexploited species exist, but in general the cost of harvesting them would not be justified at present by the revenue obtainable from the derived products.

There seems to be a better possibility of increasing the harvest of small shoaling pelagic species. Stocks of such species are subject to periods of high and low abundance, extending over decades. Prediction of potential availability is complicated further by evidence that when the abundance of one species is low other species may increase. Additional harvesting may be feasible, however, by more intensive exploitation in some areas and improved fishery management (i.e. regulation of fishing effort) in others.

Crustacean species generally are heavily exploited and many, if not most, stocks are depleted. Some local increase in catches may be expected, for example from stocks of the smaller crabs. Most stocks of shrimp in potentially productive areas already are being exploited and no major increase in the harvest from capture fisheries can be foreseen. These fisheries generally have reached a stage of uneconomic overfishing.

Very few untapped marine resources of conventional (i.e. familiar, well-accepted) species remain anywhere. Resources of the slope in tropical seas tend to be sparse and the cost of their exploitation relatively high. Squids and other cephalopods are lightly exploited in some parts of the world but are regarded as conventional foods in only a few countries. The harvest of common squid has been increasing, as a result of better targeting and (possibly) of depletion of predator species stocks.

Freshwater fisheries provide some 10 percent of the world production of aquatic organisms and, since the total harvest is used for human consumption and includes highly valued species, the contribution to the value of production is probably even higher. Production from these waters is capable of some increase, particularly from flood-plain fisheries in Latin America and Africa. These fisheries, however, are vulnerable to natural phenomena such as drought and to interference for purposes of irrigation, power generation and other interventions which almost inevitably reduce their productivity. The loss is seldom offset by increases in production from the reservoirs provided.

The production of marine and freshwater aquaculture (finfish, crustacea and molluscs) is presently about 5.5 million tonnes. Finfish production represents 65 percent of this total with about 50 percent produced in China. In addition, 2.7 million tonnes of seaweeds and aquatic plants are cultivated.

Among unconventional marine resources, those that might support fisheries in the future include mesopelagic species and krill. The latter already supports a fishery, but there are economic constraints to the development of mass production and marketing. Mesopelagic species are widely distributed throughout the oceans and are found locally in considerable abundance. For the foreseeable future, because of the nature and size of these fish, they would have to be used for fish-meal production and, at present, incentives for commercial investment for this purpose are lacking.

## Demand/supply implications

As already noted, the total demand for fish by the year 2000, assuming no changes in relative prices or in the use of fish for fish meal, might well exceed 100 million tonnes.

An increase in supply of that magnitude based on potential catches of more or less conventional species, is theoretically feasible (Table 6.3). It is stressed, however, that only a part of such an increase would be realized through more extensive or intensive fishing effort and that may have already been largely achieved. About a half of the projected increase in supply could be obtained only through better fishery management and more efficient utilization of resources.

The rough estimates of potential increased production provided in Table 6.3 are subject to considerable uncertainty, and there are substantial gaps in the data. It is significant, however, that in a number of instances present catches of demersal species are in excess of, or close to, estimates of potential yield. Prediction of potential availability of shoaling small pelagic species is

**Table 6.3** Fish for food: projected demand and supply (million tonnes)

| Increase in demand 1980–2000 | | Estimated potential for increased production (1985) | |
|---|---|---|---|
| Location | Quantity | Category | Quantity |
| Developing countries | +22.5 | Demersal | 1–8 |
| Developed countries | + 5.9 | Shoaling pelagic | 3–10 |
| Total | +28.4 | Other marine | 4–6 |
| | | Freshwater and aquaculture | 5–10 |
| | | Total | 13–34 |

especially complicated because such species are subject to long periods of high and low abundance. It would seem possible, however, that the potential for increased production lies within the ranges indicated in the table.

The already notable rise in the price for preferred species, and modern marketing methods, may bring about a shift to other species, but the process would probably take some time. For decades, the world fisheries scene has been characterized by strong demand for expensive products of fully-exploited species while abundant, low-priced fish of high quality have been difficult to market. The latter description fits most of the shoaling pelagic species, some two-thirds of the world catch of which is used at present for the production of fishmeal. This is the group of species, however, that, in spite of their unreliability, has the largest potential for increase harvesting.

In theory, the principal incentive for a shift in demand from one species to another would be provided by a rise in the price of the species in inelastic (fully exploited) supply, and there is some evidence that what is predictable in theory is being borne out in practice: certain so called 'trash fish' species are becoming marketable. More significant is the evidence from a number of countries not only of a sharp increase in the price of 'luxury' species but of fish in general, that is in the price of fish as compared with the prices of meat and other forms of animal protein, and the trend is not confined to countries of high income.

## Major implications and issues

### Fishery management

The above outlook for the world's fisheries raises issues of policy for politicians, administrators, entrepreneurs and other decision-makers concerned with the fisheries sector. The 1950s and 1960s, in most parts of the world, were a period of rapid growth, brought about by fleet expansion and the use of innovative technologies. As fish stocks became fully exploited and then overfished, however, there emerged an interest in problems of fishery management, although not yet a generalized conviction that action in this field was widely necessary.

By the 1970s, there were few major stocks left to which fishing effort could be transferred, and in the middle years of the decade, increased fuel costs rendered many fishery ventures unprofitable, temporarily or permanently. More recently, rising prices for fish in real terms has compensated, at least partially, for cost increase. If this process were to continue, however, as seems probable, the task of fishery-management authorities might be made more difficult to accomplish, as price increases attract more fishing effort despite declining yields.

With the establishment of EEZs, some problems of fishery management have been simplified; others, for example those relating to stocks occurring in two or more adjacent national zones, may have been exacerbated. Moreover, coastal State jurisdiction does not of itself ensure effective management of fisheries, even of those based on stocks found exclusively within a national zone. The difficulties and, especially, costs of establishing systems for the monitoring, control and surveillance of fishing operations to ensure compliance to regulatory schemes, also raise serious problems. Administrators, as well as political leaders (with whom the ultimate decisions rest) and donors often prefer an expansionist policy; the benefits of such a policy being perceived as immediate and tangible whereas those of good management often are long-term and hypothetical. As in the past, pressures of this kind may continue to frustrate a rational approach to fishery management.

Management must be concerned with the overall economic performance of the fisheries. To this end, government intervention in fisheries must also include measures that reduce fishing costs, improve revenues and satisfy social objectives. For example, the use of fossil fuels in fishing can represent 90 percent of the cost of production, and measures can be taken to lower these costs. Many existing fishing vessels were built during the era of low-cost fuel and now require modification to be fuel-efficient, such as fitting with nozzles and compatible propellers, which can result in a 15 percent fuel saving. Considerable efforts have been put into producing fuel-saving engines by manufacturers, but re-engining with more fuel-efficient machines would not be sufficient by itself, particularly in fisheries where over-powering has been the trend. In such cases administrations will have to set upper limits for installed horsepower if cost reductions on fuel are to be obtained. In the same way, considerable savings can be achieved by reducing the search time required for finding productive shoals of fish. The use of fish aggregating devices, spotter aircraft and satellite-generated imagery are in use today and can be expected to have a wider application by the end of the century. Other areas for consideration by governments are the targeting of fisheries on species for which prices are significantly higher, namely the management of the Australian northern prawn fishery and the Saudi Arabian prawn fishery.

Social considerations often require conscious allocation of limited fish resources to particular groups of fishermen, a policy which is most commonly achieved by legislating protected areas for use by specified fishing gears or fishermen. In addition, a number of countries regulate gear either by length of net or head-rope, as a means of equalizing the fishing opportunity of fishermen. It is particularly important to protect and enhance small-scale or artisanal fisheries, which produce over 20 million tonnes of fish a year, almost all of which is used for direct human consumption. These fisheries are characterized by high labour involvement (some 10 million small-scale and some 5 million part-time fishermen), low capital investment, low levels of mechanization and often the use of passive fishing methods.

In addition, environmental degradation will become increasingly a serious problem in maintaining important fishery resources in coastal waters. More effort will be required to adopt measures to enhance productivity, such as stricter monitoring and prevention of environmental degradation and pollution, protection of nursery grounds and juvenile fish, stocking of appropriate species in suitable areas and strategic placement of artificial reefs.

## Aquaculture

It has been evident for several years that the upward trend of prices has especially important implications for the development of aquaculture. Output from this source, which at present accounts for about 10 percent of total fishery production, may increase at an average annual rate of 5.5 percent and thus be doubled by the end of the century. It should be noted, however, that the distribution of production among the four main species groups (finfish, crustaceans, molluscs and seaweeds) and the five geographic regions (Asia, North America, South America, Europe/Near East and Africa) probably would change significantly.

The farming of shrimps and prawns, given the capital-intensity required, is not expected to contribute significantly to global production. The intensive rearing of shrimp has not been commercially justifiable to date. Production increases over the next decade may be achieved through expansion of extensive culture (currently a fast-growing industry), which, however, requires substantial areas of land. In any event, aquacultural production of shrimp, although important, is likely to remain a minor component of total production by the end of the century.

Any greater contribution to the expansion of overall aquacultural production may come from the culture of finfish species. Major gains in quantity may be obtained from culture-based fisheries, that is extensive aquaculture systems, fishery enhancement in reservoirs, lakes and even the open seas. Semi-intensive and intensive systems in land-based and coastal farms are becoming attractive. For example, US production of finfish from aquaculture increased more than twofold from 1980 to 1984, while salmon culture in cages is increasing in a similarly dramatic way in Canada, Norway and the UK.

In almost all countries with a favourable natural environment for aquaculture, the initial requirement is for organization, that is an agency (governmental, parastatal or private) to convince enterpreneurs (farms, etc.) of the benefits of aquacultural enterprises, to organize the supply of inputs (particularly seed fish) and to assist with the marketing of products. When the commercial feasibility of a technology is demonstrated, the main requirement is for an extension service which, in most countries, implies a need for training.

Encouragement of small farmers/aquaculturists, if successful, could make a significant nutritional impact in the rural areas of low-income countries. The development of commercial aquaculture, on the other hand, is likely to be largely involved with luxury species or those that fetch a price sufficiently high to permit recovery of the not inconsiderable cost of inputs.

Much of the application of technology is likely to be undertaken by large firms with the financial resources to support innovative product introduction, but there will continue to be a need for research by universities and State agencies to advance technology, for example extension to new species, disease control and so on, and to supply technologists for the staff of commercial enterprises.

## Improved utilization

Improvements in utilization practices could make a significant contribution to increasing the supply of fish to meet the demand anticipated in the year 2000. Three main areas merit priority attention: rescuing discards from trawling operations, reduction in post-harvest losses, and better utilization of small-pelagics species.

An estimated quantity of between 5 million and 16 million tonnes of fish per year is caught and discarded at sea by trawlers, especially those engaged in shrimping. Perhaps between 20 and 70 percent represents marketable species and sizes, depending on the fishing area. Ensuring that discards are landed for human consumption is essentially an economic and logistical problem; where increased demand opens up a market for previously unacceptable species, the problem largely disappears. Some governments have taken the step of linking joint-venture licensing to participation in schemes to land discards as a contribution to national food supplies.

It is difficult to estimate the post-harvest losses which result from lack of facilities to preserve fish or from lack of technical knowledge; however, they probably amount to about 10 percent of food fish supplies. To reduce these losses will require investment in better infrastructure for landing, storage and distribution and trained staff to operate it.

The third area—better utilization of small pelagic species—has a greater potential but is perhaps more speculative. As noted previously, only about one-third of world catches of these species is used for direct human consumption, the balance going to fishmeal and fish oil. In addition, there is a further unexploited potential of up to 10 million tonnes. These species can be made into a wide range of highly acceptable products, including frozen, canned, smoked, salted and dried. Economies of scale are necessary to reduce production costs, but requirements for full exploitation will include technological research, consumer promotion and investment in facilities. There is a possibility for spectacular changes as these species contain the highest concentrations of the n-3 marine lipids which have been shown to be effective in preventing coronary heart disease. As an example, the perceived health benefits of fish are expected to double per caput consumption in the USA.

Two possible scenarios for the future of small pelagic fish utilization emerge depending on whether consumers prefer to take their fish oil in capsules or in the natural state, as part of the fish. The former route will encourage the use of fish for industrial purposes, with high oil prices perhaps making fish meal a by-product of the meal and oil industry. The alternative, direct consumption of fish will require investment in handling and processing facilities. Although this will result in increased availability, the prices must necessarily be sufficient to cover the increased production costs.

These trends will also have an impact on fishmeal production and prices. In the absence of other factors, demand for fishmeal in animal feed declines as many other protein sources (e.g. soyabeans) become increasingly competitive. However, the possibility of an increased demand from aquaculture, either as meal or as industrial species in wet feed, will probably balance out any decrease in animal feed requirements. In the light of these uncertainties, it would probably be realistic to assume that fishmeal and fish oil production will continue to represent about 25 percent of world catches.

## Conclusions

The projected increase in demand for direct human consumption of an additional 30 million tonnes by the year 2000 might therefore be satisfied by better fisheries management (10 million tonnes), possible increases from aquaculture (about 5 million to 10 million tonnes), and improved utilization of resources (15 million to 20 million tonnes). Delays in improving management and therefore alleviating supply constraints can be expected to increase prices, which in turn will improve the viability of aquacultural production but, at the same time, constrain overall demand.

For capture fisheries, with the natural resources under mounting pressure, the need for management is becoming acute if production is to be maintained, let alone enhanced, to the year 2000. Without management, fisheries development becomes increasingly difficult to sustain. Indeed, once fishery resources become fully exploited, catches fall and the potential wealth of an over-exploited fishery is dissipated in higher than necessary costs. In resolving this issue both technical assistance and capital investment under concessionary terms have important roles.

Within the context of technical assistance in support of fisheries management, a need of many developing countries is for a greater support of research on tropical fisheries, including the improvement of statistical services.

Governments and donors will also have to give further consideration to ways in which capital aid may be directed towards alleviation of the problems of conflicts between types of fisheries, overcapacity and dissipation of economic rents so as to create a more orderly and sustainable industry. Governments without access to funds for compensating fishermen for losses incurred from management measures will not be able to achieve significant changes in the conduct of fishing. In the inshore areas of most tropical fisheries, the closure or restriction of a fishery has extreme economic implications on the livelihood of artisanal fishermen. More attention is required to the matching of fishing effort to the sustainable yield from the resources, whereby direct control over fishing effort can relieve fishing pressure, improve incomes to fishermen as well as providing them with important collateral for credit acquisition.

Just as the extension of fisheries jurisdictions to 200 miles placed under national control fisheries that were previously under free and open access, national fisheries will also require division into areas for exclusive use by specified fishing gears or fishermen if conflicts are to be avoided and the consequences of 'open' access overcome. The enforcement of these areas will require a greater physical presence 'at sea'; indeed, the concept of fisheries protection vessels should be viewed from the same perspective as that of fences for agricultural lands.

While the production levels from capture fisheries can be improved through management, the costs of production also can be reduced by immediate attention to energy-saving methods directed at engine-efficiency horsepower limits, and reductions in search time for productive shoals of fish. Particular attention is required to improving the living standards of small-scale fishermen in recognition of their important contribution to sustained supplies of fish for direct human consumption.

Without sufficient government infrastructures to undertake fisheries management, the fisheries sector will fail to reach its potential. In the past, many governments have not given sufficient priority to improving the capability of their fishery institutions to enable them to undertake the complex tasks of fisheries management.

The development of aquaculture will require long-term government assistance for the promotion of adaptive technologies, marketing programmes and credit services. The future growth of the aquaculture industry and its successful establishment as a viable enterprise throughout the world depend principally on the effective application of financial assistance and private investment, rather than on other factors such as advances in technology.

A significant contribution to increased supplies could also result from making better use of what is already caught. Ensuring that the present discards from trawl fisheries are landed for human consumption, investing in facilities to reduce post-harvest losses and better utilizing the small pelagic species as food could all have an important impact.

The challenges created by these prospective demand and supply scenarios and the various issues involved in meeting them were the subjects of international consideration at the FAO World Conference on Fisheries Management and Development convened in 1984 to confront the realities of adjusting to the new regime of the oceans and of ensuring a better future for the fisherman and his family.

To this end, the World Fisheries Conference adopted by consensus a Strategy which embodies principles and guidelines on the best courses for the future management and development of fisheries (FAO 1984). It also approved five associated Programmes of Action for implementation by FAO, in collaboration with donor agencies and other concerned international and national organizations, to enhance the capabilities of developing countries as they seek to promote the sustained development and rational management of their fish resources.

# 7 Issues of international trade and adjustment

## Recent developments in world agricultural trade and current issues

In many respects, the state of international agricultural trade, and the conditions which govern it, have deteriorated, in some cases markedly, since the beginning of the decade. Prospects to the end of the century for international trade growth for most agricultural commodities, have also worsened compared with the previous, already discouraging, assessment (FAO 1981). Three major sets of factors, all of them interrelated, are at the heart of this situation. One is the slow growth, and even decline in recent years, of import demand, stemming partly from the effects of slow economic growth, debt-servicing problems, the decline in petroleum prices and, on the positive side, stronger growth in agricultural production in some developing countries. The second set of factors comprises continuing rapid technological advances which in some ways have been allowed to frustrate the orderly growth of international trade. The third set of factors comprises the national agricultural policies which, in many surplus producing countries have, by and large, so far failed to adjust sufficiently so as to provide appropriate signals to producers in the face of substantial changes in market requirements. In many developing countries, structural adjustments have been made, aiming to stimulate production and reduce imports. Policies have thus contributed to the depressed conditions on world markets in recent years.

Naturally, the part of the slow-down in world agricultural trade which reflected genuine cost-efficient gains in the self-sufficiency of some developing countries, rather than slow-down in their consumption, is a positive development.

By 1985 the volume of world agricultural trade was only 8 percent more than in 1980, compared with growth of over 30 percent in the preceding five-year period. The slow-down predominantly reflects a drastic curtailment of the growth of import demand: supplies have been ample, international market prices have generally collapsed and surplus stocks of many products have risen to very high levels, including not only cereals but also dairy products, sugar, cotton, coffee and natural rubber to name the main ones. While the slow-down in growth of import demand partly reflects macro-economic factors, such as slower general economic growth in many countries and debt-servicing problems in nearly half the developing countries, requiring them to give first priority to the servicing of foreign debts in allocating such earnings rather than to imports of food and other products, a number of other factors have also contributed to that situation.

In particular, demand in high-income countries for the traditional agricultural export commodities of developing countries has been approaching saturation levels; some of the new 'epi-centres' of import demand for food commodities in the 1970s, such as the petroleum-exporting developing countries and the USSR, have become less buoyant markets; and a number of countries, both developed and developing, have given increased emphasis to raising their degrees of self-sufficiency. As analysed in Chapter 3, Western Europe, and the EEC in particular, has switched in the past decade from being a significant importer to being a large exporter of major commodities in world agricultural trade, including cereals, meats and sugar. The region has also accumulated large stocks, particularly of cereals and dairy products which could not find markets on normal commercial terms. Globally, carryover stocks of cereals have mounted, notably in North America, to the equivalent of 27 percent of world annual consumption, against a figure of 18 percent estimated by FAO as adequate to meet world food security needs. This implies that up to 150 million tonnes of cereals were surplus to market requirements by 1987.

There is a long history of concerns about the underlying tendency towards 'surpluses' in developed countries, testifying to the difficulties which confront policy-makers in adapting supplies to match market requirements (see for example FAO 1972). Indeed, in industrialized countries as a whole, self-sufficiency ratios for most basic foods have shown a secular tendency to increase, notably in the case of cereals and sugar, but also for meat and meat products and dairy products. In part, this tendency reflects the rapid technological advances which have led to significant increases in the potential yields of both crops and livestock and to large increases in actual yields, stimulated in many cases by price policies which have favoured expansion of output.

Moreover, price policies which have acted as incentives to production have also provided an umbrella which has, over time, made artificially profitable the research, development and production of substitutes for commodities which in the 1980s have been in any event in surplus at global level. The development of alternative sweeteners to sugar in some developed country markets is one major example. The related penetration of corn gluten meal into some markets for feed concentrates thus, in combination with other feed ingredients, displacing grains, is another example. Technological advances and their application are not by themselves called into question; indeed, they are the essence of the productivity improvements which are needed to enable mankind to raise living standards. What are called into question are the national agricultural policies which facilitate such developments at the expense of competitive agricultural industries, and incomes and employment, in other parts of the world, again by providing grossly distorted signals (sometimes far above and sometimes far below long-term equilibrium levels) regarding prices to domestic producers.

This brings us to the third of the major factors which accounts, in large measure, for the present disarray in world agricultural commodity markets. By extrapolation, a continuation of present policies points to the perpetuation of severe problems in several such markets, implying more radical policy adjustments than have so far occurred. In particular, as Chapter 3 pointed out, long-standing structural-adjustment problems seem likely to confront policy-makers in the dairy sector. Grain policies also require serious adjustment or, it would appear, the world cereal economy will also show continuing structural surpluses in developed countries, despite increasing import needs of developing countries as a whole. A range of other commodities of export interest to both developed and developing countries will yield, at best, only moderate world market growth in the future; and the growth of markets for tropical products and agricultural raw materials will similarly be constrained if current policies persist. In short, world agriculture in the mid-1980s was producing more than could be absorbed even at extremely low international prices, in spite of measures to curb production growth in a number of developed countries. The potential to produce exceeds actual production and is likely to continue to do so towards the year 2000, according to the projections. There are therefore two overall choices: stimulate demand or curb production growth. Until demand growth exceeds production growth, and excess supplies are reduced, the developed countries should work together and share the cost of holding production below potential.

In this connection, major asymmetries exist among countries in the levels and types of protection afforded to their agricultural sectors. Although precise quantification of levels of protection is beset with well-known measurement difficulties, broad conclusions can be established from the large amount of research completed or underway in this area.

Among developing countries, with some notable exceptions in certain commodity sectors, very low and even negative protection of agricultural producers is typical, particularly on export commodities. Hence, in general agriculture in developing countries is taxed, in both absolute terms and in relation to domestic manufacturing sectors. In particular, export taxes, especially indirect ones, form a major instrument of agricultural policy, although in recent years many developing countries have reduced or eliminated such taxation in order to increase export earnings and maintain positive balances on trade accounts or to remain competitive in the face of sharply lower prices on world markets. Currency devaluation and, when necessary, controls have slowed or reduced growth in their imports.

In contrast, industrialized countries, again with some exceptions, have adopted measures designed to curb production growth but have tended to maintain relatively high price or producer-income supports, thus generally leading to higher production than would otherwise occur. Moreover, the response of major industrialized countries to depressed conditions in agricultural export markets has been to grant export subsidies and other aids to exporters, which has reduced their export earnings appreciably. On average in the early 1980s domestic producer prices in OECD countries exceeded world market prices by about 40 percent; budgetary expenditures, principally on price supports, storage subsidies and export aids, but also to withhold land from production in some cases, have increased massively; and although the total return to producers has declined, in some cases sharply, costs to taxpayers, as a consequence of both direct and indirect elements of protection, have reached huge levels. According to recent estimates of the OECD (OECD 1987), such transfers in 1979/81 averaged 32 percent of the gross domestic value of production of all major commodities in member countries as a group. Among individual countries, these producer subsidy equivalents were estimated at 16 percent of the value of production in the USA, 23.9 percent in

Canada, 42.8 percent in the EEC and Austria and 59.4 percent in the case of Japan, but only 4.7 percent in Australia. In some of these countries domestic consumers have benefited from price declines, but in general both foreign buyers and domestic non-agricultural sectors have been the main beneficiaries.

In global terms, the broad result of policy interventions in agriculture has been that too little is produced in developing countries and too much in developed countries. In this situation a particular responsibility rests on the shoulders of policy-makers in developed countries to unwind the major distortions of agricultural trade which have resulted from the pursuit of policies which encourage excessive production. Key issues, however, concern the ways in which the necessary adjustments could and should be effected.

## Adjustment policies and scope for further action

In recent years, a number of governments of industrialized countries have taken steps to stem the growth of structural surpluses. These steps were taken in response to rising government expenditure and were thus oriented toward those commodities in most serious surplus, notably dairy products and cereals which are also projected to remain in surplus if production trends are not checked. Typically, the primary objective was not to constrain a country's exports but rather to control surpluses and limit the government's support expenditures.

Dairying is one of the most protected agricultural sub-sectors and is in costly surplus in many industrialized countries. As a result, many governments have implemented quota systems which in effect limit the amount of milk receiving full government price support. Among these countries are Austria, the EEC, Finland, Norway, Sweden and Switzerland. Canada has already had a quota system for a number of years, while Japan limits the quantity of milk receiving direct government payments under its deficiency payments scheme. The United States has implemented a dairy termination programme under which producers are paid to terminate dairy production for at least five years, and the Food Security Act of 1985 made provision for further cuts in the milk support price.

The purpose of these restraints is above all to control production and government spending as well as to protect farm incomes as far as possible. Given the high support prices existing in most of the above countries, it is questionable whether the over-quota production penalties, which also apply in most cases, will have much of a restraining influence on production. For example, in the EEC quotas on milk deliveries were introduced in 1984 as a temporary measure because of the rapid increase in milk production during the early 1980s and led to a total reduction in deliveries of 2.4 percent by 1986 compared with 1983, the last non-quota year. Moreover, the quota system has been extended with the aim of reducing deliveries by nearly 10 percent by 1988/9. Mechanisms therefore exist to bring dairy surpluses under control provided such restraints remain in effect and that quotas are adjusted in order to clear the world market for dairy products. Indeed, even on the hypothesis that only the major supplier of dairy products to world markets, the EEC, were to adjust in isolation in the role of a 'residual supplier', the projections suggest that growth in world import demand to the year 2000—provided it materializes as effective demand—could still allow some expansion of dairy production in the Community. However, against this it should be borne in mind that huge 'hidden reserves' of milk products exist in Western Europe in the form of highly subsidized disposals onto domestic markets for food and non-food uses. In 1987, such sales amounted to about 15 million tonnes of milk equivalent in the EEC alone, more than average exports of the Community in recent years.

In the case of grains, important recent policy initiatives have been taken in the major cereal-exporting country, the United States. The Food Security Act of 1985 retains many of the same policy instruments previously used in the United States but gives the Secretary of Agriculture added flexibility to change programme parameters as market conditions warrant. In addition, the goals of the Act are somewhat different. Intervention prices (loan rates) are to be reduced substantially in order to enhance the United States' export competitiveness.

In order to cushion the effect of lower prices on farm incomes, target prices in the United States are kept at previous levels with the difference between target prices and market prices or loan rates (whichever is the higher) made up by direct government payments. To limit these payments, the Act calls for new and more severe acreage-reduction programmes for wheat and coarse grains. Included under the Act are the usual set-aside programmes under which farmers must set aside a certain percentage of their acreage in order to qualify for programme benefits; a paid acreage diversion programme; and a new conservation acreage-reserve programme under which 45 million acres of highly erodable land would be removed from crop production for a 10–15 year period. Given the acreage reduction provisions of the Act up to 1989, and assuming that the area under grains in the United States would then be held constant, the tendency towards global surpluses of wheat and coarse grains could be partly held in check. Indeed, these assumptions about the United States' adjustments would be sufficient in theory to bring world coarse grain markets into equilibrium and still allow an expansion of that country's production even if its measures were not accompanied by significant adjustments in other countries. In wheat, however, the tendency toward surplus global production is projected to be so pronounced (mainly because the US intervention price tends to keep the price of wheat above a competitive level in feedgrain markets) as to call for significant adjustments also elsewhere in the world.

Indeed, in wheat and coarse grains trade, according to the trend projections, the United States would suffer a sharp drop in market share—mostly to the benefit of the EEC. This makes the hypothesis that the United States would be willing to act as the 'residual supplier' in world grain markets very unlikely. In fact, the intent of the grain provisions of the Food Security Act is to increase United States' exports and most forecasters project increasing exports in spite of the Act's acreage reduction programme. The increase in exports would be accompanied by a run-down of stocks. Once stocks are depleted, it is unlikely that the United States would allow its market share to deteriorate by keeping cropland out of production. This is especially the case in regard to the paid acreage diversion programme. Thus expansion of the present conflict over world grain markets would appear likely unless the other grain exporters, and the EEC in particular, take strong action to limit grain production. Many alternative combinations of policy adjustment could be hypothesized which would bring about statistical equilibrium in world wheat and coarse grain markets. On top of the assumption made above concerning constraints in the United States on grain production, it would also be necessary, for example, for the EEC to reduce the growth of grain production to about 1 percent a year (instead of 2.5 p.a. in 1970–85) in order to contain fully the tendency to global surpluses, assuming that no other countries were to make significant downward adjustments in their own production compared with projected levels.

## The scenario of trade conflict amongst OECD countries

With the exception of wheat, the tendencies toward trade imbalances projected in Chapter 3 appear relatively small in relation to production and consumption in the DME group of countries. In theory, therefore, the adjustments needed in volumes and prices should be quite manageable, whether shared or whether the main onus of adjustment is assumed by major suppliers, or even by the single major supplier to world markets. In practice, however, the problem is more serious for three important reasons.

Firstly, the policies of most governments (developed or developing, market or centrally planned) insulate producers and consumers from conditions on world markets. Even if world prices fall in response to the surpluses projected on the basis of current production trends, domestic prices may not be seriously affected. This changes the margin between domestic support levels and world market prices even with no overt change in government policy. For net exporters, the wider margin or lower export tax is financed by the government and the former is viewed as an increase in direct or indirect export subsidies by the rest of the world.

Secondly, because of the high degree of insulation of many domestic markets from world market conditions, market equilibrium could be achieved in a statistical sense, without any improvement in market access for low-cost suppliers.

Thirdly, adjustments of the type discussed above, regardless of whether visible surpluses exist, presuppose that major exporters would be satisfied with their market shares. Certainly the evidence in recent years suggests that the large changes in market shares which have already occurred have not been acceptable to losers. There is no reason to suppose that the future would be different unless agriculture were to be brought into a framework of international rules and disciplines.

Indeed, it would seem that major exporters have been on the brink of an agricultural trade war for several years. Trade tensions have been reflected in a large number of agricultural disputes brought before the GATT, threats of new restrictions on market access and of retaliatory action, bilateral accommodations, and the growth of public expenditure devoted to export assistance in order to capture, defend or regain export shares in a fiercely competitive market. In this situation, it cannot be ruled out that one scenario might comprise a perpetuation of the trade skirmishes of the past and their intensification in the case of commodities in structural surplus. What might be the effects of such a 'trade war'?

Dairy products are an excellent illustration of the problem. These are among the most protected of all temperate zone agricultural products, and most government policies insulate producers and consumers from changes in world prices. The exceptions, broadly stated, are policies in Australia and New Zealand among the developed countries. In these circumstances, a conflict in which all countries attempt to maintain their trade shares using policy mechanisms currently in place would imply further increases in the already high subsidization of dairy trade, and the economically absurd consequence that lowest-cost producers could become large importers of dairy products unless they also adopt defensive measures.

Wheat is the commodity for which the projected tendency to surplus is the most serious and thus the commodity with the greatest potential for causing a trade war. In this case, assuming that countries with insulatory policies attempt to maintain exports and keep domestic prices or income supports constant, and that the United States would allow its intervention (loan) prices to fall in response to declining world market prices, a substantial decline in world wheat prices would ensue.

Measured solely by market share, the United States is likely to be slightly better off under this scenario than in a situation where it is the sole residual adjuster on world markets. This is because a number of other countries which also allow world prices to pass through on to domestic prices would bear part of the burden of adjustment. Even so, the United States and these other countries would suffer a substantial loss of market share to the EEC, unless they also adopted similar policies of protection and export subsidization. In response, however, if the United States were to maintain its target prices and production, its deficiency payments would rise accordingly. In these circumstances, it seems likely that even more drastic price reductions would be necessary to bring about equilibrium, particularly if adjustments were confined to OECD countries.

In practice, however, developing countries would not be immune from the effects of an intensification of subsidized production and export in developed countries. While some benefits, in terms of lower import prices, would accrue to chronic food-deficit countries, many developing countries would suffer setbacks to the long-term development of their food production. In particular, although it would be possible—and even desirable—to tax low-priced imports in order to prevent disruption of domestic production, it would become increasingly difficult to sustain domestic production incentive policies in developing countries generally, and especially in those which attain a high level of self-sufficiency and occasional surpluses. Already, in recent years, the conjuncture of such surpluses in a number of these countries with exceptionally low prices on world grain markets, have caused them to scale back incentives to grain production and to incur burdensome costs of storage of unmarketable export supplies.

## The scenario of trade liberalization and enhanced access to international markets

Both of the scenarios of trade adjustment discussed above—the 'residual supplier' approach to achievement of market equilibrium in the case of commodities in excessive surplus, and battles for market share based on direct or indirect subsidies—have obvious limitations. In particular, they would achieve nothing in terms of enhancing the export earnings of developing countries which, as Chapter 3 shows, are expected to remain tightly constrained in the years ahead due to, primarily, inadequate access to markets for their primary and processed export commodities. Further, domestic policies of nearly all countries seek to increase domestic agricultural production. This leads to either lower import requirements or higher export availabilities, both of which tend to depress world market prices.

Clearly, the impact of trade liberalization on trade flows, prices in international markets, export earnings and domestic agricultural sectors, would depend on many factors. These factors include the approaches selected for implementation of trade liberalization measures and the intensity of their application, for instance whether liberalization takes the form of harmonization of domestic and international market prices or involves specific concessions on market access to particular countries in particular commodities; and which countries adapt their policies. For instance, the outcome would also depend on the commodity coverage to which selected approaches are applied, due to the existence of close economic and technical links in both demand and supply between commodity sectors, such as the cereals, feed and livestock sectors.

Tackling these aspects within a single analytical framework capable of quantifying the possible outcome of agricultural trade liberalization, is difficult. Nevertheless, in the recent past a number of studies have attempted to measure the various effects of agricultural trade liberalization. In most cases, the approach employed involved the construction of partial equilibrium single or multi-commodity trade models. Starting from an initial level of protection for the commodities analysed, these models then estimate what could happen to production, consumption, world prices and trade under the assumption of a reduction or elimination of protectionist price-oriented policies. Experiments conducted using such trade models generally abstract from many of the complexities of the real world, especially the swings which characterize currency exchange rates. Their results consequently reflect in large measure the macro-economic factors prevailing in the selected base period. None the less, they indicate the broad directions of the impact and implications of trade liberalization.

Most of the studies undertaken so far refer to partial or full trade liberalization by the industrialized countries. In general their results suggest that world market prices would rise, world price variability would decline, domestic price variability would rise, and that the volume of world trade would expand. In a number of cases, however, their results point to reductions in import expenditures by developing countries following trade liberalization, despite higher world market prices, as these higher prices would stimulate their domestic production, reduce their consumption and lead to import substitution. As regards the main food commodities, the general effects would tend to be larger if all market economies were to participate in such liberalization. For illustrative purposes, however, the discussion which follows focuses on the possible effects of agricultural trade liberalization by the industrialized countries, bearing in mind the commitment made in the

Ministerial Declaration of Punta del Este that 'the developed countries do not expect the developing countries, in the course of trade negotiations, to make contributions which are inconsistent with their individual development, financial and trade needs'.

## Benefits and costs to developing countries from trade liberalization[1]

*Basic food commodities*

The short-term impact on developing countries from higher world prices as a result of trade liberalization would depend to a large extent on the shares of developing countries in the world market of the affected commodities. For instance, during 1981–4 developing market economy countries as a group earned from exports of cereals 32 percent of what they spent on cereal imports, from meat exports 60 percent of their expenditure on meat imports and from dairy exports only 5 percent of their expenditure on dairy imports. On the other hand, their earnings from sugar exports were 112 percent higher than their expenditures on imports of the same commodity.

These aggregate figures give a rough idea of the impact of higher prices of basic food commodities as a result of liberalization on developing countries. Net gains to developing countries as a whole would be expected from liberalization in sugar, whereas their net position from liberalization in meats, dairy products and especially cereals is less obvious. These observations are generally confirmed by the results of several analytical studies which have estimated the impact of trade liberalization on developing countries.

*Sugar*: Overall, most of the gains from liberalization in the sugar market would accrue to developing countries. These gains would be considerable. One study estimated export revenues of developing countries to increase by at least US$2.2 billion (or, based on data for 1983, by over $5 billion). Other studies, based on either earlier periods for the degree of protection in the sugar market and/or covering a smaller set of industrialized countries, estimate smaller but still considerable increases in export revenues of developing country sugar exporters. Geographically, the benefits would accrue mainly to Asian and Latin American sugar-exporting countries, accounting for 50 and 42 percent of the total increase in foreign exchange earnings, respectively. The net benefits to developing countries as a group from a reduction in protection in the sugar market would be less pronounced, to the extent that net sugar-importing developing countries would incur higher import bills for their imports and if exporting developing countries would suffer foreign-exchange losses from possible elimination of their preferential treatment in certain developed country markets. For instance, the losses of the ACP group on the EEC market have been estimated to range between $173 million to $191 million.

*Meat and dairy products*: As regards the meat sector, although estimates of benefits and costs vary widely, some studies report considerable gains in export earnings and reductions in expenditure on imports of livestock products

[1] Results of studies reported in this section are from FAO/CFS 1987. Full references to the studies are to be found in this document.

following liberalization.[2] Potential benefits would be highly concentrated. Latin America would gain over 90 percent of the potential increase in developing countries' export earnings from liberalization in the beef market. The expected effect on trade balances of the increase in the price of dairy products, following liberalization in this market, would generally be negative for developing countries.[3] For both meats and dairy products, however, the increase in the cost of imports would mainly affect the middle- and high-income developing countries, which presently account for most of the developing countries' imports of these commodities. Despite the implied overall short-term costs to developing countries from liberalization of industrialized countries' policies in meat and dairy products, there could be beneficial long-term effects to the development of their livestock sectors. Livestock development requires long-term planning and thus could benefit from higher prices and more stability in the market.

*Cereals*: As in the case of dairy products, because of the large cereal deficit of developing countries, liberalization of industrialized countries' cereal policies is estimated in most models to have a negative short-term effect on developing countries as a group. The extent of the losses, however, would depend on the degree of cereal price increases following liberalization. The change in cereal prices, in turn, depends on whether the liberalization of cereal markets was or was not accompanied by similar liberalization in related commodity sectors. Thus, in various studies the estimated changes in world cereal prices following liberalization are very different. The higher estimates (price increases of up to 20 percent) were generally based on single-commodity models which did not take into account the interactions between the cereal and livestock sectors. The lower estimates of price increases were based on those models which reflected the link between these two sectors, and in some of these models it is estimated that cereal prices on world markets could decline as a consequence of trade liberalization. Such results arise because under a likely contraction of the livestock sector, following multi-commodity trade liberalization, the demand for livestock feeds would be reduced and the price change in cereal commodities would not be as much as that estimated by single-commodity models.

### *Other commodities and overall effects*

Most of the empirical studies which have estimated the impacts of liberalization cover mainly temperate-zone products for which developing countries are typically net importers. Thus the estimates obtained are contingent upon this limited commodity coverage. Studies with a much wider commodity coverage, especially for those commodities of major interest to developing countries as exporters, are rare. However, it is in these commodities that greater access to industrialized country markets could yield important benefits to developing countries.

[2] The increase in export earnings of developing countries following liberalization of the beef and veal market was estimated by one study to range from $4.4 billion to $5.1 billion using data for 1980, while the import costs of this set of countries was estimated to decrease by between $350 million and 580 million.

[3] One study estimated that in case the EEC liberalized its dairy sector, import costs of developing countries would increase by $228 million (1981 dollars). In contrast, the benefit from an increase in their export earnings would be only $12 million.

One study with wide commodity coverage (both temperate-zone and tropical products, including processed products) gives an idea of the overall effects to developing countries.[4] It included 99 individual commodities for which it was assumed that OECD countries reduced their trade barriers (expressed in tariff equivalents) by 50 percent (1975–7 base period). World price increases for several processed tropical products, such as coffee and cocoa products, were estimated to be substantial, ranging between 10 and 15 percent. The estimated gains reflect mainly the foreign-exchange benefits to developing countries which could occur as a consequence of de-escalation of import barriers in developed countries, which generally bear more heavily on processed than on primary products. Further, the prices of many tropical products would have increased more than the prices of some temperate-zone products imported by developing countries. Thus, although developing countries would have incurred losses from higher prices of some temperate-zone products, increases in export revenues from other products would have more than compensated for such losses. According to one study, multi-commodity trade liberalization, on the above assumptions, could have provided a net foreign-exchange benefit to developing countries of about $4.6 billion (1975–7 base period).

Another potentially important benefit to developing countries from liberalization of industrialized countries' agricultural policies could be in the non-agricultural sector and the economy as a whole. Agriculture is strongly linked to other sectors of the economy through, *inter alia*, relative product prices, and the capital and labour markets. Particularly for those developing countries, in which the agricultural sector accounts for a large part of the national product and employs 70 percent or more of the labour force, any changes in the performance of that sector would be expected to have important repercussions on the whole economy.

Preliminary results, based on the application of a general equilibrium model, point, in general, to some positive overall effects for developing countries' economies following liberalization of industrialized countries' agricultural policies. Developing countries' real incomes are estimated to increase, although there are important differences in the magnitude of this increase between the various developing country economic groups and geographical regions. As in the case of trade-oriented liberalization studies, the Latin America and Caribbean region would be the major beneficiary region. All developing country regions, however, are estimated to improve their terms of trade, as a result of an estimated decrease in the real prices of manufactured and equipment goods exported by OECD countries following liberalization in their agricultural sectors. Moreover, all developing country regions are estimated to benefit in terms of improvements in rural incomes, thus contributing to a more equitable distribution of incomes between the urban and rural population.

Domestic food prices in developing countries are also estimated to increase following liberalization in OECD agriculture. This would result in increased domestic food production, but, at the same time, also in a decrease in domestic

[4] See Valdés *et al*. 1980, as well as updated information included in World Bank 1986a. (The study was originally undertaken as a contribution to the 1979 version of 'Agriculture: Toward 2000', FAO 1979.)

demand. However, despite the marginal overall decrease in food consumption, per caput food consumption of rural households is estimated to be higher, albeit at the expense of urban consumers. Nevertheless, provided that the urban poor are compensated through appropriate targeted intervention measures, this may be a desirable effect from the point of view of equity, particularly in low-income countries where a large part of the poor and food-insecure households are concentrated in rural areas.

Finally, the potential impact of liberalization of industrialized countries' policies must also take into consideration the likely response of developing countries' policies to a more open trading environment. Although to a lesser extent compared to industrialized countries, many developing countries also pursue agricultural policies to protect producer and consumer interests and to shield their agricultural sector from external shocks. To the extent that these policies would be modified as a response to parallel changes in industrialized countries' agricultural policies, the overall benefits from liberalization could be even greater.

## Current international policy initiatives

### GATT multilateral trade negotiations

In recognition of the high levels of protection in agriculture, the budgetary and economic costs that they entail and of the dangers of allowing the present indiscipline and unpredictability of world agricultural markets to continue, the contracting parties to the GATT have agreed to give special attention to agriculture in the new Uruguay Round of multilateral trade negotiations. Specifically, the negotiations 'shall aim to achieve greater liberalization of trade in agriculture and bring all measures affecting import access and export competition under strengthened and more operationally effective GATT rules and disciplines'. In particular, the Ministerial Declaration launching the new round refers to improving market access through such measures as reduction of import barriers; increasing discipline on the use of all direct and indirect subsidies and other measures affecting agricultural trade, including the phased reduction of their negative effects and dealing with their causes; and minimizing the adverse effects that sanitary and phytosanitary regulations and barriers can have on trade in agriculture.

In the Declaration, the GATT contracting parties also agree to give special attention to negotiations on tropical products and natural resource-based products (including fishery and forestry products). The aim will be to achieve fullest liberalization of trade in these products, including their processed and semi-processed forms. Recognizing the importance of trade in tropical products to a large number of less-developed contracting parties, the Declaration provides for special attention to negotiations in this area, including the timing and the implementation of results.

So far, work programmes for the newly-established Negotiating Groups, including that on agriculture, have been outlined. In agriculture, the first phase will cover identification of major problems and their causes, including all measures affecting directly or indirectly agricultural trade and elaborate an 'indicative list' of issues considered relevant to achieving the negotiating objective. In a subsequent process, there will be negotiations with a view to reaching agreement on comprehensive texts of strengthened and more operationally effective GATT rules and disciplines; the nature, content and phasing of multilateral commitments to be undertaken; any other understandings deemed necessary for fulfilment of the objective of the negotiations; and exchange of concessions.

In preliminary work undertaken in the GATT Committee on Trade in Agriculture during 1983–6, which is to be taken into account in the negotiations on agriculture, a large number of specific proposals and suggestions were put forward for consideration by individual contracting parties. These covered a wide spectrum of possible approaches for dealing with issues of market access; subsidies affecting trade in agriculture; sanitary and phytosanitary regulations and other technical matters; the review of national measures and policies; and 'general considerations' such as differential and more favourable treatment for developing countries.

None the less, it is premature to speculate on the precise form of any general approaches and combinations of specific measures that might be agreed in the GATT as a basis for the negotiations. However, the Declaration launching the new round does provide some guidance regarding the range of options which could be considered. For instance, improved market access could be achieved either directly through liberalization of non-tariff barriers, such as expansion of quotas, or indirectly by aligning domestic prices more closely to international market prices. Also, increased discipline on subsidies and measures affecting agricultural trade could be pursued either by reducing the overall levels of budgetary expenditures or by reducing the level of policy-induced transfers effected directly and indirectly through subsidies, tariff and non-tariff measures. Other possible matters for consideration could also include reinforcement of specific GATT articles, as already suggested in the Committee on Trade in Agriculture. Such proposals include regulation of production, or establishment of links between import quotas and changes in domestic production; improvements in the framework of rules and disciplines regarding equitable market shares of exporters; and limitations or prohibition of export subsidies and other forms of export assistance.

The Council of the OECD, meeting at ministerial level in May 1987, has also set out a potentially far-reaching set of principles and commitments to achieve 'a concerted reform of agricultural policies 1[which 1] will be implemented in a balanced manner' in the framework of the GATT negotiations, 'including a progressive reduction of assistance to and protection of agriculture on a multi-country and multi-commodity basis'. The principles cited refer to the long-term objective of allowing market signals to orient agricultural production; consideration of social concerns, such as food security, environment and employment; standstill and rollback of measures which stimulate supply of surplus commodities; minimizing economic distortions when production constraints are imposed; the desirability of providing farm income support directly rather than through measures linked to production; the stimulation of off-farm employment in rural areas; and the need for governments to retain flexibility in the choice of the means necessary for the fulfilment of their objectives.

## Trade liberalization among developing countries

Currently, as well as the GATT Uruguay Round, another potentially significant set of trade negotiations has commenced involving developing countries. The proposal to establish a global framework of trade preferences and other trade promoting measures to facilitate expansion of trade among developing countries received major support at the Mexico City Conference on Economic Cooperation among Developing Countries in 1976. Among the measures adopted was the establishment of a global system of trade preferences (GSTP) with the objective of promoting the development of national production and mutual trade of the developing countries. Following UNCTAD secretariat studies, the Fourth Ministerial Meeting of the Group of 77 set out in 1979 a number of principles which should guide further work on the subject. By 1982, recommendations on the principles, rules and timetable for the GSTP negotiations were endorsed by the Ministerial Meeting of the Group of 77 held in New York, and the First Round of Negotiations was launched in Brasilia in 1986. The scope of the negotiations extends to customs tariffs, direct trade measures, para-tariff concessions (border charges and fees on foreign trade transactions of a tariff-like effect which are levied solely on imports) and non-tariff barriers.

As in the case of the results of the simulation studies of trade liberalization summarized above, the dimensions of potential trade expansion among developing countries which could arise as a result of the GSTP negotiations depend on the assumption made about, among other aspects, the depth and commodity coverage of tariff preferences and other approaches still to be negotiated. As regards expansion of agricultural trade among developing countries, one UNCTAD simulation study (Erzan *et al.* 1986) concludes that the GSTP could generate additional trade amounting to about $2419 million, or nearly 17 percent more than total agricultural trade among developing countries using 1981 as a base line. Of this, it is estimated that expanded trade in refined sugar and palm oil would each account for about $250 million, with other large gains in trade flows of such commodities as soybean oil, raw sugar, unmanufactured tobacco, pulses, tea and forestry products.

## Market stabilization and related measures

Volatility in international commodity markets, particularly of prices, stems only in part from the capriciousness of nature, such as weather, pests or diseases on the supply side. In part, it also stems from cyclical variations in demand. However, an important cause of volatility is attributable to man-made factors, notably interventionist policies which insulate and thereby stabilize domestic markets in food commodities and which, as a by-product, make for greater instability in residual world markets. As indicated above, a number of studies suggest that global free trade could be expected to reduce world price fluctuations. Progress in the GATT Round could thus yield important gains in terms of reduced world market price volatility. Since fluctuations of domestic prices would be more in line with those of world market prices in a 'global free trade' scenario, such reductions in volatility in world market prices would, of course, imply some increases in domestic price volatility in those countries which currently use policies which insulate their economies from the world market.

For a number of commodities, especially tropical products and agricultural raw materials, fluctuations in supply on account of changes in weather from season to season, are very pronounced, as are the impacts on trade earnings, rural incomes, and long-term maintenance of market shares for raw materials competing against synthetic substitutes. It is therefore not surprising that much time and effort should have been spent on attempts at international commodity stabilization. The results from such efforts have, however, been generally disappointing. At present, only two commodities, cocoa and rubber, are subject to international commodity agreements which contain buffer stocking provisions. Only one other international commodity agreement, on coffee, also contains regulatory provisions, but its principal mechanism, entailing export quotas, has not always been able to stem large price fluctuation in international coffee trade.

The international environment which forms the backcloth to the negotiation of effective commodity agreements has become considerably more unfavourable in recent years. In particular, at the technical level, the strong swings in currency exchange rates have made it more difficult to establish reference points for the negotiation of price levels to trigger economic mechanisms of agreements. Secondly, the collapse of the International Tin Agreement in 1985, and the nature of the factors which led to its collapse, have undoubtedly affected political attitudes towards regulatory mechanisms. Thirdly, a greater polarization of political opinion regarding market-oriented approaches on the one hand, and regulation of commodity markets on the other hand, appears to have developed over the past decade. Such changes in the setting for intergovernmental agreements have particularly affected the major endeavour launched in 1976 to generate greater stability in primary commodity markets, with greater benefits to developing countries, namely the UNCTAD Integrated Programme for Commodities (IPC). Apart from the International Natural Rubber Agreement, no new commodities have become subject to agreements with regulatory functions since then, although agreements for the purpose of promoting commodity development projects, such as research and development, have come into force for jute and tropical timber. Besides international commodity agreements, the IPC had envisaged a Common Fund, with financial facilities to help finance both the stabilization measures undertaken by associated international commodity agreements as well as commodity development programmes and projects. However, seven years after an agreement was reached on the establishment of the fund in 1980, it had yet to come into operation as the share of the capital pledged by the countries which had ratified the agreement by end-1987 was still below, though very close to, the minimum required for the fund to become effective.

The very limited progress in stabilizing markets by means of international agreements, and the generally bleak prospects for such action, means that special importance attaches to other means of dealing with both the adverse impacts of market volatility, on developing countries in particular, and its causes. As regards the first of these aspects, the compensatory financing facility

(CFF) of the IMF is the major international mechanism for providing relief to countries experiencing balance-of-payments problems arising from shortfalls in export earnings (and excesses in the costs of cereal imports, since 1981). However, the most recent expansion of access to CFF resources occurred in 1979. The subsequent prolonged period of depressed prices on primary commodity markets has demonstrated both the insufficiency of resources in absolute terms, despite the expansion, and the limitations of the facility in terms of its conditions regarding the phasing of repayments of borrowings. In particular, while the CFF in its present form deals with problems caused by year-to-year fluctuations in export earnings, it provides only limited relief in situations where earnings remain low for several successive years.

A second approach for dealing with commodity market volatility is to attack the causes of the problem. In this connection, a proposal for financing, through a compensatory mechanism, export earnings shortfalls at country level caused by short-term supply instability, has been under consideration in UNCTAD in recent years. The basic idea of the proposal envisages that borrowings would be directed towards addressing the causes of the supply instability. However, no agreement is yet in sight on this issue.

## Adjustment implications and issues

The global agricultural trade environment has seriously deteriorated in recent years. The main symptoms are that agricultural commodity prices on world markets became depressed as seldom before, surplus stocks reached record levels, costs of agricultural support programmes rocketed, agricultural export revenues of many countries declined, and encounters in agricultural trade policy, in particular over export subsidies, have intensified. Experience demonstrates that it would be imprudent to extrapolate this situation far into the future as a forecast of what is in store. Yet certain underlying factors and trends, based on the outcome of Chapter 3 and summarized at the beginning of this chapter, point to a difficult future international trade environment for agricultural exporters unless more substantial policy adjustments bearing on trade are undertaken, compared with the past. The necessary adjustments involve all countries, both developed and developing. The consequences of maladjustments are most visible in the area of international trade, and thus the improvements to be sought include trade-oriented measures. However, trade policies are essentially supportive of a wider spectrum of objectives which domestically-oriented measures seek to achieve. It is therefore necessary to address these domestic policies, which primarily affect production and consumption, as a fundamental part of any lasting improvement in the international trading environment. Thus the ultimate goal of greater market orientation in world agriculture, which would enable comparative advantages to play a greater role in determining global resource use in the sector, is now on the international agenda.

While agricultural trade practices of many countries in recent years have acted in such a way as to aggravate international market conditions, there appears now to be a greater consensus on the need to bring more effective rules and disciplines to bear on such practices. Against this background, the 'trade war' scenario, which has already in some respects emerged, will hopefully be seen by history as only an unfortunate interlude in the quest for an improved international environment based on multilateral principles.

# 8 Other policy issues of agricultural development and adjustment in developing countries

In addition to issues discussed in separate chapters—international trade, poverty and equity, the environment and technological developments—a number of other policy issues will confront developing countries as they strive to develop their agriculture along the broad lines explored in this study. The issues discussed below, some of long standing, others comparatively new, are all interrelated and are separated only for clearer presentation. While partly common to developed countries, they are examined here in relation to developing countries.

## Macro-economic policies and agriculture

*The setting of macro-economic policies*: Many governments of developing countries now face the need to bring about structural adjustments in the economies of their countries. It is widely agreed that the thrust of these policies as regards agriculture must be to redress the disadvantages frequently imposed on the sector by past development strategies. It is also increasingly recognized that country-specific economic and social settings exert a powerful influence on both the feasibility of particular measures and on their success.

The external situation has been distinctly adverse since the first years of the 1980s. Depressed agricultural commodity prices and poor trade prospects; heavy debt-servicing burdens for a number of developing countries and a reversal of capital inflows; and the slow growth and lack of confidence as to the economic outlook in major, industrialized countries have in many cases severely reduced resources needed by developing countries in applying adjustment policies. These adverse conditions have borne most heavily, but not exclusively, on Latin American and African countries.

Domestic situations are varied, particularly as to the capacity of individual countries to apply policies effectively. Some developing countries now have good administrative capacity and can choose amongst a wide range of measures with confidence that they can be applied effectively. In other countries, however, relatively weak administrative capacity restricts severely the kinds of measures governments can choose or the extent to which hoped-for results will actually emerge. The following discussion of selected issues must therefore be seen in the light of the many and serious constraints which in different measure confront developing countries in their efforts to resolve problems of concern to agriculture.

*The importance of macro-economic policies to agriculture*: Governments use a variety of economy-wide or macro-economic policies—fiscal, monetary, trade and so on—as well as others more limited to one sector or problem. When farming in developing countries was almost entirely subsistence agriculture, these macro policies had little influence on it except for the small export enclaves. Agriculture, still a leading sector in most developing countries, is however becoming much more commercialized, both as to output and inputs, and thus increasingly more open to the influences of macro policies and the national and external conditions and policies which they reflect. The linkage works in the opposite direction also; how agriculture performs in such matters as generating a trade surplus, holding down food prices, providing employment or generating savings also influence the constraints on the scope and effectiveness of macro policies.

There is an important issue here for agriculture. Impacts on the sector of macro policies can be weighty and experience shows that they have often been adverse to agriculture. The possibility of such damage to the sector, and in the longer run to the whole economy, appears to have often been overlooked or underestimated.

Pressures for increased efficiency in agriculture can be expected to mount, driven by the needs of developing countries to continue to increase production, remain competitive in difficult world markets and enhance economic performance to improve their creditworthness. Measures to bring about a more rational allocation of resources and to raise the efficiency of their use will therefore be at the centre of the policy stage in developing countries in the years ahead. Macro policies are basic instruments for achieving these economic objectives, and several are particularly relevant to agriculture in developing countries.

Some interventions arising from macro policies improve the profitability of agriculture, for example expenditure of public funds on infrastructures which benefit agriculture also, or the insulation of the economy from the full impact of windfall gains from non-agricultural exports. In many developing countries, however, macro-policy applications, particularly in the areas of industrialization-based development strategy and exchange rates and other influences on producer prices, have often worked against agriculture. These disincentives to agriculture have probably been introduced inadvertently at times, particularly when they originated in abrupt and unforeseen changes in economic circumstances. The negative effects on agriculture of the rapid increase in incomes and foreign earnings in the 1970s from oil exports by some predominantly agricultural countries are a striking example, though other countries used such additional resources to promote agricultural growth.

The full implications in developing-country conditions of the indirect effects of policies through the changes they bring about in the relative profitability of different sectors are now increasingly recognized. While in the short term the response of agricultural supply to prices of farm products relative to those in other sectors is low, in the longer term, when the quantity and mix of production resources and technologies are more flexible, supply responses are higher.

*Protected industrialization*: A development strategy under which the industrial sector is very highly protected compared with agriculture has been typical, at least at a certain stage of development, of most developing countries. (The reverse holds true at present in most developed market economy countries.) The direct effects of this protection, however undertaken, are first to raise the profitability of manufacturing relative to agriculture, thus stimulating investment in manufacturing and drawing resources out of agriculture. In the second place, prices of industrial inputs used by agriculture and locally manufactured consumer goods purchased by farmers will be raised.

Developing countries are understandably reluctant to dismantle completely the protection typically accorded manufacturing because they fear that this might halt the process of industrialization. Manufacturing built up under very high protective walls will, however, inevitably hold back agricultural and overall economic development. Some protection is usually essential but its typical extent should be greatly reduced.

*Exchange rates*: Inappropriate exchange rate policies can directly damage agriculture. Overvalued currencies are a disincentive to the production of agricultural exports and of import-competing foodstuffs. They are instrumental in establishing or encouraging patterns of consumption which tend to generate additional import demand and so detract from demand for domestically produced foods.

The correction of an exchange rate by a shift in the direction of the value likely to be set by a free exchange market is often difficult, politically and administratively. The distribution of income within a country is changed. Uncertainties may be created. If pressures on domestic price levels consequent upon a devaluation cannot be resisted, its effectiveness will be undermined and the change in the nominal rate will not be reflected in relative sectoral prices, that is in the actual exchange rate within the economy. The strength of monetary and fiscal instruments to buttress the effects of changes in the exchange rate are therefore crucial in determining its effectiveness.

Within agriculture, the effects of an exchange rate change must not be offset by institutional arrangements which introduce a wedge between external and internal prices such as a price-setting mechanism that does not allow local prices to reflect export parities. The influence of high-cost marketing parastatals has at times caused agricultural producers to be worse off after a currency devaluation than before. An improvement in producer prices through an exchange rate change usually requires attention also to be given to other influences on output for an effective incentive to be created.

Exchange rate and other policies of concern to agriculture which are being applied concurrently may work in the same direction or they may offset each other. For example, studies of several Latin American countries which attempt to take into account all policy influences for the period from the 1960s to the early 1980s show that macro policies either added to existing disincentive effects of direct agricultural price measures or otherwise reduced or reversed the positive effects (Cavallo and Mundlak 1982; Garcia 1981). The same picture emerges from recent work by FAO which examines changes in producer price bias before and after correction for estimated exchange rate bias (FAO 1987b). In many instances, the result of exchange rate policy was not simply to lessen the incentive given by sector price support measures but to turn the overall effect of policy interventions negative. The intent of the agricultural policy was thereby reversed.

*Fiscal policy*: The raising of government revenue by taxes on agricultural export commodities is a traditional fiscal instrument in many developing countries. At early stages of development, the paucity of alternative sources of revenue and the administrative ease of collecting levies on exports makes this choice virtually inevitable. Such taxes, however, distort producer prices (even if the agricultural sector later becomes a net recipient of public funds). In a number of instances, the taxes have been very heavy and they have sometimes become the income of monopolistic marketing bodies. While economic development makes available other sources of revenue and decreases the share of total revenue obtained by taxes on agricultural commodities, governments have been reluctant to abolish them. The feasibility of accelerating the shift to other means than commodity taxes for collecting the contribution of agriculture to government revenues is, therefore, a fiscal policy issue of considerable importance to the sector.

Budget deficits tend to affect agriculture adversely. Financing the deficit usually adds to inflationary pressures which raise the general level of costs in the country. Prices of agricultural products, however, which are open to both international market influence and to government interventions designed to check rises in food prices, are likely to be prevented from sharing fully in the general inflationary rise.

*Monitoring agricultural implications of macro policies*: Well-chosen macroeconomic policies adapted to particular country circumstances are required for the good of the national economy and not simply for that of one of its sectors. There is, however, a clear need to reduce inconsistencies which have existed between macro and sector policies and to avoid serious distortions in price relationships and resource flows. An evident need exists for on-going and rigorous analysis and monitoring of the potential effects of such macro policies as exchange rates, sectoral protection and fiscal policy, to reveal their implications for agriculture. Since agriculture tends to be the victim, even if accidental, rather than the beneficiary of some macro policies, its own sectoral economic institutions should develop the technical competence to make authoritative analyses of the bearing of actual or proposed macro policies on the sector.

## Debt management, structural adjustment and agriculture

The high level of external indebtedness now poses a major issue. A steep fall in the availability of new loans and the depressed level of most commodity prices have critically intensified the problem. In the face of adversely affected incomes, expenditures have had to be reduced, including government expenditures on investment and on welfare schemes, and strong pressures have arisen for export surpluses to be generated in order to provide funds for debt-servicing. Not all developing countries have been affected by the debt crisis; the bulk of the heavily indebted countries and others with debt-servicing difficulties are in Latin America and in Africa.

*Impacts of recent indebtedness*: Agriculture was not the focus of the surge of borrowing which gathered force in the 1970s but it did benefit from the stimulus given to economic growth in the borrowing countries and from the greater availability of internal and external resources. Governments were able to maintain or raise public expenditure, including capital expenditure in agriculture. Larger food imports by a number of countries contributed to higher levels of food consumption.

The abrupt and severe tightening of the external financial situation from 1982 led to a reversal of the macro-economic conditions in developing borrowing countries. For 61 countries classified by the IMF as capital-importing developing countries with debt payments difficulties, the growth rate of GDP declined progressively: 5.6 percent for 1968–77, 4.5 percent for 1978–80 and only 0.8 percent for 1981–5. Per caput GDP, therefore, fell in the latter period. Gross capital formation for 1981–85 fell to 79 percent of the 1978–80 average. As a major part of the adjustment to the collapse of new capital inflows, the trade deficit of $7.1 billion in 1982 was transformed into a surplus of $33.7 billion in 1985. In a smaller and partly overlapping group of countries classified by the IMF as heavily-indebted capital-importing developing countries, whose average debt-servicing ratio had reached 40 percent in 1982, a trade balance of $3.7 billion in 1982 was raised to no less than $40.7 billion by 1985.

Because the impacts of the debt crisis on agriculture are indirect, lagged and partly offset by other developments, they cannot be quantified. However, their nature and direction are evident. The growth of domestic demand facing agriculture in countries with debt problems has been checked by the reduction in per caput GDP and by an increase in unemployment in some countries. The availability of food calories per caput in these countries fell off fractionally after having risen by towards 1 percent a year in the second half of the 1970s. Food subsidies have been reduced in the wake of budgetary stringencies.

The debt crisis must also have reinforced the shift away from input subsidies which was already underway. Government developmental expenditures on agriculture in a sample of 35 countries studied by FAO generally rose in real terms in the second half of the 1970s but then declined in the early 1980s in a number of countries with debt-servicing problems. The full effects on production will be felt only later.

*Agriculture and future debt management*: The future involvement of food and agriculture in debt management will depend chiefly on measures adopted by governments of indebted countries to (a) raise revenue and to economize on expenditures so as to meet the domestic costs of debt servicing and (b) improve the trade balance in order to meet the external costs of debt-servicing.

There appears to be only limited scope for agriculture to contribute to increased government revenue. The sector is a relatively small direct contributor to public funds—5–6 percent of total revenue in a sample of 35 countries but up to 30 percent or more in some low-income countries—and appears in a number of instances to be now a net recipient of central government funds. Taxes on commodity exports, while slowly declining as a major source of revenue from the sector, still remain important, particularly in poorer countries. Pressures arising from debt management will tend to maintain such taxes. The same pressures should support their replacement by the more economically desirable form of taxing incomes, although in practice political and administrative constraints may preclude such changes being made.

Budgetary constraints arising from future debt management will make it essential that governments limit public expenditures, but reductions on food and agricultural items may entail high social and economic costs. The continuation of food subsidies should be considered essential, but the greatest attention will need to be given to effective targeting and to administrative efficiency. It is neither acceptable nor desirable that the food consumption of the poorest of people should suffer in order to assist the efforts of governments to raise funds for external debt management; external assistance should not be made contingent on such action. Within indebted countries, the issue is one of expenditure priorities.

The future growth of agricultural exports and imports could contribute to the creation or increase of a trade surplus needed to service external debt. Agricultural products, however, account for only about one-quarter of total exports of indebted countries. Of the 51 countries with recent debt-servicing difficulties, this study projects 23 to improve their agricultural net trade balances in volume terms compared with 11 out of the 36 countries without such difficulties. In the projections, the indebted countries as a group would improve their initial positive agricultural trade balance while the initial deficit of the countries without debt problems would also increase. The importance of agricultural trade to individual countries differs widely. Of the 51 countries with debt-servicing problems, agricultural products accounted for half or more of total exports in 23 countries and for one-third or more in 30 countries. Faster growth of agricultural export earnings in these countries could make a significant contribution to debt-servicing, but such a result would depend as much or more on improved conditions in international markets as on domestic stimulus to export expansion.

Agricultural imports during 1983/5 accounted for only 16 percent of total imports of the 51 countries with debt-servicing problems and were more than a fifth of imports in only 20 of these countries. Fifteen were sub-Saharan Africa countries. Imports supplied 20 percent of food calorie supplies in these countries, more than double the share in countries without debt-servicing problems. While a slower growth in agricultural imports would contribute to a saving in foreign exchange, this would check estimated improvements in food consumption. Overall, a significant contribution to the saving of foreign exchange needed for debt-servicing made by reducing agricultural imports does not seem feasible.

It therefore appears that for agriculture to play a substantial role in the management of external debt, much will depend on future commodity prices. Experience shows that there is little that developing countries can do by themselves to improve the prices of their agricultural exports and hence to increase the contribution of agricultural exports in debt management. Constraints in present international circumstances on the ability of indebted countries to expand agricultural export earning except at the cost of lower world prices and reduced earnings of all developing countries as a group, are therefore a factor which must be taken into account in any international discussions or negotiations on rescheduling of debt.

## Price policies in developing countries

Few aspects of agriculture have given rise to as much controversy as price policies. There are compelling reasons why this is so. Price interventions are almost universal in agriculture, but their effective design and implementation is remarkably difficult. They frequently entail multiple targets—levels of producer prices, levels of consumer prices and price stability—and multiple instruments, such as price-setting arrangements, marketing institutions and government subsidies. They can become remarkably expensive. Price interventions in many countries, often carried out by monopoly marketing agencies, have also introduced large distortions in prices and, because of misunderstandings of the relationship of price and production response, the price distortions have too often become disincentives.

The production projections presented in Chapter 3 assume that prices will be sufficiently remunerative to induce growth in production in line with the general objective of improving self-sufficiency or slowing down its rate of decline, depending on the particular country/commodity situation.

## Producer prices

At the heart of the issue of producer prices in developing countries has been the frequent assumption—perhaps implicit as often as explicit—that agricultural production growth in the aggregate did not depend to any marked extent on the level of real prices received by farmers. This view has been challenged. While common sense would indeed say that prices matter very much to farmers' production decisions, agricultural production response is actually a complex matter. It is influenced not only by product prices but also by conditions such as the availability and costs of inputs and of credit to purchase them, the adequacy of prior investment in agricultural infrastructure and the confidence of the farmers as to the future effectiveness of price support measures. The elasticity of aggregate supply to prices inevitably varies widely amongst countries and over time.

A consensus appears to have been reached, at least amongst economists, as to how supply responds to price. FAO views, as reported in its recent study 'Agricultural Price Policies' are quite definite as to the general situation. 'The usual direction of the response 1[of aggregate supply to price 1] is well established: it is positive' (FAO 1987b: 187). When the factors of production are more or less fixed, prices can exert only a weak influence on output. Over the longer run, however, when the use of additional land, water and other resources or improved technologies can be drawn on, supply responses of the sector as a whole are greater.

These values of long-run supply response of the agricultural sector as a whole not only indicate that price incentives must be part of any policy to raise agricultural production but they also warn that if the prices of agricultural products fall in relation to other products, there can be considerable adverse effects. At the same time, however, the supply elasticities are low enough to rule out the possibility of fuelling sustained growth in agricultural production by positive pricing inducements alone. In contrast to the relatively moderate extent of the aggregate supply response, there is a high positive degree of supply responsiveness to price changes for a specific commodity. Price policy is thus a powerful instrument for influencing the commodity composition of output.

Incentives given by producer price policies have also been a controversial issue because of a school of thought that other measures could provide more effective incentives than output prices. Thus, it was argued, controlled prices and subsidies for credit or fertilizer or other inputs would increase their use by farmers and so lead to an increase in productivity and lower per unit production costs. In this way, producer returns could be enhanced without the need for any politically difficult rise in food prices. Experience, however, showed that while input subsidies could be effective in stimulating the spread of improved technologies which required greater use of purchased inputs and that they were at times essential to offset sudden jumps in the prices of inputs, serious drawbacks became apparent.

Input subsidies proved extremely difficult to administer effectively and fairly. When provided through public bodies, such as the monopoly purchase and distribution of fertilizer, the service often became very inflexible in practice and of greater benefit to large than to small farmers. In many cases it was also found that subsidies were maintained at initial levels instead of being reduced as productivity gains were realized, and therefore the subsidies became expensive in fiscal terms. By now a large measure of agreement has been reached: while effective if well administered in carefully chosen circumstances, producer input subsidies should have only a limited application and temporary life; they cannot replace producer price incentives.

The moderate extent of the response to price, however, underlines the need for other conditions which enable price incentives to work to full effect, particularly at a time when technology is no longer static and the marketed share of output is growing. Increased production depends critically on the adequacy of the whole infrastructure of agriculture. Technologies to raise yields and in some countries to bring additional land into production, must be made known to the farmer. Inputs of the right kind must be available when required, together with the credit for their purchase. Major public investments are required in such areas as irrigation, land clearing, research and extension services, marketing and road building. The list of such prerequisites differs amongst countries and regions but much is common to all. In all instances, consumer goods wanted by farm families must be on the shelves of their local shops at prices which can be afforded if incentive producer prices are to have any real meaning. Finally, meeting such non-price requirements but omitting to give farmers the assurance of prices which they consider to be profitable, is likely to disappoint hopes of improved production growth. The two sets of influences, price and non-price, are complementary.

Where policies have seriously distorted the level of prices received by farmers, it has become imperative that price measures and price setting mechanisms are revised. Attitudes to producer price incentives have in fact been changing and in the right direction, particularly in African agriculture, where adverse price bias had become extreme; but further change will be required. Price measures should also contribute to improved income distribution within the sector; with unequal distribution of land, price incentives will, however, benefit large farmers more than small ones. In order to mitigate these adverse effects on distribution, all farmers with a marketable surplus, even if small, need assured access to marketing systems through which price measures are applied; products important in the output of small farmers and not only those of which large farmers are the suppliers should be included in price support schemes to the fullest extent possible; and small farmers and landless labourers must be able to participate adequately in services provided to the sector, such as institutional credit, transport networks or extension services, which facilitate an increase in their productivity and marketable production.

### Stabilization

The large price fluctuations to which agricultural products are inherently subject impose hardships on both producers and consumers, weaken the role of price in guiding production and give rise to instability in the economy as a whole. A reasonable degree of price stability is therefore a basic objective of agricultural policy. Stabilization schemes may contain elements of both food-price subsidization and producer-income support.

The objective of price stabilization is worth pursuing, despite problems likely to be encountered, in order to protect both producers and needier consumers. It will be necessary, however, under the stricter budgetary constraints which now widely prevail, for the subsidy element to be reduced and for a somewhat greater degree of price flexibility to be accepted.

Large fluctuations in world prices have made stabilization more desirable but more difficult to achieve in recent years. The very limited progress in international measures, notably commodity agreements, puts more weight on domestic approaches. While in principle it remains essential that price stabilization goals—in terms of floor and ceiling prices—should be related to international price trends, in present circumstances governments must make judgements as to the appropriateness of international prices as guides to domestic price targets in the case of heavily subsidized commodities in world trade.

### Consumer subsidies

Consumer food subsidies, a particularly sensitive area of price policy, have been employed in many developing countries. In a sample of 37 countries studied in the recent FAO study on agricultural price policies, 31 countries had provided food subsidies (FAO 1987b). The importance given to them by consumers in improving the quality of life, especially for the urban poor, is demonstrated by the civil unrest that their removal or reduction frequently provokes. Although, chiefly because of budgetary pressures, a number of countries have recently scaled down or eliminated food subsidies or have been advised to do so, humanitarian as well as political considerations support the view that some form of intervention should continue to be widely employed.

All measures which shift most of the cost of cheap food from the budget to food producers—procurement by state monopolies, cheap food imports, export taxes—reduce the incentive to produce and invest in agriculture, thus confronting policy-makers with a choice of short-term fiscal benefit versus long-term cost to society. The alternative of shifting a greater share of the burden of a sizeable scheme on the budget implies the near-certainty of increased fiscal deficits or of sacrificing expenditures needed for future growth.

Rural poor, who are usually the most numerous in developing countries, tend to benefit much less than urban populations in the distribution of subsidized food. Urban groups have a stronger political voice, and for practical reasons they have better access to distribution centres. Beneficiaries of food subsidies have frequently included better-off urban people.

Experience shows how difficult it is to design a food subsidy scheme that benefits only the needy, extends in practice to rural areas and avoids high budgetary and administrative costs. Targeting the beneficiaries by various criteria—such as subsidizing products consumed mainly by the poor or locating urban distribution centres in poor neighbourhoods only and extending distribution centres to rural areas also, rationing subsidized quantities and providing benefits through food-for-work schemes—constitutes the most appropriate approach, but its administrative requirements are demanding. A firm ceiling must be imposed in advance on the cost of the scheme to the budget.

These are all issues which must be faced by governments deciding to continue with or to introduce targeted food subsidy schemes of moderate overall cost. Finally, food subsidies cannot be used as a panacea for ailments elsewhere in the food and agricultural system. They work best in the context of a coherent and consistent food policy.

Within the field of agricultural price policy, it is suggested that in order to ensure that incentives are actually provided to their farmers and that the poorest of consumers have assurance of access to enough food, developing countries should:

(1) remove or lessen serious distortions affecting producer prices, for example industrial and urban policy bias, extreme commodity export taxes, overvalued exchange rates, pan-territorial prices administered by a government marketing body, and ensure that unless there are very strong reasons to the contrary, producer prices do not move too far and for long periods away from long-term international price trends. That current levels of international prices for some commodities are an inappropriate guide is undoubtedly true and must be allowed for in any price policy interventions.

(2) provide administratively strong and well-funded arrangements permanently in place to provide guaranteed floor and ceiling prices for major products. The floor price should not interfere with the operation of markets except when the market price is abnormally depressed. The ceiling price should be high enough to encourage producers to increase production but low enough to prevent large increases in food prices. There is no sure way of avoiding consumer opposition to any essential food price rises but gradualism and prior education of the public as to the rationale of the change appear to be needed.

(3) operate welfare food distribution schemes to assist the poorest of consumers in rural as well as urban areas (and as far as is practicable, only those) so that, without incurring fiscal burdens which are not viable in the long run, producer prices of food commodities need not be held down artificially for the protection of such vulnerable populations.

(4) consider providing limited and temporary input subsidies in kind to the

poorest of producers so that, again without heavy fiscal burdens being incurred, they will be encouraged to increase productivity in the output of food.

## The role of the public sector in developing country agriculture

The appropriate role of the public and private sectors has become the focus of increasing attention in recent years. In general, a smaller role is being given to the public sector, a reversal of earlier emphasis.

All countries, developed and developing alike, accord an essential role to the public sector in the development of the agricultural sector. This is especially so in providing its infrastructure—transport, research and extension systems, large-scale irrigation, technical standards, control of animal diseases and agricultural pests and so on—but amongst developing countries other influences have also been prominent. Some countries at the time of independence inherited well-established systems of public marketing channels. Many developing countries faced serious inadequacies in agricultural institutions and in physical infrastructures—rural credit, input supply and agricultural services systems, storage, price information—and direct public provision of these services appeared the quickest solution. The need was widely felt to control food prices in the interest of poor consumers and to prevent rising wage costs from impeding industrialization.

The overall result was typically a substantial presence of government controls and public or quasi-public bodies. There was considerable public activity in marketing and significant transfers of public funds from and to the sector. There was also some direct public participation in production, although in most countries agricultural production remained in the private sector.

Since around the beginning of the present decade the extent and forms of many government activities in agriculture have, however, come under increasing criticism. Private sector initiatives and institutions are being advocated in place of their public sector counterparts. This change is supported by financial constraints and by the realization of frequent low cost-effectiveness of public enterprises. The reduction of balance-of-payments and budget deficits have become primary objectives of economic policy in many countries in recent years. With the decline in external capital inflows and the extreme difficulty in increasing revenue from domestic sources, public spending cuts have often appeared the only option. Agriculture has had to bear a share. The main targets have been public expenditures on agricultural marketing of output and inputs, distribution and transport, and on transfer payments, that is subsidies of various kinds. Some loss-making public enterprises have been privatized.

Government marketing agencies have attracted considerable attention. In some countries, food and agricultural export marketing agencies have had their role diminished by exposure to competition from the private sector or have been directly phased out, except, in certain cases, as 'buyers of last resort'. Although public agencies in this category vary significantly in their functions, background and performance, they generally face demanding operational tasks while being open to pressures for staffing and management. The frequent result has been high-cost and inefficient operations. They have also attracted criticism through being the instrument by which governments have extracted excessive tax revenue from agricultural exports with a significant share of the proceeds used to meet inflated administrative costs. Some agencies were given the power to formulate pricing and trade policies which were then inevitably influenced by considerations of their own revenue and status.

Changes now being adopted or considered are for pricing and tax decisions to be made outside the public marketing agencies, with the role of the latter being to operate the pricing policy of the government and to provide quality control and provision of technical advice and information, leaving the actual domestic and external aspects of marketing to private enterprise. More prices of agricultural products are being deregulated so that price levels will reflect supply and demand influences, although basic foods generally remain subject to government intervention. Transfer payments in the form of food and input subsidies are being reduced.

As exemplified in the area of marketing, there are both advantages and dangers in this reduction of the scope of the public sector. Public marketing monopolies came to deserve much of the criticism made of their inefficiency and high costs. They were also an integral part of the process by which price bias adverse to producers was introduced or maintained. On the other hand, however, there are enough efficient public marketing agencies to suggest that high costs and inefficiencies are often a consequence of underdeveloped conditions such as transport, storage and training rather than an inherent characteristic of such organizations. In many countries, furthermore, they are an indispensable means of providing access to markets of small or distant farmers who, as tends to be the case in some Latin American countries, would be bypassed by private marketing channels which cater predominantly for the larger, commercialized farms. In brief, state action is necessary in order to provide equitable institutional means to transmit price policy signals to all producers and to avoid excessive profits being made by private marketing channels which develop local monopolistic powers.

Governments face three major issues regarding the respective roles of the public and private sectors in agriculture. The first is that of keeping an appropriate balance between private and public sector roles. Enthusiasm for reform must not induce governments to curtail too severely the involvement of the public sector. Provision of the infrastructure of agriculture, protection against violent price fluctuations, and access of the poor to food, are examples of functions which will continue to require a substantial government presence. In the field of marketing, a competitive coexistence of private and public channels is a better means of promoting efficiency and equity of treatment than the complete phasing out of either public institutions or private enterprises. The provision of agricultural credit will continue to need some backing of governments, especially as regards credit to small farmers and assurance against losses. The focus should be on improving efficiency and this will often require some shifts in the composition of activities of the public sector, for example more of its resources devoted to building rural roads and fewer to the commercial marketing of food, rather than a diminution in its overall extent.

The second issue is that a withdrawal of the public sector may lead to a collapse of the particular service. Experienced and competent private enterprises are usually lacking after a period when the private sector has not been active in that field. The change-over from the public to the private sector must therefore be a phased one, and assistance must be given to enable private enterprises to become established and effective. For instance, credit must be extended to the private sector to take over existing marketing facilities and establish new ones. While the transfer is a transitional problem, the lack of sufficient assistance and a general readiness on the part of government to nurture the incoming organizations can be a serious deterrent to the willingness or the ability of the private sector to assume a wider role.

In the third place, governments are faced with decisions as to the balance between long-term and short-term objectives. Policy reforms associated with smaller government expenditures and a greater influence of markets are very likely to augment temporarily hardships faced by the poorest people. Unemployment may increase, food prices rise, welfare schemes provided with fewer funds and subsidies on production inputs reduced. The public sector will, however, continue to have the duty of alleviating these hardships. The choice appears to be between a broader protective coverage and faster economic growth in the longer run. The selection of the latter can be made politically viable only by skilful interventions in terms of targeting beneficiaries of foods and, in some special cases, inputs to be made available below cost, and a determination to continue to allocate public funds to these welfare schemes.

## Financing agricultural development

The magnitude of the investment requirements of agriculture in the developing countries presented in Chapter 4 point to the importance of the financing of agricultural development. At the early stages of economic growth, agricultural investment is largely own-time activities such as land clearing, building ditches and construction of simple farm buildings and in increases in livestock numbers. As agriculture modernizes, however, the share of such items in total investment decreases and that of monetized investment rises, although fully one-third of investment still takes place in activities where own-time labour work dominates.

### Sources of development finance

Issues of development finance are now increasingly focused on monetized expenditures. Three overlapping flows of financial resources dominate the financing of agricultural development: private financing, public expenditure and external financing, the latter being channelled largely through the public sector. Reliable estimates of total private investment in agriculture, especially including the own-labour component, are generally lacking, but private financing is thought typically to be more than half of total sectoral investment expenditure and public expenditure less than one-half. External flows, comprising official assistance and the relatively small private external financing, has recently accounted for around one-third of public development spending on the sector. Agriculture can also be a source of development resources for other sectors, and its ability to generate an investible surplus has been traditionally exploited to provide resources for economic growth, particularly in the early stages of development.

In the post-war period, the public sector was given a primary role in accelerating development through its fiscal policies. The recognized dual constraint to development, the difficulty of accumulating capital for investment and the chronic shortage of foreign exchange, led to calls for development finance from external sources, generally on concessional terms and so representing a transfer of resources. Such government-to-government assistance is normally disbursed through the public sector budget; excluding technical assistance, it is a capital inflow either as a grant or loan and generally in the form of foreign exchange or aid-in-kind. Traditionally agriculture, broadly defined, has been a major recipient of external assistance, with increases in the emphasis given to agriculture during the 1970s, led by the World Bank. Agriculture usually receives 15–20 percent of total official disbursements which were around $48 billion in 1985 but more than 20 percent of total concessional disbursements (approximately $36 billion 1985).

Overall, official commitments to agriculture (OCA), that exclude food aid, grew by 5–6 percent a year in real terms between 1974 and 1984, but the rate of increase has slowed down. Over the four years ending 1978–80, the real increase was 37 percent, but it was only 18 percent over the following four years.

A major event in development finance was the surge in external private borrowing (i.e. from banks or through supplier credits) that took place in the 1970s. For agriculture, however, such flows were less important, averaging $2 billion a year in 1980–2, before halving in 1982–4. They were concentrated in a few countries. For example, in the early 1980s, 60 percent of total external disbursements to agriculture in Nigeria comprised external private flows, but the corresponding figure for Bangladesh was only 1 percent.

Foreign direct investment (FDI) takes the form of risk or equity capital which is not usually guaranteed by governments. In agriculture, FDI has been concentrated in a few, generally middle-income countries, in a few sub-sectors such as forestry or food-processing, by a few transnational corporations. While important for some countries, particularly in Latin America and Asia, its gross flows to the agricultural sector in the early 1980s were estimated at only around $500 million a year.

The increase in external flows of resources during the 1970s, coupled with the surge in revenues arising from the rise in commodity prices, was reflected in a rise in public sector spending on agriculture through the development and current budgets. Development budgets usually finance capital investments in irrigation schemes, large-scale land development and the establishment of research centres, while current budgets provide for services and the maintenance of past investment. For all regions, the rise in spending was 4 percent a year in real terms between 1974 and 1983, with a particularly rapid increase in Asia, but with a decline in Latin America. The rates of increase lost their momentum from the early 1980s as governments began to be forced to reduce their fiscal deficits.

The direct contribution of agriculture to the government budget through taxes and fees is usually small or moderate. In the early 1980s, total direct and indirect taxation on agriculture by central government amounted to about 5–6 percent of total tax revenue in a sample of 35 countries, although it ranged up to 30 percent or more in some low-income countries. Agriculture was, therefore, a net receiver of central government finance. This estimate, however, does not take account of implicit taxes, price biases against agriculture, such as through overvalued exchange rates or industrial protection policies, which often are well in excess of total direct and indirect taxes.

## Issues in financing agricultural development

Some broad conclusions follow from the above brief review and provide a framework for an identification of issues. Firstly, while external financing has been a dynamic force in agricultural financing, it constitutes a relatively small source of total development resources to the sector, apparently around 10–15 percent for developing countries as a whole (excluding China). Furthermore, with the levelling off in the rates of increase in OCA and a sharp drop in private lending to the sector, it has noticeably lost momentum in recent years. It does not seem likely that OCA will expand in the future as it did during the decade 1974–84. The economies of donor countries are projected to expand more slowly, only a very small increase, if any, in the share of their GDP allocated to development assistance is expected, and agriculture already has a relatively large share of their total development assistance. Private lending continues to be affected by debt-servicing problems, low commodity prices and poor market growth prospects.

Secondly, while public sector spending on agriculture rose appreciably, there has been a less than proportionate response in agricultural production. However, the infrastructure and institutions surrounding agriculture were often so manifestly lacking that it could take much more than a decade of rising expenditures to make a noticeable impact. Studies have shown that sustained public sector expenditures do have a positive impact on agricultural performance. Nevertheless, the efficiency of public-sector expenditures must come under scrutiny.

Another issue is how to mobilize rural savings—the major source of development finance for the agriculture—and stimulate private investment in rural activities, including the local service and industrial sectors as well as agriculture itself.

Resolving the first two sets of issues—externally provided resources and public expenditures—will require greater effectiveness. This is now widely considered to require a more balanced composition of assistance as between project and programme or sectoral approaches and away from an undue concentration on projects. Such a change in emphasis would also shift more responsibility for the application of assistance to national institutions and allow quicker disbursement of funds. Sectoral or programme lending also facilitates policy dialogue between donor and recipient.

As regards public sector expenditures, the focus also is on cost-effectiveness, and where appropriate, government interventions are being withdrawn or minimized. In times of budgetary stringency, provisions to meet current expenditures are often more vulnerable than those for development expenditures. The current budget, however, may include an important component of recurrent expenditure needed to maintain and operate past capital investment. It is essential to guide expenditure-cutting exercises by careful assessments of the cost effectiveness of on-going projects.

The financing of agriculture also carries implications for sectoral contributions to government revenues. An agricultural-led development strategy implies that agriculture can become a more important source of investment capital and government revenue. Some agricultural taxes are difficult to administer and all are unpopular, but a thriving agricultural community reaping the benefits of increasing productivity promoted in part from public expenditures on such activities as research, extension and transport, can and should sustain a tax load. Fees may also be charged for public services such as veterinary attention or the provision of irrigation water.

Conversely, in other situations, tax breaks or concessions may be justified, for example in forestry investment where the financial returns are often low and postponed but the economic benefits for the society as a whole considerably greater. Fees, too, may be waived where the social benefits may exceed private benefits, such as in animal disease control programmes.

The main issue concerning the role of the private sector in financing agriculture centres on the mobilization of rural savings and their channeling to investment opportunities in rural areas. The classic argument is that poor people cannot save. The widely-held view then follows that the promotion of improved agricultural technology demands programmes operated by parastatal institutions with credit often financed by external sources, at low or negative real rates of interest, and targeted to groups of farmers or to the output of particular products. Credit at low rates of interest may also be used to offset distorted agricultural product prices.

The counter-argument is that subsidized credit can be used for purposes other than that designated, and often ends up in urban areas or in the hands of the richer farmers. The parastatal credit agencies, being absorbed by the management of their credit programmes, are neither motivated nor, indeed, set up to mobilize savings or look for rural investment opportunities. As a consequence, the rural financial market is split into two separate parts: the formal agricultural credit agency and the informal sector, which may charge high nominal rates, but is quick, flexible and provides a service that is needed.

Experience is now indicating, however, that even poor people will usually save if they have access to suitable saving mechanisms. Where such means exist for mobilizing potential savings, ranging from informal savings groups to rural branches of commercial banks, substantial investment funds can be generated from the small savings of many individuals. The Grameen Bank in Bangladesh has shown that there is a wide range of investment opportunities in rural areas waiting to be financed.

High real rates of interest are not an essential requirement for mobilizing savings, although the real rate should be positive, possibly requiring an upward shift in nominal interest rates. Similarly, relatively high interest rates are not necessarily a disincentive for rural credit needs, which usually are short term only. What is more important is the reliability of the banking service and the ease with which deposits may be made and applications for loans acted upon.

Institutional development is usually needed, ranging from supporting informal savings groups which subsequently may become cooperatives, to encouraging commercial banks to establish rural branches operating thrift deposits as well as providing managerial and financial guidance to small-scale rural enterprises.

As noted earlier, much agricultural and rural investment is own-account, self-help activities. For the promotion of such non-monetized savings and investment, at the level of individual households, security of tenure is essential. This prerequisite is often lacking. At the community level, where self-help activities can create assets such as irrigation works or feeder roads, self-help will be promoted by a reasonably egalitarian socio-economic structures so that the benefits of the assets created are not expropriated by the better-off. Land reform may be a key factor.

Finally, an expansion of non-debt-creating foreign direct investment is a possible means of replacing the declining flows of private borrowing. This form of investment is usually a transnational corporation package comprising advanced technology, management skills, access to markets and foreign exchange. This is a relatively small source of investment in developing country agriculture. Nevertheless, increased investment of this kind in agricultural enterprises such as production for export or agro-industrial enterprises, would allow more concessional funds to be allocated to less commercial activities. Forms of joint ventures and schemes to insure foreign investors against expropriation, such as the Multilateral Investment Guarantee Agency (MIGA) proposed by the World Bank, would facilitate such an expansion and reduce the profit margins with which the overseas firms may seek to offset their investment risks. A developing country needs a well-developed capability by the government to control and negotiate with the firms.

To sum up, as agriculture modernizes and as the pressure for more rural employment intensifies, the expanding needs for agricultural and rural investment will require the exploitation of all possible means of raising the volume and effectiveness of development finance. Savings by rural people, which together with their own-labour activities are the largest source of agricultural investment in developing countries, could be expanded considerably if institutional arrangements were made more adequate. Public expenditure on agricultural development complements private investment and, in view of budget stringencies in most developing countries, raising its efficiency will be increasingly important. Again, there appears scope for doing this. The third component of investment, external resource flows, will continue to be of critical importance in expanding overall investment in agriculture but appears unlikely to expand appreciably.

# 9 Rural poverty, growth and equity[1]

The need to reduce rural poverty remains one of the most pressing economic and social issues in developing countries. Poverty is very widespread, and so far efforts to improve the lot of the rural poor have usually had only limited success. It is also a very complex problem with the circumstances of poverty, and hence the detailed nature of measures to combat it, varying considerably amongst countries as well as within them. The present chapter reviews the extent of rural poverty and recent experience with measures to reduce it, as a background to a consideration of future approaches to the issue.

## Extent and characteristics of rural poverty

The World Bank estimated the number of absolute poor in 1980 to be around 780 million in the developing world apart from China and other Asian centrally planned economies. Half of the poor lived in South Asia, mainly in India and Bangladesh. A sixth lived in East and South-East Asia. Another sixth were in sub-Saharan Africa, and the rest were divided among Latin America, North Africa and the Middle East. The estimate is conservative in the sense that it used a poverty threshold based on the Indian minimum consumption 'basket' which is low in relation to general living standards in many other developing countries.

There is a close correspondence between national poverty and rural poverty in the developing countries; 90 percent of the poor as estimated above were rural people who worked on farms, or did non-farm work that depended in part on agriculture. Latin America, where 40 percent of the poor lived in urban areas, was a partial exception.

Alternative estimates based on data from a World Bank sample of 52 developing countries indicate that about half the rural population of Asia (excluding China and other centrally planned countries) and Latin America could be considered as living in poverty, with the incidences sharply higher in sub-Saharan Africa and lowest in the Near East/North Africa region. While the estimation procedure may result in some overstatement of the numbers, the data do point to the serious extent of the problem in all developing regions (Table 9.1).[2]

In addition to numbers of the poor, estimates are available on two other dimensions of poverty: how poor are the poor (i.e. the difference between the poverty cut-off point and the average per caput income of the poor) and how unequal is the income distribution among them.

[1] This chapter draws heavily on FAO 1987c.

[2] The estimation procedure uses country specific poverty cut-off points and involves: (i) identifying the food basket consumed by low-income groups in the country (taken to be the 20th percentile of the household income distribution); (ii) adjusting the quantities of that food basket necessary to provide the minimum calories and proteins required for nutritional needs; (iii) costing the minimum food basket at appropriate retail market prices; and (iv) adding the estimated monetary equivalent of essential non-food needs (clothing, shelter, etc.).

Data for nine developing countries show that per caput incomes of the bottom decile of the rural population in almost all of the countries were less than a third of per caput national income. Direct comparison with the poverty cut-off point was possible in India and Indonesia where, in both cases, average per caput incomes of the poorest 10 percent in rural areas came to only 42 percent of the level of income at the poverty cut-off point. The Gini coefficient of income distribution among the rural poor in India was over 0.41 in the early 1970s, implying a high degree of income inequality.

*Heterogeneity of rural poor*: The rural poor are a heterogeneous group, comprising landless, nomads and pastoralists, fishermen, and so on. However, they share the common disabilities of limited assets, if any, environmental vulnerability and lack of access to public services and amenities, specifically access to education and medical facilities.

According to an estimate for 1979, 30 million agricultural households were landless and another 138 million were near-landless (FAO 1986b). In terms of total numbers, landlessness is largely a South Asian problem, and the bulk of the landless are poor, as illustrated by Box 9.1 on India. Landlessness and near-landlessness are nevertheless growing in South-East Asia, Africa and Latin America.

**Box 9.1** *Rural poverty in India*

Indian data on the incidence of rural poverty are summarized below:

*Occupational classification of poor in rural India, 1977–8*

| Household type (main source of income) | Share in all rural households (%) | Incidence of poverty within each household type (%) | Share in all rural households below the poverty line (%) |
|---|---|---|---|
| 1. Self-employed in agricultural occupations | 46.1 | 30.1 | 35.0 |
| 2. Self-employed in non-agricultural occupations | 10.6 | 38.1 | 10.1 |
| 3. Agricultural labour households | 29.9 | 58.8 | 44.2 |
| 4. Other labour households | 6.9 | 38.5 | 6.7 |
| 5. Other rural households | 6.5 | 23.5 | 3.9 |
| 6. All households | 100.0 | 39.6 | 100.0 |

*Source*: National Sample Survey, Draft Report No. 298 (8), Government of India. Cited in Lipton (1985).

A very large proportion of 'agricultural labour households' (the majority of which would be landless) were poor, followed by 'other labour households' and 'self-employed in non-agricultural occupations' (consisting mainly of village artisans—blacksmiths, potters, tailors, etc.). A little under one-third of the 'self-employed in agricultural occupations' (consisting mainly of tenants and/or owners of small plots of arable land) were also poor.

As a proportion of the total number of poor, the two largest occupational groups were 'agricultural labour households' and 'self-employed in agricultural occupations'. Despite the fact that the proportion of 'agricultural labour households' in all rural households was distinctly smaller than that of 'self-employed in agricultural occupations', the poor within the former accounted for the larger share of the rural poor.

**Table 9.1** Rural poverty by region (different years in period 1975–80)*

| Region | Rural population in poverty (%) |
|---|---|
| 1. Latin America | 53.4 |
| 2. Asia | 49.8 |
| 3. Near East/N. Africa | 32.0 |
| 4. Africa (sub-Saharan) | 65.2 |

* Country details are given in FAO 1987c.

In certain situations (e.g. when agriculture is not so important or when access to land is equitable), there may be little connection between poverty and landlessness, but in most rural communities the two are closely related. The quality of land being farmed is also influential in determining the existence or degree of poverty. It has been estimated that in Indian conditions a household's risk of poverty would not be greatly reduced if it moved from landlessness up to about 1–4 semi-arid rain-fed hectares, depending on land quality.

Of a total population of 26 million to 30 million pastoralists and nomads, roughly half live in Africa and about one-third in the Near East. They are vulnerable to adverse environmental conditions, which can cause a high death rate among stock, thus depleting their major asset. This vulnerability was tragically evidenced during recent famines in Ethiopia and Sudan, where many pastoralists and nomads who had lost or sold off their animals later died from famine. While not all pastoralists or nomads are poor—incomes of Somalian nomads equalled those of small farmers—they have less access to education and agricultural services.

Another group prone to poverty is small-scale fishermen of whom there are over 10 million, living mainly in the tropics. While data are limited, it is thought that the majority of these households live below the poverty cut-off point.

## Conditions associated with poverty

*Undernutrition*: Household income/expenditure surveys in a number of countries (India, Bangladesh, the Philippines, Somalia, Kenya, Tunisia, Haiti and Peru) confirm that undernutrition is largely concentrated among the landless, share croppers, small farm holders and small-scale fishermen. As discussed in more detail later, increases in domestic production of food may result in only limited improvement in food consumption of the poor, especially when production increases consist largely of items consumed mainly by middle- and high-income consumers and produced on large- and medium-sized farms, especially those highly mechanized.

Seasonality in food production is often associated with acute undernutrition, especially among landless and near landless. Hunger increases in many rural areas during the pre-harvest months, when food reserves are low, food prices high and energy requirements for farm work increasing. During this period, adults have been found to lose up to a tenth of their body weight, child mortality rates reach a peak and sickness is prevalent. Poor and landless families headed by women or families with large numbers of children are particularly vulnerable.

The health of children is particularly at risk in conditions of undernutrition. Anthropometric surveys carried out during 1975–83 show that high percentages of children (under 5 years) in developing countries were below normal weight for age—54 percent in Asia, 26 percent in Africa and 18 percent in Latin America (excluding Argentina and Uruguay). Measured in this way, undernutrition appeared to be much higher among rural children than urban children. The implications are disturbing, since studies show that mortality rates increase rapidly as the weight-for-age indicator declines, reaching 112 per 1000 in Bangladesh when the indicator fell to under 60 percent of normal.

*Illiteracy*: A high incidence of illiteracy among sections of rural poor is confirmed in country surveys. A survey in Nigeria showed that 67 percent of hired agricultural labourers and small farmers were illiterate and had incomes below those with some schooling. In Sri Lanka the rate of illiteracy among hired and unemployed landless labourers was three times higher than the average in rural areas. Infant mortality in rural areas is higher when the mothers are illiterate. In India a survey showed a mortality rate of 139 per 1000 among infants born to illiterate mothers in rural areas, but only 64 where mothers had completed primary education, and a death rate of 101 per 1000 among infants of illiterate mothers, compared with 82 among those whose mothers had from one to six years of education. A study in Bangladesh showed that the child mortality rate in landless agricultural households was much lower when the worker had between one and six years of schooling than when he was illiterate, and that in the former circumstances it was close to child mortality rates of small landowning households.

*Dependency burden, household size and poverty*: Poor households tend to be larger in developing countries, with higher child/adult ratios (or dependency burden). A high child/adult ratio is both a cause and effect of poverty. It is a cause of poverty in as much as it implies a high consumer/earner ratio, but on the other hand, a high proportion of children may also imply a high replacement fertility overcompensating for a high mortality of children among poor households. Large families are also still widely considered desirable in rural communities in order to provide security in the future to the parents.

*Commercial disadvantages*: Links between transactions concerned with farming may aggravate the disadvantages of the poor through the imposition of some form of 'forced commerce'. For instance, trading in one market, say, the credit market in the form of consumption loans, usually induced by a threat to survival, leads to involuntary participation in exchange in some other markets (say, sale of output at a predetermined price by a small cultivator). One party tends to dictate the terms of exchange which the weaker party is obliged to accept within limits. A monopolistic landlord/moneylender who faces legally stipulated norms of maximum permissible rents or interest rates may be able to extract additional rent or interest in the form of underpaid labour services from the tenant/borrower. Such practices are considerable barriers to the improvement of living conditions of low-income households in rural areas.

## Economic performance and poverty

*Recent structural adjustment and poverty*: Developing countries faced with economic difficulties in recent years have resorted to adjustment policies, and as a result, at least in the shorter run, poverty and undernutrition have worsened in a number of countries.

A recent study of ten developing countries (Cornia *et al*. 1987), representative of all regions except the Near East/North Africa, for the period between the late 1970s to the early 1980s, confirms this general picture. Real wages declined in all but one country following widespread declines in GDP including, in six countries, a decline in per caput GDP. In the latter six countries, unemployment rose. The fall in real wages was especially heavy in sectors producing agricultural exports whose world market prices had slumped. Inflation accelerated in all countries in the early 1980s with food prices generally rising faster than overall prices.

In these circumstances, in a number of countries, the distribution of income changed to the disadvantage of the poor and the incidence of poverty rose. There is also some indication of a relative deterioration of rural conditions, for example where expenditures such as on health and education fell, there was a disproportionate decrease in social services in the rural sector.

*Agricultural growth and rural poverty*: The relationship between rural poverty and the performance of the agricultural sector remains a controversial issue. In general, it appears that a better agricultural performance results in a lower price of food, higher agricultural wage rates and employment and consequently a lower incidence of rural poverty.

This generalization is supported by recent empirical evidence in Asia, for instance:

- an unchanging inverse relationship in India between agricultural growth and rural poverty, including the period of the spread of the new technology;
- comparative village studies in the Philippines and Indonesia. Where high-yielding varieties of rice were adopted, real wages remained approximately

constant between 1960 and 1976 despite rapid population growth and in-migration. Where HYV rice was not accepted, real wages declined between 1966 and 1976, although population growth was low.
– adoption of the new technology in a Malaysian area resulted in landowning households gaining most but with real incomes of landless paddy workers almost doubling between 1967 to 1974 despite a considerable shift to the use of tractors for land preparation.

While agricultural growth should therefore generally have a favourable effect on rural poverty, the actual outcome in each specific case will be conditioned by the institutional setting. In particular, very unequal distribution of assets and access to resources may result, as has been noted in some Latin American situations, in the benefits of growth in the agricultural sector as a whole largely bypassing small farmers and agricultual workers. Subsidized mechanization can have the same effect.

*Alleviation of poverty and economic growth*: The bearing of the alleviation of poverty on economic growth has remained as an important and complex issue. A number of influences have been found to affect the outcome. If more income is consequently spent on consumption, savings, investment and subsequently growth are all seemingly reduced. Actual outcomes will, however, depend also on the composition of consumption and investment expenditure. For instance, increased purchases by the poor will do more to stimulate overall economic growth than consumption expenditure on imports of luxury consumer goods.

The time horizon may also be critical to the trade-off between growth and poverty. While a redistributional strategy may involve a loss of savings and consequently a lowering of growth of aggregate output, these immediate unfavourable effects may be more than neutralized by productivity gains as a consequence of nutritional improvement among the poorer sections over a period of time. The assumption that the poor save little is also questionable in the light of recent experience of schemes which are designed to attract and mobilize the small savings of the many individuals.

Given the composition of aggregate output and the time horizon, the trade-off between the growth of output and poverty may also depend on the labour-intensity of production. The greater the labour intensity, the lower may be the trade-off. In brief, the empirical evidence suggests that anti-poverty intervention does not necessarily lower growth over a period of time.

## Reducing rural poverty: experience and policy approaches

The incidence of rural poverty, its characteristics and causes vary across agro-climatic environments, across social and political systems and over time. Generalizations on the appropriate policy actions towards poverty alleviation are therefore fraught with difficulties. Nevertheless, certain policy conclusions are emerging which, though not necessarily applicable in each and every developing country, merit serious attention in most.

The broad theme is that accelerated per caput agricultural growth, stimulated by technological change, is central to solving rural poverty in low-income countries with large agricultural populations. However, important qualifications must be made in terms of the type of technological change, its diffusion and the access to productive resources. Even when these conditions are met, in many cases agricultural growth alone will not be enough. Thus, complementary policy initiatives must be taken within agriculture to tackle rural poverty directly. Finally, since the rate of expansion of the non-farm sector will be a key factor, particular attention must also be focused on the creation of non-farm employment opportunities.

*Promoting agricultural growth*: Backward agricultural technologies and sluggish growth in output, together with rapid population growth within a rigid institutional setting merely serves to worsen the position of the poor. On the other hand, accelerated agricultural growth, promoted by sustained technological change, can make a significant contribution to poverty alleviation. For agricultural growth to benefit the poor, however, new technologies should be spread widely throughout the rural sector, with care being taken to ensure that the extent of use of herbicides and mechanization (particularly at harvest), does not cause serious labour displacement, and the availability of food products on domestic markets should be allowed to increase. If these conditions are met, the poor gain as landless labourers employed for longer periods (even if real wage rates may not change much), as producers with lower production costs and a greater marketed surplus, and as consumers enjoying a more nutritious diet and a smaller food bill.

These circumstances, however, though favourable to the rural poor in terms of their absolute income levels, do not necessarily improve their position in the overall income distribution. A dynamic agricultural sector may be yet more advantageous to other income groups (including the urban poor). In addition, the employment-creation opportunities offered by the new technologies may be smaller in the future partly because more marginal areas are being brought into cultivation.

While the production projections of this study are based on a plausible set of technological conditions, alternative changes in technology, which are yet more 'pro-poor', could be envisaged. These technologies, however, would require greater research efforts and policy incentives to promote progress in crops grown in less favourable environments (particularly the dryland areas), and in crops grown and/or consumed by the poor.

New technologies can directly benefit the poor producer if they are designed to improve small farm systems or to increase yields of staple crops grown on small farms. To take a specific example, there appears to be considerable scope, notwithstanding the difficulties discussed in Chapter 4, for raising the productivity of root crops, the traditional staple food of much of Africa and the Pacific, with the result of improving diets and increasing food security of small producers. Yet relatively little research has been undertaken on improved planting material and cultivation practices, and governments often show more interest in agricultural products for urban or export markets.

An important determinant of labour requirements in agriculture and, it may be inferred, of the incidence of rural poverty, is the choice of cropping pattern. Indeed, the employment creation effects of changes in the crop mix can exceed those of specifically designed rural employment programmes. The range of employment outcomes will depend on the type of crops grown (some crops are relatively more labour intensive than others), and on the scope for multiple and inter-cropping. These choices of cropping pattern must, however, be made within the constraints imposed by the commodity pattern of demand growth.

The seasonal character of much agricultural production (with peaks in labour demand at planting and harvesting) can increase the vulnerability of the casual worker to undernutrition (in the slack season). In the scenario projections, about a tenth of the growth in agricultural output will be due to greater cropping intensity. To the extent that this entails multiple cropping (taking advantage of short-duration modern varieties) and inter-cropping (where the crops may have different harvest periods), fluctuations in the demand for labour are usually reduced. Moreover, those who obtain employment as a result of the expansion of livestock production will also enjoy a more steady stream of earnings throughout the year. These changes are favourable to better nutritional conditions for small farmers and landless labourers.

Agricultural prices, particularly of food, exert a dominant influence on poverty. At the national level, an increase in agricultural production will lower domestic prices if domestic availability is allowed to expand. Provided that changes in farm level prices get passed on to the consumer (i.e. there is no collusion or serious inefficiency in the marketing chain), cheaper food prices are highly favourable to those poor, particularly the landless labourer, with a high dependence on market purchases for his food requirements. (This will not be so if money wages fall in line with food prices.) On the other hand, low farm-level prices are detrimental to the poor producer who has a marketed surplus but may have been unable to adopt cost-reducing technology. The importance of ensuring a widespread diffusion of new technologies is thus apparent. However, trade policy will be the critical determinant of whether or not these changes in domestic prices and income distribution take place. If the additional agricultural production is not absorbed domestically but is used to reduce imports or increase exports, the price effects on poverty will not occur. Only the producer who has been able to adopt the new technology will enjoy an increase in net income; non-adopters and consumers will be unaffected.

Technical choices which improve the well-being of the poor, exist or can be made the subject of future research efforts. The policy-makers' tasks are to make these choices widely available and economically attractive to the producer, and to enable the poor as consumers to benefit from a lower cost of living.

*Adding to the assets of the poor through land reform*: Land redistribution and tenancy reforms are the most fundamental of direct anti-poverty measures in the rural sectors of developing countries, and most countries have attempted to introduce such measures.

The history of land reforms is largely, but by no means entirely, one of failures. Usually only a small fraction of the surplus land (land above prescribed ownership ceilings) was actually redistributed (e.g. Bangladesh, Brazil, Chile, India, Nepal, Pakistan). Often it is the poor-quality land which has been surrendered and redistributed (e.g. Sri Lanka and Colombia). The achievements in tenancy reforms have also been disappointing. Either rent regulatory measures were not implemented (as in India and Indonesia) or if implemented did not result in any improvements. Evidence points in fact to a worsening of the position of tenants in some countries, with large-scale evictions of tenants, continuation of high rents and unregistered tenancies.

Lack of political will and opposition from landlords have been key factors and some attempted reforms have been technically underprepared.

Despite numerous failures to achieve significant results, sufficient examples exist to show quite conclusively that land reform can be made to work, for example in the Republic of Korea, the Indonesian transmigration programme and the West Bengal land redistribution and tenancy reforms.

Land reform programmes have two major advantages. First, since the distribution of income depends to a great extent upon the distribution of productive assets, a more equitable redistribution of these assets would bring about a more equitable distribution of income and a substantial improvement in the living standards of the poor, without reducing aggregate output, at least in the longer term. Even if the objective is not fully achieved, some redistribution will improve equity. Second, the benefits of such a programme are not easily reversible. There is, in fact, no real substitute for a significant degree of land reform to reduce rural poverty in situations where agricultural land is very unequally distributed.

How drastic a redistribution of assets would be feasible is a country-specific matter. The production projections indicate that arable land per caput (of the agricultural labour force) will decline in Asia, the Near East and Africa, but in Latin America, where the agricultural labour force is growing at a much slower rate (and in some countries is declining), average land availability per caput will rise (Table 9.2).

**Table 9.2** Land availability per caput

| | Arable land (ha) per caput of agricultural labour force | | Growth of agricultural labour force (% p.a.) |
|---|---|---|---|
| | 1982/4 | 2000 | 1982/4–2000 |
| 93 Developing Countries | 1.4 | 1.3 | 1.3 |
| Africa (sub-Saharan) | 1.6 | 1.4 | 1.8 |
| Near East/N. Africa | 2.8 | 2.5 | 0.6 |
| Latin America | 4.9 | 5.5 | 0.3 |
| Asia (excl. China) | 0.8 | 0.7 | 1.2 |

In *Asia*, the reduction in the already limited land availability per caput has been associated with a higher incidence of landlessness in Bangladesh and of near-landlessness in India, Sri Lanka, Thailand and the Philippines. The pressure on sub-division and fragmentation may be counteracted to some degree by land settlements. However, despite programmes of agrarian reform in most countries, little change in the relatively unequal distribution of land in the region generally has been evident (although these programmes may have prevented matters getting worse). Nevertheless, in partial offset to reduced land availability the producer, on average, has achieved higher yields.

In *Latin America*, in the opposite situation of increasing availability of land per caput (in all countries in the region except Haiti and Paraguay), the problem of national land scarcity has not arisen. Nevertheless, smallholders have very limited access to land, especially the better-quality land. The small-farm sector has had to accommodate most of the increase in rural population (with 'mini-minifundia' resulting), and at the same time it is being crowded out of the food market by the expanding commercial sector, comprising the medium- and large-sized farms, which are better placed to take advantage of technological change and market opportunities. Indeed, the small-farm sector is becoming less and less important both as a productive unit (in terms of contribution to agricultural GDP) and as a source of labour (as the large farms adopt labour-saving technology). In the absence of intervention, these trends are likely to continue, despite increasing availability of land per caput, and to aggravate the existing severe problem of poverty and lack of equity in agriculture.

In regions with relatively higher availability of land per caput, there is more scope for promoting greater rural equity and reducing poverty by enhancing access to land. However, in other regions, for example Asia, where a relatively large proportion of the land is currently farmed by smallholders and most countries are at or close to their land frontier, other approaches to a reduction in poverty must play a larger role than the necessarily more limited but still significant degree of potential land redistribution.

*Adding to the productivity of the poor—access to inputs, markets and services*: Improved access to productivity-raising inputs, markets and services have been a major part of efforts to solve rural poverty. In view of commercial disadvantages often suffered by the poor because of the possible linking of agricultural-related transactions referred to earlier, these measures are best combined as far as possible rather than applied separately. They should also be adapted to the requirements of women as well as to men working in agriculture.

*Credit*: Access to institutional credit (e.g. banks, cooperatives), as opposed to borrowing from the local moneylender, remains confined to certain segments of small cultivators, rendering it difficult for a majority of small farmers and landless labourers to invest in yield-improving methods/techniques. There are, however, a number of credit-based programmes designed to assist small and marginal farmers, for example Integrated Rural Development Programme (IRDP) in India, Grameen Bank in Bangladesh and Small Farmers' Development Programme (SFDP) in Nepal. They have achieved varying degrees of success, but there has been considerable under-representation of target groups among the beneficiaries. For instance, in IRDP in India, a substantial percentage of the beneficiaries were small farmers who were not formally eligible for the assistance.

In the recently introduced pilot credit schemes (Kredit Untuk Pedesaan—KUPEDES) in several areas of Indonesia, credit is provided and chanelled through small-farm groups and no collateral is required. Furthermore, the credit is not restricted to agricultural investment but also covers other productive activities of small-farming households. With a repayment rate of 90 percent, the performance of the scheme has been impressive.

Such programmes tend to be one-shot injections of resources without adequate provision for working capital and consumption loans required to support the investments over critical periods before returns begin to be received or during their temporary cessation. Moreover, the capital stock created may be too small and fragile; and the flow of new additional income may also be insufficient for enabling the poor to escape poverty. However, a number of the schemes are of recent origin or limited application and sufficient time has not yet elapsed for the full benefits to become available or for the modifications suggested by experience to be made. Initial results have generally been sufficiently promising for substantial longer-term results to be possible.

In order to give more poor farmers access to credit, either the problem of lack of collateral must be overcome by redistribution of productive assets or a less rigid view of the need for collateral must be taken. Moreover, when credit is provided it is best not restricted unduly to single activities, crops or products, but rather the credit institutions, recognizing the occupational multiplicity of the poor, should aim to facilitate related productive activities. Encouragement should be given to schemes which encourage and mobilize, for local use, savings of individual poor people.

*Irrigation*: The choice of irrigation scheme (e.g. large or small scale, new or rehabilitated) can influence the incidence of poverty through employment creation for landless labourers during construction and maintenance, and through the provision of adequate and reliable water supplies to small producers. As with any technical choice, of which irrigation is a major example, the appropriateness of a given system cannot be judged without reference to the particular socio-economic and agro-climatic environment in which the scheme is to be placed. Past experience suggests that causes of failure are not so much a function of size as a lack of appreciation, in the design of irrigation schemes, of the needs and contraints of indigenous small-farm systems.

Moreover, one of the major problems, particularly with large schemes, has been that many administrative structures became very cumbersome, slow to respond to producers' changing requirements, and very complex. If smaller-scale systems (for instance, based on swamp management, river diversion or tubewells) can be operated within a cooperative management framework, they can give the small producer a voice in the decision-making process, as well as provide a more equitable distribution of water supplies.

*Extension services*: To ensure the spread of new, improved technologies there is a primary need for extension and manpower training services and to assure access to them by the small farmer and landless labourer. Yet these requirements have been neglected in many parts of the developing world but notably in Africa. There are of course exceptions, but often in these cases the services have strongly favoured the larger-scale, wealthier and apparently more progressive farmers, leaving many smaller, poorer producers disadvantaged. Where facilities do exist, they are often underfinanced or poorly maintained. The inadequate deployment of extension staff is mainly due to lack of funds for transport and other expenditures. There is then considerable scope, particularly in Africa, for improving the effectiveness of extension and training services and for augmenting them in a substantial way, through budgetary support, as part of the approach to improving equity and reducing poverty within agriculture.

*Investment in human capital*: Access to formal education can raise the productivity of small farmers, facilitate adoption of improved agricultural practices and open up new avenues of employment for labourers in rural areas. As a result, especially among cultivators, formal education is typically associated with a marked reduction in the risk of poverty. In addition, female education is associated with a lower risk of infant mortality and lower levels of fertility.

From a policy perspective, the options are to either raise the general educational level in rural areas, or to have more targeted programmes addressed to improved skills in farming. In the latter approach, there is much scope for the greater participation of female members of the farming community and other neglected groups such as remote resource-poor farmers and landless labourers.

*Employment*: The potential for additional employment and labour-intensive technological change will be a critical factor in determining the impact of intensification on the poor. The production projections of this study are founded on feasible changes in input usage and involve adaptation and transfer of existing technologies across regions. The relatively labour-intensive strategy results in a growth of demand for labour man-days which exceeds the growth of the agricultural workforce in all regions and country groups. Additional days of work could be found in livestock production and in the fishery and forestry sectors, not explicitly considered in the analysis.

In addition to an expanding demand for employment arising from the growth of agricultural production, governments have frequently introduced specific employment-creating schemes. These are essentially rural works programmes or food for work programmes—for example, Employment Guarantee Scheme (EGS) in India, Rural Works Programme in Bangladesh, the Kabupaten programme in Indonesia. While the major objective has been the creation of employment, particularly during agricultural slack seasons, the creation of durable assets (especially agricultural infrastructure) has also been emphasized. In some schemes the participation of the target groups has not been altogether satisfactory. For instance, in the case of the EGS in India, slightly fewer than half of the workers came from the landless population and the very small farmers while half or more came from larger landowners. Sharing of benefits of the assets created through the EGS, however, was even more unequal than the sharing of employment. On the other hand, although the Kabupaten programme of rural development in Indonesia was not specifically targeted on the rural poor, most of the workers involved represented the poorer rural families. In Bangladesh, the Rural Works Programme, which undertakes construction and renovation of irrigation channels, flood protection works and so on has become the single most important programme for poverty alleviation in rural areas.

Schemes of these kinds have therefore brought about increased employment, although the increases have not been as large as was hoped. They can also absorb underemployed or unemployed workers in the slack season without interfering with crop production. The underlying situation of an unequal distribution of assets invariably leads to unequal sharing of power in a community. As a consequence, a leakage of benefits is bound to occur. However, because numerous very poor people do share in the benefits, such a consequence should be looked on as an unavoidable cost in the circumstances rather than a reason to abolish or reduce such schemes.

*Producer price policies and marketing services*: The importance of producer price policies has been discussed in Chapter 8. This section needs only to re-emphasize that unless careful attention is given in their design and application to the circumstances of small farmers, the benefits of price supports and incentives, they will benefit little from them. The distribution of benefits from price supports would mirror to a large extent the distribution of land. It is also essential that small farmers have assured access to marketing channels through which producer price policies are applied. Likewise, the marketing of inputs must not be organized so that they primarily benefit large purchasers.

*Consumer food prices*: Many developing countries have introduced supplementary feeding programmes for the benefit of nutritionally vulnerable groups or broader subsidies to reduce the cost of food to poor people. These policies were also discussed briefly in the preceding chapter. Here it can be noted that while often expensive in fiscal terms, welfare food distribution schemes have become in many countries an integral part of policies to combat the worst effects of poverty. The limitation of benefits to target groups, increasingly necessary for keeping costs down, remains a major problem, but experience has indicated various ways in which this aim can be achieved to a reasonable degree. The schemes, however, have been of greater benefit to urban rather than rural poor, despite the much greater numbers of the rural poor. Their progressive extension to rural areas is therefore needed.

Reasonable stability in consumer food prices is also important in the fight against poverty. Abrupt rises in food prices almost invariably hurt poor people whose incomes, even if they rise to the same extent, will do so only with a lag. Reasonable price stability does not, however, mean complete price rigidity. In that case, price adjustments finally called for are likely to be more damaging still to poor people.

*Promoting the non-farm sector*: Labour-intensive agricultural growth will by itself prove an inadequate means of alleviation of rural poverty. In order to raise or maintain per caput incomes in agricultural households and to provide work for those members who cannot be productively employed in agriculture, an increasing proportion of employment will have to be provided by non-farm activities. The importance of the growing non-agricultural labour force in rural areas is reflected in its 30–40 percent share of the total rural labour force in most developing countries. The agricultural labour force has grown at a much slower rate than the rural non-agricultural labour force in all developing regions (e.g. in Latin America the growth rates were 0.9 percent and 2.6 percent p.a. and for South-East Asia 4.5 and 1.3 percent, respectively, in the period 1950–80). The degree of involvement of rural households in non-farm activities has thus been steadily increasing.

The importance of non-farm employment for the poor is underscored by two additional factors: many rural poor households derive a significant proportion of their income from non-farm activities, and the counter-cyclical nature of non-farm employment smooths the seasonal pattern of earnings. In most countries the share of off-farm employment in total employment is significantly higher for the smaller holdings. Since, typically, rural households with inadequate access to land seek non-farm employment in the slack agricultural season and return to farming in the peak season, a counter-cycle to the peaks and troughs of agricultural employment and earnings is generated.

The macro-economic projections used in this study imply that in many developing countries the growth rate of the non-agricultural GDP would not be much above that projected for agriculture. Under these circumstances there might well be very limited opportunities for absorption of labour in the non-agricultural sector. If so, the agricultural labour force may grow at rates above those indicated earlier (see Table 4.9).

There is, however, considerable potential for an expanding agricultural sector itself to stimulate growth in the non-farm sector—through its need for marketing, processing and distribution services, its increased demand for farm inputs and its greater expenditure on household consumption. These developments can be facilitated and encouraged by policy intervention which, however, must be designed and implemented with great care, as illustrated in Box 9.2 on rural industrialization in China. An expanding non-farm sector does not lead automatically, however to a reduction in poverty. It is also important that the objectives of policy interventions should go beyond mere employment creation. There are a sufficient number of case studies indicating that workers in rural industry receive low wages not significantly different from those of landless agricultural workers, to caution that attention must also focus on conditions of employment including wage rates, hours of work, health and safety standards and worker participation. From the perspective of assisting the rural poor, the issue is not only the size of the non-farm sector, but the conditions and environment within which it can perform a poverty alleviating role.

**Box 9.2** *Rural industrialization in China*

The vigorous rural industrialization programme in China exemplifies how, through an allocation of surpluses generated in industrial enterprises, social goals can also be achieved.

One basic problem confronting rural industries in developing countries is the deficiency of demand for their products, in part due to poor quality of their products and also to their inability to compete with the larger enterprises located mainly in urban areas. Therefore, when income rises in rural areas, it does not result in an appreciable increase in the demand for the products of rural industries. Such a problem, however, did not confront rural industries in China which enjoyed an adequate local market in the commune itself. Also, intra-industrial competition (from the state-run urban industrial enterprises) was precluded in most areas, especially in the early phase of development.

The surpluses generated in these industrial enterprises were distributed through general welfare programmes which improved the standard of living of all members of the communes and financed schemes of agricultural development tending to favour underdeveloped parts of the commune. But a sizeable part was also used for the expansion and diversification of the commune's industrial sector. Such a mechanism thus became dynamically cumulative, allowing a widening of the product and technology range, an increasing involvement with large-scale state factories in sub-contracting arrangements, and a steady improvement in the standard of living of all members in the commune.

An important institutional feature was the full integration of the agricultural and the industrial sectors, within the same ownership and decision-making unit. Thus peasant labour, having generated the industrial surpluses, could gain through direct welfare transfers, and also through the higher incomes generated through the higher agricultural productivity financed by such surpluses.

There is also the question of whether non-farm enterprises should be rural-based. Location in rural areas has been viewed as essential in those cases (e.g. Kenya, Lesotho, Tanzania) in which urban areas have been unable to absorb an increasing number of rural migrants. Rural industrialization then serves to limit further large-scale out-migration, and the diversification of the rural economy offers a more direct and in the end less expensive way of alleviating poverty. However, what may be more important from the point of view of rural poverty alleviation is not location *per se*, but rather whether non-farm enterprises generate significant development linkages with the rural sector. While a rural-based non-farm enterprise may obtain most of its resources from, and return most of its surplus to, urban areas or even abroad, if the infrastructure is well developed and if rural resources including labour are sufficiently mobile, a firm can be urban-based and still generate significant rural income. For example, the textile (especially silk) industry of the Republic of Korea developed in urban areas, but the rural linkages were established through the supply of raw materials and labour.

The success of rural industrialization programmes as a long-term strategy for poverty alleviation will depend on the ability of rural enterprises to adapt to changing market conditions and demands. Positive government support can take the form of advice on product quality control and marketing, and the provision of marketing research information. In addition, rural enterprises must adapt to changing means of production as new technologies emerge, if they are to remain competitive with alternative sources of supply. Again, the government can assist by undertaking research, extension and training services. An example of policy intervention along these lines is provided by India, where the promotion of village industries is an integral part of the national development programme. District Industries Centres provide support at the district level by undertaking feasibility studies in the area, arranging credit, supplying extension and training services and assisting with marketing. A basic requirement for the success of rural industrialization is that, as in China and in some schemes in Bangladesh, rural people are given the opportunity to save and invest in local industry.

*People's participation and organization*: Regardless of the quality and comprehensiveness of government policies, rural poverty can be abolished only with the voluntary and active participation of the rural people themselves. Experience indicates that when the poor fail to benefit from rural development programmes—including specific anti-poverty programmes—it is largely because they are isolated and unorganized. Governments can, however, encourage and assist the organization of local communites in numerous ways, such as those described in the Programme of Action of the World Conference on Agrarian Reform and Rural Development.

The difficulties of forming trade unions in rural areas are well known. Labour is abundant and cheap, often seasonally unemployed, widely dispersed and unable to resist the demands of employers. Nevertheless, some progress may be possible, particularly among landless and near landless workers.

It is doubtful whether rural trade unions can significantly raise either total employment or the real wage rate, and to the extent that they do the latter, this may be partly at the expense of other workers. Unions can, however, negotiate successfully for improved working conditions, in ensuring that labour and wage laws are enforced and in ending the physical abuse of workers by landowners. Support by government policy of the union movement and protection of its members is particularly important while they are still at the early stages of organization.

# 10 Technological developments of the future

The main technological determinants of agricultural progress during the remainder of this century are well established. The realization of the scenario presented in Chapter 3 and the projected resource use discussed in Chapter 4 therefore are not heavily dependent on new technologies. Most of the required gains in productivity are achievable with the evolutionary progress in the application or adaptation of available technologies.

Looking further ahead it is apparent that the technological determinants will not simply echo those of the past, although many of the dominant features will be the same. Factor scarcity, particularly in land, water and labour, will be the main driving force. But as described below, environmental conservation, agricultural pollution abatement and sustainability of agricultural production will be objectives more dominant than in the past, and biotechnology is expected to create new opportunities to meet these aims.

## Technological innovation in agriculture: past and future

In the industrialized countries, science has made an increasing contribution to agricultural technology from the beginning of the nineteenth century onward. Agricultural research institutions have played an increasing role in encouraging and testing innovations in agricultural technology, whether initiated by farmers, scientists or engineers. Organized plant breeding also had its origins in the nineteenth century, largely through outbreeding crops, such as sugar beet, where farmers had difficulty in producing their own seed.

In this accelerating application of science to agriculture, contributions from the private sector have been complementary to those of the publicly funded institutions. In fact, the private sector has been the chief promoter in important areas like seed production and pesticides development, the breeding of broiler and laying hens, the development of farm machinery, in processing techniques, and so on. The collective outcome has been an expanding flow of agricultural technology soundly based on scientific investigation.

The intensification of production that these new technologies have permitted, coupled with a favourable economic environment, has led to the now familiar problems of agricultural surplus in the majority of industrialized countries (see Chs. 3 and 8). Moreover, the cultivation of marginal land and the indiscriminate use of chemicals have induced the equally familiar problems of ecological change and environmental pollution (see Ch. 11).

In many developing countries the response to population pressure has been to reduce the period of land resting between crops, leading at best to a low-level production equilibrium or, at worst, to soil degradation and erosion. The consequences can be serious, especially when there is migration into areas of tropical rain-forest or on to land that is marginal for arable cropping because of unreliable rainfall or infertile soils. In both situations there are considerable risks of soil erosion and environmental degradation, as well as declining yields and crop failure in some seasons (see Ch. 11).

Consequently, some of the issues for both the industrialized and the developing countries, though arising from different causes, are essentially similar in the scientific challenges they pose. In both, for example, there is an urgent need to develop and promote technologies that increase or sustain productivity at lower costs and do not harm the environment.

*Considerations for developing countries*: In any discussion of research, it is useful to distinguish among the various levels at which it is conducted, even though such distinctions represent arbitrary divisions of a continuum of activities. In the Second Review of the Consultative Group on International Agricultural Research (CGIAR) the terms 'basic', 'strategic', 'applied' and 'adaptive' were used and will be adopted here (CGIAR 1981). In this usage, basic research means the quest for new knowledge; strategic research relates to the solution of specific research problems such as devising a new research technique; applied research relates to the creation of new technology; and adaptive research denotes the fine adjustment of new technologies to suit the needs of particular environments of farming systems.

Because adaptive research has been closely linked to development strategies, priorities for adaptive research in the developing countries have been strongly influenced by the prevailing economic policies. In general, development plans and economic policies have not focused specifically on the problems of the resource-poor farmer but have concentrated on the most obvious ways of generating wealth, such as from irrigation, exportable cash crops or by expanding production on the large commercial farms. Problems of the resource-poor farmer have not always been omitted from the research agenda, but results have been unspectacular and progress in their application often limited not necessarily because of poor technologies but due to problems of their acceptance and use.

With renewed emphasis on social equity and the role of women in agriculture, however, national development strategies are now giving increasing emphasis to problems of the resource-poor farmer. Consequently, changes are required in priorities for adaptive research, as well as in the applied research on which it draws, even though research policy is not the best instrument to pursue distributional objectives.

Fortunately, there already exists a substantial body of relevant knowledge built up from basic, strategic and applied research during the present century and, in more recent years, sustained and developed by the International Agricultural Research Centres (IARCs). The application of this knowledge and the creation of new knowledge to meet effectively the challenges of overcoming poverty and malnutrition however require changes in the programmes of both national and international research systems.

## Requirements to meet new challenges

The search for technological innovations to help farmers in less favourable circumstances and to sustain development in more favoured areas must be based on a thorough understanding of:

— the physical and biological production environments;
— the genetic potential for increased productivity;
— the socio-economic circumstances in which the farmer operates.

The implications of these basic considerations will vary from country to country, but may include greater emphasis on rain-fed agriculture in the less favourable areas, while remaining alert to the possibilities for irrigation; greater attention to nutrient recycling without discounting the crucial importance of mineral fertilizers; greater attention to traditional patterns of intercropping while not prejudicing the opportunities for mechanization and the use of herbicides; investigating possibilities for integrated and biological control of pests while exploiting suitable opportunities for the proper use of chemical pesticides; breeding for stress tolerance, in both crops and livestock, without restricting performance under favourable conditions; greater understanding of the farming systems of the small producer, while not neglecting the problems of large-scale production; greater attention to the basic food commodities, while recognizing the place of cash crops in income generation; greater attention to small ruminants; and intensified efforts to resolve the dry season feed-supply and feed-quality problem.

A balanced approach is essential, but the nature of the balance will depend on local circumstances. Broadly, the aims of research and technology development must be to raise productivity in ways that do not aggravate fluctuations in production, do not reduce the potential of the environment to sustain production indefinitely into the future and that contribute to increased rural incomes.

In addition, there are many problems of food-processing, storage and preparation that currently lack suitable solutions and therefore require urgent attention, particularly with respect to the use of fuel for cooking given the increasing scarcity of fuelwood, and the need to expand the production of processed forms of foods from traditional staples.

*Rainfall and water conservation*: Some 80 percent of the developing world's potential arable land is in areas with sub-humid or semi-arid climates and erratic rainfall. But the economically available surface and groundwater resources can only irrigate a small fraction of this potential. Therefore the exploitation and sustained use of this potential is dependent on developments in research and technology that improve understanding of soil-plant-atmosphere systems; that modify such systems and improve water use efficiency through run off management and water harvesting, and changes in cropping patterns and rotations; and that manipulate soil fertility and water interactions to increase crop yields through improved fertilizer and water use efficiency, for example by using modern tillage practices to raise available soil water.

In the absence of irrigation, tropical agriculture is dominated by the amount, distribution and reliability of rainfall. These parameters are the primary determinants of productivity. They largely determine optimum maturation periods for crops, optimum grazing patterns for livestock, optimum practices for soil management and optimum responses to soil nutrients. They also have profound effects on the activity of soil micro-organisms as well as on the occurrence and severity of pests and diseases, all of which contribute to the biological production environment.

Early work in East Africa showed how rainfall patterns varied over relatively small areas and that probability analysis could be used to give greater predictability to the results of both agronomic experiments and variety trials. In conjunction with knowledge of crop water requirements, such analysis could also be used to define the desirable plant ideotype. These conclusions were applied in the development of short-term maize varieties for the low-rainfall areas of Kenya. The Katumani composite varieties produced did much to improve the reliability of food supply in large areas of Kenya. Although this essentially agro-meteorological approach has been adopted by others, it has not received great emphasis in research programmes, either at the national or international levels, but this must happen if the full potential of areas with low and erratic rainfall is to be exploited.

Such efforts in plant breeding need to be complemented by others to reap the maximum benefit from rainfall. No increase in productivity can be achieved in many sub-humid and semi-arid areas without the more efficient use of rainfall, the aim being to devise systems of soil management that prevent both erosion and excessive leaching. Finding methods of achieving this that do not compete with the more immediate needs for inputs of labour is often difficult and constitutes one of the major challenges for the future.

For example, tie-ridging on the sandy soils of Tanzania proved unpopular for this reason even though substantial increases in yield had been demonstrated in addition to the long-term benefits of preventing soil erosion. In earlier years, however, a practice that effectively amounted to tie-ridging was the normal method of soil management on Ukara Island (Tanzania), until the pressure of population on the island was relieved by migration to the mainland. The issue that arises is how to create incentives for the prevention of soil erosion before the forces of dire necessity take their toll. It is an issue for which there is no obvious solution but one with which researchers and policy-makers must continue to grapple.

Another approach which needs further development is minimum tillage systems for soil moisture conservation that are appropriate to developing-country conditions. Minimum tillage has substantially boosted crop productivity and reduced soil erosion in North America, but the techniques used are unsuitable for peasant agriculture and for certain soil types. Cheaper and less toxic herbicides are required together with simple but reliable sprayers and planters. Work in Nigeria and the Gambia shows great promise, but it needs to be extended to other environments.

*Soil productivity*: Improved soil-management practices to increase efficiency in the use of rainfall can help to alleviate the effects of unreliable rainfall amounts or distribution, but they cannot entirely avert the dangers of drought or prevent crop failure in exceptional seasons. The application of relatively small amounts of water at critical periods of crop growth can have disproportionate effects on the yield of crops such as sorghum, by reducing the effects of water-stress. Consequently, the use of simple techniques to build ponds or wells for supplementary irrigation must remain at the forefront of approaches to increase the stability of production in marginal areas.

Technologies to reduce the risk of water-stress are entirely complementary to those directed to increasing and sustaining the supply of nutrients and to overcoming problems of toxicity. In spite of the obvious futility of attempts to increase productivity without adding nutrients to the soil, plant breeders and agronomists are not infrequently urged to develop technologies for increasing yields with minimum use of commercial fertilizers.

Where soils are already on the verge of degradation, technologies that use minimum inputs are unlikely either to increase yields significantly or to prevent further degradation in adverse seasons. In these circumstances, the primary requirement for beginning the process of restoring soil structure and fertility is to induce more vigorous crop growth through the use of mineral fertilizers or relatively large dressings of organic manure.

*Pests and diseases*: Perhaps the most consistent cause of depressed yields in tropical environments arises from competition for water and nutrients from weeds. Attempting to maintain crops weed-free is also one of the most frequent causes of bottlenecks in labour. It follows that there could probably be no greater contribution to increasing productivity in tropical environments than by solving the problems of weed control, partly because effective weed control demands well-grown crops which, in turn contribute greatly to the prevention of soil erosion and, through vigorous root growth, to the maintenance of soil structure. Consequently, technologies that reduce competition from weeds and increase the productivity of labour in weed control deserve high priority in research.

There are three basic strategies to enhance weed control:

- giving greater emphasis in crop rotations to crops, such as maize or sorghum that establish quickly and smother the weeds;
- encouraging mechanization through draught animals or simple machines; and
- using herbicides.

In addition, given the biotechnical methods now available for transferring genes between unrelated plant species, there are interesting possibilities, in the long term, for the development of allelopathic plants. These strategies are clearly not mutually exclusive and are usually applied in a complementary or integrated approach, with the aim of reducing labour requirements where labour is scarce and achieving effective control of weeds.

Pest and disease problems are and will continue to become more serious in developing countries as a result of the intensification of agricultural production practices and the replacement of generally low-yielding but disease-resistant traditional cultivars by more susceptible modern varieties. In response to this challenge many modern varieties have multiple resistance bred into them, but more needs to be done in this field. Moreover, the use of pesticides is having two negative effects: 'New' pests and diseases are appearing at an accelerating rate because of the impact of pesticides on non-target species, and prolonged exposure to pesticides is leading to genetic adaptation or selection of pesticide-resistant pest strains. These problems require major research efforts, particularly on the ecology of crops and their pests, whether weeds, insects, mites or diseases. Strategies that, amongst other actions, combine the use of resistant varieties, changed cultural practices and limited use of pesticides, have demonstrated ways of reducing the rate of build-up of the pest problem, which in most circumstances may be all that is required to allow natural enemies of the pest to gain effective control. This integrated approach to pest management is increasingly becoming recognized as the preferred alternative to the indiscriminate use of chemical pesticides.

*The genetic potential for increased productivity*: The development and use of improved varieties will continue to provide the farmer with one of the most easily adopted and cost-effective innovations. Although during the past 50 years, great strides have been made in raising the potential yield of the world's most important staple food crops, there is no reason to suppose, even in the most advanced varieties of crops such as wheat, that the potential for further improvement has yet been exhausted. Further contributions may be expected not only in yield potential but also in resistance to pests and diseases, the improvement of quality and the adaptation of the crop to more efficient production practices, such as by lending itself more readily to mechanized establishment, harvesting or mixed cropping.

Moreover, through breeding for resistance to crop hazards, such as water stress and storm damage, as well as pests and diseases, the breeder can contribute to reducing the severity of fluctuations in production. Given the complexity of the problem, however, the contribution that the breeder can make to stability of production in regions of unreliable rainfall will be relatively small compared to the overriding influence of rainfall distribution. Moreover, in all regions, stability is strongly influenced by economic policies and by such considerations as the distribution and timely availability of fertilizers and other production inputs.

Similar considerations apply to breeding for resistance to adverse soil conditions, such as salinity and aluminium toxicity. Although significant advances have already been made in breeding for tolerance to both these conditions, it would be unwise to expect too much from plant breeding alone. An integrated approach is required, in which tolerant varieties constitute only one element in the attempted solution.

The rapid application of the benefits of new varieties continues to be hampered, however, by inadequate facilities for seed multiplication and distribution. These limitations are particularly apparent for cross-pollinating crops such as maize. Similar limitations apply in some countries to the dissemination of improved planting material for perennial crops.

*Socio-economic considerations*: The need to gear adaptive research to the socio-economic circumstances of the resource-poor farmer has found increasing practical expression through the promotion of 'farming systems research', perhaps more appropriately thought of as an approach or a perspective, rather than as an entirely new or separate form of research. Traditionally, results of research on experiment stations have been exposed to wider evaluation through district, national or international trials, conducted in collaboration with other organizations, or with farmers themselves. In spite of this wide evaluation, some technologies that appeared to offer advantages in terms of increased yields, or greater efficiency, were not adopted by farmers.

It was primarily this lack of adoption that led to increased research on the socio-economic circumstances of the small-farm family. It was found that assumptions about constraints to increased productivity were sometimes based on inadequate knowledge of farmers' goals and management strategies and that, consequently, the suggested new technologies were inappropriate. Adaptive research must therefore be based on a thorough understanding of farmer circumstances and conducted through on-farm evaluation, in which both the technical and socio-economic factors can be taken into account. In the farming systems approach, on-farm research is used not only to evaluate new technologies but also as a feedback mechanism to guide scientists at all levels in planning their work. It therefore introduces a further iterative element into the research process, incorporating the reactions of the farmer to the prospects and limitations of the technology under test.

## New opportunities

Confronted by the magnitude of the challenges for the future, it is essential for agricultural scientists to monitor continuously the advancing frontiers of knowledge in the natural sciences. Both scientists and policy-makers must remain alert to new opportunities for technological innovation, recognizing the dangers of abusing the environment and the benefits from preserving, through sound agriculture and agro-forestry, the essential features of natural eco-systems.

In this general context, it is recent advances in biotechnology that have led to the greatest speculation on future possibilities for technological breakthrough. While some of these claims have been exaggerated, and others simply ill-informed, the outcome of this new knowledge is already such that all those concerned with agricultural research planning will have to take it into account when formulating future programmes and strategies. However, the actual impact on levels and costs of production is unlikely to be appreciable until after the year 2000.

*Biotechnology and crop improvement*: In plant breeding, for example, contributions from molecular genetics, cell biology and tissue culture will increasingly contribute to the speed and extent to which the plant can be modified. The application of such techniques, however, will not change in any significant way the requirements for producing successful varieties, nor the need to tailor them precisely to the production system for which they are intended.

Techniques in biophysics, molecular genetics and cell biology are already contributing to the breeding process through new ways of manipulating genetic variation and through the development of new and extremely precise techniques for evaluation and selection. The prospect of being able to transform plants in directed ways opens up new possibilities for breeders, but does not justify undue optimism for the creation of entirely new plant-types.

In the foreseeable future it will be possible to transfer genes from one species to another, regardless of how unrelated they are, and the transferred gene need not carry with it any of the unwanted genes that are normally transferred using prevailing techniques. The consequence will be a large reduction in the number of generations of breeding required to integrate an introduced gene into a desirable genotype. Moreover, in theory at least, the breeder will have at his or her disposal an infinite library of candidate genes for possible transfer. In practice, however, the extent to which such technology will assist in the production of improved varieties is somewhat speculative.

More general opportunities for applications of recombinant DNA technology in the evaluation and selection part of the plant breeding process may arise. For example, the technique known as 'probing', which allows genetic material to be labelled, could be used to monitor the presence of any known genes that have been isolated and identified. The great advantage with this technique is that the breeder does not have to wait for expression of the character concerned in the mature plant, but can eliminate unwanted material at the seedling stage, or even as seed. Moreover, with characteristics such as disease resistance, where one gene may mask the expression of another, it should eventually be possible to build up multiple gene complexes, giving a stability to host-plant resistance that has not previously been possible.

The other main area of technological innovation with applications to crop improvement is tissue culture, primarily for the production of improved clones of a wide range of plants, including ornamentals and perennial crops.

*Biotechnology in animal production and health*: The rapidly growing science of biotechnology can offer considerable possibilities in livestock improvement programmes in the future. In animal breeding, genetics and reproduction techniques to increase livestock production are already available and clearly applicable to developing countries. Their impact, however, will depend on the creation of a favourable infrastructure for implementation of the techniques. For example, embryo transfer (ET) as a tool in livestock improvement programmes may contribute to increased production using low-grade animals as recipients and foster mothers for embryos from improved types, either produced locally or imported. Its implementation until now has been hampered due to lack of infrastructure and high costs for animals and drugs for oestrus synchronization and superovulation treatment and equipment. Overcoming these problems will be a first step for development. In animal breeding traditional improvement and selection programmes are hampered by lack of infrastructure and basic essentials. New approaches are imperative in order to overcome these problems without the least possible delay. Open Nucleus Breeding Systems applying ET could be a means to speeding up progress. Other more advanced techniques being even more promising like cloning, sexing, genome mapping and *in vitro* fertilization need further research before application can be envisaged and justified. Close follow-up of research has to be guaranteed in order not to miss developments which could be useful in Africa.

Biotechnology, through plant breeding, will play a part in the development of new feed sources and the increase of feed supplies; it may also provide new ways of improving the feeding value of poor feeds. There are also indications that new techniques may, in the longer term, provide the means of modifying rumen fermentation or of altering the rumen micro-organisms; costs, convenience and safety will determine the feasibility of such applications in small-scale farming. While the economic use of genetically engineered hormones, such as growth hormone, in developing countries at present seems unlikely, even if it were permitted, this application may be only the vanguard of long-term possibilities.

In animal health, the development of diagnostic techniques, using monoclonal antibodies, is already proving useful for the early diagnosis of certain diseases of livestock (such as foot-and-mouth disease and rinderpest) and will no doubt find progressively wider application. The technique is precise, sensitive and can readily be automated. Recombinant DNA techniques also have applications in this area of diagnostics, as well as in their possible contribution to the synthesis of antigens and the production of vaccines.

*Applications to fish farming*: Similar diagnostic techniques to those being developed for livestock diseases could also be developed for important diseases of fish. As stocking intensities increase, and the risk of disease becomes greater, early diagnosis becomes increasingly important.

Because of the importance of inducing spawning in fish farming, there is scope for further research using recombinant DNA technology to produce sex hormones in the quantities required. Other applications of this technology also suggest themselves, such as the development of growth hormones to increase productivity.

*Policies for research in biotechnology*: Faced with the realities of limited budgets for agricultural research, policy-makers and scientific leaders in developing countries have difficult decisions to make. Extensive investment in basic research in the biological sciences from which these new technologies are emerging can hardly be accorded highest priority when solutions to urgent problems can be achieved from smaller resources. Nevertheless, no country would wish to miss opportunities for significant technological breakthroughs because of a lack of trained individuals who could exploit the new opportunities.

## Prerequisites for further progress

Prior to the present century, intensification of production through the application of science had hardly begun. By the end of this century, comparatively little suitable land will be available for increasing the area of arable crops. Thus, within the period of a single century, there will have been an enormous transition from extensive to intensive production systems, for most crops, and for pig and poultry systems that account for the bulk of the marketed output.

This growing awareness of present and potential land shortage, coupled with the need to sustain production at increasingly higher levels of yield, is one consideration in the new synthesis that is emerging. Among others are concerns stemming from the rate of consumption of fossil fuels; pollution of the environment through the misuse of chemicals; and the reckless destruction of forests and other stable ecosystems, to make way for arable production.

All of these considerations point to the need to maintain the impetus of agricultural research and technology development on a world scale. Advances in agricultural technology and their widespread application will depend on three sets of factors: the generation, or availability of new technologies;

appropriate technology diffusion to ensure the knowledge of, or accessibility to the new technology by farmers; the economic and social policy setting needed to achieve progress in technology development and application. These factors reflect the complexity of achieving the conditions required for sustainable growth, at adequate and balanced levels, in agriculture based on technology. The main considerations and requirements involved under each of the foregoing headings are discussed below.

*Generation of new technologies*: The prerequisites for progress in the generation of new technologies depend on their final use and the level of technologies which one wishes to obtain. At an advanced level, they may include access to biotechnological methods for the manipulation of genes for improving plant or animal production or combat diseases. But in most developing countries and for the bulk of their farmers progress in less sophisticated technology is needed to improve farm tools, design simple irrigation systems or to plant indigenous crops and trees for soil and water conservation. Consequently the generation of low and high levels of technologies should be undertaken simultaneously.

There are, however, a number of prerequisites which are necessary for all levels of technology development. Some of these will be mentioned here:

- The highest priority should certainly be given to the development of *human resources* who will not only be well-trained and experienced research workers but should also have the ingenuity to see the problems of their agricultural production system and generate the appropriate technologies their national and natural conditions may warrant.
- Equally important is the provision of an adequate infrastructure for research and the testing of research results. But this does not necessarily mean that sophisticated research facilities are needed; often simple workshops and laboratories may go a long way in achieving improved technologies.
- A constant *resource flow* to the research system from both public and private sources would be indispensable.
- The development of effective new technologies does not only depend on a strong research base, particularly for high-technology levels, but also on *strong links and cooperative arrangements* with researchers and institutions elsewhere.
- Led by the CGIAR System, more emphasis is being put on socio-economic research and the so-called second-generation problems, that is on income generation, distribution and on developing technologies for sustainable agriculture. Such a reorientation of research priorities would have considerable consequences on the generation of new technologies.

*Technology diffusion*: For applied agricultural research to contribute to agricultural development, the technology generated should be targeted to the real needs of producers, and properly made available to them. Research institutions, development agents and farmers should cooperate closely from the start of the technology generation process up to its full mass diffusion in an iterative manner.

Frequently research is focused on themes of little relevance to the farmers, or is conducted under non-representative conditions. It has been shown that farmers are purposeful in their behaviour, responsive to opportunities offered by their environment and reasonably efficient in managing their resources and selecting production technologies. Recommendations therefore should be made with sufficient consideration of the farmers' circumstances and focused on the farmer and his or her farm situation.

In many developing countries, manpower and other resources are often so thinly spread in research and extension that neither functions effectively. Competition for meagre resources combined with mutual mistrust between research and extension personnel can lead to situations where extension blames the researchers for the inappropriateness of a technological package, while the researchers blame extension for not understanding its nuances. The result is low impact and loss of credibility and support for both systems.

Improved communication between research and extension agencies, often in different ministries, is required. Extension should be interpreted not in its narrow sense of providing inputs, services and advice as needed by farmers but as an instrument for intelligent communication of new technology's potentials and limitations. Research scientists should look upon extension agents not as passive conduits of communication but as active articulators of field problems and invaluable guides who enable researchers to tackle 'real world' problems. The role of policy-makers and administrators is to ensure active collaboration betweeen the two services.

Several innovations have been tried to forge functional links between research and extension services and to make both effective. The most widely propagated in recent years have been the Training and Visit system of extension, and the farming systems research approach. Another is to set up a separate establishment to promote technology. This approach often tends to give greater emphasis to the choice of extension media and the behavioural patterns of farmers, but its isolation from research establishments may cause a lack of technical content. Yet another approach is to deploy a part of the research system to promote available technology (e.g. the National Demonstrations Programme in India). This is inadvisable where research resources are limited.

Researchers often promote technologies they believe to be viable on the basis of their experiments, while extension workers tend to emphasize weaknesses in technology in relation to farmers' resources. As noted before, only improved communication can bring these two positions together. Many developing countries, particularly in Africa, are without elaborate national research systems and cannot adopt the methods described above. But every country must foster institutionalized communication between its research and extension wings if they are to become both productive and supportive of agricultural development.

Several approaches may help to popularize and disseminate technologies: that is, on-farm research and demonstration, use of a minikit, and the pilot project approach, the three-in-one scheme of extension and extension work of colleges/faculties/universities of agriculture.

On-farm experimentation is conducted in farmers' fields with the active participation of the farmers, which ensures that technologies are formulated in accordance with the farmers' conditions. Because of this, *on-farm research* actually identifies the farmers for whom the research is intended, and efforts must be focused on relatively homogeneous groups of farmers.

This approach was pursued by FAO in promoting the use of fertilizer

(FAO's Fertilizer Programme) and new crop varieties and management practices in the Farm Demonstrations Programme. The demonstration approach exposes a new technology to a wide range of farmers with differing skills and resources. These programmes help planners to delimit those areas and situations where the new technology has the best chance of rapid adoption and beneficial results. The type of programme undertaken by FAO's Fertilizer Programme for more than 20 years should be greatly expanded in Africa and incorporated as an on-going element of national programmes for agricultural development. This will require substantial increase of international fertilizer aid.

As in some FAO's Fertilizer Programme trials and demonstrations, the response to both manure and mineral fertilizer should, where practicable, be covered. There are, however, practical limits to analysis where the number of variables is increased and a large number of demonstrations involved. Field trials should be conducted under the control of national research bodies to obtain more data on varietal responses, and the rotation of plants for biological nutrient fixation should be incorporated. The benefits of technology established by trials should be incorporated in demonstrations at village level.

The second approach uses a *minikit*. Participating farmers are encouraged to commit only small portions of their holdings to the new technology in order to minimize the risk of failure. Many FAO field projects adopt the minikit approach to promote new crop varieties and management practices by demonstrating their superiority over the farmers' own practices and/or varieties. The choice of technologies must be sound and particular account should be taken of agro-ecological conditions and labour availability. Their potential effectiveness has been well illustrated in Zambia and Zimbabwe, where small maize kits were introduced, and Nigeria, where minikits comprising small quantities of hybrid seed, fertilizer, and sometimes insecticide, were made available. This approach has also been widely used in Asia, particularly in India.

The *pilot project* approach takes a particular area and in it intensifies institutional support and extension advice. This is recommended when promoters are convinced that farmers will not be worse off if they adopt the technology even under adverse conditions, but will in fact gain substantially in good environments. FAO's area development projects and the World Bank's integrated rural development projects follow this approach. Although the improved technology is targeted to farmers in the project area, many outside this area are expected to adopt and benefit from the new technology.

The three-in-one scheme of extension as being practised in hundreds of counties in China puts the three functions of 'experimentation, training and extension' in one County Agro-technological Extension Centre. New technology and recommendations received from the provincial or national research institutes are verified and tested in these centres. Extension workers and farmer leaders are trained with the new approved (tested) technology and practices in the centre, and then they are deployed for extension work with farmers in their respective areas of coverage.

An increasing number of colleges/faculties or universities of agriculture in developing countries are adding to the function of teaching and research a third function—extension. Generally, this is being carried out by higher agricultural education institutions which have had a mature agricultural research programme generating technology which is not only useful for teaching but also for farming. The extension work is confined to a limited area near the institution but a more far-reaching contribution in some countries is the extension support these educational institutions provide to the national extension service in terms of training and as a source of subject-matter specialists and extension materials. Other related emerging means of diffusing agricultural technology are the use of mass media by agricultural education institutions and the use of distance education in agriculture by an increasing number of developing countries.

The success of technology diffusion depends on linkage mechanisms built up between farmers, researchers, extension workers, administrators and policy-makers. Such interactions foster a spirit of cooperation among these partners while helping to clarify the potentials and limitations of the new technology. Crossing the institutional boundaries and finding a way to concerted effort at the farm level, while keeping each one's specific responsibilities, will be a necessary condition for more successful research and development.

*Socio-economic aspects*: For agricultural research to yield its full benefits, it is essential that government policies provide the appropriate economic incentives. Inadequate economic policies retard the desired technical changes and production increases and reduce the return of funds to research. It is therefore essential that the policy setting (prices, credit, land tenure, marketing, etc.) for agriculture be such that it induces and facilitates the adoption of new technologies by farmers. Substantial economic (and socio-cultural) analysis related to the recommended technologies is needed to ensure their appropriateness to the farmers' circumstances. Although this socio-economic component of agricultural research has been given increasing attention in international research centres, it is often still too limited and weak in the national agricultural research systems (NARs) of many developing countries.

A good example of appropriate socio-economic analysis is the introduction of the farming systems research approach, which integrates socio-economic analysis with the research and extension functions. Further development and implementation of this approach in the NARs will be required for speeding up the adoption of technological innovations among the resource-poor farmers.

## Prospects for the future

There is growing evidence of an increased public awareness that only through greater application of new, science-based agricultural technology at the individual country level can food and nutrition problems be overcome. The large investments in international research through the CGIAR and other multilateral arrangements, as well as the growing funding of NARs by international lending and aid agencies, are proof of the confidence placed in agricultural research as a powerful instrument for human improvement. A greater emphasis on agriculture in many developing countries leads to a more favourable environment both for research and for farmers' adoption of innovations.

A substantial stock of research knowledge has been accumulated internationally, which with some adaptations can be readily moved out to farmers fields. Also, the large investments incurred since early 1970s, for creating the CGIAR system of centres and for strengthening some NARs, such as Brazil's EMBRAPA and others, will be maturing over the last decade of this century, considering a research time-lag of about 10 to 15 years.

The fast progress of scientific knowledge that has been occurring in the advanced countries is also enlarging the frontiers for innovative applied agricultural research. The potential of biotechnology, already discussed, particularly opens up unpredictable advances that may revolutionize some aspects of agriculture in the next century. Discoveries and innovations in science and technology are proceeding at such a pace that accessibility to them by the developing countries' scientific community is becoming an important issue, as there is fear that innovations may become restricted to a few institutions and experts. Hence some observers consider that, with few exceptions, the gap in the access to innovative research between developing and developed countries may widen in the years ahead.

Finally, in recent years, many developing countries embarked upon significant training programmes for agricultural researchers that now gradually are bearing fruit. Particularly, agricultural universities and research institutes are being strengthened and upgraded, appointing full- time staff and creating graduate research programmes aimed at generating locally the bulk of human resources required for research. The countries where this is the case are beginning to create and to be able to retain the critical mass of scientists necessary to render productive the national agricultural research systems established in the past two decades. However in many low-income countries, particularly in sub-Saharan Africa, this process of establishing a viable research community is just beginning, and is hampered by the small size of many countries and the difficulties in running jointly regional research centres.

In so far as the developing countries are concerned, the CGIAR and the IARCs in close cooperation with national systems are selectively changing from applied and adaptive research to strategic research. On the other hand, developed countries, after having made technological advances in agriculture, are investigating ways and possibilities of reducing overproduction. Thus while in developing countries research efforts are aimed at boosting agricultural production, research in the developed countries is directed to viable low-input, environment preserving, but efficient agricultural technology. It may be expected that these trends in research will in fact become complementary, facilitating the generation of agricultural technology in developing countries that will foster production under ecologically safer conditions and ensuring the long-term sustainability of agriculture.

# 11 Environmental aspects of agricultural development

By the year 2000 the global population will be 25 percent above that of the mid-1980s with 90 percent of the increase concentrated in developing countries. Fulfilling the global needs for agricultural products without damaging the environment and redressing existing disparities presents a formidable challenge.

Most countries have sufficient natural resources to meet this challenge, but the availability and quality of these resources are dependent upon complex ecological systems which are not fully understood and cannot be fully controlled by man. Moreover, the ability of these resources to sustain agriculture is being diminished by factors which range from industrial pollution in developed countries to the reduction in fallow periods in shifting cultivation and bush fallow systems in developing countries.

The relationship between sustainable agriculture and the environment is one of complementarity and interdependence. Agricultural production systems are heavily dependent upon the capacity of natural resources to sustain their development. Advances in agriculture have modified this dependency and reduced environmental constraints upon production through the use of irrigation, plant breeding, mineral fertilizers and pest control. However, these advances have not supplanted agriculture's fundamental dependence upon the productive capacity of the natural environment. In fact, technical advances have reinforced the need for appropriate policies and technologies and sound land-use planning in both developed and developing countries.

Agriculture, if well managed, can assist in conserving natural resources. Much of the rural landscape that appears to be 'natural' in developed countries is the result of natural resource planning and management. And many productive areas, such as Japan and the south-eastern United States, formerly had poor quality soils until the fertility was improved through sound farming practices.

None the less, the increasing strains on the environment have led to mounting concern about the sustainability of development activities. This was recently discussed in the report of the World Commission on Environment and Development (1987). Mounting concern has led to greater awareness of the relationships between environment, population and development, particularly when linked to trade and equity.

Chapter 3 presents projections for the year 2000 that involve a 20 and 60 percent increase in agricultural output for developed and developing countries respectively. The achievement of these projections in the developing countries is, as described in Chapter 4, dependent on the opening up of new land, the more intensive use of existing land, and the greater use of production inputs, such as mineral fertilizers and pesticides. In the past such actions have caused environmental degradation when improperly implemented. Therefore, similar degradation is possible in the future.

## Agricultural and environmental interactions in the 1970s and 1980s

### Global and transnational problems

*Carbon dioxide*: Since the early 1970s, there has been mounting concern about climatic changes resulting from the increasing concentration of carbon dioxide ($CO_2$) and other gases in the earth's atmosphere. If current rates of increase continue, it is predicted that by the end of the next century the concentration will be double that at the start of the Industrial Revolution. This may create a greenhouse effect resulting in a warming of the atmosphere by 1.5°C or more. Although existing models cannot yet confidently predict the effects upon the climate, the sea level or agriculture, there is considerable risk that by the time effects upon agriculture become apparent, the process will be difficult to change. The potential risks to agriculture consist of shifts in agro-ecological zones, in the productivity of crop and grazing lands, as well as both decreases and increases in the availability of water depending on location, and alteration in the distribution and viability of forests.

An issue which is difficult to resolve is the relative contribution of fossil fuel consumption by more-developed countries versus the contribution of deforestation in less-developed countries to the increased global levels of carbon dioxide.

*Atmospheric pollution and acid deposition*: Acid deposition is primarily found in the developed countries. There are a number of atmospheric pollutants which contribute to acid deposition, however the two most significant are sulphur dioxide ($SO_2$) and oxides of nitrogen ($NO_x$). The main sources of these pollutants are fossil fuel power stations, motor vehicles, industrial processes, oil refining and heating of residential and commercial buildings. The volatilization of nitrogen-based fertilizers may also play a role in emitting $NO_x$ to the atmosphere; however, there is insufficient evidence to estimate agriculture's contribution to acid deposition.

Although lakes and forests can be significantly affected by acidic conditions, the environmental effects of acid deposition on agricultural crops appear to be small in comparison to other factors such as fluctuations in weather conditions. The synergistic effects resulting from different mixes of pollutants may be more damaging to crops than the impact of a single pollutant.

*Ozone*: The depletion of ozone in the stratosphere due to increased levels of nitrous oxide (NO) and chlorofluorocarbons is also of concern. This could decrease crop productivity, but present evidence is inconclusive and it is not known whether this phenomenon will have a negative impact in this century.

### National and local problems

A number of significant changes in the longer-term agricultural trends have occurred during the past 15 years, which can be expected to intensify during the remainder of this century. Developed-country problems can be typified as consequences of intensive agricultural production, such as pest resistance to biocides, contamination of groundwater due to improper use of mineral fertilizers, and soil erosion. Some of these problems have become critical even though there has been a reduction in the activities that cause them. For example, although there has been a reduction in fertilizer use—in fact in some countries an actual decline in the past two years—the incidence of high nitrate concentrations in groundwater has increased.

The problems of the developing countries are primarily the consequence of overexploitation and area extension, particularly the reduction in fallows, deforestation, desertification and soil erosion. Some large irrigated areas are seriously affected by salinization. The rapid increase in the use of pesticides and mineral ferilizers in Asia and the Pacific region can lead to environmental problems too—unless due care is taken.

## Problems in developed countries

During the past 50 years, most developed countries have moved from small-scale farming systems to larger, more intensive systems of crop and livestock production. There has been a corresponding shift from relatively self-contained units, adapted to and dependent upon natural ecological processes, to more specialized enterprises reliant upon external supplies of mineral fertilizers, pesticides, improved seed varieties and mechanical power. Environmental systems and natural resources still form the foundation for agriculture, but improved technologies and materials, including mechanization, have permitted the modification of natural factors which formerly constrained agricultural production.

The shift toward more intensive agriculture has resulted in significant increases in both productivity per unit area and total production. These advances have helped individual nations cope with the loss of agricultural land due to urban expansion, transport and communications, recreation and wildlife conservation, as well as meet changing demands for agricultural products. However, intensification of agriculture has had negative environmental effects resulting mainly from overreliance on the technical advances in machinery, chemicals and seed. Some of the main problems are excessive application of fertilizers, heavy use of pesticides, soil erosion and water pollution.

Figure 11.1 presents the main environmental effects of intensive agriculture. The spatial distribution and severity of effects will vary between different countries. For example, leaching of nitrates into groundwater supplies is potentially a more serious human health problem in the Netherlands than in parts of the United States because application rates of nitrogen are higher and population densities greater.

Agriculture makes use of a number of toxic and potentially hazardous materials, the majority of which are used in biocides, although non-purified fertilizers can contain metals and metalloids. The two primary concerns surrounding the use of these materials are the adverse effects they may have

| AGRICULTURAL PRACTICES | SOIL | GROUNDWATER | SURFACE WATER | FLORA | FAUNA | OTHERS Air, noise, landscape, agri-cultural products |
|---|---|---|---|---|---|---|
| Land development, land consolidation programmes | Inaccurate management leading to soil degradation | Other water management influencing ground water table | | Loss of species | | Loss of ecosystem, loss of ecological diversity. Land degradation if activity not suited to site |
| Irrigation, drainage | Excess salts, water-logging | Loss of quality (more salts), drinking water supply affected | Soil degradation, siltation, water pollution with soil particles | Drying out of natural elements affecting river ecosystems | | |
| Tillage | Wind erosion, water erosion | | | | | |
| Mechanization, large or heavy equipment | Soil compaction, soil erosion | | | | | Combustion gases noise |
| Fertilizer use<br>- Nitrogen | | Nitrate leaching affecting water | | | | |
| - Phosphate | Accumulation of heavy metals (Cd) | | Run-off, leaching or direct discharge leading to eutrophication | Effect on soil microflora | | |
| - Manure, slurry | Excess: accumulation of phosphates, copper (pig slurry) | Nitrate, phosphate (by use of excess slurry) | | Eutrophication leads: to excess algae and water-plants | to oxygen depletion affecting fish | Stench, ammonia |
| - Sewage sludge, compost | Accumulation of heavy metals, contaminants | | | | | Residues |
| Applying pesticides | Accumulation of pesticides and degradation products | Leaching of mobile pesticide residues and degradation products | | Affects soil microflora: resistance of some weeds | Poisoning resist-ance | Evaporation: spray drift, residues |
| Input of feed additives, medicines | Possible effects | | | | | Residues |
| Modern buildings: e.g. silos and intensive livestock farming | See: slurry | See: slurry | See: slurry | | | Ammonia, offensive odours, noise, resi-dues. Infrastructure: aesthetic impacts |

Source: OECD (1984).

**Figure 11.1** Selected environmental effects of agriculture

upon human health as a result of consuming contaminated food or water, and upon the long-term productivity of soils.

The use of sophisticated chemical formulations for fertilizers and biocides have generally had a highly beneficial effect upon agricultural production and have helped to improve human welfare, nutrition and health. Mismanagement and overuse of these materials, however, can overwhelm the ability of natural processes to disperse, dilute or break them down. The hazard they pose is related to their toxicity, persistance or accumulation in soil, plants or animals.

*Problems associated with mineral fertilizers*: The timing and rates of fertilizer applications are critical to both good crop production and avoidance of potential hazards of soil and water pollution. Excessive applications can result in excessive uptake of nitrates in plant tissues (leaf vegetables and fodder) and contamination of soil by heavy-metal impurities.

Secondary effects resulting from excessive and ill-timed use of mineral fertilizers include:

— leaching of nitrate into groundwater and its accumulation therein;
— surface water contamination by nitrate and phosphates;
— reduction in soil organisms such as earthworms and nitrogen fixing bacteria which help maintain natural soil fertility;
— inhibition of nitrogen fixation and nitrification in soils due to increased concentrations of cadmium.

Intensification of agriculture, coupled with increased geographic specialization, commonly results in the separation of animal and crop production systems. This has two effects. The first is the shortage of animal manure resulting in increased dependence on mineral fertilizers in arable areas. The second is the production of more manure than can be safely incorporated into the soil, associated with intensive stock-rearing operations. An extreme example is the Netherlands, where intensive animal production has created a surplus of manure. Due to high levels of nitrate in adjacent ground and surface water bodies, strict controls over rates of manure application to fields have been introduced. Dutch farmers are consequently faced with the costs and difficulties of storage and safe disposal of this otherwise beneficial organic source of nutrients and soil conditioner. Similar problems exist in some intensively farmed valleys of Switzerland where the high levels of farmyard manure from dairy operations have been applied to fields and resulted in dangerous levels of coli bacteria in drinking-water supplies.

It is, however, by no means just a Dutch problem. Most OECD countries have introduced or strengthened legislation in recent years. This has not prevented the discharge of inadequately treated wastes into surface waters. In Britain, for example, the accidental discharge into water bodies of liquid manures and silage effluents from intensive stock-rearing operations is growing rapidly. In 1984 the number of incidents of pollution of watercourses by farm wastes was approximately double the number reported in 1979. The main effect of silage and liquid manures is to create an increased demand for biological oxygen (BOD), thereby consuming the oxygen needed by fish and other aquatic life.

Assessing the impact of excessive fertilizer application on the environment and on human health is difficult. The transformation of high nitrates in vegetables or water into nitrites by bacterial reduction in the body can be hazardous. Nitrates have been linked to methaemoglobinaemia (blue baby syndrome) and are believed to contribute to the risk of gastric cancer. However, there is considerable debate as to whether nitrates play a major role in determining the risk of cancer because of the complex biochemical aspects of the disease. Epidemiological studies have not conclusively demonstrated the link between environmental nitrates and gastric cancer, or that controlling the level of nitrate in drinking water would reduce the risk of contracting the disease.

*Biocide-associated problems*: The control of diseases and pests has played a major role in improving yields and reducing post harvest losses for most crops. Such control will continue to be important in future food production. Some high-yielding crop varieties are less resistant to pests and disease than older varieties, and modern biocides are essential in realizing the full value of these varieties.

However, the increases in productivity which have been achieved so far have also introduced new management problems, namely increasing resistance of pests to chemical control, emergence of new pests, and unintentional hazards to human health.

Intense agronomic practices, such as monocultures, provide ideal conditions for increased pest populations. This is often controlled by an increased use of biocides, which may kill predator species as well as pests, and may facilitate the development of resistant strains of pests. The short-term effects of this strategy may be beneficial, but in the long term the effect may favour the pest. It is estimated that 1,600 arthropod pest species have developed significant resistance to major pesticides. The long-term use of non-selective chemicals is considered the main reason for the development of resistance.

Beneficial species which are natural enemies of the pests or diseases are also reduced or eliminated by the non-selective nature of many chemicals applied. As natural predators are eliminated, other previously innocuous organisms increase in number and their influence on crops can elevate them to the role of pests. Mites are a particularly good example of non-pest species which have been transformed into pests due to pesticides reducing the number of beneficial predators.

As little as 1 percent of pesticides and other materials used actually reach the target organism. The persistence of some of these materials allows them to be taken up by plants and animals, where they increase in concentration due to bio-accumulation within food chains.

Direct exposure to biocides or ingestion of contaminated foodstuffs can be a health hazard to human beings. The incidence of contamination and poisoning is influenced by the growth in biocide use, the rate and timing of application, its toxicity and rate of breakdown. Currently, the use of pesticides in the United States is some eleven times greater than in Africa, although the application of agro-chemicals in the United States has remained nearly constant since 1981. The use of pesticides is growing at approximately 4.5 percent annually world-wide, but with wide country to country variation, and rates of increase of up to 20 percent per annum (an effective doubling every four years) are reported for some developing countries. In order to minimize negative impacts, FAO's member governments have adopted the International Code of Conduct on the Distribution and Use of Pesticides.

A variety of environmental effects could be added to Figure 11.1 if agriculture is considered in a wider rural development perspective where employment and amenity are altered by agricultural intensification. Agriculture can be beneficial in the maintenance of an essentially man-made rural landscape with amenities such as recreation and nature conservation. Rationalization of farm holdings, the removal of hedgerows and the drainage and filling of wetlands may improve the short-term efficiency of agriculture but eliminate other land-use options. Intensification and mechanization also reduce the demand for on-farm labour which can lead to unemployment and rural–urban migration. These factors are increasingly the subject of debate on agricultural policy. A recent EEC Green Paper, for example, calls for improved environmental and agricultural policies whose main aims would be:

- rational use and long-term conservation of the soil, combined with the protection of all natural riches and resources;
- the maintenance and development of rural life, starting with the maintenance of agricultural employment and the opportunity for those who work the land to receive a reasonable income; and
- the production of food of good quality in sufficient quantity to meet needs.

## Problems facing developing countries

Ninety percent of the projected global increase in population to the year 2000 will take place in developing countries. Some of these countries do not produce enough food to be self-sufficient at present, but with the proper use of fertilizers and pesticides, improved plant material and agricultural systems which are adapted to environmental, social and cultural needs, many countries can increase the volume and improve the sustainability of their production. A critical challenge facing most developing countries is to halt and reverse present degradation, and to introduce sustainable production systems. Some of the more serious problems to be addressed in meeting that challenge are deforestation, desertification, resource degradation of cultivated lands, and loss of biological diversity. Other important environmental problems are the contamination of water with agricultural chemicals and waste products from water borne diseases associated with irrigation.

*Deforestation*: The total area of closed forest in the world is estimated at 2500 million ha. Tropical forest extends over an area of about 1935 million ha, of which 1200 million ha are closed forest and 735 million ha are classified as open tree formations. The rate of deforestation for both closed and open tropical forests is estimated to be some 11.5 million ha per year (see Ch. 5). Reafforestation and afforestation help to offset this loss but only amount to approximately one-tenth the annual rate of deforestation. The quality of the regenerated forest is generally inferior due to the narrow range of species used and the common use of poorer lands. However, some of the functions of natural forests, such as erosion control in upland watersheds, can also be performed by conservation farming/agroforestry systems, perennial crops and man-made forests.

The main cause of deforestation is the expansion of agriculture and the overexploitation of wood, especially fuelwood. Consequently a major factor which will influence the future clearance of forests is the improvement of crop production and grazing systems on existing agricultural areas. The increased demand for land up to the year 2000 in the developing countries (excluding China) is estimated at about 80 million ha (see Ch. 4). Most of this land will have to be transferred from tropical forests, but two important factors must be taken into consideration.

First, many tropical forest soils are unsuitable for continuous cultivation or intensive grazing unless the sites are carefully selected, cleared and prepared, and unless the new agricultural system can maintain soil fertility. This requires levels of investment and management which are generally underestimated by policy-makers. The sustainability and stability of production of the ensuing agricultural use will depend upon the advances which can be achieved in assessing their fragile, low-fertility soils and developing appropriate farming systems. This approach, combined with improved and more intensive agricultural systems for existing cultivated areas, appears the most practical way to meet increased needs for both food and forest-based environmental goods and services.

Second, natural forest systems provide goods and services which can last indefinitely and which man cannot easily replicate. Forests, for example, reinforce the sustainability and improvement of agricultural production by regulating hydrologic regimes within watersheds which helps to ensure reliable supplies of surface water and groundwater, wildlife, medicinal plants and various native foods.

A major cause for concern is the accelerating rate of forest loss in upland watersheds, which often leads to increased flooding followed by extended periods of low water flow during the dry season. This can have a severe influence on agriculture located in floodplains and in the bottomland of valleys, where the more fertile soils are generally found. In India more than 20 million ha of land are affected annually by flooding due to climatic conditions, geological erosion and deforestation in the Himalayan region. In the Ganges Plain alone, flood damage regularly exceeds US$1 billion per year.

Erosion resulting from deforestation, in addition to land degradation in the uplands, leads to the siltation of river channels and increases the incidence and severity of downstream flooding. Sediments also collect in still water areas formed by dam storage schemes built to supply power, regulate floods and ensure adequate irrigation water supplies. Sedimentation reduces the economic life of these schemes and their long-term potential for improving and sustaining agricultural production.

*Desertification*: In the distant past, climatic fluctuations resulted in the expansion and contraction of deserts. Today, most desertification is caused by increasing human and livestock populations, overgrazing, bushfires, expansion of agricultural crops and deforestation due to demand for fuelwood. Mismanagement of resources is considered to be responsible for over 80 percent of recent world-wide desertification.

The rate of desertification is accelerating throughout Sahelo-Sudanian Africa, the Middle East and in Iran, Pakistan and north-west India. The semi-arid area in north-east Brazil is subject to desertification, and similar conditions are being created in parts of Argentina. In North Africa, areas of

Morocco, Tunisia and Libya are losing some 100 000 ha of rangeland and cropland each year due to desertification. In Somalia some 500 sq. km of previously stabilized sand dunes have been remobilized since the 1960s by overgrazing and activities such as lime burning and quarrying.

The degree of desertification varies within the drier regions; however some 3 billion ha, or approximately one-fourth of the earth's land surface, is damaged by factors which contribute to desertification. Of this area, 60 percent of the rangelands and rain-fed croplands are moderately to severly desertified, and 30 percent of irrigated dryland are similarly affected. As some areas go out of production due to desertification, others come into production due to restoration efforts, but the overall balance is a net loss.

*Poor land management*: Traditional agriculture has evolved broadly-based mixed resource utilization practices to offset the risk of failure of any one crop and to maintain the natural resource base. However, the development of market economies, foreign-exchange requirements and rapid growth in population have disrupted these traditional practices and created social and ecological instability. New and more advanced production systems, while necessary for increased production, if not adapted to local socio-cultural, economic and ecological conditions, can lead to extensive degradation.

The main forms of resource degradation associated with poor land and water management are erosion, salinization and alkanization, acidification, and the spread of water-borne diseases through the expansion of irrigation schemes.

Most, if not all, of the world's agricultural areas are susceptible to erosion, mainly by wind or water. Wind erosion is generally considered to be most serious in arid and semi-arid regions, including much of North Africa and the Near East, parts of southern and eastern Asia and South America.

In selected areas of Nepal, a region highly vulnerable to geologic erosion, land cleared of forests and used inappropriately in crop cultivation has resulted in the loss of between 35 and 75 tonnes of soil per hectare per year. A joint FAO/UNEP assessment of land degradation found that in Africa, north of the equator, 11.5 percent of the total land area was affected by water erosion and 22.4 percent by wind erosion. The Near East has 17.1 percent of its total area affected by water erosion and 35.5 percent by wind erosion.

Both salinization and alkalinization can lead to increased soil moisture stress and, in some cases, toxic effects. They are most commonly associated with high and rising groundwater levels, due to inadequate water management and drainage, and the presence of salts in irrigation water. Some 40 million ha, or 20 percent of the area in irrigation, are either water-logged or suffer from excessive salinity, or both, and will go out of production unless remedial measures are taken.

Acidification which affects many acid-sulphate peat soils in coastal areas occurs once the groundwater table is lowered and the sulphides in the soil are exposed to the air, leading to the production of sulphuric acid. When this happens, fish and crop production is often so poor that fields and fish ponds are abandoned. Extensive coastal areas of Indonesia, Malaysia, Thailand and the Philippines are being opened up for agriculture and aquaculture, and face this risk, unless properly managed.

The development of water resources, with the associated modification of the aquatic environment, influences the risk to human health from various water-related diseases. Among these are vector-borne diseases such as malaria, schistosomiasis and lymphatic filariasis; and diarrhoeal diseases, cholera, typhoid and dysenteries, where the pathogen is generally a component of drinking water. Therefore, water development must be accompanied by measures to offset possible health risks, such as prophylaxis, chemotherapy, chemical control, environmental manipulation and modification, sanitation and water supply. Usually a combination of measures is needed, together with community education.

## Future environmental concerns in agriculture

Looking only 15 years ahead—a short period from an environmental viewpoint—world agriculture will have to increase output by about 40 percent. Three-quarters of this additional amount will have to be produced in developing countries, whereas the developed countries will need to expand output by only one-fifth. The first implication is that the environment will come under comparatively little additional strain in developed countries, but under considerably more strain in developing countries. Developed countries will have the time and financial resources to ameliorate the environmental problems arising from agricultural development. Developing countries face severe constraints with regard to both of these factors.

Sources of additional production in developing countries: yields 63 percent, arable land area 22 percent, cropping intensity 15 percent (see Ch. 4) suggest ways in which additional pressure will be put on the environment. The projected modernization of production technology implies continuing intensive use of mineral fertilizers and pesticides and larger areas under monoculture and irrigation.

The nature and severity of environmental problems will vary widely amongst and within developing countries, but in broad terms problems will be related to: Asia—increased irrigation, and deforestation; Near East/North and West Africa—shortage of arable land and increasing desertification; Southern Africa—livestock and crop pressure on marginal lands and fragile soils, Latin America—deforestation and increased monoculture.

Assessing the future impact of agricultural production on the environment is extremely difficult. It is relatively easy to catalogue the geographic extent of forest clearance and to enumerate some of the major effects, such as increased soil erosion or increased incidence of downstream flooding. It is much more difficult to specify the degree of degradation to the environmental system itself, the loss in productivity or the condition of the resources. This is due to the limited information available for vast areas of the earth's surface and incomplete understanding of how many environmental systems actually function. The task is made more difficult by the absence of means to monitor changes in these systems in response to development pressures or to factors such as climatic change, atmospheric pollution or toxic substances.

*Erosion and productivity*: Figure 11.2 illustrates the complexity of the linkage between erosion and productivity, showing that decline in productivity may not be solely linked to erosion, due to other factors which influence production. These relationships are not fully understood. Improved farming

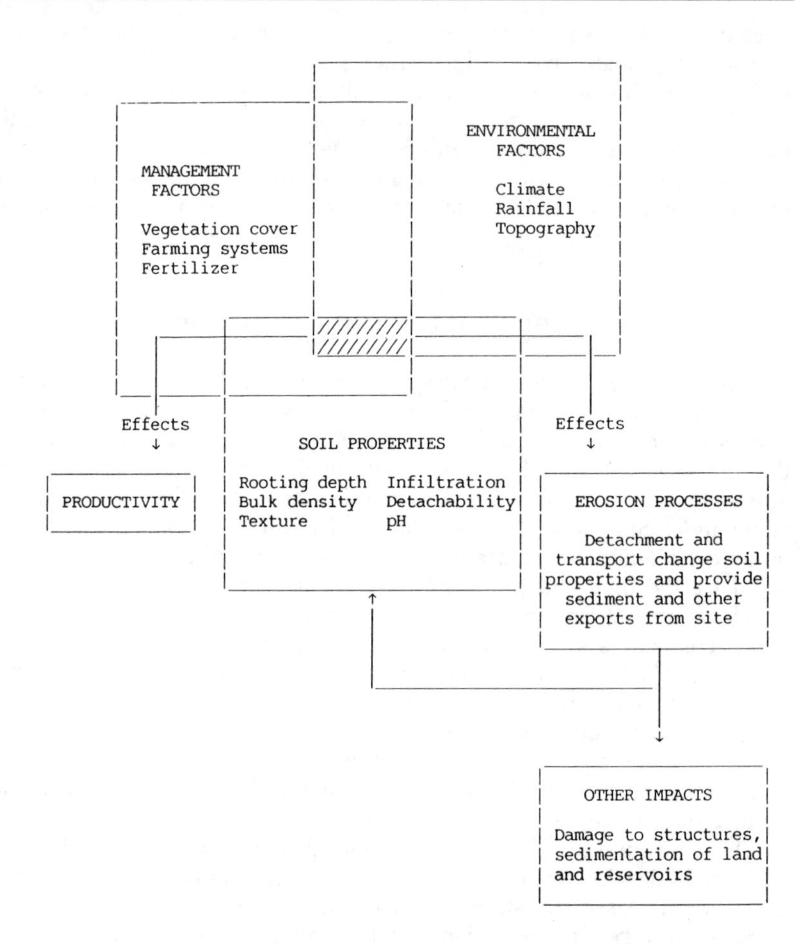


Source: Perrens and Trustrum (1984).

**Figure 11.2** Relationship between soil erosion and productivity

systems can mask the effects of erosion, hiding both the increasing cost to the farmer in terms of fertilizers required to compensate for loss of soil fertility and loss of production. The ability to compensate for potential loss of production by advances in yield-enhancing technologies and plant varieties allows production to continue but at a declining marginal rate of return. In addition, erosion can lead to secondary effects which reduce productivity, such as increased silt loads in rivers which can choke channels, lead to flooding, and reduce reservoir capacity. Erosion can either enrich flood plain soils or bury good soils under coarse-grained materials of low fertility.

Despite difficulties in assessing the environmental impact of agricultural production, possible problem areas can be identified, in addition to the serious deforestation discussed earlier. Two particular problems stand out regarding crop production. First, acute population pressure on the land, overexploitation and slow adaptation of traditional farming systems into sustainable intensive production systems. The resulting soil degradation involves soil erosion, nutrient loss and reduction in organic matter, which in turn leads to reduced moisture-holding capacity and increased vulnerability to drought. This problem is likely to be most pronounced in Africa. Second, nitrogen fertilizer application rates in, for example, parts of Korea, India and Zimbabwe, may rise by the year 2000 to levels which have led to groundwater nitrate problems in some developed countries.

Two potential problems also exist in the livestock sector. First, there is overgrazing, because the livestock population projections given in Chapter 4 represent stocking rates which, for some countries, exceed the sustainable carrying capacity of the rangeland. Most of these countries are in Africa and the Near East, where overgrazing is already serious, but the problem will also arise in parts of Asia and Latin America. The dominant impact is likely to be desertification and soil erosion.

The second problem is that of livestock waste disposal. Fast growth in intensive pig and poultry production is projected in most developing countries. Unless this expansion is accompanied by strictly enforced environmental protection legislation, water pollution and odour problems will arise.

## Policy issues

From the foregoing it is evident that the environmental aspects of agricultural development constitute serious, complex, interrelated issues. Environmental degradation reduces the potential and capacity for sustained expansion of agricultural production to meet future food and agricultural needs. This expansion will increase pressures on the environment. In addition, environmental changes originating outside agriculture may have serious implications for agriculture, notably rising carbon dioxide concentrations in the atmosphere.

Notwithstanding the limited knowledge of the full effects of some shocks to the environment, it appears that, in general, agricultural development can continue to the extent needed without seriously damaging the world's natural resources, provided policies guide that development, with environmental requirements given more weight. However, it may be difficult for some countries to implement policies quickly enough to avoid serious damage, which could lessen production potential by up to 25 percent.

Attention has focused on the strategies, plans of action and policies needed to check environmental damage. The World Conservation Strategy, the Agenda for Action resulting from the Global Possible Conference, the Tropical Forestry Action Plan, the World Soil Charter, the Plan of Action to Combat Desertification and, most recently, the Report of the World Commission on Environment and Development, all call for improved conservation of the ecological processes and natural resources essential to the sustained development of agriculture.

Persuasive as these documents are, there are a number of obstacles to achieving practical and cost-effective solutions to environmental degradation. These include, for example, the hidden nature of many forms of environmental damage and low awareness of their longer-term consequences, a tendency on the part of decision-makers not to take action on environmental problems without irrefutable scientific evidence or strong public opinion, and a reluctance on the part of politicians to allocate scarce development capital to conservation measures which may increase short-term costs in favour of distant future benefits.

One implication arising from those strategies and plans of action and from experience is that environmental considerations cannot be taken care of by the traditional market mechanisms alone. The 'invisible hand' must be guided. Government intervention is essential to encourage proper use of natural resources, to prevent misuse and to ensure that social and long-run costs of agricultural production and processing activities are met. This requires a strong commitment from politicians, an informed public, environment-oriented NGOs and senior decision-makers to act on environmental matters. The main lines of action appear to be as follows.

*Integration of agricultural and environmental policies*: At present these aspects are seldom the subject of an integrated policy, so that production technologies which raise output but damage the environment may be encouraged or permitted. Examples include the overuse of subsidized pesticides or the neglect of forseeable environmental consequences of development projects, such as soil erosion following resettlement of people after construction of a new dam. Prevention is cheaper than subsequent cure or treatment.

*Land-use planning*: This is practised in developing countries only to a limited extent, but is essential to optimize return on investment while minimizing the loss of good agricultural land to other uses, to reduce pressure to extend agriculture into marginal soils, and to link forest management and agricultural development. In some developing countries land reform is needed to ensure the rational use of land and to check misuse of marginal areas. In developed countries, less pressure on expansion of agricultural production gives the opportunity to take marginal land out of production and to encourage alternative uses, an on-going process which needs additional support.

*Improved agricultural technologies*: Some of the most promising of these are:

- mixed cropping or the use of varietal mixtures to mimic the diversity of natural ecosystems and to increase productivity based upon the combined yield of crops (multiple cropping can also improve the long-term stability of agriculture);
- exploitation of biological nitrogen-fixation techniques through the increased use of leguminous plants or non-symbiotic ferns (Azolla) and nitrogen fixing blue-green algae (Ananbaena);
- improved grazing management techniques, including fodder crops and temporary pastures in crop rotations;
- increased use of underexploited animal species, such as game ranching.

These technologies can help to increase the productivity, stability and long-term sustainability of agriculture. There is another consideration which is equally significant—the socio-economic issue of equity in access to agricultural resources and distribution of the resulting benefits. Ideally, the improvement of productivity, stability and equity will be the ultimate goal of agricultural development. This will require greater attention to the socio-economic organization of the diverse farming systems which characterize many of the regions needing help.

*Preservation of genetic resources*: Only a small proportion of the total number of plant and animal species are used to supply food and other agricultural products. Only some 150 species are used extensively; three species (wheat, maize and rice) supply over half of the human energy requirements. Within individual species, a small number of varieties account for much of the food produced under intensive agriculture. In Canada, 75 percent of the wheat crop is derived from four varieties, in the United States 72 percent of potato production is based upon four varieties, and the entire soybean production is derived from only six plants from one place in Asia.

The number of species and varieties used in developing countries is also narrowing as a result of the introduction of high-yielding varieties. While the benefits in terms of production are undeniable, many species that could be used to develop plants adapted to local conditions are being lost. Particularly relevant is the loss of genetic diversity in primitive cultivars of crop and forage species and other economic plants due to habitat conversion.

The world's stock of biological species is estimated at 10 million, 8.5 million of which have yet to be identified. However, there is ignorance of the potential they offer for crop and livestock improvement, medicinal compounds, industrial materials or energy purposes. Steps should be taken to preserve and maintain access to these species for present and future benefits.

*Integrated plant nutrition systems*: Since the Second World War, mineral fertilizers and pesticides have played an important role in increasing agricultural production. Many countries have and can continue to increase yields by greater use of mineral fertilizers and chemical pesticides, particularly in the developing world. However, where appropriate, governments should encourage the use of more organic plant nutrients to maintain soil fertility in areas—particularly semi-arid ones—where the use of mineral fertilizers is too costly or too risky; to complement mineral fertilizers; and to build up soil organic matter levels more rapidly. Such complementarity can be effected within the concept of integrated plant nutrition systems designed to make efficient use of locally available organic sources of nutrients and obtain a positive interaction with mineral fertilizers. It is wishful thinking, however, to believe that organic nutrients can replace mineral fertilizers entirely except in relatively restricted situations.

*Integrated pest control*: Single-factor approaches to improved crop yields through the control of pests and diseases dominate much of the available agricultural technology. Integrated pest control (IPC) offers an alternative approach where a wide range of factors affecting pest species can be brought into play. Among the techniques which can be applied are: introducing parasites and predators of the target pest species; reducing the growth rate of pest population by altering the physio-chemical properties and the mix and timing of crops; trapping pests by enticing them with sexual attractants (pheremones). Pesticide use can still form part of the control strategy but often as a last resort or in combination with other methods. If pesticides are used, the level of application can be minimized by timing applications to correspond with critical stages in the life-cycle of the target species where the pesticide will have maximum effect and not interfere with beneficial insects. This reduces the cost of pesticide use as well as unintended side effects.

*Expenditures on environmental protection*: As the need for increased agricultural production will probably continue for the next 75 to 100 years, integrated agricultural/environmental policies to sustain the long-term productivity potential of the land for agriculture will need increased funds.

Conservation and treatment of land and water degradation are not cheap. The task is to persuade policy-makers of the benefits of allocating scarce resources to uses which will usually have only long-term benefits. However, the rising public concern over environmental damage should facilitate efforts to have a higher priority given to such spending. Environmental protection can be profitable even on strict economic calculations. On the other hand, the costs of neglecting conservation are high in terms of human suffering and lost agricultural production.

In developing countries in particular, the task cannot be left to governments alone. Much of the motivation and expenditure will have to come from the farmers themselves. This requires an approach to environmental protection that focuses on the introduction of conservation measures into agricultural and agroforestry production systems at the farm level. Hence, FAO is promoting a shift away from purely technical approaches towards community and farmer-centred measures which produce short to medium-term benefits.

# APPENDICES

# Appendix 1 Country and commodity classification

## List of the developing countries of the study

| *Africa, sub-Saharan* | *Near East/North Africa* | *Asia* | *Latin America* |
|---|---|---|---|
| Angola | Afghanistan* | Bangladesh* | Argentina |
| Benin* | Algeria | Burma* | Bolivia |
| Botswana | Cyprus | China* | Brazil |
| Burkina Faso* | Egypt | India* | Chile |
| Burundi* | Iran | Indonesia | Colombia |
| Cameroon | Iraq | Kampuchea DM* | Costa Rica |
| Central Afr. Rep.* | Jordan | Korea DPR | Cuba |
| Chad* | Lebanon | Korea Rep. | Dominican Rep. |
| Congo | Libya | Lao* | Ecuador |
| Côte d'Ivoire | Morocco | Malaysia | El Salvador |
| Ethiopia* | Saudi Arabia | Nepal* | Guatemala |
| Gabon | Syria | Pakistan* | Guyana |
| Gambia* | Tunisia | Philippines | Haiti* |
| Ghana* | Turkey | Sri Lanka* | Honduras |
| Guinea* | Yemen AR | Thailand | Jamaica |
| Kenya* | Yemen PDR | Vietnam* | Mexico |
| Lesotho | | | Nicaragua |
| Liberia | | | Panama |
| Madagascar* | | | Paraguay |
| Malawi* | | | Peru |
| Mali* | | | Suriname |
| Mauritania | | | Trinidad and Tobago |
| Mauritius | | | Uruguay |
| Mozambique* | | | Venezuela |
| Niger* | | | |
| Nigeria | | | |
| Rwanda* | | | |
| Senegal* | | | |
| Sierra Leone* | | | |
| Somalia* | | | |
| Sudan* | | | |
| Swaziland | | | |
| Tanzania* | | | |
| Togo* | | | |
| Uganda* | | | |
| Zaire* | | | |
| Zambia* | | | |
| Zimbabwe | | | |

*Note*: In the tables '94 developing countries' refers to all developing countries given above; '93 developing countries' refers to the same countries excluding China.

* Low-income country (1985 GNP per caput less than US$400). All other countries are classified as middle income.

## List of the developed countries of the study

*Market economies*: Australia, Austria, Belgium, Canada, Denmark, Finland, France, Germany FR, Greece, Iceland, Ireland, Israel, Italy, Japan, Luxembourg, Malta, Netherlands, New Zealand, Norway, Portugal, South Africa, Spain, Sweden, Switzerland, United Kingdom, United States, Yugoslavia.

*European centrally planned economies*: Albania, Bulgaria, Czechoslovakia, German DR, Hungary, Poland, Romania, USSR.

## List of the commodities and inputs

| Commodity | Commodity aggregates | | Inputs |
|---|---|---|---|
| | Name | Commodities included | |
| 1. Wheat | Coarse grains | 3–7 | Seed, traditional |
| 2. Rice, paddy | Cereals | 1–7 | Seed, improved |
| 3. Maize | Meat | 27–30 | Labour |
| 4. Barley | Cereals (value) | 1–7 | Draught animals |
| 5. Millet | Other food crops (value) | 8–19 | Tractors |
| 6. Sorghum | Basic food crops | 1–12, 14 | Fertilizer N |
| 7. Other cereals | Non-food (value) | 20–26 | Fertilizer P |
| 8. Potatoes | Livestock products (value) | 27–32 | Fertilizer K |
| 9. Sweet potatoes and yams | Total value | 1–32 | Plant protection chemicals |
| | Total food (value) | 1–19, 27–32 | |
| 10. Cassava | | | Low rainfall rain-fed land |
| 11. Other roots | | | Uncertain rainfall rain-fed land |
| 12. Plantains | | | Good rainfall rain-fed land |
| 13. Sugar, raw* | | | Problem land |
| 14. Pulses | | | Naturally flooded land |
| 15. Vegetables | | | Irrigated land |
| 16. Bananas | | | |
| 17. Citrus fruit | | | |
| 18. Other fruit | | | |
| 19. Vegetable oil and oil seeds (vegetable oil equivalent)† | | | |
| 20. Cocoa beans | | | |
| 21. Coffee | | | |

22. Tea
23. Tobacco
24. Cotton lint
25. Jute and hard fibres
26. Rubber
27. Beef, veal and buffalo meat
28. Mutton, lamb and goat meat
29. Pork
30. Poultry meat
31. Milk and dairy products (whole-milk equivalent)
32. Eggs

* Sugar production analysed separately for sugar cane and sugar beet.
† Vegetable oil production analysed separately for soybeans, groundnuts, sesame seed, coconuts, sunflower seed, palm oil/palm-kernel oil, all other oilseeds.

## Note on commodities

All commodity data and projections in this report are expressed in terms of primary-product equivalent unless stated otherwise. Historical commodity balances (Supply Utilization Accounts—SUAs) are available for about 170 primary and 200 processed crop and livestock commodities. To reduce this amount of information to manageable proportions, all the SUA data were converted to the commodity specification given in the list for commodities 1–32 applying appropriate conversion factors (and ignoring joint products to avoid double counting, e.g. wheat flour is converted back into wheat while wheat bran is ignored). In this way one SUA in homogeneous units is derived for each of the commodities of the study. Meat production refers to indigenous meat production, that is production from slaughtered animals plus the meat equivalent of live animal exports minus the meat equivalent of all live animal imports. Cereals demand and trade data include the grain equivalent of beer consumption and trade.

The commodities for which SUAs were constructed are 26 crops (nos. 1–26 in the list) and six livestock products (nos. 27–32). The production analysis was, however, carried out for 33 crops because sugar and vegetable oils are decomposed (for production analysis only) into the nine crops shown in the footnote to the list. In addition, and solely for purposes of land accounting, an allowance was made for land under cultivated fodder.

The existence of joint products and by-products makes it impossible to avoid distortions in the consumption and trade data when a large number of commodities are converted into a smaller set of equivalent (mostly primary) products. For example, in the case of dairy products expressed in fresh whole-milk equivalent, any country importing and consuming skimmed milk powder (SMP) is shown as importing and consuming the amount of fresh whole milk that went into the production of the SMP. Trade and/or consumption (perhaps in another country) of the joint product—butter—is not shown at all to avoid double counting and also because animal fats are not covered in this study. Oilseeds are another commodity with significant joint products (oils, oilmeals) and the associated problems of allocation of consumption and trade. All consumption and trade of whole oilseeds, oils and downstream products of oils are recorded in oil equivalent while the joint product oilmeal is ignored. Thus any country importing only oilmeals is not recorded as trading in oilseeds.

The above examples indicate that some further work is required to improve the commodity coverage and conversion system used in this study. It involves not only an increase in the number of commodities but also some changes in the model structure to account for the fact that production of one single primary product (soyabeans) depends simultaneously on developments in two separate markets, that for oils and that for feeding stuffs.

# Appendix 2: Methodology of projections: a summary note

## Demand, production, trade

The projections of demand, production and trade are carried out for each of the commodities and countries analysed individually (see list of commodities and countries covered). The overall quantitative framework for the projections is based on the Supply Utilization Accounts (SUAs). The SUA is an accounting identity showing for any year the sources and uses of agricultural commodities in homogeneous units (see note on commodities in Appendix 1), as follows:

FOOD + INDUSTRIAL NON-FOOD USES + FEED + SEED + WASTE + (CLOSING STOCKS—OPENING STOCKS) = PRODUCTION + (IMPORTS—EXPORTS)

There is one such SUA for each of the historical years (generally 1961 to 1985) and the bulk of the projection work is concerned with drawing up SUAs (by commodity and country) for the year 2000. Different methods are used to project the individual elements of the SUA, as follows.

*Food demand* per caput is projected using the base year data for this variable (the three-year average 1982/4) the FAO food demand model (a set of estimated food demand functions—Engel curves—for up to 52 separate commodities in each country) and the assumptions of the growth of per caput incomes (GDP). The results are adjusted as required by the commodity and nutrition specialists taking into account the historical evolution of per caput demand. Subsequently, total projected food demand is obtained by simple multiplication of the projected per caput levels with projected population.

The terms 'food demand', 'food consumption' and 'food availability' are used interchangeably to denote the element 'Food', that is the use of agricultural commodities for direct human consumption in the SUAs. Projected food demand will equal consumption or availability on the assumption that the projected values of the other elements in the SUA (in particular production and net imports) would also materialize.

*Industrial demand* for non-food uses is projected as a function of the GDP growth assumptions and/or the population projections and subsequently adjusted in the process of inspection of the results.

*Feed demand* for cereals is derived simultaneously with the projections of livestock products by multiplying projected production of each of the livestock products with country-specific input/output coefficients (feeding rates) in terms of metabolizable energy supplied by cereals and brans. The part that can be met by projected domestic production of brans is deducted, and the balance represents cereals demand for feed. Feed use of non-cereal products is obtained by *ad hoc* methods using historical data mostly as a proportion of total production or total demand. The study does not project feed use of oilmeals. This is a serious lacuna planned to be filled in future development of the analytical framework.

*Seed use* is projected as a function of production using seeding rates per hectare. This is part of the projections of input requirements, discussed below.

*Waste* is projected as a proportion of total supply (production plus imports).

The study does not project year-2000 *stock changes*. This does not mean that present stocks are assumed to remain constant but rather that changes to adjust them to 'desired' or 'required' levels will occur in the years between now and 2000. It is impossible to project country- and commodity-specific adjustments in any one particular year. The general point is made in the report that current stocks of particular commodities and countries are out of balance with 'desired' or 'required' levels. If the adjustments occur in any year(s) before 2000, the impact on production will appear only as temporary deviation(s) from the smooth growth path represented by a curve joining the base-year production level to that of the year 2000, ignoring fluctuations in the intervening years. Whether or not year-2000 production includes a provision for 'normal' stock changes (i.e. to maintain stocks at the desired percentage of consumption already achieved before 2000) makes little difference to the average growth rate of production for 1983/5–2000 if the deviations from the constant growth rate path in the intervening years are ignored.

*Production and trade* projections for each country involve a number of iterative computations and adjustments as follows:

(1) Commodities in deficit in the base year (developing countries only): a preliminary 'target' level is set for the year 2000 taking into account the projected demand, production growth possibilities (evaluated in more detail in subsequent steps of the analysis) and the general objective that self-sufficiency should be raised or, as the case may be, its past rate of decline should be contained if possible, depending on the country/commodity situation.

(2) Commodities exported in the historical period and the base year (developing countries only): it is assumed that they will continue to be exported in amounts which will depend on the country's possibilities to increase production, a preliminary assessment of import demand on the part of all the other countries which are deficit in that commodity and an assessment of the country's possibility to have a share in total world import demand resulting from an analysis of trends and other relevant factors. Since for world balance total deficits of the importing countries must be equal to total surpluses of the exporting countries there is an element of simultaneity in the determination of the production levels of all commodities in all countries. This is solved in a number of successive iterations rather than through a formal model, the key element being expert judgements of market shares in world exports and of somewhat more formal evaluations of the production possibilities, as explained below. Based on the above considerations, preliminary production 'targets' are therefore set for the export commodities of each developing country. They are equal to their own domestic demand plus the preliminary export levels. Once the preliminary production targets are set for all commodities, the missing elements of the demand side of the SUA which depend on the levels of production (feed, seed, waste) can be filled in.

At this stage complete preliminary SUAs are available for the year 2000 for all commodities and all the developing countries, showing for each commodity and country all the demand elements and production. The differences between total demand and production are the preliminary net trade positions (imports or exports). The next step is to derive preliminary world balances. Similar SUAs are therefore constructed for the developed countries.

(3) For the European centrally planned economies (CPEs) the procedure followed is more or less the same as that described above for the developing countries, though the judgemental element concerning objectives of self-sufficiency and exports may not be identical. Moreover, there is no further evaluation of the projected production levels in terms of land and yields in different agro-ecological land classes, an operation carried out for the developing countries only (see below).

(4) For the developed market economies (DMEs) the demand components of the SUA are projected in the same manner as for the other countries. Production is, however, projected as trend in the manner described in Chapter 3. The net trade balances thus obtained for the DMEs are subsequently reviewed together with those of the developing countries and the European CPEs as follows.

(5) For the commodities not produced, or produced only in insignificant quantities in the DMEs (tea, coffee, cocoa, bananas, natural rubber, jute, cassava), nearly all their demand translates into import requirements. This, together with the import requirements of the developing countries in deficit and those of the European CPEs, define the total market available to the developing exporting countries. Their provisional production and export levels, set as described above, are then adjusted judgementally to equate them to the total import requirements.

(6) A second set of commodities comprises those produced in substantial quantitites in both the DMEs and the developing countries but for which the latter have been traditionally substantial net exporters (mainly sugar, vegetable oils and oilseeds, citrus, tobacco, cotton). DME production trends of some of these commodities, particularly sugar and oilseeds, have been strong resulting in import substitution and declining net imports from the developing countries. If these production trends continued, net DME imports from the developing countries of some of these commodities would decline further and the DMEs could turn into net exporters. Assumptions were therefore introduced that farm protection policies in the DMEs would be adjusted to check production growth so as to enable the developing countries to continue to be net exporters. No radical departures from past trends in the net exports of the developing countries are, however, incorporated into these assumptions. The results, which in practice reflect the above assumptions for the DMEs as well as those concerning export availabilities of the major developing exporters, are shown in Table 3.8 (pp. 90–1). It is emphasized that these assumptions reflect present evaluations of possible policy stances as revealed by past trends in policies. As such they represent only one possible trade outcome, and the scope for different results for some of these commodities is very wide, particularly for those in which the developing countries are low-cost

producers, for example of sugar. In such cases the outcome is overwhelmingly determined by the farm protection policies of the major DME consumers and producers. Therefore a much higher degree of uncertainty applies to these trade projections compared with those of the other commodities.

(7) The last group of commodities comprises those for which the developing countries and the European CPEs are major importers and the DMEs are the major suppliers of these imports (mainly wheat, coarse grains, milk). For these commodities, the net exports of the developing exporters are determined first (step 2, above) and subsequently the net export balances resulting from the trend projections of the DMEs are confronted with the remaining deficits of the developing importers and the CPEs. As discussed in Chapter 3, these projected DME export balances generally exceed the import requirements of the rest of the world. The final step of this analysis computes the extent to which the production trends of the DMEs must be modified for world balance.

At this stage the projections of demand, production and trade are complete: there is one projected SUA for each country and commodity and world imports equal world exports. These projections are, however, still provisional pending a more detailed evaluation of the feasibility of the production projections of the developing countries.

## Evaluation of production projections

(8) For each developing country (excluding China) the base-year data set is expanded to include a complete description of crop and livestock production systems in terms of the main parameters. For crops this is a matrix (size 33 × 21) with data on area, yield and production of each crop in each of the six agro-ecological land categories (described in Ch. 4). In steps 1 and 2 above, the crop production projections were specified only in terms of aggregate production and occasionally also in terms of area and yields, total not by land classes. The more detailed production analysis is therefore concerned with evaluation of these production projections in terms of land and yield by agro-ecological class. This is equivalent to creating for the year 2000 a matrix (a crop production programme) similar to that of the base year. In doing so, certain land and yield constraints by agro-ecological class have to be respected.

(9) For this purpose two additional data sets are used. The first one (land data set) has data for each country of potential agricultural land by class and how much of it is used in the base year. The second (global technology data set) comes from a survey of yields prevailing in different parts of the developing world and the inputs associated with such yields in each of the agro-ecological classes. The crop production programme for the year 2000 is constructed judgementally and iteratively by specialists on different countries and on crop production. Assumptions are first made of what are feasible rates of harvested land expansion by agro-ecological class (through use of more land from the reserves and or through increased cropping intensities, including expansion of irrigation). Similar assumptions are made for yield increases and the land allocation to each crop. Since a multitude of detailed assumptions and different

specialists are involved, continuous iterative computations of the whole system are made to ensure that the constraints of land availability and the permissible levels of yield increases (both by land class) are respected. The end result is that either the initial production target is accepted or is revised downwards for some crops because land resources (of the required class, where applicable) are not sufficient or because it requires yield increases considered by the specialists to be beyond achievement by the year 2000 even under reasonably improved policies. A more formal description of the procedures presented here is to be found in Bruinsma *et al.* (1983).

(10) Similar production analysis procedures are applied to the livestock production, except that the relevant parameters are animal numbers and yields (off-take rates, carcass weight, milk yields, eggs per laying hen) for the livestock species considered.

## Final adjustments

(11) For the commodities and countries for which the provisional production 'targets' had to be lowered during the feasibility tests, the resulting import requirements would be higher than originally estimated. This means that the provisional world balance achieved in steps 1 to 7 is disturbed. A final iteration is made to adjust production and trade balances of other countries to make up the shortfall in production in the developing countries whose initial provisional 'targets' were found to be unfeasible.

At this stage, the world demand, production and trade picture is completely quantified. The remaining steps in the analysis are concerned with quantifying the projected requirements of the developing countries for inputs and investments as well as the mechanization and employment implications.

## Input requirements

The crop production projections and the global technology data set described above are subsequently used to estimate the inputs required for the projected production. These inputs are fertilizer (N,P,K), power in terms of man-day equivalents (subsequently decomposed into the parts to be provided by draught animals, labour and machinery), seed (distinguishing traditional and improved seed) and crop protection chemicals (in monetary units, given the great diversity of the products actually used).

The input use coefficients in the global technology data set are specified as the amounts of, for example, N fertilizer required per hectare for a given yield in each agro-ecological land class and crop. These coefficients are made country-specific (calibrated) on the basis of data on total input use in the base year. Subsequently, total input requirements in the year 2000 are calculated by simple multiplication of these input coefficients by the projected harvested land areas.

The above discussion covers the inputs into crop production. For livestock, only the cereals feed requirements are estimated, as explained earlier. In addition, in countries which use significant areas for cultivated fodder production, an allowance is made for future land requirements for this purpose. This is, however, done in order to complete the land-use accounts rather than in relation to livestock production. It proved impossible to draw-up complete balance sheets of feed resources and uses, including grazing land, crop residues and non-cereal concentrates. This is an area for future improvement of the study's data base and methodology.

## Employment and mechanization

The methodology for projecting labour use and requirements of mechanization is explained in Chapter 4, and is not repeated here. A more formal description of an earlier version of the method is given in Alexandratos *et al.* (1982). Some significant improvements were introduced in the present application.

## Investments

The methodology for estimating investment requirements for the developing countries (excluding China) and the main items covered are presented summarily in Chapter 4.

In the first place, the investment goods to be added to the base year capital stock of agriculture are estimated in physical units. Most of the required additions are taken from the projections of production and inputs which identify, for example, the additional land to be developed, to be irrigated, the additions to the tractor part and to livestock needs. These additions are the cumulative net investment requirements of the entire period between the base year and the year 2000. Subsequently, requirements for replacement investment are derived for the capital goods which must be replaced periodically. These are added to the net requirements to obtain estimates of gross investment.

Once the estimates in physical units are made they are valued at average unit prices in 1979/81 dollars to obtain the investment requirements in monetary terms. The problems encountered in this evaluation (assumptions on unit prices, derivation of the dollar values for more recent years) are discussed in Chapter 4.

# Appendix 3: A summary evaluation of the methodology

The preceding discussion highlighted the key characteristics of the methodology which may be summarized as follows: (i) all analyses are conducted in a great amount of detail (individual countries, commodities, inputs), (ii) behavioural relationships are used explicitly only rarely, for example in the projections of food demand and in the determination of the rate of mechanization; (iii) some other projections, mostly those of current inputs, are derived from fixed-coefficient technological relationships; (iv) the more important projections of land use (by agro-ecological class), production and trade depend heavily on 'expert judgement' of different specialists reflecting the multidisciplinary nature of the study; (v) links with rest of the economy are not accounted for except for the influence of income growth on demand; and (vi) prices play no explicit role in bringing about demand–supply balance. The latter is established iteratively in a framework of accounting consistency in successive rounds of inspection and adjustment of the preliminary projections by country and commodity specialists.

This methodology has positive and negative aspects. On the positive side, the great detail of analysis means that the projections and related statements contained in this book for country groups, regions or the world as a whole as well as those for large commodity aggregates and the whole of agriculture are underpinned by detailed country/commodity quantifications. In practice, each global statement is derived from a summation of, and can be decomposed back into, a number of constituent single-country or commodity statements. This characteristic sets this study apart from most other 'global' studies in which analyses are carried out at the level of major countries and/or regions and large commodity groups. As a consequence of the great detail of analysis, the results of this study can be viewed with greater confidence, and are more relevant for policy analysis, than if they had been derived from analyses at more aggregate level. For example, knowledge on constraints and opportunities for increased cereal production in Africa is normally available for individual grains in specified agro-ecological zones and countries but not for 'cereals' in 'Africa'. Production prospects for cereals in Africa can therefore be evaluated with a higher degree of confidence because they can be better recognized and cross-checked by experts if the methodology allows for the distinction of individual grains, zones and countries than if it does not. Similarly, some key trade policy issues are commodity-specific and cannot be meaningfully analysed if the demand/supply situation is not defined in the required commodity detail, for example bananas and citrus separately rather than fruit in general. Without this detail the evaluation of the production and trade prospects of individual countries becomes difficult.

The great country and commodity detail is in practice an integral part of the methodology because the projections are heavily dependent on expert judgement. Only in this way is it possible for the study to exploit the wide range of expertise available in FAO, which is one of its strongest points. The required contributions from the experts on the different countries and disciplines (e.g. agronomy, animal production, commodity specialists, etc.) are forthcoming only if the questions are asked in what they consider to be meaningful detail. This means, for example, that yield prospects and production potential must be evaluated for millet in semi-arid conditions, or for flooded and upland rice separately and so on, not for cereals in general. Similarly, export prospects and the related trade policy issues must be evaluated separately for bananas or citrus, not for fruit in general.

This heavy dependence on great detail and expert judgement is at the same time the major weakness of the methodology. Projections based on expert judgement suffer from the fact that the criteria and assumptions used and the implicit decision-making mechanism cannot be formally described and they can vary from one person to another and over time. It follows that the projections cannot be strictly replicated at will, including for estimating alternative scenarios by varying certain assumptions only. This would have been possible if a formal model had been used for the projections.

There are advantages and disadvantages in the use of formal models for this type of work (Alexandratos 1976). In the case of this study, the great amount of detail makes it impossible to conduct the analysis using one single formal model representing behaviour of the different actors (producers, consumers, governments) and with price-based market clearing mechanisms. Many of the data required for such an effort are just not available. For a formal modelling approach, the choice would have been between having (i) a roughly estimated formal model with much less commodity, input and country detail or (ii) a huge model with all the detail of this study but with the bulk of the parameters and coefficients being 'guesstimates' rather than data. The former case is a clearly inferior option since it would make it impossible to evaluate the results using the expertise available in FAO. Moreover, the findings of the study would be of limited value for policy analysis work because of the much reduced commodity and country detail.

The second option (large model with a wide range of guesstimates for the parameters) is really a formal variant of the expert judgement-based approach used in this study, the difference being that expert judgements would be contained in the guesstimates of the values of the model parameters and coefficients. Such an approach is superior to the one of this study, since the utilization of the expert judgement input is subject to the discipline that the implied values of the parameters and coefficients must fall within a certain acceptable range. Iterations and dialogue would be greatly facilitated, alternative scenarios can be estimated and greater transparency is assured. These advantages must be set against the greater resources and time required for model preparation, particularly for the development of the computing algorithms. This can be daunting for a global model that could recognize more than 100 countries communicating through trade flows, over 35 commodities, up to six sets of production conditions per crop, and so on. It could easily absorb a disproportionate part of the resources of the study without assurance of a satisfactory end-product.

In conclusion, future improvements in the methodology should aim at introducing some of the advantages of formal models in the form of explicit statements of the assumed behavioural relationships and their empirical verification, replication of results and derivation of alternative scenarios in a consistent manner. It is, however, important that the strong points of the present methodology be preserved, namely the detail of analysis as regards countries, commodities and production conditions as well as the associated possibility to use multidisciplinary input. Given 'reasonable' resource and time limitations, it is unlikely that this could be achieved by an attempt to build a formal model in all the detail of this study. Scarce resources could be used more productively if they are concentrated on improving selected components of the present methodology, for example developing a more complete submodel to link the cereals, oilseeds and livestock subsectors in the analysis and projections of demand for animal feed.

# Appendix 4: Statistical tables

Notes to the tables appear in a separate section (pp. 326–7).

**Table A.1** Total population and agricultural labour force

| | Total population | | | | | Agricultural labour force | | | | | | | | |
|---|---|---|---|---|---|---|---|---|---|---|---|---|---|---|
| | thousands | | growth rates (% p.a.) | | | thousands | | % of total labour force | | | | growth rates (% p.a.) | | |
| | 1985 | 2000 | 70–80 | 80–5 | 85–2000 | 1985 | 2000 | 1970 | 1980 | 1985 | 2000 | 70–80 | 80–5 | 85–2000 |
| World | 4836958 | 6122101 | 1.9 | 1.7 | 1.6 | 1053001 | 1157668 | 55 | 51 | 9 | 42 | 1.2 | 1.2 | 0.6 |
| All developing countries | 3626521 | 4793355 | 2.3 | 2.0 | 1.9 | 993069 | 1122860 | 71 | 66 | 63 | 53 | 1.6 | 1.5 | 0.8 |
| 94 developing countries | 3591393 | 4745698 | 2.3 | 2.0 | 1.9 | 988787 | 1118141 | 71 | 66 | 63 | 53 | 1.6 | 1.5 | 0.8 |
| 93 developing countries | 2531872 | 3489803 | 2.5 | 2.4 | 2.2 | 550251 | 662774 | 67 | 61 | 58 | 50 | 1.3 | 1.4 | 1.2 |
| Africa (sub-Saharan) | 416452 | 675345 | 3.0 | 3.1 | 3.3 | 128010 | 168267 | 81 | 76 | 74 | 66 | 1.9 | 1.7 | 1.8 |
| Angola | 8754 | 13234 | 3.3 | 2.5 | 2.8 | 2671 | 3313 | 78 | 74 | 72 | 66 | 2.3 | 1.2 | 1.4 |
| Benin | 4050 | 6532 | 2.6 | 3.0 | 3.2 | 1295 | 1465 | 81 | 70 | 66 | 52 | 0.6 | 0.8 | 0.8 |
| Botswana | 1107 | 1917 | 3.9 | 3.9 | 3.7 | 254 | 343 | 86 | 70 | 67 | 55 | 1.1 | 2.4 | 2.0 |
| Burkina Faso | 6942 | 10538 | 2.0 | 2.4 | 2.8 | 3222 | 4260 | 88 | 87 | 86 | 82 | 1.6 | 1.7 | 1.9 |
| Burundi | 4721 | 7226 | 1.7 | 2.9 | 2.9 | 2319 | 3227 | 93 | 93 | 92 | 89 | 1.2 | 1.9 | 2.2 |
| Cameroon | 9873 | 15168 | 2.5 | 2.7 | 2.9 | 2597 | 2834 | 83 | 70 | 66 | 52 | −0.2 | 0.5 | 0.6 |
| Central African Rep. | 2576 | 3750 | 2.1 | 2.3 | 2.5 | 869 | 860 | 83 | 72 | 68 | 52 | −0.1 | 0.0 | −0.1 |
| Chad | 5018 | 7308 | 2.0 | 2.3 | 2.5 | 1419 | 1542 | 90 | 83 | 79 | 63 | 0.9 | 0.8 | 0.6 |
| Congo | 1740 | 2643 | 2.4 | 2.6 | 2.8 | 433 | 559 | 65 | 62 | 61 | 56 | 1.7 | 1.3 | 1.7 |
| Côte d'Ivoire | 9810 | 16006 | 3.9 | 3.7 | 3.3 | 2454 | 2724 | 76 | 65 | 61 | 46 | 1.0 | 1.2 | 0.7 |
| Ethiopia | 43557 | 66509 | 2.3 | 2.5 | 2.9 | 14827 | 18096 | 85 | 80 | 77 | 69 | 1.4 | 1.1 | 1.3 |
| Gabon | 1151 | 1603 | 1.1 | 1.6 | 2.2 | 372 | 350 | 80 | 75 | 72 | 59 | 0.3 | −0.4 | −0.4 |
| Gambia | 643 | 898 | 2.2 | 2.0 | 2.3 | 254 | 299 | 87 | 84 | 83 | 77 | 1.7 | 0.9 | 1.1 |
| Ghana | 13588 | 22607 | 3.0 | 3.3 | 3.5 | 2625 | 3378 | 58 | 56 | 53 | 44 | 1.9 | 1.6 | 1.7 |

**Table A.1** (*cont.*)

| | Total population | | | | | Agricultural labour force | | | | | | | | |
|---|---|---|---|---|---|---|---|---|---|---|---|---|---|---|
| | thousands | | growth rates (% p.a.) | | | thousands | | % of total labour force | | | | growth rates (% p.a.) | | |
| | 1985 | 2000 | 70–80 | 80–5 | 85–2000 | 1985 | 2000 | 1970 | 1980 | 1985 | 2000 | 70–80 | 80–5 | 85–2000 |
| Guinea | 6075 | 8879 | 2.1 | 2.4 | 2.6 | 2209 | 2478 | 85 | 81 | 78 | 66 | 1.3 | 0.8 | 0.8 |
| Kenya | 20600 | 38534 | 4.0 | 4.2 | 4.3 | 6634 | 10438 | 85 | 81 | 79 | 72 | 3.2 | 3.0 | 3.1 |
| Lesotho | 1520 | 2255 | 2.3 | 2.6 | 2.7 | 607 | 710 | 90 | 86 | 83 | 71 | 1.6 | 1.2 | 1.1 |
| Liberia | 2191 | 3615 | 3.2 | 3.2 | 3.4 | 584 | 780 | 77 | 74 | 72 | 65 | 2.2 | 1.6 | 1.9 |
| Madagascar | 10012 | 15550 | 2.6 | 2.8 | 3.0 | 3555 | 4492 | 84 | 81 | 79 | 71 | 1.8 | 1.4 | 1.6 |
| Malawi | 6944 | 11387 | 2.8 | 3.1 | 3.4 | 2444 | 2946 | 91 | 83 | 80 | 65 | 1.4 | 1.6 | 1.3 |
| Mali | 8082 | 12658 | 2.1 | 2.8 | 3.0 | 2165 | 2919 | 89 | 85 | 83 | 75 | 1.3 | 2.0 | 2.0 |
| Mauritania | 1888 | 2998 | 2.7 | 3.0 | 3.1 | 395 | 557 | 85 | 69 | 67 | 60 | −0.3 | 2.0 | 2.3 |
| Mauritius | 1050 | 1298 | 1.2 | 1.9 | 1.4 | 98 | 96 | 34 | 28 | 25 | 18 | 0.5 | 1.1 | −0.1 |
| Mozambique | 13961 | 21104 | 4.1 | 2.9 | 2.8 | 6372 | 8085 | 86 | 84 | 83 | 78 | 3.6 | 1.8 | 1.6 |
| Niger | 6115 | 9750 | 2.5 | 2.9 | 3.2 | 2861 | 3870 | 94 | 91 | 89 | 82 | 1.5 | 1.9 | 2.0 |
| Nigeria | 95198 | 161930 | 3.5 | 3.4 | 3.6 | 24316 | 34259 | 71 | 68 | 66 | 61 | 2.7 | 2.1 | 2.3 |
| Rwanda | 6070 | 10123 | 3.3 | 3.4 | 3.5 | 2821 | 4224 | 94 | 93 | 92 | 89 | 3.0 | 2.6 | 2.7 |
| Senegal | 6444 | 9765 | 3.5 | 2.6 | 2.8 | 2304 | 2993 | 83 | 81 | 80 | 76 | 3.0 | 1.6 | 1.8 |
| Sierra Leone | 3602 | 4867 | 1.5 | 1.8 | 2.0 | 893 | 914 | 76 | 70 | 66 | 55 | 0.1 | 0.1 | 0.2 |
| Somalia | 4653 | 6671 | 4.3 | 3.0 | 2.4 | 1458 | 1660 | 79 | 76 | 73 | 64 | 3.2 | 1.3 | 0.9 |
| Sudan | 21550 | 32926 | 3.0 | 2.9 | 2.9 | 4606 | 5348 | 77 | 71 | 66 | 49 | 1.9 | 1.2 | 1.0 |
| Swaziland | 650 | 1048 | 2.7 | 3.1 | 3.2 | 192 | 228 | 81 | 74 | 70 | 58 | 1.2 | 1.1 | 1.2 |
| Tanzania | 22499 | 39129 | 3.4 | 3.6 | 3.8 | 9098 | 12758 | 90 | 86 | 83 | 75 | 2.3 | 2.2 | 2.3 |
| Togo | 2960 | 4709 | 2.4 | 3.0 | 3.1 | 887 | 1181 | 77 | 73 | 71 | 66 | 1.6 | 1.8 | 1.9 |
| Uganda | 15477 | 26262 | 2.9 | 3.4 | 3.6 | 5892 | 8163 | 89 | 86 | 84 | 75 | 2.2 | 2.2 | 2.2 |
| Zaire | 29938 | 47581 | 2.9 | 3.0 | 3.1 | 8012 | 10154 | 79 | 71 | 69 | 60 | 0.8 | 1.4 | 1.6 |
| Zambia | 6666 | 11237 | 3.0 | 3.4 | 3.5 | 1591 | 2420 | 77 | 73 | 71 | 64 | 2.2 | 2.6 | 2.8 |
| Zimbabwe | 8777 | 15130 | 3.3 | 3.6 | 3.7 | 2405 | 3344 | 77 | 73 | 71 | 63 | 2.2 | 2.1 | 2.2 |

| | | | | | | | | | | | | | |
|---|---|---|---|---|---|---|---|---|---|---|---|---|---|
| Near East/North Africa | 265476 | 387041 | 2.7 | 2.7 | 2.5 | 33473 | 36776 | 57 | 46 | 41 | 29 | 0.3 | 0.6 | 0.6 |
| Afghanistan | 16519 | 26035 | 1.7 | 0.6 | 3.1 | 2877 | 3723 | 66 | 61 | 58 | 48 | 0.7 | —0.3 | 1.7 |
| Algeria | 21718 | 33444 | 3.1 | 3.1 | 2.9 | 1301 | 1386 | 47 | 31 | 27 | 17 | —1.0 | 0.6 | 0.4 |
| Cyprus | 669 | 762 | 0.2 | 1.2 | 0.9 | 72 | 58 | 39 | 26 | 23 | 16 | —2.7 | —1.0 | —1.4 |
| Egypt | 46909 | 63941 | 2.3 | 2.5 | 2.1 | 5526 | 6786 | 52 | 46 | 43 | 36 | 0.8 | 1.4 | 1.4 |
| Iran | 44632 | 65161 | 3.1 | 2.9 | 2.6 | 4082 | 4331 | 44 | 36 | 31 | 21 | 1.3 | 0.3 | 0.4 |
| Iraq | 15898 | 25377 | 3.6 | 3.6 | 3.2 | 1043 | 1073 | 47 | 30 | 24 | 14 | —0.5 | —0.7 | 0.2 |
| Jordan | 3515 | 6437 | 2.4 | 3.8 | 4.1 | 63 | 52 | 28 | 10 | 8 | 3 | —8.7 | —1.0 | —1.3 |
| Lebanon | 2668 | 3617 | 0.8 | 0.0 | 2.0 | 90 | 69 | 20 | 14 | 12 | 6 | —2.0 | —3.3 | —1.8 |
| Libya | 3605 | 6082 | 4.1 | 3.9 | 3.5 | 131 | 118 | 29 | 18 | 14 | 8 | —0.9 | —0.9 | —0.7 |
| Morocco | 21941 | 29512 | 2.4 | 2.5 | 2.0 | 2746 | 2950 | 58 | 46 | 41 | 28 | 1.1 | 1.1 | 0.5 |
| Saudi Arabia | 11542 | 19824 | 5.0 | 4.3 | 3.7 | 1490 | 1729 | 64 | 48 | 44 | 30 | 2.7 | 2.3 | 1.0 |
| Syria | 10505 | 17809 | 3.5 | 3.6 | 3.6 | 713 | 847 | 50 | 32 | 27 | 18 | —1.1 | 0.2 | 1.2 |
| Tunisia | 7081 | 9429 | 2.2 | 2.1 | 1.9 | 648 | 549 | 42 | 35 | 29 | 16 | 1.8 | —0.6 | —1.1 |
| Turkey | 49289 | 65351 | 2.3 | 2.1 | 1.9 | 11385 | 11335 | 71 | 58 | 53 | 39 | —0.2 | 0.4 | 0.0 |
| Yemen AR | 6848 | 10881 | 2.2 | 2.7 | 3.1 | 1103 | 1562 | 76 | 69 | 66 | 56 | —0.1 | 1.7 | 2.3 |
| Yemen PDR | 2137 | 3379 | 2.2 | 2.8 | 3.1 | 203 | 208 | 51 | 41 | 36 | 24 | —0.4 | 0.4 | 0.2 |
| Asia | 2510478 | 3143897 | 2.1 | 1.8 | 1.5 | 786986 | 870980 | 74 | 70 | 67 | 57 | 1.6 | 1.5 | 0.7 |
| Bangladesh | 101147 | 145800 | 2.8 | 2.8 | 2.5 | 20704 | 27551 | 81 | 75 | 72 | 62 | 1.2 | 1.9 | 1.9 |
| Burma | 37153 | 48499 | 2.2 | 2.0 | 1.8 | 8343 | 9020 | 59 | 53 | 50 | 41 | 1.1 | 0.7 | 0.5 |
| China | 1059521 | 1255895 | 1.8 | 1.2 | 1.1 | 438536 | 455367 | 78 | 74 | 71 | 60 | 1.9 | 1.5 | 0.3 |
| India | 758927 | 964072 | 2.2 | 2.0 | 1.6 | 199765 | 243512 | 72 | 70 | 68 | 63 | 1.4 | 1.5 | 1.3 |
| Indonesia | 166440 | 211367 | 2.3 | 2.0 | 1.6 | 33522 | 34885 | 66 | 57 | 53 | 40 | 0.6 | 0.8 | 0.3 |
| Kampuchea DM | 7284 | 9772 | —2.8 | 5.9 | 2.0 | 2603 | 2753 | 78 | 74 | 72 | 65 | 0.1 | 1.2 | 0.4 |
| Korea DPR | 20385 | 28166 | 2.6 | 2.5 | 2.2 | 3460 | 3493 | 53 | 43 | 38 | 25 | 0.7 | 0.6 | 0.1 |
| Korea Rep. | 41258 | 50981 | 1.8 | 1.6 | 1.4 | 5061 | 3594 | 49 | 36 | 30 | 16 | —0.4 | —1.1 | —2.3 |
| Lao | 4117 | 5789 | 2.0 | 2.3 | 2.3 | 1484 | 1857 | 79 | 76 | 74 | 67 | 0.9 | 1.3 | 1.5 |
| Malaysia | 15557 | 20497 | 2.4 | 2.5 | 1.9 | 2266 | 2170 | 54 | 42 | 37 | 24 | 1.1 | 0.4 | —0.3 |
| Nepal | 16482 | 23048 | 2.5 | 2.4 | 2.3 | 6346 | 8717 | 94 | 93 | 92 | 90 | 1.7 | 2.1 | 2.1 |
| Pakistan | 100380 | 140961 | 2.7 | 3.1 | 2.3 | 15539 | 20133 | 59 | 55 | 52 | 45 | 2.0 | 2.3 | 1.7 |
| Philippines | 54498 | 74057 | 2.6 | 2.4 | 2.1 | 9782 | 11935 | 55 | 52 | 49 | 42 | 1.9 | 1.5 | 1.3 |
| Sri Lanka | 16205 | 19620 | 1.7 | 1.8 | 1.3 | 3109 | 3751 | 55 | 53 | 53 | 50 | 1.9 | 1.3 | 1.3 |

**Table A.1** (*cont.*)

| | Total population | | | | | Agricultural labour force | | | | | | | | | |
|---|---|---|---|---|---|---|---|---|---|---|---|---|---|---|---|
| | thousands | | growth rates (% p.a.) | | | thousands | | % of total labour force | | | | growth rates (% p.a.) | | | |
| | 1985 | 2000 | 70–80 | 80–5 | 85–2000 | 1985 | 2000 | 1970 | 1980 | 1985 | 2000 | 70–80 | 80–5 | 85–2000 |
| Thailand | 51411 | 65503 | 2.5 | 2.0 | 1.6 | 18038 | 19686 | 80 | 71 | 68 | 57 | 1.6 | 1.5 | 0.6 |
| Vietnam | 59713 | 79870 | 2.4 | 2.0 | 2.0 | 18428 | 22556 | 77 | 67 | 64 | 53 | 0.8 | 1.8 | 1.4 |
| Latin America | 398987 | 539415 | 2.5 | 2.3 | 2.0 | 40318 | 42118 | 41 | 32 | 29 | 21 | 0.7 | 0.6 | 0.3 |
| Argentina | 30564 | 37197 | 1.7 | 1.6 | 1.3 | 1267 | 1108 | 16 | 13 | 12 | 8 | −1.1 | −1.2 | −0.9 |
| Bolivia | 6371 | 9724 | 2.6 | 2.7 | 2.9 | 873 | 1061 | 52 | 46 | 44 | 36 | 0.9 | 1.6 | 1.3 |
| Brazil | 135564 | 179487 | 2.4 | 2.3 | 1.9 | 13701 | 12458 | 45 | 31 | 28 | 18 | −0.3 | 0.0 | −0.6 |
| Chile | 12038 | 14792 | 1.6 | 1.6 | 1.4 | 615 | 527 | 23 | 16 | 14 | 10 | −1.0 | −0.1 | −1.0 |
| Colombia | 28714 | 37999 | 2.2 | 2.2 | 1.9 | 2835 | 2786 | 39 | 34 | 31 | 21 | 1.1 | 0.7 | −0.1 |
| Costa Rica | 2600 | 3596 | 2.8 | 2.7 | 2.2 | 245 | 232 | 43 | 31 | 27 | 18 | 0.5 | 0.5 | −0.4 |
| Cuba | 10038 | 11718 | 1.3 | 0.6 | 1.0 | 854 | 792 | 30 | 24 | 21 | 16 | 0.7 | 0.1 | −0.5 |
| Dominican Rep. | 6243 | 8407 | 2.6 | 2.4 | 2.0 | 755 | 765 | 55 | 46 | 41 | 27 | 1.3 | 1.0 | 0.1 |
| Ecuador | 9378 | 13939 | 3.0 | 2.9 | 2.7 | 975 | 997 | 51 | 39 | 34 | 23 | −0.1 | 0.7 | 0.1 |
| El Salvador | 5552 | 8708 | 3.0 | 3.0 | 3.0 | 737 | 944 | 56 | 43 | 40 | 32 | 0.3 | 1.5 | 1.7 |
| Guatemala | 7963 | 12222 | 2.8 | 2.9 | 2.9 | 1221 | 1662 | 61 | 57 | 54 | 45 | 1.4 | 1.8 | 2.1 |
| Guyana | 953 | 1196 | 2.0 | 2.0 | 1.5 | 83 | 90 | 32 | 27 | 25 | 18 | 2.0 | 1.3 | 0.5 |
| Haiti | 6585 | 9860 | 2.3 | 2.5 | 2.7 | 1889 | 2260 | 74 | 70 | 67 | 58 | 0.3 | 1.1 | 1.2 |
| Honduras | 4372 | 6978 | 3.4 | 3.4 | 3.2 | 752 | 1131 | 65 | 60 | 58 | 49 | 2.5 | 2.9 | 2.8 |
| Jamaica | 2336 | 2880 | 1.5 | 1.5 | 1.4 | 319 | 358 | 33 | 31 | 29 | 23 | 2.3 | 1.5 | 0.8 |
| Mexico | 78996 | 109180 | 3.1 | 2.6 | 2.2 | 8656 | 9728 | 44 | 37 | 33 | 24 | 2.5 | 1.3 | 0.8 |
| Nicaragua | 3272 | 5261 | 3.0 | 3.4 | 3.2 | 422 | 546 | 52 | 47 | 42 | 31 | 1.9 | 1.9 | 1.7 |
| Panama | 2180 | 2893 | 2.5 | 2.2 | 1.9 | 215 | 212 | 42 | 32 | 28 | 19 | −0.2 | 0.6 | −0.1 |
| Paraguay | 3681 | 5405 | 3.3 | 3.0 | 2.6 | 577 | 802 | 53 | 49 | 47 | 43 | 2.7 | 2.5 | 2.2 |
| Peru | 19698 | 27952 | 2.7 | 2.6 | 2.4 | 2315 | 2772 | 47 | 40 | 37 | 30 | 1.7 | 1.5 | 1.2 |
| Surinam | 375 | 469 | −0.5 | 1.1 | 1.5 | 21 | 23 | 25 | 20 | 18 | 13 | −1.7 | 0.0 | 0.6 |

| | | | | | | | | | | | | | |
|---|---|---|---|---|---|---|---|---|---|---|---|---|---|
| Trinidad and Tob. | 1185 | 1473 | 1.4 | 1.6 | 1.5 | 39 | 34 | 19 | 10 | 9 | 6 | −3.8 | −0.4 | −0.9 |
| Uruguay | 3012 | 3364 | 0.3 | 0.7 | 0.7 | 171 | 158 | 19 | 16 | 15 | 12 | −1.5 | −0.8 | −0.5 |
| Venezuela | 17317 | 24715 | 3.5 | 2.9 | 2.4 | 781 | 672 | 26 | 16 | 13 | 7 | −0.1 | −0.3 | −1.0 |
| Developing, low income | 2437626 | 3143021 | 2.1 | 1.7 | 1.8 | 802330 | 911140 | 76 | 73 | 70 | 61 | 1.7 | 1.6 | 0.9 |
| Low inc. excl. China | 1397255 | 1909826 | 2.4 | 2.3 | 2.1 | 371719 | 464003 | 74 | 71 | 69 | 62 | 1.5 | 1.6 | 1.5 |
| Low inc. excl. China/ India | 638328 | 945754 | 2.6 | 2.7 | 2.7 | 171954 | 220491 | 78 | 73 | 70 | 61 | 1.6 | 1.7 | 1.7 |
| Developing, middle income | 1134617 | 1579977 | 2.6 | 2.4 | 2.2 | 178532 | 198771 | 56 | 47 | 43 | 34 | 1.0 | 1.0 | 0.7 |
| Developed countries | 1210246 | 1328530 | 0.8 | 0.7 | 0.6 | 59924 | 34805 | 18 | 13 | 10 | 5 | −2.3 | −3.1 | −3.6 |
| European CPEs | 392313 | 437352 | 0.8 | 0.8 | 0.7 | 34483 | 20105 | 28 | 21 | 17 | 9 | −1.7 | −3.2 | −3.5 |
| Albania | 3050 | 4102 | 2.5 | 2.2 | 2.0 | 732 | 823 | 66 | 56 | 52 | 41 | 1.3 | 1.6 | 0.8 |
| Bulgaria | 8980 | 9439 | 0.4 | 0.3 | 0.3 | 650 | 342 | 35 | 18 | 15 | 8 | −6.2 | −4.3 | −4.2 |
| Czechoslovakia | 15498 | 16495 | 0.7 | 0.3 | 0.4 | 897 | 567 | 17 | 13 | 11 | 6 | −1.5 | −3.4 | −3.0 |
| German DR | 16660 | 17041 | −0.2 | 0.0 | 0.2 | 877 | 606 | 13 | 11 | 9 | 6 | −1.1 | −1.9 | −2.4 |
| Hungary | 10642 | 10659 | 0.4 | −0.1 | 0.0 | 755 | 391 | 25 | 18 | 15 | 7 | −3.6 | −4.5 | −4.3 |
| Poland | 37203 | 40834 | 0.9 | 0.9 | 0.6 | 4699 | 3158 | 39 | 29 | 24 | 15 | −2.4 | −2.3 | −2.6 |
| Romania | 22710 | 25230 | 0.9 | 0.4 | 0.7 | 2803 | 1554 | 49 | 31 | 25 | 12 | −4.5 | −3.6 | −3.9 |
| USSR | 277570 | 313552 | 0.9 | 0.9 | 0.8 | 23070 | 12664 | 26 | 20 | 16 | 8 | −1.0 | −3.4 | −3.9 |
| Developed market economies | 817933 | 891178 | 0.8 | 0.7 | 0.6 | 25441 | 14700 | 13 | 8 | 7 | 4 | −3.1 | −3.1 | −3.6 |
| Australia | 15691 | 18620 | 1.6 | 1.3 | 1.1 | 430 | 325 | 8 | 7 | 6 | 4 | 0.7 | −1.6 | −1.8 |
| Austria | 7555 | 7570 | 0.1 | 0.0 | 0.0 | 252 | 125 | 15 | 9 | 7 | 3 | −4.1 | −3.8 | −4.6 |
| Canada | 25379 | 28874 | 1.2 | 1.1 | 0.9 | 534 | 287 | 8 | 5 | 4 | 2 | −0.7 | −3.1 | −4.1 |
| Belgium-Lux. | 10230 | 10333 | 0.2 | 0.0 | 0.1 | 97 | 47 | 5 | 3 | 2 | 1 | −4.2 | −4.2 | −4.7 |
| Denmark | 5113 | 5073 | 0.4 | 0.0 | −0.1 | 163 | 85 | 11 | 7 | 6 | 3 | −2.9 | −3.8 | −4.2 |
| Finland | 4910 | 5075 | 0.4 | 0.5 | 0.2 | 246 | 140 | 20 | 12 | 10 | 5 | −4.0 | −2.9 | −3.7 |
| France | 55162 | 57728 | 0.6 | 0.5 | 0.3 | 1673 | 851 | 14 | 9 | 7 | 3 | −3.7 | −3.8 | −4.4 |

**Table A.1** *(cont.)*

| | Total population | | | | | Agricultural labour force | | | | | | | | |
|---|---|---|---|---|---|---|---|---|---|---|---|---|---|---|
| | thousands | | growth rates (% p.a.) | | | thousands | | % of total labour force | | | | growth rates (% p.a.) | | |
| | 1985 | 2000 | 70–80 | 80–5 | 85–2000 | 1985 | 2000 | 1970 | 1980 | 1985 | 2000 | 70–80 | 80–5 | 85–2000 |
| Germany FR | 61015 | 59619 | 0.0 | −0.2 | −0.2 | 1330 | 587 | 7 | 6 | 5 | 2 | −2.2 | −4.1 | −5.3 |
| Greece | 9970 | 10534 | 1.0 | 0.7 | 0.4 | 1046 | 746 | 42 | 31 | 27 | 19 | −2.3 | −1.6 | −2.2 |
| Iceland | 243 | 273 | 1.1 | 1.3 | 0.8 | 11 | 7 | 17 | 10 | 9 | 5 | −2.3 | −2.0 | −3.0 |
| Ireland | 3608 | 4320 | 1.4 | 1.2 | 1.2 | 216 | 167 | 26 | 19 | 16 | 10 | −2.3 | −1.6 | −1.7 |
| Israel | 4289 | 5348 | 2.6 | 2.0 | 1.5 | 84 | 65 | 10 | 6 | 5 | 3 | −1.7 | −1.3 | −1.7 |
| Italy | 57128 | 58466 | 0.5 | 0.3 | 0.2 | 2098 | 942 | 19 | 12 | 9 | 4 | −4.0 | −4.2 | −5.2 |
| Japan | 120754 | 129738 | 1.1 | 0.7 | 0.5 | 5072 | 2308 | 20 | 11 | 8 | 4 | −4.8 | −4.5 | −5.1 |
| Malta | 383 | 418 | 1.3 | 0.7 | 0.6 | 6 | 5 | 6 | 5 | 4 | 3 | 0.0 | −3.9 | −1.2 |
| Netherlands | 14484 | 15065 | 0.8 | 0.5 | 0.3 | 264 | 156 | 7 | 6 | 5 | 2 | −0.7 | −2.7 | −3.4 |
| New Zealand | 3271 | 3696 | 1.2 | 0.8 | 0.8 | 145 | 128 | 12 | 11 | 10 | 7 | 1.4 | −0.5 | −0.8 |
| Norway | 4150 | 4223 | 0.5 | 0.3 | 0.1 | 136 | 73 | 12 | 8 | 7 | 3 | −1.4 | −3.7 | −4.1 |
| Portugal | 10212 | 11211 | 1.4 | 0.7 | 0.6 | 924 | 546 | 32 | 26 | 20 | 11 | 0.4 | −3.8 | −3.4 |
| South Africa | 32392 | 46918 | 2.3 | 2.5 | 2.5 | 1700 | 1645 | 33 | 16 | 16 | 10 | −5.5 | 1.8 | −0.2 |
| Spain | 38356 | 42035 | 1.0 | 0.6 | 0.6 | 1860 | 1018 | 26 | 17 | 14 | 7 | −3.4 | −3.3 | −3.9 |
| Sweden | 8351 | 8166 | 0.3 | 0.0 | −0.1 | 198 | 117 | 8 | 6 | 5 | 3 | −2.7 | −3.5 | −3.4 |
| Switzerland | 6520 | 6486 | 0.0 | 0.4 | 0.0 | 164 | 84 | 8 | 6 | 5 | 3 | −2.2 | −3.0 | −4.4 |
| United Kingdom | 56807 | 57056 | 0.1 | 0.1 | 0.0 | 633 | 435 | 3 | 3 | 2 | 2 | −0.3 | −2.2 | −2.5 |
| United States | 238840 | 269163 | 1.0 | 1.0 | 0.8 | 3333 | 2090 | 4 | 3 | 3 | 2 | 0.1 | −2.6 | −3.1 |
| Yugoslavia | 23120 | 25170 | 0.9 | 0.7 | 0.6 | 2826 | 1721 | 50 | 32 | 27 | 15 | −3.4 | −2.5 | −3.3 |

**Table A.2** Growth rates of total agricultural demand and production and self-sufficiency ratios

| | Growth in total demand (all uses) (% p.a.) | | | | Growth in total production (% p.a.) | | | | Self-sufficiency ratios (%) | | | |
|---|---|---|---|---|---|---|---|---|---|---|---|---|
| | 1961–70 | 1970–80 | 1980–5 | 1961–85 | 1961–70 | 1970–80 | 1980–5 | 1961–85 | 1961/3 | 1969/71 | 1979/81 | 1983/85 |
| World | 3.0 | 2.4 | 2.5 | 2.5 | 3.0 | 2.4 | 2.7 | 2.5 | 101 | 100 | 100 | 100 |
| All developing countries | 3.6 | 3.7 | 3.6 | 3.5 | 3.5 | 3.0 | 3.8 | 3.2 | 106 | 105 | 99 | 100 |
| 94 developing countries | 3.6 | 3.6 | 3.7 | 3.5 | 3.5 | 3.0 | 3.9 | 3.2 | 107 | 106 | 100 | 101 |
| 93 developing countries | 3.0 | 3.6 | 3.1 | 3.3 | 2.7 | 3.0 | 3.0 | 2.9 | 110 | 108 | 101 | 101 |
| Africa (sub-Saharan) | 3.1 | 3.0 | 2.3 | 2.9 | 2.8 | 1.5 | 2.0 | 2.0 | 120 | 117 | 103 | 101 |
| Angola | 4.0 | 3.6 | 1.5 | 3.2 | 3.3 | −4.7 | −0.1 | −1.1 | 162 | 154 | 78 | 75 |
| Benin | 2.6 | 4.4 | 6.2 | 3.6 | 3.5 | 1.7 | 8.1 | 2.7 | 109 | 120 | 95 | 97 |
| Botswana | 3.1 | 3.3 | 2.6 | 3.3 | 3.4 | −0.5 | 1.6 | 1.6 | 132 | 140 | 106 | 99 |
| Burkina Faso | 2.7 | 2.6 | 3.3 | 2.4 | 3.2 | 1.8 | 4.8 | 1.9 | 110 | 110 | 101 | 101 |
| Burundi | 2.4 | 2.1 | 1.6 | 1.9 | 2.5 | 1.8 | 1.6 | 1.9 | 105 | 106 | 106 | 105 |
| Cameroon | 3.9 | 2.9 | 1.7 | 3.1 | 4.2 | 1.6 | 1.2 | 2.6 | 131 | 135 | 121 | 119 |
| Central African Rep. | 3.0 | 2.3 | 1.4 | 2.8 | 2.7 | 2.5 | 1.2 | 2.5 | 108 | 104 | 104 | 102 |
| Chad | 0.9 | 1.4 | 1.4 | 0.6 | 0.8 | 1.2 | 0.3 | 0.3 | 133 | 133 | 121 | 121 |
| Congo | 2.3 | 3.1 | 4.0 | 3.0 | 2.5 | 1.5 | 1.7 | 1.7 | 96 | 96 | 81 | 74 |
| Côte d'Ivoire | 6.1 | 6.4 | 2.4 | 5.0 | 6.0 | 5.4 | 2.3 | 5.0 | 150 | 152 | 153 | 155 |
| Ethiopia | 1.9 | 2.0 | 1.8 | 1.6 | 1.9 | 1.3 | −0.2 | 1.2 | 107 | 108 | 103 | 96 |
| Gabon | 1.5 | 4.7 | 5.5 | 3.6 | 0.1 | 0.9 | 1.0 | 0.7 | 94 | 86 | 62 | 53 |
| Gambia | 3.3 | 2.0 | 11.1 | 3.6 | 2.7 | −3.4 | 5.7 | 0.3 | 182 | 173 | 109 | 90 |
| Ghana | 4.0 | −1.6 | 4.9 | 1.4 | 1.8 | −2.9 | 1.7 | −0.3 | 163 | 147 | 130 | 112 |

**Table A.2** *(cont.)*

| | Growth in total demand (all uses) (% p.a.) | | | | Growth in total production (% p.a.) | | | | Self-sufficiency ratios (%) | | | |
|---|---|---|---|---|---|---|---|---|---|---|---|---|
| | 1961–70 | 1970–80 | 1980–5 | 1961–85 | 1961–70 | 1970–80 | 1980–5 | 1961–85 | 1961/3 | 1969/71 | 1979/81 | 1983/85 |
| Guinea | 3.0 | 2.2 | 2.3 | 2.2 | 2.6 | 1.1 | 1.6 | 1.6 | 107 | 105 | 97 | 94 |
| Kenya | 2.6 | 3.9 | 2.3 | 3.3 | 3.4 | 3.2 | 2.3 | 3.1 | 110 | 114 | 104 | 103 |
| Lesotho | 0.6 | 4.6 | 2.2 | 3.3 | 1.6 | 0.5 | 1.2 | 1.2 | 84 | 88 | 61 | 57 |
| Liberia | 2.7 | 3.8 | 2.2 | 3.3 | 4.2 | 2.0 | 3.5 | 3.2 | 107 | 120 | 104 | 109 |
| Madagascar | 3.0 | 2.4 | 2.4 | 2.7 | 2.9 | 1.6 | 2.0 | 2.1 | 111 | 110 | 101 | 99 |
| Malawi | 3.7 | 3.2 | 2.3 | 3.5 | 3.5 | 3.9 | 2.3 | 3.7 | 120 | 117 | 124 | 123 |
| Mali | 3.8 | 2.3 | 3.3 | 2.3 | 2.7 | 3.3 | 1.4 | 2.3 | 121 | 114 | 121 | 115 |
| Mauritania | 2.8 | 3.1 | 3.4 | 2.5 | 2.1 | 0.7 | −1.7 | 0.2 | 118 | 110 | 87 | 70 |
| Mauritius | 1.5 | 5.4 | 1.1 | 3.5 | 1.4 | 0.7 | 2.7 | 0.9 | 178 | 168 | 110 | 108 |
| Mozambique | 3.3 | 1.9 | 1.0 | 2.2 | 3.4 | −0.8 | −1.6 | 0.8 | 121 | 121 | 99 | 88 |
| Niger | 3.0 | 4.9 | 1.3 | 3.0 | 2.4 | 3.3 | −2.7 | 1.2 | 137 | 129 | 107 | 93 |
| Nigeria | 2.7 | 3.5 | 1.3 | 2.7 | 2.0 | 1.4 | 2.1 | 1.4 | 116 | 109 | 91 | 92 |
| Rwanda | 5.0 | 4.2 | 1.6 | 4.2 | 4.6 | 4.2 | 0.7 | 4.2 | 108 | 105 | 104 | 102 |
| Senegal | 3.6 | 4.5 | 3.3 | 3.6 | −0.9 | 0.8 | 1.6 | 0.2 | 159 | 123 | 81 | 73 |
| Sierra Leone | 3.7 | 2.0 | −0.3 | 2.0 | 3.2 | 1.4 | 0.8 | 1.6 | 101 | 98 | 89 | 94 |
| Somalia | 3.1 | 3.4 | 1.2 | 2.7 | 3.2 | 1.0 | 0.3 | 1.7 | 106 | 107 | 88 | 87 |
| Sudan | 3.5 | 4.8 | 1.3 | 4.0 | 2.7 | 3.0 | 2.0 | 3.2 | 127 | 121 | 104 | 106 |
| Swaziland | 3.0 | 4.7 | 2.6 | 3.9 | 4.5 | 3.8 | 1.2 | 4.4 | 141 | 162 | 157 | 153 |
| Tanzania | 3.8 | 5.4 | 2.1 | 4.1 | 3.4 | 4.3 | 1.1 | 3.1 | 122 | 117 | 107 | 102 |
| Togo | 2.9 | 2.1 | 3.2 | 2.4 | 3.4 | 0.3 | 1.5 | 1.3 | 122 | 128 | 106 | 98 |
| Uganda | 4.9 | −0.3 | 6.1 | 2.9 | 5.4 | −2.0 | 6.8 | 2.1 | 121 | 123 | 104 | 108 |
| Zaire | 2.4 | 1.8 | 3.7 | 2.4 | 2.0 | 1.3 | 3.1 | 2.0 | 110 | 106 | 101 | 99 |
| Zambia | 4.7 | 2.2 | 1.5 | 3.0 | 2.7 | 2.9 | 2.6 | 2.5 | 94 | 82 | 83 | 86 |
| Zimbabwe | 2.3 | 1.4 | 2.4 | 2.9 | 2.6 | 2.0 | 2.8 | 2.9 | 144 | 153 | 147 | 140 |

| | | | | | | | | | | | | |
|---|---|---|---|---|---|---|---|---|---|---|---|---|
| Near East/North Africa | 3.4 | 5.3 | 3.8 | 4.3 | 3.0 | 3.1 | 2.4 | 2.9 | 101 | 97 | 80 | 76 |
| Afghanistan | 3.2 | 1.9 | 1.2 | 1.7 | 2.7 | 2.5 | 0.7 | 1.7 | 103 | 98 | 103 | 101 |
| Algeria | 2.9 | 8.1 | 3.8 | 5.9 | 0.1 | 0.2 | 2.4 | 0.9 | 106 | 85 | 44 | 41 |
| Cyprus | 6.9 | 1.1 | 3.4 | 3.5 | 7.4 | 0.5 | 2.2 | 3.0 | 103 | 107 | 98 | 94 |
| Egypt | 3.6 | 4.4 | 4.1 | 3.9 | 3.2 | 1.7 | 2.5 | 2.2 | 104 | 101 | 80 | 74 |
| Iran | 4.7 | 6.7 | 3.8 | 5.7 | 4.8 | 4.2 | 2.1 | 4.1 | 98 | 97 | 79 | 73 |
| Iraq | 4.9 | 5.8 | 5.5 | 5.5 | 4.5 | 1.7 | 1.1 | 2.4 | 90 | 85 | 56 | 48 |
| Jordan | −1.3 | 6.0 | 7.3 | 2.7 | −4.3 | 4.0 | 2.8 | 0.2 | 75 | 61 | 52 | 49 |
| Lebanon | 2.7 | 2.4 | 0.0 | 2.7 | 3.5 | 0.6 | 0.9 | 2.4 | 61 | 64 | 60 | 62 |
| Libya | 12.6 | 10.4 | 3.0 | 10.1 | 8.3 | 8.1 | 5.6 | 7.2 | 73 | 48 | 40 | 44 |
| Morocco | 3.9 | 4.2 | 2.3 | 3.6 | 5.4 | 1.4 | 3.6 | 2.5 | 89 | 97 | 75 | 77 |
| Saudi Arabia | 6.1 | 14.3 | 11.7 | 11.7 | 3.1 | 5.1 | 20.8 | 7.2 | 64 | 59 | 25 | 32 |
| Syria | 1.8 | 8.4 | 2.3 | 5.7 | 0.4 | 8.3 | −1.2 | 4.3 | 119 | 104 | 97 | 88 |
| Tunisia | 3.1 | 5.7 | 2.0 | 4.5 | 0.3 | 3.3 | 3.0 | 3.3 | 103 | 93 | 79 | 81 |
| Turkey | 2.9 | 3.8 | 3.0 | 3.0 | 2.8 | 3.6 | 2.2 | 3.0 | 107 | 107 | 106 | 105 |
| Yemen AR | −0.2 | 7.0 | 4.4 | 4.4 | −1.4 | 2.6 | 1.2 | 1.4 | 100 | 92 | 62 | 54 |
| Yemen PDR | 2.8 | 4.5 | 6.1 | 3.4 | 1.6 | 2.5 | 1.3 | 2.1 | 59 | 57 | 48 | 40 |
| Asia | 3.6 | 3.4 | 4.4 | 3.5 | 3.8 | 3.2 | 4.9 | 3.5 | 101 | 102 | 100 | 102 |
| Bangladesh | 3.1 | 2.0 | 3.0 | 2.1 | 2.7 | 2.1 | 1.9 | 1.5 | 103 | 96 | 93 | 91 |
| Burma | 3.5 | 3.2 | 3.8 | 3.3 | 1.5 | 3.4 | 3.6 | 3.1 | 123 | 108 | 111 | 115 |
| China | 5.1 | 3.6 | 5.2 | 4.2 | 5.8 | 3.2 | 5.9 | 4.2 | 97 | 101 | 98 | 100 |
| India | 1.4 | 2.8 | 3.5 | 2.5 | 1.8 | 2.5 | 4.3 | 2.6 | 98 | 100 | 96 | 101 |
| Indonesia | 3.3 | 4.0 | 3.5 | 4.0 | 2.9 | 3.6 | 4.0 | 3.8 | 111 | 108 | 105 | 107 |
| Kampuchea DM | 3.5 | −6.1 | 9.0 | −0.7 | 3.4 | −6.8 | 9.9 | −2.3 | 127 | 119 | 88 | 97 |
| Korea DPR | 3.4 | 5.7 | 3.8 | 4.8 | 2.8 | 5.8 | 4.3 | 4.7 | 99 | 95 | 96 | 97 |
| Korea Rep. | 6.0 | 7.1 | 4.0 | 5.9 | 4.8 | 6.3 | 4.3 | 4.7 | 92 | 86 | 75 | 73 |
| Lao | 4.3 | 2.0 | 4.5 | 3.1 | 5.8 | 1.9 | 5.9 | 3.6 | 83 | 93 | 96 | 100 |
| Malaysia | 4.2 | 5.1 | 2.3 | 4.5 | 5.6 | 5.5 | 4.0 | 5.7 | 136 | 155 | 165 | 173 |
| Nepal | 3.1 | 3.0 | 3.0 | 3.0 | 1.6 | 1.8 | 3.3 | 2.0 | 116 | 106 | 96 | 97 |
| Pakistan | 4.4 | 3.1 | 5.0 | 3.7 | 4.6 | 2.6 | 3.9 | 3.4 | 102 | 103 | 99 | 96 |
| Philippines | 4.3 | 4.5 | 2.1 | 3.8 | 3.4 | 5.0 | 0.5 | 3.8 | 119 | 114 | 118 | 111 |

**Table A.2** (*cont.*)

| | Growth in total demand (all uses) (% p.a.) | | | | Growth in total production (% p.a.) | | | | Self-sufficiency ratios (%) | | | |
|---|---|---|---|---|---|---|---|---|---|---|---|---|
| | 1961–70 | 1970–80 | 1980–5 | 1961–85 | 1961–70 | 1970–80 | 1980–5 | 1961–85 | 1961/3 | 1969/71 | 1979/81 | 1983/85 |
| Sri Lanka | 3.2 | 2.0 | 4.7 | 2.4 | 2.6 | 1.5 | 2.6 | 1.9 | 118 | 113 | 110 | 104 |
| Thailand | 5.0 | 4.0 | 3.0 | 3.9 | 4.2 | 5.2 | 4.2 | 4.5 | 137 | 130 | 141 | 150 |
| Vietnam | 2.6 | 1.4 | 5.3 | 2.4 | 0.5 | 2.4 | 6.4 | 2.7 | 99 | 87 | 96 | 101 |
| Latin America | 3.6 | 3.7 | 2.0 | 3.2 | 3.0 | 3.3 | 2.3 | 3.0 | 120 | 116 | 113 | 114 |
| Argentina | 2.3 | 2.4 | 0.8 | 1.7 | 2.1 | 3.2 | 2.0 | 2.1 | 131 | 128 | 137 | 143 |
| Bolivia | 3.5 | 3.6 | 2.3 | 3.6 | 3.9 | 3.4 | 2.0 | 3.8 | 90 | 95 | 96 | 92 |
| Brazil | 4.0 | 3.9 | 2.4 | 3.4 | 2.9 | 3.7 | 3.3 | 3.6 | 118 | 112 | 115 | 120 |
| Chile | 2.7 | 0.8 | 0.1 | 1.5 | 2.7 | 1.7 | 1.0 | 1.7 | 86 | 85 | 87 | 87 |
| Colombia | 2.1 | 4.2 | 2.1 | 3.2 | 2.4 | 4.3 | 0.8 | 3.2 | 118 | 118 | 120 | 114 |
| Costa Rica | 4.4 | 4.4 | 2.0 | 4.0 | 5.7 | 3.7 | 1.0 | 4.1 | 160 | 176 | 168 | 159 |
| Cuba | 5.0 | 1.8 | 2.5 | 3.0 | 3.9 | 1.8 | 2.7 | 2.7 | 148 | 138 | 134 | 131 |
| Dominican Rep. | 3.4 | 4.0 | 3.3 | 3.8 | 1.2 | 2.4 | 2.6 | 2.7 | 153 | 135 | 119 | 114 |
| Ecuador | 2.7 | 2.9 | 0.8 | 1.9 | 2.6 | 2.0 | 0.1 | 1.5 | 126 | 125 | 119 | 114 |
| El Salvador | 3.3 | 4.8 | 0.5 | 3.4 | 2.1 | 3.8 | −0.9 | 2.2 | 160 | 152 | 136 | 123 |
| Guatemala | 3.4 | 4.0 | 1.4 | 3.5 | 4.1 | 4.7 | −2.1 | 3.7 | 139 | 148 | 154 | 133 |
| Guyana | 3.4 | 2.0 | 3.4 | 2.8 | 1.2 | 1.4 | 0.1 | 1.0 | 197 | 170 | 147 | 127 |
| Haiti | 2.5 | 2.6 | 1.4 | 2.5 | 1.7 | 1.4 | 1.5 | 1.6 | 110 | 103 | 94 | 93 |
| Honduras | 4.7 | 2.6 | 2.1 | 3.5 | 5.9 | 2.6 | 0.5 | 3.4 | 144 | 156 | 156 | 147 |
| Jamaica | 4.5 | 2.6 | 0.6 | 3.2 | 0.8 | 0.4 | −0.2 | 0.2 | 124 | 92 | 73 | 69 |
| Mexico | 4.9 | 5.4 | 3.0 | 5.0 | 4.4 | 4.1 | 2.0 | 3.7 | 117 | 112 | 97 | 93 |
| Nicaragua | 6.0 | 3.1 | 3.9 | 3.4 | 6.4 | 2.5 | 1.5 | 2.3 | 163 | 165 | 154 | 127 |
| Panama | 3.9 | 2.9 | 2.3 | 3.2 | 5.2 | 2.6 | 2.1 | 3.2 | 109 | 118 | 111 | 110 |
| Paraguay | 3.4 | 4.9 | 3.8 | 3.6 | 3.4 | 5.0 | 4.5 | 4.0 | 116 | 118 | 122 | 125 |
| Peru | 4.3 | 1.3 | 1.8 | 2.4 | 2.5 | 0.2 | 2.8 | 1.4 | 112 | 100 | 90 | 90 |
| Surinam | 6.4 | 2.3 | 2.2 | 3.2 | 8.1 | 4.6 | 2.9 | 5.2 | 81 | 90 | 113 | 116 |

|  |  |  |  |  |  |  |  |  |  |  |  |  |
|---|---|---|---|---|---|---|---|---|---|---|---|---|
| Trinidad and Tob. | 3.4 | 4.1 | 1.6 | 3.5 | 2.5 | −1.7 | −1.6 | −0.6 | 91 | 83 | 47 | 39 |
| Uruguay | 1.3 | −0.8 | −1.9 | 0.1 | 1.9 | −0.5 | −1.1 | 0.9 | 118 | 124 | 131 | 145 |
| Venezuela | 4.4 | 7.0 | 1.4 | 5.2 | 5.7 | 4.0 | 2.0 | 4.1 | 81 | 87 | 68 | 70 |
| Developing, low income | 3.5 | 3.1 | 4.4 | 3.3 | 3.7 | 2.7 | 4.8 | 3.2 | 101 | 102 | 98 | 100 |
| Low inc. excl. China | 2.3 | 2.6 | 3.5 | 2.6 | 2.3 | 2.2 | 3.7 | 2.4 | 104 | 103 | 98 | 100 |
| Low inc. excl. China/India | 3.3 | 2.4 | 3.5 | 2.8 | 2.7 | 1.9 | 3.0 | 2.3 | 111 | 106 | 101 | 100 |
| Developing, middle inc. | 3.6 | 4.3 | 2.8 | 3.8 | 3.1 | 3.5 | 2.6 | 3.2 | 115 | 111 | 103 | 102 |
| Developed countries | 2.6 | 1.5 | 1.4 | 1.8 | 2.6 | 1.9 | 1.6 | 2.0 | 97 | 97 | 100 | 100 |
| European CPEs | 3.7 | 2.0 | 1.5 | 2.3 | 3.7 | 1.5 | 2.1 | 2.0 | 99 | 99 | 93 | 95 |
| Albania | 2.9 | 4.1 | 2.0 | 3.2 | 3.9 | 4.6 | 2.6 | 3.6 | 94 | 100 | 102 | 104 |
| Bulgaria | 4.1 | 2.3 | −1.5 | 2.2 | 4.1 | 1.7 | −0.6 | 2.0 | 114 | 114 | 112 | 114 |
| Czechoslovakia | 2.5 | 1.4 | 0.8 | 1.5 | 2.8 | 1.9 | 2.8 | 2.2 | 84 | 87 | 90 | 98 |
| German DR | 2.1 | 1.8 | 1.9 | 1.6 | 3.1 | 1.8 | 2.4 | 1.9 | 83 | 88 | 91 | 91 |
| Hungary | 1.9 | 2.4 | 1.0 | 2.2 | 2.7 | 3.5 | 1.7 | 3.1 | 102 | 109 | 118 | 124 |
| Poland | 2.4 | 1.2 | 0.6 | 1.2 | 2.2 | 0.6 | 2.4 | 1.0 | 100 | 98 | 93 | 99 |
| Romania | 2.9 | 5.5 | 2.5 | 4.1 | 2.8 | 5.2 | 3.5 | 3.8 | 106 | 106 | 101 | 104 |
| USSR | 4.3 | 2.0 | 1.6 | 2.5 | 4.1 | 1.2 | 2.0 | 1.9 | 100 | 99 | 91 | 92 |
| Developed market economies | 2.1 | 1.2 | 1.4 | 1.5 | 2.2 | 2.1 | 1.4 | 1.9 | 96 | 96 | 104 | 103 |
| Australia | 1.8 | 0.7 | 1.9 | 1.1 | 3.2 | 2.6 | 2.9 | 2.4 | 139 | 152 | 182 | 185 |
| Austria | 1.1 | 0.8 | 0.1 | 0.8 | 1.6 | 1.3 | 1.4 | 1.3 | 90 | 92 | 94 | 99 |
| Belgium-Lux. | 1.3 | 0.5 | 2.3 | 1.2 | 2.2 | 0.4 | 0.8 | 1.4 | 81 | 87 | 90 | 82 |
| Canada | 2.7 | 1.3 | 1.2 | 1.7 | 3.1 | 2.2 | 2.0 | 2.2 | 116 | 117 | 124 | 131 |
| Denmark | 0.5 | −0.2 | 0.6 | −0.1 | −0.1 | 1.7 | 3.1 | 1.0 | 140 | 135 | 160 | 176 |
| Finland | 0.7 | 0.8 | −0.5 | 0.5 | 1.3 | 1.0 | 1.6 | 1.1 | 90 | 97 | 97 | 105 |

**Table A.2** (*cont.*)

| | Growth in total demand (all uses) (% p.a.) | | | | Growth in total production (% p.a.) | | | | Self-sufficiency ratios (%) | | | |
|---|---|---|---|---|---|---|---|---|---|---|---|---|
| | 1961–70 | 1970–80 | 1980–5 | 1961–85 | 1961–70 | 1970–80 | 1980–5 | 1961–85 | 1961/3 | 1969/71 | 1979/81 | 1983/85 |
| France | 0.7 | 1.3 | 0.6 | 0.9 | 1.6 | 1.6 | 2.0 | 1.7 | 96 | 103 | 110 | 116 |
| Germany FR | 1.8 | 0.5 | 0.5 | 0.8 | 1.9 | 0.9 | 1.3 | 1.2 | 77 | 77 | 80 | 83 |
| Greece | 4.2 | 3.0 | 0.7 | 3.3 | 3.4 | 3.2 | 0.4 | 3.2 | 106 | 101 | 103 | 103 |
| Iceland | 0.4 | 2.0 | 1.2 | 1.4 | 0.4 | 2.0 | 0.7 | 1.0 | 93 | 91 | 88 | 84 |
| Ireland | 1.2 | 0.3 | 0.6 | 0.9 | 2.1 | 3.5 | 2.5 | 2.6 | 127 | 137 | 169 | 175 |
| Israel | 6.3 | 2.2 | 4.1 | 3.8 | 6.0 | 3.1 | 2.1 | 4.2 | 84 | 83 | 90 | 88 |
| Italy | 3.6 | 1.2 | 1.2 | 1.8 | 2.4 | 1.7 | 0.2 | 1.5 | 87 | 80 | 82 | 81 |
| Japan | 4.4 | 2.4 | 1.7 | 3.0 | 3.4 | 1.7 | 2.0 | 1.9 | 77 | 70 | 63 | 62 |
| Malta | 2.7 | 1.5 | 2.8 | 1.7 | 3.5 | 1.1 | 4.0 | 1.9 | 34 | 35 | 35 | 37 |
| Netherlands | 2.8 | 3.7 | 3.4 | 2.9 | 3.1 | 3.4 | 2.4 | 3.5 | 104 | 109 | 115 | 115 |
| New Zealand | −1.3 | 0.4 | 1.6 | 0.1 | 2.9 | 1.3 | 3.2 | 1.9 | 205 | 277 | 294 | 309 |
| Norway | 1.4 | 1.5 | −0.7 | 1.1 | 0.9 | 1.4 | 0.6 | 1.2 | 79 | 76 | 76 | 80 |
| Portugal | 2.8 | 2.3 | 0.6 | 2.1 | 1.2 | 0.5 | −0.1 | 0.6 | 93 | 80 | 70 | 66 |
| South Africa | 4.0 | 2.4 | 2.6 | 2.9 | 3.0 | 2.9 | −1.7 | 2.6 | 112 | 106 | 114 | 94 |
| Spain | 3.5 | 3.1 | 0.9 | 3.0 | 3.0 | 3.3 | 1.8 | 3.0 | 100 | 95 | 95 | 98 |
| Sweden | 0.2 | 1.4 | 0.2 | 0.7 | −0.1 | 1.4 | 1.7 | 1.0 | 91 | 88 | 91 | 97 |
| Switzerland | 2.0 | 0.7 | 0.3 | 1.1 | 1.6 | 1.6 | 1.1 | 1.4 | 74 | 71 | 75 | 77 |
| United Kingdom | 0.8 | −0.4 | 0.5 | 0.1 | 1.6 | 1.5 | 1.8 | 1.7 | 59 | 63 | 76 | 82 |
| United States | 2.1 | 0.8 | 2.1 | 1.4 | 1.9 | 2.3 | 1.1 | 2.0 | 105 | 104 | 120 | 112 |
| Yugoslavia | 2.6 | 3.5 | 1.5 | 2.9 | 3.1 | 3.2 | 0.9 | 2.6 | 99 | 101 | 96 | 95 |

**Table A.3** Growth rates of total agricultural exports and imports and shares of agriculture in total economy

| | Growth in exports (% p.a.) | | | | Growth in imports (% p.a.) | | | | Share of agriculture in total (%) | | | | |
|---|---|---|---|---|---|---|---|---|---|---|---|---|---|
| | | | | | | | | | Exports | | Imports | | GDP |
| | 1961–70 | 1970–80 | 1980–5 | 1961–85 | 1961–70 | 1970–80 | 1980–5 | 1961–85 | 1969/71 | 1983/5 | 1969/71 | 1983/5 | 1980 |
| World | 3.3 | 3.9 | 1.5 | 3.6 | 3.1 | 3.8 | 1.8 | 3.5 | — | — | — | — | — |
| All developing countries | 2.6 | 1.8 | 3.3 | 2.1 | 3.4 | 8.0 | 1.7 | 5.8 | — | 14 | 18 | 14 | — |
| 94 developing countries | 2.6 | 1.7 | 3.3 | 2.1 | 3.0 | 8.2 | 1.2 | 5.7 | — | 18 | 18 | 15 | — |
| 93 developing countries | 2.3 | 1.8 | 2.6 | 2.0 | 3.5 | 8.0 | 2.6 | 5.8 | — | 18 | 18 | 15 | — |
| Africa (sub-Saharan) | 2.3 | −2.2 | 0.4 | 0.0 | 3.1 | 6.6 | 1.6 | 5.3 | — | 26 | 15 | 17 | — |
| Angola | 4.7 | −14.6 | −17.9 | −7.9 | 5.7 | 15.6 | 4.5 | 7.5 | 48 | 9 | 14 | 36 | 43.1 |
| Benin | 20.7 | −12.4 | 21.8 | 3.2 | 3.5 | 1.9 | 10.7 | 4.3 | 92 | 77 | 19 | 11 | 48.7 |
| Botswana | 3.5 | 4.5 | 6.1 | 4.3 | 4.6 | 11.1 | 7.2 | 7.1 | 53 | 10 | 27 | 17 | 11.7 |
| Burkina Faso | 7.0 | 1.7 | 0.6 | 2.6 | −0.2 | 9.1 | 7.5 | 6.7 | 95 | 89 | 24 | 30 | 40.5 |
| Burundi | 5.6 | −0.2 | 9.2 | 3.7 | 8.1 | 8.5 | 7.5 | 8.8 | 96 | 90 | 17 | 15 | 55.3 |
| Cameroon | 5.3 | 0.5 | 0.1 | 1.8 | 6.3 | 5.6 | 8.8 | 5.7 | 71 | 45 | 13 | 12 | 27.2 |
| Central African Rep. | 2.8 | 0.0 | 5.7 | 1.3 | 6.0 | −2.1 | 8.0 | 1.4 | 56 | 50 | 24 | 26 | 40.4 |
| Chad | 2.8 | 2.2 | −2.8 | 0.7 | −0.2 | −1.5 | 51.6 | 3.8 | 95 | 80 | 20 | 23 | 40.5 |
| Congo | 21.6 | −15.4 | 15.8 | −3.7 | 0.8 | 5.8 | 15.4 | 4.9 | 33 | 1 | 17 | 13 | 11.7 |
| Côte d'Ivoire | 5.5 | 3.6 | 4.7 | 4.9 | 10.2 | 5.3 | −4.0 | 6.3 | 68 | 70 | 21 | 21 | 34.7 |
| Ethiopia | 3.1 | −4.2 | −3.1 | −0.5 | 15.7 | 12.4 | 33.8 | 11.5 | 93 | 81 | 9 | 23 | 45.9 |

**Table A.3** (*cont.*)

| | Growth in exports (% p.a.) | | | | Growth in imports (% p.a.) | | | | Share of agriculture in total (%) | | | | |
|---|---|---|---|---|---|---|---|---|---|---|---|---|---|
| | | | | | | | | | Exports | | Imports | | GDP |
| | 1961–70 | 1970–80 | 1980–5 | 1961–85 | 1961–70 | 1970–80 | 1980–5 | 1961–85 | 1969/71 | 1983/5 | 1969/71 | 1983/5 | 1980 |
| Gabon | 3.7 | −0.6 | −14.2 | −0.9 | 2.9 | 13.2 | 13.3 | 7.8 | 2 | 0 | 15 | 17 | 5.6 |
| Gambia | 5.7 | −1.2 | 0.8 | −1.2 | 8.8 | 13.8 | 17.4 | 10.1 | 95 | 52 | 28 | 37 | 25.3 |
| Ghana | −2.0 | −6.5 | −5.2 | −4.1 | 1.9 | −5.9 | 2.3 | −2.2 | 76 | 28 | 17 | 10 | 57.9 |
| Guinea | 0.4 | −8.3 | −14.6 | −5.0 | −0.8 | 9.7 | 3.8 | 4.5 | 37 | 6 | 12 | 15 | 46.3 |
| Kenya | 4.4 | 3.6 | 4.0 | 3.8 | 1.0 | −2.2 | 4.4 | 1.9 | 56 | 68 | 12 | 12 | 27.5 |
| Lesotho | 6.5 | −7.3 | 0.6 | −1.9 | 2.8 | 12.2 | 5.0 | 7.1 | 86 | 59 | 36 | 25 | 19.3 |
| Liberia | 7.8 | −0.1 | 1.2 | 3.0 | 1.5 | 3.7 | −1.3 | 3.0 | 17 | 28 | 17 | 24 | 17.3 |
| Madagascar | 3.6 | −2.8 | −2.8 | −0.8 | 1.4 | 2.8 | −3.3 | 2.6 | 80 | 82 | 14 | 19 | 36.1 |
| Malawi | 7.7 | 7.3 | 1.9 | 5.6 | 10.9 | −4.8 | −8.1 | 0.6 | 88 | 92 | 14 | 7 | 37.6 |
| Mali | −0.1 | 6.3 | 0.2 | 5.1 | 8.1 | −2.6 | 21.8 | 7.9 | 75 | 95 | 39 | 27 | 28.2 |
| Mauritania | 0.8 | −1.8 | −3.0 | −0.8 | 2.3 | 10.6 | 10.8 | 7.5 | 22 | 12 | 26 | 51 | 32.2 |
| Mauritius | 1.4 | 0.6 | 0.4 | 0.3 | 0.1 | 6.5 | 0.3 | 3.6 | 93 | 51 | 34 | 23 | 10.5 |
| Mozambique | 5.1 | −7.9 | −24.4 | −4.1 | 2.5 | 7.0 | 7.4 | 3.2 | 77 | 49 | 12 | 23 | 43.4 |
| Niger | 3.2 | −5.7 | −6.2 | −4.1 | 2.5 | 13.4 | 5.8 | 10.4 | — | 19 | 16 | 21 | 42.5 |
| Nigeria | −1.6 | −6.8 | −5.7 | −4.3 | 3.5 | 20.5 | −8.0 | 11.9 | 32 | 3 | 13 | 15 | 20.9 |
| Rwanda | 7.4 | 9.0 | 7.3 | 8.3 | 110.8 | 12.9 | 16.0 | 28.3 | 63 | 82 | 11 | 17 | 45.8 |
| Senegal | −3.5 | −1.8 | 1.8 | −5.9 | 1.4 | 1.9 | 2.2 | 1.6 | 58 | 24 | 39 | 27 | 19.1 |
| Sierra Leone | 1.3 | −0.3 | 5.1 | 0.9 | 6.4 | 0.0 | −8.1 | 1.0 | 17 | 35 | 23 | 31 | 30.9 |
| Somalia | 3.8 | −1.3 | −11.7 | 0.4 | −0.2 | 10.1 | 3.1 | 7.8 | 94 | 53 | 36 | 33 | 40.7 |
| Sudan | 2.4 | −3.0 | −4.1 | −0.6 | 2.7 | −0.7 | 8.4 | 2.5 | 98 | 86 | 19 | 22 | 36.5 |
| Swaziland | 8.5 | 4.7 | 2.5 | 6.3 | 3.0 | 5.9 | 4.7 | 4.9 | 43 | 52 | 16 | 11 | 20.1 |
| Tanzania | 4.3 | −4.4 | −4.9 | −1.6 | −0.8 | −0.1 | −3.9 | 1.7 | 72 | 79 | 10 | 12 | 41.6 |
| Togo | 5.5 | −5.6 | 0.2 | 0.1 | 5.6 | 4.6 | 17.3 | 5.3 | 64 | 38 | 19 | 33 | 26.6 |
| Uganda | 4.8 | −8.4 | 5.5 | −1.5 | 1.9 | −3.6 | −15.5 | −0.6 | 84 | 91 | 11 | 5 | 73.1 |

| | | | | | | | | | | | | | |
|---|---|---|---|---|---|---|---|---|---|---|---|---|---|
| Zaire | 0.3 | −5.1 | −1.2 | −1.4 | 3.2 | −5.3 | 8.3 | 1.5 | 16 | 17 | 12 | 23 | 31.4 |
| Zambia | 7.3 | −5.5 | 7.6 | −4.7 | 11.1 | −5.5 | −8.3 | 1.5 | 1 | 2 | 11 | 8 | 14.2 |
| Zimbabwe | −0.9 | 3.8 | 2.6 | 3.7 | −11.1 | −3.4 | 8.9 | −2.4 | 35 | 41 | 3 | 6 | 13.5 |
| Near East/ North Africa | 1.6 | −2.6 | −0.1 | −0.1 | 2.6 | 12.7 | 6.1 | 8.8 | 16 | 5 | 20 | 18 | — |
| Afghanistan | 4.5 | 6.1 | −4.0 | 3.6 | 7.7 | 2.7 | −3.4 | 4.1 | 75 | 30 | 28 | 12 | 75.9 |
| Algeria | −3.2 | −12.7 | −9.6 | −9.5 | −1.4 | 14.8 | 7.0 | 8.1 | 18 | 0 | 16 | 21 | 7.7 |
| Cyprus | 7.7 | 0.3 | 2.4 | 3.5 | 5.3 | 3.5 | 7.3 | 5.0 | 58 | 39 | 16 | 15 | 9.7 |
| Egypt | 2.1 | −8.6 | −2.4 | −3.1 | 0.8 | 16.0 | 9.0 | 8.4 | 69 | 22 | 32 | 34 | 19.0 |
| Iran | 2.6 | −9.5 | −15.1 | −7.1 | 0.8 | 19.0 | 7.1 | 13.5 | 6 | 1 | 9 | 20 | 15.6 |
| Iraq | 2.6 | −5.3 | −18.5 | −4.9 | 0.1 | 16.5 | 6.1 | 10.4 | 4 | 0 | 25 | 18 | 4.7 |
| Jordan | 6.6 | 15.1 | −5.9 | 9.4 | 4.9 | 9.6 | 4.9 | 7.2 | 45 | 19 | 34 | 21 | 6.6 |
| Lebanon | 10.0 | 0.6 | −14.8 | 1.9 | 4.0 | 3.5 | −3.7 | 3.1 | 34 | 15 | 25 | 16 | 9.1 |
| Libya | 0.0 | 0.0 | 0.0 | 0.0 | 18.9 | 9.6 | −1.4 | 12.0 | 0 | 0 | 19 | 17 | 1.6 |
| Morocco | 3.4 | −3.1 | −8.4 | −1.5 | 0.9 | 7.0 | 1.3 | 4.2 | 47 | 16 | 25 | 21 | 26.7 |
| Saudi Arabia | 14.2 | 15.2 | −3.8 | 14.6 | 9.7 | 18.3 | 6.0 | 13.3 | 0 | 0 | 30 | 14 | 1.2 |
| Syria | 0.2 | −3.8 | 3.8 | −3.1 | 4.7 | 5.1 | 9.9 | 7.3 | 71 | 17 | 27 | 19 | 20.0 |
| Tunisia | −4.8 | −0.7 | 2.9 | −0.1 | 3.7 | 8.2 | 3.1 | 6.9 | 33 | 7 | 28 | 16 | 14.1 |
| Turkey | 4.4 | 1.6 | 5.0 | 4.2 | −4.4 | −4.0 | 15.9 | 3.4 | 82 | 33 | 11 | 5 | 21.7 |
| Yemen AR | −10.7 | −1.0 | −28.7 | −8.2 | 19.6 | 22.1 | 5.5 | 17.9 | 56 | 33 | 47 | 35 | 28.3 |
| Yemen PDR | −13.9 | −9.8 | −9.9 | −12.6 | −0.5 | 6.6 | 6.8 | 1.7 | 10 | 2 | 25 | 13 | 10.1 |
| Asia | 2.6 | 4.0 | 4.4 | 3.6 | 3.1 | 5.4 | 1.8 | 3.4 | — | 18 | 23 | 11 | — |
| Bangladesh | −0.6 | −2.1 | −2.0 | −3.0 | 4.7 | −0.9 | 9.8 | 2.8 | 36 | 23 | 31 | 27 | 46.7 |
| Burma | −14.5 | 0.3 | −3.2 | −3.3 | −9.7 | 2.0 | −7.8 | −3.1 | 67 | 55 | 8 | 10 | 46.5 |
| China | 11.6 | 0.5 | 15.7 | 4.6 | −1.7 | 11.1 | −13.8 | 4.5 | 37 | 16 | 24 | 10 | 39.1 |
| India | −1.0 | 2.4 | −3.2 | 1.6 | 1.8 | −2.7 | 7.6 | −2.0 | 33 | 28 | 29 | 14 | 33.7 |
| Indonesia | 3.5 | 4.4 | 5.2 | 3.3 | 2.9 | 11.7 | −13.6 | 7.2 | 43 | 11 | 26 | 8 | 25.0 |
| Kampuchea DM | −2.9 | 7.7 | 25.0 | −7.4 | −9.4 | −1.8 | −25.9 | 8.0 | 92 | 67 | 13 | 14 | 38.0 |
| Korea DPR | 12.5 | 9.5 | −27.3 | 5.0 | 19.2 | 2.1 | −12.9 | 6.1 | 11 | 4 | 18 | 9 | 24.0 |
| Korea Rep. | 15.4 | 7.6 | 4.6 | 9.8 | 16.7 | 9.7 | 2.9 | 12.7 | 9 | 2 | 23 | 11 | 14.2 |

**Table A.3** (*cont.*)

| | Growth in exports (% p.a.) | | | | Growth in imports (% p.a.) | | | | Share of agriculture in total (%) | | | | |
|---|---|---|---|---|---|---|---|---|---|---|---|---|---|
| | | | | | | | | | Exports | | Imports | | GDP |
| | 1961–70 | 1970–80 | 1980–5 | 1961–85 | 1961–70 | 1970–80 | 1980–5 | 1961–85 | 1969/71 | 1983/5 | 1969/71 | 1983/5 | 1980 |
| Lao | 23.0 | 23.7 | 61.6 | 10.5 | −6.2 | 6.4 | −16.5 | −3.2 | 7 | 19 | 23 | 12 | 34.9 |
| Malaysia | 5.8 | 5.4 | 5.6 | 5.8 | −0.1 | 4.0 | 7.6 | 2.7 | 45 | 26 | 22 | 12 | 25.1 |
| Nepal | −1.2 | −12.1 | −22.9 | −10.1 | 3.3 | 0.3 | 3.9 | 2.3 | — | 12 | 23 | 11 | 57.9 |
| Pakistan | 5.0 | 5.2 | −4.9 | 4.2 | 2.0 | 9.1 | 10.6 | 5.8 | 32 | 29 | 16 | 18 | 24.8 |
| Philippines | −0.7 | 4.3 | −9.5 | 2.0 | 0.3 | −2.0 | 7.7 | 0.7 | 44 | 28 | 13 | 9 | 23.3 |
| Sri Lanka | 0.0 | −2.1 | 2.9 | −0.9 | 2.2 | 0.0 | 6.4 | −0.7 | 95 | 55 | 42 | 17 | 26.2 |
| Thailand | 2.5 | 9.2 | 7.2 | 6.9 | 4.8 | 7.5 | 2.7 | 5.1 | 69 | 50 | 7 | 6 | 25.4 |
| Vietnam | −16.4 | 10.5 | 14.5 | 0.8 | 27.8 | −6.7 | −6.9 | 0.1 | 20 | 43 | 68 | 20 | 45.0 |
| Latin America | 3.0 | 2.7 | 3.8 | 2.5 | 3.0 | 8.3 | −3.2 | 5.5 | 46 | 30 | 13 | 14 | — |
| Argentina | 2.6 | 6.2 | 7.6 | 3.3 | 1.5 | 0.7 | −9.5 | 0.5 | 84 | 72 | 8 | 6 | 8.6 |
| Bolivia | 16.9 | 5.1 | −11.4 | 8.5 | 3.3 | 3.6 | −1.0 | 2.2 | 8 | 4 | 20 | 19 | 17.6 |
| Brazil | 3.8 | 1.7 | 5.6 | 3.9 | 2.8 | 12.7 | −5.2 | 5.5 | 71 | 39 | 10 | 9 | 12.5 |
| Chile | −0.8 | 21.2 | 8.2 | 9.0 | −0.6 | −0.2 | −13.4 | −0.3 | 4 | 12 | 20 | 13 | 7.2 |
| Colombia | 2.6 | 4.3 | −1.1 | 2.9 | 2.4 | 6.4 | 1.7 | 5.9 | 79 | 68 | 11 | 11 | 19.4 |
| Costa Rica | 7.2 | 2.1 | 2.9 | 4.3 | 10.9 | 0.3 | −4.5 | 4.5 | 78 | 66 | 11 | 9 | 17.8 |
| Cuba | 1.4 | 2.6 | 1.9 | 2.1 | 4.3 | 2.8 | 2.3 | 3.9 | 83 | 83 | 22 | 14 | 5.2 |
| Dominican Rep. | −1.3 | −0.4 | 0.7 | 1.4 | 13.9 | 11.0 | −3.4 | 8.4 | 88 | 62 | 15 | 14 | 20.2 |
| Ecuador | 3.7 | 3.3 | −1.2 | 2.3 | 5.7 | 11.8 | 0.0 | 7.7 | 84 | 20 | 10 | 11 | 12.1 |
| El Salvador | 1.5 | 2.3 | 0.5 | 1.5 | 1.3 | 8.4 | 1.5 | 2.8 | 68 | 64 | 15 | 14 | 27.8 |
| Guatemala | 4.5 | 5.8 | −0.7 | 3.6 | 4.2 | 6.9 | −3.3 | 2.8 | 71 | 63 | 11 | 10 | 24.8 |
| Guyana | 0.1 | −0.5 | −6.1 | −1.5 | 3.2 | 1.9 | −19.6 | −1.7 | 42 | 48 | 16 | 8 | 20.7 |
| Haiti | −3.9 | −0.4 | 3.6 | −1.3 | 0.8 | 14.0 | 1.1 | 7.7 | 57 | 38 | 26 | 25 | 38.1 |
| Honduras | 8.6 | 4.8 | −0.6 | 4.2 | 8.4 | 14.7 | −8.9 | 5.5 | 75 | 71 | 11 | 9 | 25.4 |

| | | | | | | | | | | | | | |
|---|---|---|---|---|---|---|---|---|---|---|---|---|---|
| Jamaica | −2.1 | −6.6 | 3.6 | −4.8 | 8.2 | −1.0 | 1.2 | 3.2 | 25 | 24 | 17 | 18 | 8.1 |
| Mexico | 5.3 | −1.1 | 3.0 | −1.8 | 4.7 | 18.3 | −4.3 | 14.6 | 54 | 7 | 9 | 20 | 8.4 |
| Nicaragua | 4.9 | 2.7 | −1.1 | 1.3 | 11.0 | 6.4 | −5.5 | 7.6 | 75 | 80 | 10 | 14 | 22.6 |
| Panama | 10.3 | 4.8 | 0.9 | 5.5 | 4.0 | 3.6 | 1.7 | 5.0 | 64 | 53 | 10 | 10 | 9.0 |
| Paraguay | 3.7 | 9.2 | 11.5 | 7.6 | −1.9 | 6.0 | −3.5 | 0.8 | 68 | 92 | 19 | 8 | 29.5 |
| Peru | −3.3 | −3.2 | 4.2 | −2.9 | 4.5 | 2.3 | −6.3 | 2.3 | 18 | 8 | 20 | 17 | 8.5 |
| Surinam | 7.4 | 12.6 | 0.6 | 8.8 | 7.0 | 1.9 | −0.7 | 3.6 | 6 | 12 | 15 | 12 | 9.8 |
| Trinidad and Tobago | −0.5 | −7.0 | −6.2 | −5.2 | 0.7 | 5.6 | 3.9 | 4.1 | 8 | 2 | 11 | 20 | 2.1 |
| Uruguay | 3.1 | 1.4 | −0.8 | 2.6 | −1.8 | −1.6 | −5.8 | −1.5 | 83 | 60 | 15 | 11 | 9.6 |
| Venezuela | 19.6 | −18.3 | 11.2 | −7.7 | 3.2 | 15.0 | −0.6 | 8.3 | 1 | 1 | 12 | 22 | 5.7 |
| Developing, low income | 1.7 | −0.9 | 3.1 | 0.6 | 2.3 | 3.8 | −1.4 | 2.2 | 48 | 27 | 24 | 14 | — |
| Low inc. excl. China | 0.3 | −1.2 | −1.5 | −0.3 | 3.7 | 0.0 | 6.8 | 1.0 | 51 | 38 | 24 | 17 | — |
| Low inc. excl. China/India | 0.6 | −2.0 | −1.0 | −0.7 | 4.8 | 1.0 | 6.4 | 2.8 | 58 | 44 | 23 | 19 | — |
| Developing, middle inc. | 2.9 | 2.4 | 3.3 | 2.6 | 3.3 | 10.1 | 1.9 | 7.2 | 34 | 17 | 16 | 15 | — |
| Developed countries | 3.8 | 5.2 | 0.6 | 4.5 | 3.0 | 2.6 | 1.9 | 2.9 | 13 | 10 | 17 | 11 | — |
| European CPEs | 3.9 | 0.1 | −0.3 | 0.9 | 2.3 | 5.8 | −0.4 | 5.1 | 12 | 5 | 18 | 16 | — |
| Albania | 6.3 | 7.6 | −7.6 | 4.2 | −7.2 | 1.7 | −8.6 | −0.6 | 0 | 0 | 0 | 0 | 34.0 |
| Bulgaria | 7.2 | 0.2 | −2.1 | 1.2 | 10.2 | 3.0 | 10.1 | 4.6 | 27 | 10 | 10 | 7 | 16.9 |
| Czechoslovakia | −1.3 | 2.6 | 4.3 | 1.7 | 2.0 | −1.1 | −3.6 | −0.3 | 5 | 3 | 21 | 10 | 8.4 |
| German DR | 7.0 | 7.8 | −2.7 | 5.2 | 1.5 | 0.6 | −0.9 | 1.8 | 2 | 2 | 17 | 9 | 11.0 |
| Hungary | 8.9 | 5.2 | 5.5 | 7.1 | 3.3 | 1.4 | −0.5 | 2.0 | 24 | 23 | 15 | 9 | 14.6 |

**Table A.3** *(cont.)*

| | Growth in exports (% p.a.) | | | | Growth in imports (% p.a.) | | | | Share of agriculture in total (%) | | | | |
|---|---|---|---|---|---|---|---|---|---|---|---|---|---|
| | | | | | | | | | Exports | | Imports | | GDP |
| | 1961–70 | 1970–80 | 1980–5 | 1961–85 | 1961–70 | 1970–80 | 1980–5 | 1961–85 | 1969/71 | 1983/5 | 1969/71 | 1983/5 | 1980 |
| Poland | −3.1 | −1.7 | 11.7 | −2.2 | 1.6 | 6.9 | −12.1 | 3.1 | 12 | 7 | 17 | 13 | 15.8 |
| Romania | 7.2 | 5.5 | −7.7 | 2.2 | 7.8 | 10.4 | −15.6 | 7.8 | 19 | 8 | 11 | 9 | 14.1 |
| USSR | 4.1 | −4.6 | −4.4 | −1.8 | 1.9 | 8.2 | 1.9 | 7.0 | 12 | 2 | 20 | 23 | 14.9 |
| Developed market economies | 3.8 | 5.7 | 0.7 | 4.9 | 3.1 | 2.0 | 2.5 | 2.5 | 13 | 11 | 17 | 11 | — |
| Australia | 3.0 | 2.9 | 0.1 | 2.7 | 3.5 | 1.2 | 5.5 | 2.3 | 51 | 34 | 6 | 5 | 5.8 |
| Austria | 7.7 | 5.6 | 9.9 | 6.5 | −0.9 | 2.2 | 0.9 | 1.4 | 5 | 5 | 12 | 8 | 4.5 |
| Belgium-Lux. | 13.4 | 7.4 | 4.0 | 9.3 | 5.4 | 4.6 | 3.5 | 4.8 | 10 | 11 | 14 | 13 | 2.2 |
| Canada | 0.7 | 2.8 | 2.7 | 3.8 | 3.1 | 1.7 | 2.3 | 2.1 | 11 | 10 | 9 | 7 | 4.0 |
| Denmark | 0.2 | 2.7 | 2.6 | 1.6 | 0.9 | 2.1 | 2.0 | 1.9 | 36 | 28 | 12 | 11 | 4.8 |
| Finland | 7.8 | 1.7 | 6.2 | 5.8 | 2.7 | 1.0 | −6.1 | 1.3 | 6 | 5 | 10 | 7 | 8.6 |
| France | 7.8 | 5.6 | 3.7 | 7.1 | 2.4 | 4.4 | 0.4 | 3.2 | 18 | 17 | 18 | 12 | 4.1 |
| Germany FR | 15.5 | 11.0 | 3.9 | 12.4 | 3.1 | 2.3 | 1.9 | 2.9 | 4 | 6 | 21 | 13 | 2.1 |
| Greece | 4.3 | 2.3 | 11.4 | 2.7 | 7.8 | 4.1 | 7.5 | 5.1 | 53 | 32 | 14 | 14 | 15.8 |
| Iceland | 5.1 | 8.0 | −5.4 | 2.6 | 1.6 | 3.1 | 3.0 | 2.4 | 5 | 3 | 13 | 11 | 18.4 |
| Ireland | 3.0 | 5.4 | 0.6 | 3.2 | 1.8 | 4.0 | 0.9 | 3.0 | 50 | 26 | 15 | 13 | 10.0 |
| Israel | 6.8 | 3.8 | −1.5 | 4.3 | 7.4 | 2.6 | 3.5 | 4.1 | 24 | 15 | 15 | 10 | 4.8 |
| Italy | 2.8 | 4.0 | 4.1 | 4.4 | 7.8 | 2.7 | 4.5 | 4.4 | 9 | 7 | 24 | 16 | 6.4 |
| Japan | 3.4 | −10.6 | −15.7 | −3.3 | 8.3 | 2.8 | 2.2 | 4.5 | 2 | 1 | 22 | 13 | 3.8 |
| Malta | 13.8 | 2.6 | −17.7 | −0.5 | 0.2 | 1.7 | 1.9 | 0.6 | 15 | 6 | 28 | 16 | 3.4 |

| | | | | | | | | | | | | | |
|---|---|---|---|---|---|---|---|---|---|---|---|---|---|
| Netherlands | 7.2 | 6.3 | 3.6 | 6.8 | 5.8 | 6.1 | 3.8 | 5.7 | 27 | 22 | 16 | 16 | 3.5 |
| New Zealand | 3.0 | 0.7 | 2.5 | 1.9 | 0.6 | 0.1 | 4.2 | 1.8 | 83 | 61 | 8 | 7 | 10.3 |
| Norway | 2.2 | −0.3 | 1.5 | 1.8 | 3.1 | 1.2 | −2.7 | 1.4 | 4 | 2 | 9 | 7 | 3.9 |
| Portugal | 3.9 | −3.0 | 7.5 | −0.5 | 6.4 | 5.1 | 2.0 | 5.3 | 16 | 9 | 19 | 18 | 10.3 |
| South Africa | 1.1 | 2.3 | −11.3 | 0.7 | 8.6 | −4.1 | 31.2 | 4.0 | 27 | 6 | 8 | 7 | 6.5 |
| Spain | 4.4 | 2.7 | 5.2 | 4.0 | 8.6 | 5.0 | −0.9 | 5.0 | 30 | 15 | 20 | 13 | 7.1 |
| Sweden | 0.6 | 1.7 | 10.6 | 3.2 | 3.0 | −1.0 | −1.0 | 0.3 | 3 | 3 | 11 | 7 | 3.2 |
| Switzerland | 6.3 | 0.5 | 2.1 | 2.6 | 3.4 | −1.1 | −0.1 | 1.0 | 7 | 4 | 14 | 9 | — |
| United Kingdom | 0.3 | 11.4 | 4.1 | 6.3 | −0.7 | −1.6 | 0.2 | −1.3 | 7 | 7 | 27 | 13 | 1.9 |
| United States | 2.2 | 8.1 | −5.0 | 5.0 | 1.2 | 0.2 | 4.0 | 0.9 | 17 | 17 | 15 | 6 | 2.7 |
| Yugoslavia | 1.9 | 0.6 | 11.5 | 1.0 | 0.2 | 3.0 | −4.8 | 2.2 | 20 | 11 | 14 | 9 | 11.7 |

**Table A.4** Food per caput

| | Calories per caput per day | | | | | | | | Cereals | |
|---|---|---|---|---|---|---|---|---|---|---|
| | Total | | | | By major commodities, 1983/5 | | | | 1983/5 (kg p.a.) | |
| | 1961/3 | 1969/71 | 1979/81 | 1983/5 | Cereals | Roots and plaintains | Livestock | Other | Food | Other uses |
| World | 2316 | 2450 | 2599 | 2665 | 1407 | 155 | 350 | 753 | 166 | 170 |
| All developing countries | 1957 | 2113 | 2321 | 2424 | 1517 | 157 | 176 | 574 | 172 | 62 |
| 94 developing countries | 1956 | 2111 | 2319 | 2423 | 1521 | 157 | 171 | 574 | 173 | 61 |
| 93 developing countries | 2069 | 2174 | 2333 | 2364 | 1370 | 156 | 171 | 667 | 154 | 58 |
| Africa (sub-Saharan) | 2045 | 2097 | 2150 | 2051 | 945 | 507 | 102 | 497 | 113 | 22 |
| Angola | 1818 | 2034 | 2158 | 1946 | 675 | 632 | 143 | 496 | 79 | 7 |
| Benin | 1987 | 2078 | 2138 | 2138 | 769 | 762 | 76 | 531 | 94 | 39 |
| Botswana | 2033 | 2139 | 2140 | 2165 | 1328 | 22 | 277 | 538 | 162 | 21 |
| Burkina Faso | 1863 | 1967 | 2034 | 1962 | 1378 | 36 | 90 | 458 | 172 | 22 |
| Burundi | 2282 | 2363 | 2345 | 2216 | 701 | 504 | 40 | 971 | 83 | 11 |
| Cameroon | 2050 | 2185 | 2173 | 2074 | 859 | 510 | 71 | 634 | 110 | 14 |
| Central African Republic | 2065 | 2160 | 2114 | 2046 | 413 | 1036 | 82 | 515 | 49 | 6 |
| Chad | 2290 | 2137 | 1817 | 1577 | 768 | 256 | 108 | 445 | 98 | 17 |
| Congo | 2212 | 2174 | 2443 | 2532 | 547 | 1145 | 83 | 757 | 73 | 2 |
| Côte d'Ivoire | 2154 | 2369 | 2570 | 2445 | 941 | 843 | 105 | 556 | 109 | 32 |
| Ethiopia | 1783 | 1702 | 1797 | 1692 | 1194 | 52 | 93 | 353 | 133 | 12 |
| Gabon | 1953 | 1895 | 2226 | 2434 | 467 | 1237 | 154 | 576 | 62 | 7 |
| Gambia | 2130 | 2249 | 2177 | 2229 | 1339 | 28 | 106 | 756 | 158 | 63 |
| Ghana | 2033 | 2200 | 1783 | 1682 | 506 | 835 | 29 | 312 | 61 | 10 |
| Guinea | 1805 | 1907 | 1767 | 1725 | 714 | 410 | 50 | 551 | 77 | 13 |
| Kenya | 2250 | 2244 | 2191 | 2163 | 1346 | 196 | 177 | 444 | 158 | 19 |

| | | | | | | | | | | |
|---|---|---|---|---|---|---|---|---|---|---|
| Lesotho | 2012 | 2020 | 2346 | 2346 | 1798 | 14 | 136 | 398 | 218 | 39 |
| Liberia | 2093 | 2210 | 2381 | 2343 | 1090 | 546 | 68 | 639 | 121 | 17 |
| Madagascar | 2395 | 2494 | 2511 | 2467 | 1456 | 488 | 158 | 365 | 147 | 40 |
| Malawi | 2058 | 2325 | 2473 | 2429 | 1703 | 156 | 51 | 519 | 210 | 35 |
| Mali | 1827 | 1836 | 1752 | 1793 | 1339 | 49 | 111 | 294 | 160 | 21 |
| Mauritania | 1997 | 1987 | 2000 | 2076 | 1018 | 9 | 485 | 564 | 120 | 7 |
| Mauritius | 2400 | 2301 | 2723 | 2721 | 1467 | 37 | 251 | 966 | 172 | 11 |
| Mozambique | 2007 | 2074 | 1804 | 1664 | 579 | 695 | 46 | 344 | 68 | 6 |
| Niger | 2067 | 2002 | 2364 | 2265 | 1531 | 90 | 149 | 495 | 223 | 64 |
| Nigeria | 2181 | 2131 | 2245 | 2062 | 831 | 635 | 52 | 544 | 101 | 23 |
| Rwanda | 1742 | 1968 | 2073 | 2010 | 432 | 890 | 58 | 630 | 53 | 10 |
| Senegal | 2306 | 2370 | 2389 | 2341 | 1513 | 12 | 128 | 688 | 186 | 27 |
| Sierra Leone | 1617 | 1956 | 2049 | 1833 | 1030 | 128 | 32 | 643 | 118 | 21 |
| Somalia | 1972 | 2182 | 2054 | 2059 | 1015 | 21 | 437 | 586 | 112 | 71 |
| Sudan | 1794 | 2117 | 2320 | 2004 | 948 | 36 | 385 | 635 | 114 | 16 |
| Swaziland | 2111 | 2225 | 2498 | 2562 | 1336 | 18 | 290 | 918 | 153 | 144 |
| Tanzania | 1916 | 1949 | 2428 | 2315 | 1056 | 688 | 100 | 471 | 128 | 32 |
| Togo | 2199 | 2194 | 2218 | 2203 | 995 | 647 | 56 | 505 | 124 | 30 |
| Uganda | 2299 | 2282 | 2171 | 2293 | 626 | 1038 | 95 | 534 | 86 | 18 |
| Zaire | 2155 | 2253 | 2128 | 2154 | 373 | 1320 | 25 | 436 | 46 | 5 |
| Zambia | 2092 | 2192 | 2203 | 2123 | 1569 | 102 | 76 | 376 | 197 | 35 |
| Zimbabwe | 2117 | 2117 | 2110 | 2095 | 1330 | 30 | 92 | 643 | 172 | 77 |
| Near East/North Africa | 2222 | 2371 | 2845 | 2985 | 1724 | 55 | 260 | 946 | 212 | 160 |
| Afghanistan | 2200 | 2185 | 2221 | 2196 | 1755 | 28 | 182 | 231 | 231 | 38 |
| Algeria | 1767 | 1825 | 2618 | 2712 | 1524 | 60 | 316 | 812 | 199 | 82 |
| Cyprus | 2407 | 3066 | 3280 | 3497 | 1282 | 77 | 886 | 1252 | 155 | 650 |
| Egypt | 2344 | 2499 | 3029 | 3263 | 1999 | 46 | 194 | 1024 | 234 | 111 |
| Iran | 1968 | 2218 | 2883 | 3115 | 1880 | 60 | 277 | 898 | 219 | 91 |
| Iraq | 2058 | 2250 | 2740 | 2901 | 1680 | 16 | 274 | 931 | 195 | 152 |
| Jordan | 2193 | 2616 | 2764 | 2962 | 1505 | 27 | 353 | 1077 | 178 | 121 |
| Lebanon | 2453 | 2478 | 2938 | 3014 | 1035 | 100 | 444 | 1435 | 136 | 65 |
| Libya | 1711 | 2368 | 3653 | 3618 | 1488 | 51 | 515 | 1564 | 195 | 173 |

**Table A.4** (*cont.*)

| | Calories per caput per day | | | | | | | | Cereals | |
|---|---|---|---|---|---|---|---|---|---|---|
| | Total | | | | By major commodities, 1983/5 | | | | 1983/5 (kg p.a.) | |
| | 1961/3 | 1969/71 | 1979/81 | 1983/5 | Cereals | Roots and plaintains | Livestock | Other | Food | Other uses |
| Morocco | 2244 | 2424 | 2727 | 2688 | 1711 | 35 | 146 | 796 | 222 | 72 |
| Saudi Arabia | 1832 | 1887 | 2827 | 3092 | 1324 | 19 | 540 | 1209 | 149 | 546 |
| Syria | 2311 | 2356 | 2883 | 3199 | 1507 | 52 | 383 | 1257 | 189 | 145 |
| Tunisia | 2117 | 2272 | 2772 | 2827 | 1616 | 38 | 214 | 959 | 204 | 113 |
| Turkey | 2631 | 2820 | 3104 | 3180 | 1690 | 102 | 239 | 1149 | 220 | 333 |
| Yemen AR | 1993 | 1842 | 2198 | 2255 | 1462 | 49 | 216 | 528 | 176 | 15 |
| Yemen PDR | 1766 | 2077 | 2212 | 2293 | 1502 | 14 | 199 | 578 | 175 | 7 |
| Asia | 1856 | 2027 | 2236 | 2380 | 1656 | 109 | 137 | 478 | 184 | 47 |
| Bangladesh | 1939 | 2012 | 1850 | 1854 | 1556 | 35 | 43 | 220 | 160 | 20 |
| Burma | 1823 | 2069 | 2376 | 2518 | 1916 | 31 | 83 | 488 | 206 | 15 |
| China | 1713 | 1976 | 2289 | 2564 | 1885 | 158 | 170 | 351 | 219 | 69 |
| India | 2037 | 2022 | 2104 | 2161 | 1382 | 43 | 118 | 618 | 151 | 25 |
| Indonesia | 1743 | 2013 | 2441 | 2504 | 1691 | 208 | 32 | 573 | 166 | 22 |
| Kampuchea DM | 2098 | 2286 | 1860 | 2116 | 1776 | 48 | 57 | 235 | 184 | 23 |
| Korea DPR | 2297 | 2502 | 3061 | 3131 | 2208 | 171 | 115 | 637 | 244 | 192 |
| Korea Rep. | 2045 | 2529 | 2823 | 2822 | 1839 | 31 | 195 | 757 | 185 | 132 |
| Lao | 1860 | 2024 | 2086 | 2243 | 1691 | 107 | 188 | 257 | 192 | 34 |
| Malaysia | 2263 | 2410 | 2596 | 2634 | 1318 | 72 | 281 | 963 | 149 | 92 |
| Nepal | 1878 | 1996 | 1975 | 2047 | 1647 | 49 | 131 | 220 | 180 | 33 |
| Pakistan | 1704 | 2027 | 2222 | 2185 | 1333 | 9 | 224 | 619 | 153 | 14 |
| Philippines | 1838 | 2053 | 2355 | 2312 | 1411 | 177 | 150 | 574 | 160 | 28 |
| Sri Lanka | 2081 | 2261 | 2227 | 2411 | 1397 | 176 | 70 | 768 | 152 | 14 |
| Thailand | 2011 | 2258 | 2405 | 2440 | 1639 | 63 | 105 | 633 | 166 | 58 |

| | | | | | | | | | | |
|---|---|---|---|---|---|---|---|---|---|---|
| Vietnam | 2037 | 2171 | 2067 | 2235 | 1624 | 181 | 123 | 307 | 162 | 26 |
| Latin America | 2383 | 2517 | 2678 | 2703 | 1137 | 160 | 391 | 1015 | 136 | 133 |
| Argentina | 3134 | 3318 | 3252 | 3196 | 1076 | 144 | 894 | 1082 | 145 | 273 |
| Bolivia | 1794 | 1972 | 2085 | 2115 | 1007 | 207 | 232 | 669 | 118 | 60 |
| Brazil | 2315 | 2472 | 2623 | 2637 | 1050 | 190 | 315 | 1082 | 125 | 140 |
| Chile | 2563 | 2674 | 2642 | 2588 | 1286 | 106 | 345 | 851 | 161 | 93 |
| Colombia | 2230 | 2159 | 2506 | 2578 | 899 | 392 | 328 | 959 | 101 | 35 |
| Costa Rica | 2197 | 2406 | 2621 | 2772 | 1051 | 87 | 377 | 1257 | 122 | 53 |
| Cuba | 2246 | 2574 | 2834 | 3094 | 1145 | 206 | 501 | 1242 | 143 | 117 |
| Dominican Republic | 1864 | 2083 | 2316 | 2469 | 824 | 253 | 266 | 1126 | 94 | 48 |
| Ecuador | 1819 | 1957 | 2063 | 2031 | 706 | 206 | 271 | 848 | 86 | 25 |
| El Salvador | 1767 | 1854 | 2153 | 2148 | 1256 | 32 | 152 | 708 | 139 | 35 |
| Guatemala | 1947 | 2101 | 2221 | 2299 | 1330 | 22 | 167 | 780 | 147 | 53 |
| Guyana | 2236 | 2292 | 2412 | 2492 | 1422 | 68 | 220 | 782 | 154 | 24 |
| Haiti | 1999 | 1920 | 1903 | 1837 | 715 | 285 | 76 | 761 | 82 | 8 |
| Honduras | 1924 | 2151 | 2197 | 2209 | 1231 | 71 | 194 | 713 | 137 | 37 |
| Jamaica | 2055 | 2533 | 2572 | 2577 | 937 | 243 | 299 | 1098 | 114 | 66 |
| Mexico | 2558 | 2703 | 3054 | 3147 | 1540 | 24 | 469 | 1114 | 184 | 202 |
| Nicaragua | 2274 | 2432 | 2326 | 2424 | 1123 | 79 | 232 | 990 | 126 | 72 |
| Panama | 2244 | 2346 | 2322 | 2420 | 1022 | 98 | 333 | 967 | 116 | 37 |
| Paraguay | 2429 | 2754 | 2780 | 2814 | 898 | 445 | 456 | 1015 | 104 | 146 |
| Peru | 2225 | 2290 | 2179 | 2144 | 1042 | 223 | 205 | 674 | 120 | 29 |
| Surinam | 2044 | 2339 | 2553 | 2666 | 1462 | 72 | 304 | 828 | 170 | 181 |
| Trinidad and Tobago | 2404 | 2567 | 2853 | 2966 | 1088 | 122 | 510 | 1246 | 134 | 80 |
| Uruguay | 2782 | 3002 | 2832 | 2721 | 949 | 106 | 819 | 847 | 136 | 88 |
| Venezuela | 2221 | 2412 | 2665 | 2550 | 1002 | 107 | 494 | 947 | 128 | 131 |
| Developing, low income | 1869 | 2014 | 2182 | 2314 | 1577 | 142 | 141 | 454 | 179 | 42 |
| Low inc. excl. China | 1998 | 2045 | 2098 | 2126 | 1345 | 130 | 119 | 532 | 149 | 22 |
| Low inc. excl. China/India | 1947 | 2075 | 2090 | 2085 | 1300 | 234 | 120 | 431 | 145 | 20 |
| Developing, middle income | 2161 | 2337 | 2624 | 2657 | 1400 | 188 | 235 | 834 | 160 | 103 |

**Table A.4** (*cont.*)

| | Calories per caput per day | | | | | | | | Cereals | |
|---|---|---|---|---|---|---|---|---|---|---|
| | Total | | | | By major commodities, 1983/5 | | | | 1983/5 (kg p.a.) | |
| | 1961/3 | 1969/71 | 1979/81 | 1983/5 | Cereals | Roots and plaintains | Livestock | Other | Food | Other uses |
| Developed countries | 3090 | 3264 | 3371 | 3372 | 1085 | 149 | 869 | 1269 | 146 | 488 |
| European CPEs | 3165 | 3332 | 3405 | 3410 | 1316 | 201 | 794 | 1099 | 185 | 600 |
| Albania | 2425 | 2556 | 2767 | 2740 | 1797 | 65 | 376 | 502 | 244 | 97 |
| Bulgaria | 3237 | 3500 | 3628 | 3626 | 1567 | 60 | 697 | 1302 | 223 | 667 |
| Czechoslovakia | 3384 | 3417 | 3434 | 3479 | 1243 | 158 | 989 | 1089 | 173 | 566 |
| German DR | 3153 | 3348 | 3645 | 3768 | 1141 | 288 | 1181 | 1158 | 162 | 659 |
| Hungary | 3122 | 3338 | 3496 | 3522 | 1206 | 105 | 861 | 1350 | 167 | 1072 |
| Poland | 3195 | 3333 | 3433 | 3252 | 1167 | 223 | 901 | 961 | 185 | 522 |
| Romania | 2930 | 3068 | 3351 | 3394 | 1511 | 141 | 639 | 1103 | 198 | 763 |
| USSR | 3172 | 3349 | 3385 | 3403 | 1326 | 210 | 763 | 1104 | 185 | 580 |
| Developed market economies | 3055 | 3231 | 3355 | 3353 | 974 | 124 | 904 | 1351 | 127 | 435 |
| Australia | 3163 | 3295 | 3367 | 3257 | 898 | 105 | 980 | 1274 | 126 | 389 |
| Austria | 3313 | 3303 | 3453 | 3484 | 837 | 121 | 1074 | 1452 | 112 | 495 |
| Canada | 3156 | 3350 | 3401 | 3443 | 926 | 130 | 1059 | 1339 | 109 | 860 |
| Belgium-Lux. | 3359 | 3483 | 3583 | 3700 | 778 | 190 | 1245 | 1476 | 123 | 322 |
| Denmark | 3457 | 3395 | 3585 | 3529 | 887 | 147 | 1278 | 1217 | 118 | 1184 |
| Finland | 3203 | 3141 | 3075 | 3008 | 786 | 185 | 1192 | 845 | 102 | 552 |
| France | 3254 | 3247 | 3322 | 3318 | 808 | 146 | 1046 | 1318 | 108 | 387 |
| Germany FR | 3032 | 3273 | 3433 | 3475 | 925 | 146 | 1088 | 1316 | 128 | 300 |
| Greece | 2912 | 3189 | 3572 | 3660 | 1147 | 134 | 807 | 1572 | 149 | 327 |
| Iceland | 3164 | 2920 | 3140 | 3040 | 606 | 131 | 1170 | 1133 | 84 | 82 |
| Ireland | 3476 | 3508 | 3713 | 3795 | 1066 | 260 | 1284 | 1185 | 149 | 507 |

| | | | | | | | | | | |
|---|---|---|---|---|---|---|---|---|---|---|
| Israel | 2805 | 3020 | 2993 | 3048 | 1072 | 72 | 612 | 1292 | 140 | 339 |
| Italy | 2985 | 3423 | 3622 | 3486 | 1139 | 78 | 824 | 1445 | 162 | 234 |
| Japan | 2519 | 2751 | 2851 | 2804 | 1264 | 73 | 361 | 1106 | 142 | 162 |
| Malta | 2853 | 3057 | 2735 | 2590 | 967 | 48 | 657 | 918 | 136 | 230 |
| Netherlands | 3190 | 3247 | 3352 | 3355 | 739 | 170 | 1035 | 1411 | 101 | 224 |
| New Zealand | 3330 | 3412 | 3399 | 3402 | 845 | 122 | 1360 | 1075 | 113 | 205 |
| Norway | 3071 | 3078 | 3376 | 3203 | 852 | 152 | 969 | 1230 | 111 | 304 |
| Portugal | 2528 | 3008 | 3058 | 3135 | 1303 | 193 | 479 | 1160 | 163 | 245 |
| South Africa | 2508 | 2718 | 2933 | 2945 | 1637 | 46 | 382 | 880 | 202 | 157 |
| Spain | 2848 | 2868 | 3337 | 3335 | 915 | 214 | 829 | 1377 | 124 | 472 |
| Sweden | 2884 | 2924 | 3068 | 3053 | 718 | 143 | 1032 | 1160 | 94 | 500 |
| Switzerland | 3478 | 3495 | 3494 | 3440 | 763 | 94 | 1252 | 1331 | 108 | 232 |
| United Kingdom | 3355 | 3337 | 3174 | 3130 | 784 | 210 | 957 | 1179 | 108 | 241 |
| United States | 3263 | 3467 | 3605 | 3652 | 781 | 116 | 1159 | 1596 | 106 | 709 |
| Yugoslavia | 3083 | 3327 | 3588 | 3598 | 1700 | 113 | 553 | 1232 | 225 | 577 |

**Table A.5** Total cereals (including rice in milled form)

| | 1969/71 (thousand tonnes) | | | | | 1969/71 | 1983/5 (thousand tonnes) | | | | | 1983/5 | 1970–85 (growth % p.a.) | |
|---|---|---|---|---|---|---|---|---|---|---|---|---|---|---|
| | Food | Feed | Tot. dem. | Prod. | Net trade | SSR (%) | Food | Feed | Tot. dem. | Prod. | Net trade | SSR (%) | Tot. dem. | Prod. |
| World | | | | 1129633 | 1688 | | | | | 1610048 | 4834 | | | 2.6 |
| All developing countries | | | | 483535 | −19469 | | | | | 767266 | −68580 | | | 3.4 |
| 94 developing countries | 375727 | 53786 | 491133 | 480280 | −16834 | 98 | 604509 | 126338 | 820258 | 762236 | −60792 | 93 | 3.8 | 3.4 |
| 93 developing countries | 251578 | 37729 | 331857 | 322417 | −14355 | 97 | 379957 | 81986 | 524557 | 472103 | −54548 | 90 | 3.4 | 2.9 |
| Africa (sub-Saharan) | 30306 | 1176 | 37628 | 36512 | −2441 | 97 | 45816 | 2002 | 54454 | 43078 | −9186 | 79 | 2.9 | 1.5 |
| Angola | 427 | 33 | 520 | 574 | 60 | 111 | 678 | 13 | 732 | 336 | −377 | 46 | 2.7 | −4.0 |
| Benin | 207 | 0 | 288 | 264 | −20 | 92 | 371 | 12 | 523 | 464 | −74 | 89 | 4.7 | 3.8 |
| Botswana | 101 | 4 | 118 | 53 | −70 | 45 | 173 | 4 | 196 | 14 | −214 | 7 | 3.3 | −9.1 |
| Burkina Faso | 908 | 0 | 1029 | 983 | −25 | 96 | 1168 | 0 | 1312 | 1251 | −135 | 95 | 2.1 | 2.3 |
| Burundi | 250 | 3 | 276 | 261 | −12 | 95 | 383 | 13 | 432 | 393 | −30 | 91 | 3.7 | 3.5 |
| Cameroon | 757 | 24 | 872 | 771 | −103 | 88 | 1056 | 26 | 1192 | 971 | −226 | 81 | 2.2 | 1.5 |
| Central African Republic | 93 | 0 | 104 | 93 | −13 | 89 | 124 | 0 | 138 | 112 | −24 | 81 | 1.8 | 1.4 |
| Chad | 578 | 15 | 685 | 671 | −10 | 98 | 478 | 6 | 565 | 486 | −88 | 86 | −0.9 | −2.0 |
| Congo | 36 | 0 | 37 | 8 | −29 | 21 | 124 | 0 | 127 | 8 | −119 | 6 | 8.7 | −1.7 |

| | | | | | | | | | | | | | | |
|---|---|---|---|---|---|---|---|---|---|---|---|---|---|---|
| Côte d'Ivoire | 541 | 6 | 666 | 529 | −155 | 79 | 1029 | 97 | 1336 | 835 | −492 | 63 | 5.7 | 3.8 |
| Ethiopia | 3959 | 4 | 4387 | 4362 | −51 | 99 | 5655 | 18 | 6154 | 5012 | −615 | 81 | 2.9 | 1.9 |
| Gabon | 23 | 0 | 24 | 8 | −15 | 35 | 71 | 0 | 78 | 11 | −70 | 14 | 9.2 | 2.7 |
| Gambia | 80 | 2 | 92 | 80 | −15 | 87 | 99 | 6 | 139 | 78 | −60 | 56 | 3.2 | 0.1 |
| Ghana | 620 | 15 | 799 | 720 | −124 | 90 | 809 | 21 | 928 | 580 | −300 | 63 | 0.3 | −2.7 |
| Guinea | 361 | 0 | 427 | 391 | −35 | 92 | 459 | 0 | 531 | 397 | −144 | 75 | 1.3 | −0.4 |
| Kenya | 1778 | 17 | 2184 | 2662 | 91 | 122 | 3131 | 56 | 3489 | 2396 | −291 | 69 | 3.1 | −1.3 |
| Lesotho | 216 | 12 | 271 | 208 | −75 | 77 | 323 | 20 | 382 | 141 | −224 | 37 | 3.1 | −1.8 |
| Liberia | 143 | 0 | 166 | 123 | −54 | 74 | 258 | 0 | 292 | 204 | −96 | 70 | 4.1 | 2.8 |
| Madagascar | 1043 | 69 | 1396 | 1388 | −19 | 99 | 1428 | 78 | 1821 | 1575 | −212 | 87 | 1.8 | 0.8 |
| Malawi | 958 | 61 | 1204 | 1160 | −31 | 96 | 1414 | 89 | 1652 | 1549 | 144 | 94 | 2.1 | 1.7 |
| Mali | 918 | 0 | 1045 | 998 | −45 | 95 | 1255 | 0 | 1419 | 1144 | −285 | 81 | 2.2 | 1.9 |
| Mauritania | 145 | 0 | 157 | 86 | −69 | 55 | 220 | 0 | 233 | 35 | −266 | 15 | 3.1 | −2.1 |
| Mauritius | 125 | 0 | 129 | 1 | −126 | 1 | 177 | 6 | 189 | 3 | −181 | 2 | 2.9 | 4.5 |
| Mozambique | 681 | 0 | 739 | 652 | −106 | 88 | 924 | 0 | 998 | 561 | −409 | 56 | 2.2 | −1.5 |
| Niger | 912 | 26 | 1203 | 1261 | 39 | 105 | 1326 | 33 | 1702 | 1536 | −119 | 90 | 3.4 | 3.5 |
| Nigeria | 5767 | 237 | 8135 | 7936 | −389 | 98 | 9312 | 408 | 11397 | 9417 | −1871 | 83 | 3.0 | 1.8 |
| Rwanda | 170 | 0 | 202 | 198 | −10 | 98 | 311 | 5 | 370 | 314 | −36 | 85 | 4.4 | 3.5 |
| Senegal | 770 | 1 | 921 | 664 | −294 | 72 | 1168 | 16 | 1336 | 784 | −583 | 59 | 3.1 | 2.5 |
| Sierra Leone | 331 | 1 | 397 | 340 | −68 | 86 | 416 | 2 | 492 | 404 | −70 | 82 | 1.7 | 1.3 |
| Somalia | 249 | 0 | 285 | 233 | −89 | 82 | 508 | 0 | 826 | 489 | −283 | 59 | 9.0 | 5.7 |
| Sudan | 1982 | 26 | 2173 | 2117 | −163 | 97 | 2390 | 111 | 2719 | 2633 | −462 | 97 | 2.0 | 1.9 |
| Swaziland | 66 | 27 | 111 | 83 | −33 | 75 | 96 | 67 | 187 | 86 | −102 | 46 | 3.5 | −1.9 |
| Tanzania | 1186 | 54 | 1370 | 1292 | −30 | 94 | 2789 | 337 | 3477 | 3105 | −247 | 89 | 7.3 | 7.1 |
| Togo | 225 | 0 | 285 | 296 | −18 | 104 | 357 | 0 | 442 | 375 | −91 | 85 | 3.1 | 1.8 |
| Uganda | 1024 | 159 | 1399 | 1564 | −49 | 112 | 1280 | 66 | 1555 | 1305 | −4 | 84 | 0.2 | −2.1 |
| Zaire | 836 | 10 | 918 | 688 | −233 | 75 | 1333 | 30 | 1487 | 1085 | −338 | 73 | 3.0 | 3.3 |
| Zambia | 817 | 69 | 1062 | 915 | −202 | 86 | 1267 | 90 | 1496 | 1032 | −237 | 69 | 2.0 | −1.0 |
| Zimbabwe | 1026 | 303 | 1554 | 1881 | 184 | 121 | 1460 | 373 | 2113 | 1957 | 81 | 93 | 1.9 | 0.4 |

**Table A.5** *(cont.)*

| | 1969/71 (thousand tonnes) | | | | | 1969/71 | 1983/5 (thousand tonnes) | | | | | 1983/5 | 1970–85 (growth % p.a.) | |
|---|---|---|---|---|---|---|---|---|---|---|---|---|---|---|
| | Food | Feed | Tot. dem. | Prod. | Net trade | SSR (%) | Food | Feed | Tot. dem. | Prod. | Net trade | SSR (%) | Tot. dem. | Prod. |
| Near East/ North Africa | 32684 | 10020 | 52614 | 45862 | −6461 | 87 | 54698 | 25406 | 95907 | 60062 | −35117 | 63 | 4.6 | 2.1 |
| Afghanistan | 3195 | 115 | 3775 | 3498 | −224 | 93 | 3802 | 138 | 4421 | 4294 | −49 | 97 | 1.0 | 1.3 |
| Algeria | 2069 | 54 | 2544 | 1881 | −492 | 74 | 4200 | 1096 | 5913 | 1934 | −4314 | 33 | 6.5 | −0.3 |
| Cyprus | 83 | 170 | 272 | 165 | −120 | 61 | 103 | 403 | 532 | 118 | −425 | 22 | 4.4 | 1.5 |
| Egypt | 6142 | 1285 | 8464 | 6530 | −1088 | 77 | 10728 | 3444 | 15778 | 7721 | −8210 | 49 | 4.9 | 1.1 |
| Iran | 4697 | 921 | 6438 | 5745 | −451 | 89 | 9493 | 2854 | 13430 | 8544 | −4918 | 64 | 5.2 | 3.1 |
| Iraq | 1472 | 521 | 2410 | 1969 | −426 | 82 | 2986 | 1857 | 5322 | 1547 | −3806 | 29 | 6.8 | −1.7 |
| Jordan | 256 | 51 | 340 | 152 | −149 | 45 | 461 | 270 | 777 | 100 | −667 | 13 | 6.6 | −3.3 |
| Lebanon | 373 | 155 | 553 | 50 | −535 | 9 | 360 | 155 | 533 | 24 | −514 | 4 | −0.5 | −7.7 |
| Libya | 289 | 126 | 456 | 113 | −347 | 25 | 677 | 484 | 1280 | 309 | −969 | 24 | 6.6 | 7.5 |
| Morocco | 3239 | 692 | 4796 | 4548 | −307 | 95 | 4760 | 577 | 6287 | 4226 | −2310 | 67 | 1.8 | −1.0 |
| Saudi Arabia | 741 | 18 | 807 | 428 | −522 | 53 | 1654 | 4295 | 7697 | 1373 | −5703 | 18 | 19.4 | 11.8 |
| Syria | 1025 | 302 | 1628 | 1229 | −393 | 76 | 1917 | 956 | 3386 | 2322 | −1572 | 69 | 5.6 | 5.5 |
| Tunisia | 872 | 115 | 1174 | 718 | −421 | 61 | 1415 | 512 | 2198 | 1373 | −983 | 63 | 4.6 | 2.8 |
| Turkey | 7231 | 5464 | 17867 | 17945 | −757 | 100 | 10606 | 8336 | 26706 | 25676 | 260 | 96 | 3.4 | 3.3 |
| Yemen AR | 809 | 32 | 894 | 801 | −93 | 90 | 1173 | 28 | 1270 | 388 | −638 | 31 | 2.4 | −4.2 |
| Yemen PDR | 190 | 0 | 198 | 90 | −122 | 46 | 364 | 0 | 377 | 115 | −286 | 30 | 4.9 | 1.6 |
| Asia | 279213 | 20722 | 338345 | 332044 | −11430 | 98 | 450816 | 58119 | 565042 | 559004 | −14972 | 99 | 3.7 | 3.7 |
| Bangladesh | 11208 | 9 | 12734 | 11220 | −1300 | 88 | 15765 | 4 | 17711 | 15654 | −1681 | 88 | 2.6 | 3.0 |
| Burma | 4537 | 14 | 4920 | 5558 | 678 | 113 | 7513 | 28 | 8068 | 10223 | 743 | 127 | 3.8 | 5.4 |
| China | 124149 | 16056 | 159276 | 157863 | −2478 | 99 | 224553 | 44352 | 295701 | 290133 | −6244 | 98 | 4.5 | 4.2 |

| | | | | | | | | | | | | | | |
|---|---|---|---|---|---|---|---|---|---|---|---|---|---|---|
| India | 79588 | 1100 | 91723 | 90259 | −3617 | 98 | 112718 | 1457 | 130775 | 135560 | −1673 | 104 | 2.5 | 2.9 |
| Indonesia | 14895 | 314 | 16249 | 15339 | −867 | 94 | 27029 | 1577 | 30648 | 29988 | −1937 | 98 | 4.3 | 5.0 |
| Kampuchea DM | 1358 | 17 | 1704 | 2137 | 111 | 125 | 1303 | 0 | 1467 | 1370 | −84 | 93 | −1.6 | −1.5 |
| Korea DPR | 2700 | 1167 | 4576 | 4350 | −181 | 95 | 4844 | 2554 | 8681 | 8362 | −195 | 96 | 4.7 | 4.7 |
| Korea Rep. | 6025 | 703 | 7429 | 5652 | −2509 | 76 | 7527 | 4094 | 12872 | 6126 | −6443 | 48 | 3.8 | 0.5 |
| Lao | 563 | 19 | 664 | 606 | −70 | 91 | 771 | 28 | 912 | 900 | −46 | 99 | 2.4 | 3.3 |
| Malaysia | 1677 | 257 | 2024 | 1146 | −940 | 57 | 2257 | 1250 | 3662 | 1191 | −2373 | 33 | 4.6 | −0.1 |
| Nepal | 2075 | 2 | 2454 | 2710 | 253 | 110 | 2903 | 17 | 3437 | 3413 | 3 | 99 | 2.5 | 1.2 |
| Pakistan | 9505 | 76 | 10524 | 10531 | 136 | 100 | 14860 | 89 | 16212 | 16545 | 556 | 102 | 3.2 | 3.7 |
| Philippines | 5599 | 340 | 6366 | 5664 | −786 | 89 | 8514 | 558 | 9984 | 8928 | −1488 | 89 | 3.4 | 3.8 |
| Sri Lanka | 1696 | 10 | 1800 | 1008 | −952 | 56 | 2417 | 58 | 2638 | 1726 | −852 | 65 | 2.1 | 4.8 |
| Thailand | 6015 | 491 | 7300 | 11196 | 2893 | 153 | 8345 | 1754 | 11278 | 17894 | 7052 | 159 | 3.1 | 3.6 |
| Vietnam | 7626 | 148 | 8604 | 6807 | −1791 | 79 | 9500 | 301 | 10998 | 10992 | −300 | 100 | 1.5 | 3.0 |
| Latin America | 33527 | 21867 | 62549 | 65866 | 3500 | 105 | 53186 | 40813 | 104862 | 100097 | −1518 | 96 | 3.8 | 3.2 |
| Argentina | 3347 | 6011 | 11051 | 20090 | 9401 | 182 | 4355 | 6344 | 12588 | 30321 | 20166 | 241 | 0.4 | 2.9 |
| Bolivia | 423 | 188 | 651 | 471 | −187 | 72 | 732 | 308 | 1105 | 707 | −335 | 64 | 4.2 | 3.4 |
| Brazil | 9524 | 8965 | 21296 | 20073 | −995 | 94 | 16626 | 14496 | 35164 | 29769 | −4789 | 85 | 3.9 | 2.9 |
| Chile | 1509 | 532 | 2262 | 1767 | −482 | 78 | 1902 | 923 | 3011 | 1922 | −932 | 64 | 2.1 | 0.4 |
| Colombia | 1699 | 256 | 2031 | 1671 | −382 | 82 | 2837 | 879 | 3830 | 2656 | −991 | 69 | 4.5 | 3.4 |
| Costa Rica | 185 | 43 | 241 | 142 | −109 | 59 | 309 | 111 | 443 | 302 | −130 | 68 | 4.5 | 5.6 |
| Cuba | 1074 | 356 | 1477 | 294 | −1228 | 20 | 1423 | 1065 | 2594 | 451 | −2161 | 17 | 3.8 | 2.5 |
| Dominican Rep. | 260 | 32 | 306 | 196 | −110 | 64 | 575 | 259 | 867 | 443 | −418 | 51 | 7.4 | 5.9 |
| Ecuador | 473 | 66 | 625 | 555 | −78 | 89 | 784 | 112 | 1010 | 629 | −324 | 62 | 3.4 | 1.1 |
| El Salvador | 418 | 73 | 522 | 514 | −46 | 98 | 750 | 141 | 937 | 660 | −242 | 70 | 4.2 | 2.0 |
| Guatemala | 743 | 114 | 928 | 849 | −98 | 92 | 1135 | 293 | 1552 | 1235 | −149 | 80 | 3.7 | 2.7 |
| Guyana | 87 | 10 | 110 | 132 | 26 | 120 | 144 | 9 | 166 | 192 | 41 | 115 | 3.2 | 3.3 |
| Haiti | 411 | 97 | 550 | 509 | −46 | 93 | 523 | 15 | 579 | 338 | −213 | 58 | 0.6 | −3.0 |
| Honduras | 350 | 54 | 438 | 395 | −44 | 90 | 579 | 104 | 738 | 604 | −107 | 82 | 3.8 | 3.0 |
| Jamaica | 214 | 71 | 293 | 5 | −292 | 2 | 263 | 137 | 414 | 7 | −425 | 2 | 2.0 | 0.4 |
| Mexico | 8820 | 3878 | 14218 | 14422 | 164 | 101 | 14136 | 12292 | 29754 | 24175 | −6237 | 81 | 5.6 | 4.1 |

**Table A.5** (*cont.*)

| | 1969/71 (thousand tonnes) | | | | | 1969/71 | 1983/5 (thousand tonnes) | | | | | 1983/5 | 1970–85 (growth % p.a.) | |
|---|---|---|---|---|---|---|---|---|---|---|---|---|---|---|
| | Food | Feed | Tot. dem. | Prod. | Net trade | SSR (%) | Food | Feed | Tot. dem. | Prod. | Net trade | SSR (%) | Tot. dem. | Prod. |
| Nicaragua | 253 | 67 | 363 | 351 | −19 | 97 | 398 | 171 | 627 | 470 | −170 | 75 | 4.1 | 3.1 |
| Panama | 181 | 34 | 229 | 162 | −71 | 71 | 247 | 64 | 327 | 214 | −105 | 65 | 2.7 | 2.9 |
| Paraguay | 226 | 57 | 323 | 273 | −56 | 84 | 374 | 426 | 892 | 861 | −67 | 97 | 8.3 | 8.8 |
| Peru | 1472 | 299 | 1883 | 1275 | −698 | 68 | 2311 | 409 | 2854 | 1548 | −1201 | 54 | 3.3 | 1.0 |
| Suriname | 54 | 14 | 84 | 88 | −5 | 105 | 63 | 35 | 130 | 194 | 70 | 149 | 3.9 | 6.3 |
| Trinidad and Tob. | 134 | 46 | 185 | 9 | −183 | 5 | 157 | 85 | 250 | 5 | −238 | 2 | 2.7 | −6.3 |
| Uruguay | 384 | 221 | 708 | 780 | 94 | 110 | 406 | 155 | 669 | 945 | 350 | 141 | −1.2 | 1.4 |
| Venezuela | 1287 | 384 | 1774 | 842 | −1038 | 48 | 2159 | 1980 | 4362 | 1450 | −2892 | 33 | 7.0 | 5.7 |
| Developing, low income | 266844 | 18192 | 323595 | 316956 | −10862 | 98 | 427466 | 47474 | 528920 | 520207 | −14865 | 98 | 3.6 | 3.5 |
| Low inc. excl. China | 142696 | 2135 | 164318 | 159093 | −8384 | 97 | 202914 | 3122 | 233219 | 230074 | −8620 | 99 | 2.6 | 2.8 |
| Low inc. excl. China/India | 63109 | 1036 | 72596 | 68835 | −4765 | 95 | 90196 | 1666 | 102444 | 94514 | −6946 | 92 | 2.6 | 2.6 |
| Developing, middle income | 108885 | 35594 | 167539 | 163325 | −5971 | 98 | 177045 | 78864 | 291341 | 242030 | −45928 | 83 | 4.1 | 3.0 |
| Developed countries | 161715 | 385347 | 626773 | 646462 | 22488 | 103 | 175665 | 473640 | 762393 | 843247 | 75688 | 111 | 1.4 | 2.0 |

| | | | | | | | | | | | | | | |
|---|---|---|---|---|---|---|---|---|---|---|---|---|---|---|
| European CPEs | 68980 | 120844 | 236695 | 231026 | −133 | 98 | 72145 | 176099 | 305528 | 266781 | −41672 | 87 | 1.7 | 0.6 |
| Albania | 485 | 67 | 611 | 534 | −66 | 87 | 729 | 206 | 1016 | 1071 | 8 | 105 | 3.9 | 5.3 |
| Bulgaria | 2165 | 3157 | 6435 | 6627 | 230 | 103 | 1993 | 4663 | 7976 | 7538 | 66 | 95 | 1.5 | 0.6 |
| Czecho-slovakia | 2596 | 5707 | 9229 | 8017 | −1423 | 87 | 2666 | 7242 | 11422 | 11606 | −355 | 102 | 1.3 | 2.2 |
| German DR | 2593 | 6059 | 9342 | 7040 | −2533 | 75 | 2698 | 9872 | 13686 | 11008 | −2883 | 80 | 2.1 | 2.6 |
| Hungary | 1889 | 5914 | 8651 | 9039 | 21 | 105 | 1783 | 9966 | 13215 | 14753 | 1643 | 112 | 2.8 | 3.3 |
| Poland | 6490 | 11640 | 20584 | 18236 | −2348 | 89 | 6828 | 16006 | 26097 | 23414 | −2516 | 90 | 1.3 | 1.0 |
| Romania | 4277 | 6258 | 12395 | 12639 | 576 | 102 | 4487 | 12477 | 21742 | 22040 | −43 | 101 | 4.2 | 4.2 |
| USSR | 48487 | 82044 | 169448 | 168896 | 5412 | 100 | 50961 | 115669 | 210375 | 175352 | −37587 | 83 | 1.5 | −0.2 |
| Developed market economies | 92736 | 264502 | 390078 | 415435 | 22622 | 107 | 103522 | 297541 | 456865 | 576466 | 117361 | 126 | 1.2 | 2.7 |
| Australia | 1691 | 2973 | 5583 | 13905 | 9006 | 249 | 1956 | 3697 | 7969 | 28272 | 16663 | 355 | 2.7 | 4.9 |
| Austria | 1050 | 2176 | 3562 | 3341 | −267 | 94 | 849 | 3346 | 4587 | 5330 | 690 | 116 | 1.8 | 3.5 |
| Belgium-Lux. | 1183 | 2613 | 4327 | 1923 | −2688 | 44 | 1260 | 2368 | 4552 | 2214 | −2130 | 49 | 0.0 | 0.8 |
| Canada | 2290 | 18052 | 22874 | 34516 | 13312 | 151 | 2735 | 18167 | 24360 | 46732 | 25069 | 192 | 0.7 | 2.9 |
| Denmark | 543 | 5899 | 7087 | 6678 | −363 | 94 | 602 | 5504 | 6654 | 7892 | 928 | 119 | −0.6 | 1.4 |
| Finland | 514 | 1898 | 2711 | 2875 | 59 | 106 | 499 | 2271 | 3193 | 3726 | 457 | 117 | 1.4 | 1.2 |
| France | 5701 | 15051 | 22963 | 33952 | 10763 | 148 | 5933 | 18499 | 27170 | 53654 | 25189 | 198 | 1.2 | 3.0 |
| Germany FR | 7290 | 15033 | 24410 | 19063 | −5145 | 78 | 7814 | 16146 | 26168 | 25156 | −2033 | 96 | 0.3 | 1.9 |
| Greece | 1389 | 1544 | 3347 | 3196 | −255 | 96 | 1471 | 2681 | 4715 | 4839 | 864 | 103 | 2.2 | 3.4 |
| Iceland | 20 | 26 | 46 | 0 | −45 | 0 | 20 | 20 | 40 | 0 | −53 | 0 | −0.8 | 0.0 |
| Ireland | 417 | 1214 | 1875 | 1452 | −425 | 77 | 530 | 1545 | 2339 | 2200 | −253 | 94 | 1.6 | 3.9 |
| Israel | 433 | 751 | 1341 | 199 | −1150 | 15 | 586 | 1197 | 2008 | 254 | −1728 | 13 | 2.6 | −1.6 |
| Italy | 10148 | 10432 | 22142 | 15831 | −6028 | 72 | 9202 | 11776 | 22587 | 18343 | −4061 | 81 | 0.0 | 1.3 |
| Japan | 15508 | 10053 | 27131 | 12172 | −14378 | 45 | 17004 | 17502 | 36442 | 10606 | −26577 | 29 | 2.0 | −0.8 |
| Malta | 53 | 57 | 115 | 4 | −113 | 3 | 52 | 82 | 139 | 10 | −127 | 7 | 0.4 | 8.5 |
| Netherlands | 1198 | 2950 | 4508 | 1564 | −2935 | 35 | 1455 | 2655 | 4685 | 1339 | −3333 | 29 | −0.2 | −0.4 |

**Table A.5** (*cont.*)

| | 1969/71 (thousand tonnes) | | | | | 1969/71 | 1983/5 (thousand tonnes) | | | | | 1983/5 | 1970–85 (growth % p.a.) | |
|---|---|---|---|---|---|---|---|---|---|---|---|---|---|---|
| | Food | Feed | Tot. dem. | Prod. | Net trade | SSR (%) | Food | Feed | Tot. dem. | Prod. | Net trade | SSR (%) | Tot. dem. | Prod. |
| New Zealand | 324 | 363 | 739 | 709 | −16 | 96 | 367 | 458 | 1029 | 1067 | 132 | 104 | 1.6 | 2.8 |
| Norway | 391 | 984 | 1477 | 777 | −670 | 53 | 458 | 1119 | 1717 | 1245 | −405 | 73 | 1.1 | 3.2 |
| Portugal | 1251 | 845 | 2394 | 1661 | −837 | 69 | 1657 | 2216 | 4138 | 1321 | −2799 | 32 | 4.2 | −2.3 |
| South Africa | 4288 | 2283 | 7366 | 8761 | 926 | 119 | 6370 | 4093 | 11335 | 8094 | −1198 | 71 | 3.0 | −0.1 |
| Spain | 4038 | 8728 | 13901 | 11689 | −1999 | 84 | 4736 | 16509 | 22743 | 18429 | −4260 | 81 | 3.3 | 2.9 |
| Sweden | 709 | 2902 | 4127 | 4789 | 610 | 116 | 779 | 3591 | 4956 | 6027 | 1152 | 122 | 1.2 | 1.1 |
| Switzerland | 798 | 1261 | 2146 | 683 | −1495 | 32 | 700 | 1392 | 2212 | 1024 | −1274 | 46 | 0.0 | 2.6 |
| United Kingdom | 6590 | 13258 | 22384 | 13941 | −9165 | 62 | 6139 | 10682 | 19772 | 23523 | 1986 | 119 | −1.1 | 3.9 |
| United States | 20182 | 136596 | 168585 | 208653 | 36260 | 124 | 25182 | 138868 | 192947 | 288112 | 93478 | 149 | 1.2 | 2.9 |
| Yugoslavia | 4742 | 6565 | 12939 | 13105 | −320 | 101 | 5169 | 11161 | 18407 | 17060 | 999 | 93 | 2.2 | 1.8 |

**Table A.6** Past and projected commodity balances of main commodities: aggregates for 94 developing countries (million tonnes)

| Commodity | Year | Food | Feed | Other use | Domestic disappearance | Exports | Imports | Net trade | Production | SSR (%) |
|---|---|---|---|---|---|---|---|---|---|---|
| Wheat | 1961/63 | 65.5 | 2.2 | 14.2 | 81.8 | 2.5 | 21.4 | −18.9 | 64.3 | 78.6 |
| | 1969/71 | 97.7 | 3.9 | 18.6 | 120.2 | 2.4 | 26.5 | −24.0 | 96.5 | 80.3 |
| | 1979/81 | 171.2 | 7.4 | 26.9 | 205.5 | 5.3 | 52.3 | −47.0 | 157.3 | 76.5 |
| | 1983/85 | 209.7 | 9.6 | 30.6 | 249.8 | 10.5 | 58.6 | −48.1 | 200.6 | 80.3 |
| | 2000 | 296.1 | 25.8 | 44.4 | 366.3 | | | −63.8 | 302.4 | 82.6 |
| Rice, paddy | 1961/63 | 182.0 | 1.4 | 23.7 | 207.2 | 8.3 | 7.0 | 1.3 | 205.5 | 99.2 |
| | 1969/71 | 245.4 | 2.8 | 30.0 | 278.2 | 8.0 | 8.5 | −0.5 | 283.3 | 101.8 |
| | 1979/81 | 330.6 | 4.9 | 37.3 | 372.9 | 11.2 | 12.7 | −1.5 | 367.6 | 98.6 |
| | 1983/85 | 379.0 | 7.4 | 41.4 | 427.8 | 11.7 | 11.4 | 0.3 | 436.1 | 102.0 |
| | 2000 | 515.6 | 20.9 | 55.5 | 592.0 | | | −2.7 | 589.3 | 99.5 |
| Maize | 1961/63 | 42.0 | 16.1 | 8.3 | 66.4 | 4.0 | 1.8 | 2.2 | 69.5 | 104.6 |
| | 1969/71 | 51.2 | 32.2 | 11.0 | 94.4 | 9.2 | 2.3 | 6.9 | 102.5 | 108.6 |
| | 1979/81 | 72.9 | 67.0 | 16.2 | 156.1 | 9.1 | 16.8 | −7.7 | 149.0 | 95.4 |
| | 1983/85 | 78.4 | 76.6 | 18.5 | 173.5 | 12.8 | 18.1 | −5.3 | 168.4 | 97.1 |
| | 2000 | 94.8 | 188.0 | 31.8 | 314.5 | | | −16.3 | 298.2 | 94.8 |
| Other coarse grains | 1961/63 | 56.8 | 10.5 | 12.4 | 79.7 | 1.8 | 2.1 | −0.3 | 80.9 | 101.6 |
| | 1969/71 | 63.2 | 15.8 | 12.1 | 91.0 | 3.1 | 2.4 | 0.7 | 92.3 | 101.4 |
| | 1979/81 | 63.9 | 27.9 | 11.8 | 103.6 | 5.1 | 8.9 | −3.9 | 100.1 | 96.7 |
| | 1983/85 | 63.7 | 35.2 | 12.7 | 111.6 | 6.1 | 13.7 | −7.6 | 102.3 | 91.7 |
| | 2000 | 84.6 | 68.1 | 18.7 | 171.3 | | | −13.3 | 158.0 | 92.3 |
| Total cereals (rice included in milled form) | 1961/63 | 285.7 | 29.7 | 50.6 | 366.1 | 13.9 | 30.0 | −16.1 | 351.8 | 96.1 |
| | 1969/71 | 375.7 | 53.8 | 61.6 | 491.1 | 20.0 | 36.9 | −16.8 | 480.3 | 97.8 |
| | 1979/81 | 528.6 | 105.6 | 79.8 | 713.9 | 26.9 | 86.5 | −59.5 | 651.6 | 91.3 |

**Table A.6** *(cont.)*

| Commodity | Year | Food | Feed | Other use | Domestic disappearance | Exports | Imports | Net trade | Production | SSR (%) |
|---|---|---|---|---|---|---|---|---|---|---|
| | 1983/85 | 604.5 | 126.3 | 89.4 | 820.3 | 37.2 | 98.0 | −60.8 | 762.2 | 92.9 |
| | 2000 | 819.4 | 295.8 | 131.8 | 1247.0 | | | −95.3 | 1151.7 | 92.4 |
| Roots and plantains | 1961/63 | 156.2 | 24.3 | 42.0 | 222.5 | 2.2 | 0.8 | 1.5 | 227.1 | 102.1 |
| | 1969/71 | 207.8 | 39.5 | 56.5 | 303.7 | 5.8 | 0.6 | 5.2 | 309.6 | 101.9 |
| | 1979/81 | 229.3 | 60.7 | 66.5 | 356.5 | 18.2 | 1.2 | 16.9 | 370.0 | 103.8 |
| | 1983/85 | 221.7 | 75.4 | 69.3 | 366.5 | 20.9 | 1.8 | 19.1 | 386.9 | 105.6 |
| | 2000 | 282.6 | 172.3 | 104.6 | 559.6 | | | 25.2 | 584.8 | 104.5 |
| Sugar (raw equivalent) | 1961/63 | 27.1 | 2.5 | 2.8 | 32.4 | 11.6 | 4.2 | 7.4 | 39.3 | 121.3 |
| | 1969/71 | 37.1 | 2.6 | 3.8 | 43.5 | 13.3 | 4.8 | 8.5 | 52.8 | 121.3 |
| | 1979/81 | 55.3 | 2.2 | 8.8 | 66.3 | 16.8 | 10.3 | 6.5 | 71.7 | 108.0 |
| | 1983/85 | 62.6 | 3.0 | 14.9 | 80.5 | 17.7 | 11.3 | 6.4 | 88.8 | 110.4 |
| | 2000 | 104.6 | 5.4 | 14.3 | 124.3 | | | 6.9 | 131.2 | 105.6 |
| Pulses | 1961/63 | 25.3 | 2.1 | 4.0 | 31.4 | 0.8 | 0.4 | 0.3 | 31.9 | 101.8 |
| | 1969/71 | 24.0 | 2.2 | 4.0 | 30.2 | 0.9 | 0.5 | 0.5 | 30.7 | 101.6 |
| | 1979/81 | 24.7 | 2.5 | 4.0 | 31.3 | 1.2 | 1.3 | −0.1 | 31.3 | 100.1 |
| | 1983/85 | 27.1 | 2.9 | 4.3 | 34.2 | 1.6 | 1.3 | 0.2 | 33.9 | 99.1 |
| | 2000 | 40.8 | 3.0 | 5.6 | 49.5 | | | 0.4 | 49.9 | 100.9 |
| Bananas | 1961/63 | 11.8 | 0.6 | 4.6 | 17.1 | 3.4 | 0.3 | 3.1 | 20.2 | 118.2 |
| | 1969/71 | 16.5 | 0.8 | 6.2 | 23.5 | 5.0 | 0.4 | 4.6 | 28.1 | 119.8 |
| | 1979/81 | 22.0 | 0.7 | 6.7 | 29.4 | 6.2 | 0.7 | 5.6 | 35.0 | 118.9 |
| | 1983/85 | 23.1 | 0.6 | 6.9 | 30.6 | 5.9 | 0.4 | 5.5 | 36.1 | 118.0 |
| | 2000 | 39.3 | 1.0 | 10.7 | 51.1 | | | 6.9 | 58.0 | 113.5 |
| Citrus fruit | 1961/63 | 8.5 | 0.0 | 1.1 | 9.6 | 1.2 | 0.1 | 1.1 | 10.7 | 111.6 |
| | 1969/71 | 12.3 | 0.0 | 1.6 | 13.9 | 2.3 | 0.2 | 2.1 | 15.9 | 115.0 |
| | 1979/81 | 17.4 | 0.0 | 2.3 | 19.7 | 7.9 | 0.8 | 7.1 | 26.7 | 135.8 |

| | | | | | | | | | | |
|---|---|---|---|---|---|---|---|---|---|---|
| | 1983/85 | 19.9 | 0.0 | 2.6 | 22.5 | 10.3 | 0.7 | 9.6 | 32.0 | 142.7 |
| | 2000 | 33.3 | 0.0 | 3.9 | 37.2 | | | 14.6 | 51.8 | 139.2 |
| Vegetable oils and oilseeds (in oil equivalent) | 1961/63 | 8.9 | 0.3 | 2.5 | 11.7 | 3.9 | 1.0 | 2.9 | 15.1 | 129.0 |
| | 1969/71 | 12.4 | 0.3 | 3.4 | 16.1 | 3.9 | 1.5 | 2.4 | 18.9 | 117.5 |
| | 1979/81 | 20.3 | 0.4 | 5.8 | 26.5 | 7.7 | 6.0 | 1.7 | 28.5 | 107.6 |
| | 1983/85 | 25.1 | 0.5 | 6.9 | 32.6 | 9.9 | 7.4 | 2.5 | 35.0 | 107.6 |
| | 2000 | 43.5 | 1.1 | 12.3 | 56.8 | | | 2.3 | 59.1 | 104.0 |
| Cocoa beans | 1961/63 | 0.1 | 0.0 | 0.0 | 0.2 | 1.0 | 0.0 | 1.0 | 1.2 | 769.0 |
| | 1969/71 | 0.1 | 0.0 | 0.0 | 0.2 | 1.2 | 0.1 | 1.2 | 1.5 | 817.7 |
| | 1979/81 | 0.2 | 0.0 | 0.1 | 0.3 | 1.4 | 0.1 | 1.3 | 1.6 | 543.0 |
| | 1983/85 | 0.3 | 0.0 | 0.0 | 0.3 | 1.6 | 0.1 | 1.5 | 1.7 | 550.5 |
| | 2000 | 0.5 | 0.0 | 0.1 | 0.5 | | | 1.8 | 2.3 | 431.8 |
| Coffee | 1961/63 | 1.0 | 0.0 | 0.1 | 1.1 | 2.8 | 0.1 | 2.7 | 4.4 | 405.1 |
| | 1969/71 | 1.3 | 0.0 | 0.1 | 1.4 | 3.2 | 0.2 | 3.1 | 4.2 | 297.9 |
| | 1979/81 | 1.5 | 0.0 | 0.1 | 1.6 | 3.6 | 0.2 | 3.4 | 5.2 | 321.7 |
| | 1983/85 | 1.6 | 0.0 | 0.2 | 1.8 | 4.1 | 0.3 | 3.8 | 5.6 | 315.0 |
| | 2000 | 2.6 | 0.0 | 0.3 | 2.9 | | | 4.4 | 7.3 | 251.6 |
| Tea | 1961/63 | 0.7 | 0.0 | 0.0 | 0.7 | 0.6 | 0.2 | 0.4 | 1.1 | 160.6 |
| | 1969/71 | 0.8 | 0.0 | 0.0 | 0.9 | 0.7 | 0.2 | 0.5 | 1.3 | 153.7 |
| | 1979/81 | 1.3 | 0.0 | 0.0 | 1.3 | 0.9 | 0.3 | 0.5 | 1.9 | 138.3 |
| | 1983/85 | 1.6 | 0.0 | 0.0 | 1.6 | 1.0 | 0.4 | 0.6 | 2.2 | 135.6 |
| | 2000 | 2.6 | 0.0 | 0.1 | 2.6 | | | 0.7 | 3.3 | 124.9 |
| Tobacco | 1961/63 | 0.0 | 0.0 | 1.6 | 1.6 | 0.4 | 0.1 | 0.3 | 2.0 | 120.6 |
| | 1969/71 | 0.0 | 0.0 | 2.2 | 2.2 | 0.5 | 0.2 | 0.4 | 2.6 | 116.9 |
| | 1979/81 | 0.0 | 0.0 | 2.9 | 2.9 | 0.8 | 0.3 | 0.5 | 3.4 | 117.5 |
| | 1983/85 | 0.0 | 0.0 | 3.7 | 3.7 | 0.8 | 0.3 | 0.5 | 4.2 | 112.3 |
| | 2000 | 0.0 | 0.0 | 7.5 | 7.5 | | | 0.5 | 8.0 | 106.6 |
| Cotton lint | 1961/63 | 0.0 | 0.0 | 3.6 | 3.6 | 2.1 | 0.5 | 1.6 | 5.2 | 145.5 |
| | 1969/71 | 0.0 | 0.0 | 5.7 | 5.7 | 2.6 | 0.6 | 1.9 | 7.6 | 134.3 |

**Table A.6** (*cont.*)

| Commodity | Year | Food | Feed | Other use | Domestic disappearance | Exports | Imports | Net trade | Production | SSR (%) |
|---|---|---|---|---|---|---|---|---|---|---|
| | 1979/81 | 0.0 | 0.0 | 8.0 | 8.0 | 1.9 | 1.6 | 0.3 | 8.3 | 103.4 |
| | 1983/85 | 0.0 | 0.0 | 10.2 | 10.2 | 2.0 | 1.1 | 0.9 | 11.1 | 108.4 |
| | 2000 | 0.0 | 0.0 | 13.0 | 13.0 | | | 0.7 | 13.7 | 105.4 |
| Jute and hard fibres | 1961/63 | 0.0 | 0.0 | 2.9 | 2.9 | 1.8 | 0.2 | 1.6 | 4.5 | 154.9 |
| | 1969/71 | 0.0 | 0.0 | 3.3 | 3.3 | 1.6 | 0.3 | 1.3 | 4.6 | 137.8 |
| | 1979/81 | 0.0 | 0.0 | 4.3 | 4.3 | 0.9 | 0.3 | 0.6 | 4.9 | 113.7 |
| | 1983/85 | 0.0 | 0.0 | 5.2 | 5.2 | 0.7 | 0.3 | 0.4 | 5.7 | 108.2 |
| | 2000 | 0.0 | 0.0 | 5.4 | 5.4 | | | 0.4 | 5.9 | 108.1 |
| Rubber | 1961/63 | 0.0 | 0.0 | 0.4 | 0.4 | 2.1 | 0.3 | 1.8 | 2.2 | 601.2 |
| | 1969/71 | 0.0 | 0.0 | 0.7 | 0.7 | 2.8 | 0.5 | 2.3 | 3.0 | 437.3 |
| | 1979/81 | 0.0 | 0.0 | 1.2 | 1.2 | 3.2 | 0.7 | 2.6 | 3.8 | 310.2 |
| | 1983/85 | 0.0 | 0.0 | 1.4 | 1.4 | 3.5 | 0.7 | 2.8 | 4.2 | 293.6 |
| | 2000 | 0.0 | 0.0 | 2.6 | 2.6 | | | 3.6 | 6.2 | 239.7 |
| Milk and dairy products (whole-milk equivalent) | 1961/63 | 55.3 | 7.3 | 5.5 | 68.1 | 0.1 | 4.4 | −4.3 | 63.8 | 93.7 |
| | 1969/71 | 68.3 | 8.8 | 5.7 | 82.8 | 0.2 | 7.2 | −6.9 | 75.9 | 91.7 |
| | 1979/81 | 100.8 | 12.5 | 6.9 | 120.2 | 0.4 | 16.2 | −15.8 | 104.9 | 87.3 |
| | 1983/85 | 117.5 | 12.6 | 7.5 | 137.7 | 0.4 | 17.9 | −17.5 | 119.9 | 87.1 |
| | 2000 | 193.2 | 23.2 | 12.8 | 229.2 | | | −24.6 | 204.6 | 89.3 |
| Total meat | 1961/63 | 17.3 | 0.0 | 0.0 | 17.3 | 1.4 | 0.5 | 0.9 | 18.1 | 104.7 |
| | 1969/71 | 25.2 | 0.0 | 0.0 | 25.2 | 1.9 | 0.6 | 1.3 | 26.5 | 105.2 |
| | 1979/81 | 40.1 | 0.0 | 0.1 | 40.1 | 2.2 | 1.9 | 0.3 | 40.4 | 100.7 |
| | 1983/85 | 47.6 | 0.0 | 0.1 | 47.7 | 2.5 | 2.2 | 0.3 | 47.9 | 100.6 |
| | 2000 | 88.0 | 0.0 | 0.1 | 88.1 | | | 0.2 | 88.2 | 100.2 |

**Table A.7** Agricultural resources and input use in 1982/4

| | Arable land | | | | | Fertilizers | | Cereals | |
|---|---|---|---|---|---|---|---|---|---|
| | Potential (mill.ha) | In use (mill.ha) | In use as % of potential | Irrigated as % of total | ha per agric. worker | Total (thousand tonnes) | per ha (kg) | Harv. land as % of total | Yield (tonnes/ha) |
| 93 developing countries | 2142.9 | 767.8 | 36 | 14 | 1.4 | 25819.5 | 43 | 54 | 1.6 |
| Africa (sub-Saharan) | 815.7 | 201.3 | 25 | 2 | 1.6 | 989.7 | 9 | 48 | 0.8 |
| Angola | 77.3 | 4.5 | 6 | 0 | 1.7 | 6.3 | 4 | 47 | 0.5 |
| Benin | 6.3 | 3.0 | 47 | 0 | 2.4 | 5.0 | 5 | 52 | 0.7 |
| Botswana | 1.7 | 1.4 | 81 | 0 | 5.6 | 1.4 | 14 | 58 | 0.2 |
| Burkina Faso | 10.7 | 6.7 | 63 | 0 | 2.1 | 10.2 | 3 | 65 | 0.5 |
| Burundi | 1.0 | 1.0 | 97 | 1 | 0.4 | 2.0 | 2 | 34 | 1.1 |
| Cameroon | 31.5 | 7.7 | 24 | 0 | 3.0 | 44.3 | 12 | 27 | 1.0 |
| Central African Republic | 35.8 | 4.8 | 13 | 0 | 5.5 | 0.9 | 1 | 23 | 0.5 |
| Chad | 7.0 | 7.6 | 45 | 0 | 5.5 | 6.1 | 4 | 56 | 0.5 |
| Congo | 21.7 | 0.7 | 3 | 0 | 1.7 | 2.1 | 8 | 6 | 0.6 |
| Côte d'Ivoire | 14.1 | 7.0 | 50 | 0 | 2.9 | 37.3 | 8 | 22 | 0.9 |
| Ethiopia | 25.0 | 14.5 | 58 | 0 | 1.0 | 39.0 | 5 | 60 | 1.2 |
| Gabon | 12.9 | 0.3 | 3 | 0 | 0.9 | 1.8 | 13 | 5 | 1.5 |
| Gambia | 0.5 | 0.3 | 62 | 4 | 1.3 | 2.3 | 11 | 38 | 1.0 |
| Ghana | 11.0 | 4.5 | 41 | 0 | 1.8 | 19.0 | 6 | 26 | 0.7 |
| Guinea | 7.5 | 4.2 | 56 | 1 | 1.9 | 0.6 | 1 | 47 | 0.9 |
| Kenya | 6.7 | 4.4 | 66 | 1 | 0.7 | 78.3 | 27 | 54 | 1.6 |
| Lesotho | 0.3 | 0.3 | 85 | 0 | 0.5 | 4.5 | 24 | 87 | 0.8 |
| Liberia | 4.2 | 0.7 | 18 | 0 | 1.3 | 1.7 | 3 | 39 | 1.2 |
| Madagascar | 32.8 | 3.1 | 9 | 29 | 0.9 | 12.1 | 5 | 54 | 1.7 |
| Malawi | 4.1 | 2.5 | 61 | 1 | 1.1 | 41.6 | 18 | 57 | 1.2 |
| Mali | 16.8 | 8.0 | 48 | 2 | 3.8 | 14.8 | 7 | 69 | 0.7 |
| Mauritania | 1.4 | 0.9 | 61 | 2 | 2.3 | 0.5 | 3 | 56 | 0.3 |

**Table A.7** (*cont.*)

| | Arable land | | | | | Fertilizers | | Cereals | |
|---|---|---|---|---|---|---|---|---|---|
| | Potential (mill.ha) | In use (mill.ha) | In use as % of potential | Irrigated as % of total | ha per agric. worker | Total (thousand tonnes) | per ha (kg) | Harv. land as % of total | Yield (tonnes/ ha) |
| Mauritius | 0.1 | 0.1 | 100 | 14 | 1.1 | 26.6 | 272 | 1 | 2.4 |
| Mozambique | 41.4 | 5.6 | 14 | 1 | 0.9 | 19.9 | 8 | 37 | 0.6 |
| Niger | 11.8 | 11.0 | 93 | 0 | 4.0 | 2.0 | 0 | 70 | 0.4 |
| Nigeria | 47.9 | 32.3 | 67 | 0 | 1.4 | 247.5 | 9 | 50 | 0.7 |
| Rwanda | 0.8 | 0.8 | 99 | 0 | 0.3 | 1.1 | 1 | 24 | 1.2 |
| Senegal | 9.7 | 5.2 | 54 | 3 | 2.3 | 28.0 | 11 | 43 | 0.6 |
| Sierra Leone | 2.6 | 1.8 | 71 | 0 | 2.1 | 0.9 | 1 | 49 | 1.5 |
| Somalia | 1.8 | 1.2 | 68 | 4 | 0.8 | 2.4 | 3 | 68 | 0.6 |
| Sudan | 64.2 | 14.7 | 23 | 13 | 3.3 | 53.8 | 8 | 67 | 0.5 |
| Swaziland | 0.9 | 0.2 | 25 | 23 | 1.2 | 14.3 | 101 | 41 | 1.3 |
| Tanzania | 36.6 | 9.2 | 25 | 1 | 1.1 | 27.1 | 5 | 50 | 1.1 |
| Togo | 2.1 | 1.5 | 70 | 0 | 1.8 | 4.2 | 6 | 48 | 1.0 |
| Uganda | 10.7 | 5.3 | 49 | 0 | 0.9 | 0.5 | 0 | 19 | 1.7 |
| Zaire | 177.7 | 14.7 | 8 | 0 | 1.9 | 9.4 | 2 | 22 | 0.9 |
| Zambia | 51.1 | 5.3 | 10 | 0 | 3.5 | 73.7 | 87 | 64 | 1.6 |
| Zimbabwe | 15.9 | 4.1 | 26 | 3 | 1.8 | 146.5 | 59 | 77 | 0.9 |
| Near East/North Africa | 94.7 | 91.7 | 97 | 20 | 2.8 | 4558.4 | 72 | 67 | 1.4 |
| Afghanistan | 8.2 | 8.1 | 98 | 27 | 2.8 | 53.1 | 13 | 83 | 1.3 |
| Algeria | 7.7 | 7.4 | 97 | 4 | 5.8 | 154.4 | 42 | 70 | 0.6 |
| Cyprus | 0.4 | 0.4 | 91 | 25 | 5.4 | 19.6 | 91 | 31 | 1.7 |
| Egypt | 2.9 | 2.8 | 95 | 100 | 0.5 | 859.0 | 175 | 41 | 4.2 |
| Iran | 14.0 | 13.7 | 98 | 38 | 3.4 | 957.5 | 90 | 79 | 1.1 |
| Iraq | 7.8 | 7.4 | 95 | 49 | 7.0 | 94.1 | 34 | 72 | 0.7 |
| Jordan | 0.5 | 0.5 | 92 | 8 | 7.1 | 15.3 | 65 | 60 | 0.7 |

| | | | | | | | | | |
|---|---|---|---|---|---|---|---|---|---|
| Lebanon | 0.3 | 0.3 | 94 | 27 | 3.2 | 43.6 | 184 | 10 | 1.2 |
| Libya | 2.1 | 2.0 | 91 | 7 | 14.7 | 95.5 | 95 | 51 | 0.6 |
| Morocco | 7.7 | 7.5 | 97 | 11 | 2.8 | 241.3 | 40 | 74 | 0.9 |
| Saudi Arabia | 1.3 | 1.1 | 83 | 35 | 0.8 | 187.4 | 253 | 64 | 2.0 |
| Syria | 6.0 | 5.7 | 95 | 8 | 8.0 | 184.4 | 45 | 66 | 0.8 |
| Tunisia | 4.6 | 4.4 | 96 | 3 | 6.8 | 80.5 | 22 | 39 | 0.8 |
| Turkey | 28.0 | 27.5 | 98 | 8 | 2.4 | 1554.9 | 78 | 67 | 1.9 |
| Yemen AR | 2.8 | 2.8 | 98 | 9 | 2.6 | 15.6 | 16 | 78 | 0.7 |
| Yemen PDR | 0.2 | 0.2 | 94 | 32 | 1.0 | 2.4 | 17 | 50 | 1.6 |
| Asia | 342.8 | 280.0 | 82 | 27 | 0.8 | 13791.1 | 46 | 59 | 1.9 |
| Bangladesh | 9.4 | 9.1 | 97 | 16 | 0.5 | 542.6 | 41 | 84 | 2.0 |
| Burma | 20.9 | 10.3 | 49 | 10 | 1.3 | 172.1 | 21 | 61 | 2.9 |
| India | 169.0 | 169.0 | 100 | 25 | 0.9 | 6829.1 | 38 | 58 | 1.5 |
| Indonesia | 47.9 | 21.5 | 45 | 26 | 0.7 | 1640.2 | 65 | 48 | 3.3 |
| Kampuchea DM | 8.0 | 3.3 | 41 | 3 | 1.3 | 5.8 | 3 | 87 | 1.0 |
| Korea DPR | 2.3 | 2.3 | 97 | 47 | 0.7 | 768.2 | 221 | 67 | 4.2 |
| Korea Rep. | 2.2 | 2.2 | 97 | 55 | 0.4 | 703.2 | 253 | 58 | 5.4 |
| Lao | 3.7 | 0.9 | 24 | 13 | 0.6 | 0.4 | 1 | 82 | 1.7 |
| Malaysia | 10.0 | 4.5 | 45 | 11 | 2.0 | 539.2 | 118 | 15 | 2.6 |
| Nepal | 3.8 | 2.4 | 64 | 24 | 0.4 | 40.5 | 13 | 81 | 1.6 |
| Pakistan | 23.1 | 20.5 | 89 | 72 | 1.4 | 1233.6 | 62 | 57 | 1.6 |
| Philippines | 13.3 | 11.3 | 84 | 14 | 1.2 | 320.4 | 27 | 54 | 1.7 |
| Sri Lanka | 2.7 | 2.1 | 77 | 28 | 0.7 | 170.0 | 73 | 37 | 2.8 |
| Thailand | 16.4 | 14.2 | 87 | 20 | 0.8 | 452.5 | 27 | 65 | 2.0 |
| Vietnam | 10.1 | 6.7 | 66 | 17 | 0.4 | 373.8 | 44 | 71 | 2.5 |
| Latin America | 889.6 | 194.8 | 22 | 7 | 4.9 | 6481.3 | 53 | 43 | 2.0 |
| Argentina | 85.8 | 43.8 | 51 | 4 | 33.8 | 133.2 | 4 | 42 | 2.4 |
| Bolivia | 44.4 | 3.6 | 8 | 4 | 4.2 | 5.4 | 5 | 50 | 1.2 |
| Brazil | 504.3 | 82.5 | 16 | 3 | 6.0 | 2809.7 | 57 | 40 | 1.6 |
| Chile | 5.7 | 4.9 | 86 | 19 | 7.9 | 140.9 | 73 | 36 | 2.4 |
| Colombia | 37.9 | 6.7 | 18 | 7 | 2.4 | 335.0 | 78 | 31 | 2.5 |

**Table A.7** (*cont.*)

| | Arable land | | | | | Fertilizers | | Cereals | |
|---|---|---|---|---|---|---|---|---|---|
| | Potential (mill.ha) | In use (mill.ha) | In use as % of potential | Irrigated as % of total | ha per agric. worker | Total (thousand tonnes) | per ha (kg) | Harv. land as % of total | Yield (tonnes/ ha) |
| Costa Rica | 2.6 | 0.6 | 24 | 15 | 2.6 | 85.0 | 171 | 31 | 2.1 |
| Cuba | 5.4 | 3.2 | 59 | 31 | 3.8 | 558.5 | 263 | 11 | 2.8 |
| Dominican Republic | 1.7 | 1.0 | 61 | 15 | 1.4 | 50.9 | 52 | 16 | 3.7 |
| Ecuador | 11.9 | 2.5 | 21 | 22 | 2.6 | 76.5 | 47 | 24 | 1.8 |
| El Salvador | 1.0 | 0.7 | 70 | 15 | 1.0 | 65.7 | 86 | 48 | 1.7 |
| Guatemala | 4.5 | 1.9 | 42 | 4 | 1.6 | 82.4 | 52 | 53 | 1.5 |
| Guyana | 10.6 | 0.4 | 4 | 34 | 5.0 | 10.8 | 65 | 53 | 3.2 |
| Haiti | 0.9 | 0.9 | 100 | 9 | 0.5 | 3.9 | 3 | 33 | 1.0 |
| Honduras | 3.9 | 1.0 | 25 | 9 | 1.4 | 29.1 | 35 | 49 | 1.4 |
| Jamaica | 0.4 | 0.3 | 61 | 14 | 0.8 | 15.9 | 81 | 2 | 1.8 |
| Mexico | 45.4 | 23.7 | 52 | 19 | 2.8 | 1656.9 | 100 | 63 | 2.1 |
| Nicaragua | 5.4 | 1.2 | 23 | 7 | 3.1 | 47.5 | 67 | 38 | 1.8 |
| Panama | 3.1 | 0.6 | 19 | 4 | 2.8 | 26.2 | 68 | 46 | 1.4 |
| Paraguay | 22.7 | 6.3 | 28 | 1 | 11.4 | 8.6 | 5 | 27 | 1.3 |
| Peru | 30.2 | 3.3 | 11 | 35 | 1.5 | 83.4 | 46 | 42 | 2.4 |
| Surinam | 11.3 | 0.1 | 1 | 49 | 3.5 | 10.2 | 119 | 84 | 4.0 |
| Trinidad and Tobago | 0.2 | 0.2 | 70 | 14 | 4.0 | 6.2 | 58 | 2 | 3.1 |
| Uruguay | 10.6 | 1.4 | 14 | 6 | 8.3 | 47.9 | 59 | 69 | 1.9 |
| Venezuela | 39.7 | 4.0 | 10 | 10 | 5.1 | 191.7 | 111 | 41 | 2.0 |
| Low inc. excl. China | 845.6 | 374.2 | 44 | 18 | 1.0 | 9879.6 | 32 | 58 | 1.5 |
| Low inc. excl. China/India | 676.6 | 205.2 | 30 | 12 | 1.2 | 3050.6 | 23 | 58 | 1.5 |
| Developing, middle income | 1297.3 | 393.6 | 30 | 11 | 2.2 | 15940.9 | 56 | 50 | 1.9 |

**Table A.8** Yields of selected crops in 1983/5 (tonnes/ha)

| | Wheat | Rice (paddy) | Coarse grains | Cassava | Sugar cane | Pulses | Soy-beans | Ground-nuts | Seed-cotton | Tobacco | Coffee | Tea |
|---|---|---|---|---|---|---|---|---|---|---|---|---|
| World | 2.19 | 3.22 | 2.29 | 9.45 | 58.48 | 0.73 | 1.75 | 1.08 | 1.46 | 1.46 | 0.54 | 0.97 |
| All developing countries | 2.04 | 3.14 | 1.49 | 9.45 | 57.18 | 0.61 | 1.55 | 1.02 | 1.24 | 1.32 | 0.54 | 0.93 |
| 94 developing countries | 2.04 | 3.14 | 1.49 | 9.47 | 57.28 | 0.61 | 1.55 | 1.02 | 1.24 | 1.32 | 0.54 | 0.92 |
| 93 developing countries | 1.68 | 2.49 | 1.18 | 9.36 | 57.27 | 0.54 | 1.65 | 0.86 | 0.88 | 1.10 | 0.54 | 1.50 |
| Africa (sub-Saharan) | 1.31 | 1.44 | 0.76 | 7.34 | 58.80 | 0.42 | 0.67 | 0.68 | 0.70 | 0.98 | 0.34 | 1.41 |
| Angola | 0.63 | 1.10 | 0.46 | 15.00 | 16.44 | 0.36 | | 0.50 | 0.58 | 0.50 | 0.14 | |
| Benin | | 1.07 | 0.74 | 6.88 | | 0.50 | | 0.70 | 1.46 | 0.61 | 0.58 | |
| Botswana | 5.00 | | 0.22 | | | 0.47 | | 0.53 | 2.73 | | | |
| Burkina Faso | | 1.87 | 0.60 | 7.23 | 82.50 | 0.36 | | 0.61 | 1.07 | 0.60 | | |
| Burundi | 0.58 | 2.78 | 1.07 | 11.35 | | 0.87 | | 1.23 | 1.00 | 1.16 | 0.94 | 0.61 |
| Cameroon | 1.38 | 3.26 | 0.94 | 1.60 | 17.51 | 0.55 | 0.55 | 0.40 | 1.34 | 0.94 | 0.28 | 2.13 |
| Central African Republic | | 0.88 | 0.53 | 2.98 | | 0.50 | | 0.97 | 0.48 | 1.00 | 0.30 | |
| Chad | 0.94 | 0.45 | 0.50 | 4.16 | 87.50 | 0.43 | | 0.51 | 0.75 | 1.43 | | |
| Congo | | 0.50 | 0.61 | 6.42 | 20.74 | 0.63 | | 0.75 | | 0.29 | 0.79 | |
| Côte d'Ivoire | | 1.12 | 0.76 | 5.26 | 62.43 | 0.67 | 1.84 | 0.91 | 1.15 | 0.28 | 0.21 | |
| Ethiopia | 1.12 | | 1.06 | | 107.78 | 0.96 | 4.58 | 0.91 | 1.32 | 0.64 | 0.31 | |
| Gabon | | 1.92 | 1.46 | 5.99 | 40.00 | 0.56 | | 0.87 | | | 0.39 | |
| Gambia | | 1.61 | 0.91 | 3.00 | | 0.27 | | 1.13 | 0.81 | | | |
| Ghana | | 0.89 | 0.73 | 8.75 | 23.82 | 0.09 | | 0.99 | 0.74 | 0.60 | 0.19 | |
| Guinea | | 0.76 | 0.60 | 7.05 | 50.00 | 0.69 | | 0.58 | | 0.86 | 0.33 | |
| Kenya | 1.59 | 4.06 | 1.43 | 8.97 | 105.12 | 0.42 | | 0.69 | 0.14 | 1.58 | 0.67 | 1.54 |
| Lesotho | 0.53 | | 0.71 | | | 0.43 | | | | | | |
| Liberia | | 1.30 | | 3.68 | 15.50 | 0.52 | 0.40 | 0.67 | | | 0.39 | |
| Madagascar | 1.50 | 1.81 | 1.03 | 6.08 | 28.51 | 0.85 | 1.10 | 0.95 | 1.50 | 0.82 | 0.36 | 1.84 |
| Malawi | 1.08 | 1.60 | 1.19 | 6.24 | 119.60 | 0.61 | | 0.67 | 0.70 | 0.76 | 0.94 | 1.87 |

**Table A.8** (*cont.*)

| | Wheat | Rice (paddy) | Coarse grains | Cassava | Sugar cane | Pulses | Soy-beans | Ground-nuts | Seed-cotton | Tobacco | Coffee | Tea |
|---|---|---|---|---|---|---|---|---|---|---|---|---|
| Mali | 1.00 | 0.96 | 0.73 | 8.90 | 52.13 | 1.00 | | 0.48 | 1.46 | 0.86 | | 0.64 |
| Mauritania | 0.90 | 3.52 | 0.26 | | | 0.27 | | 0.73 | | | | |
| Mauritius | | 5.39 | 4.26 | 15.00 | 69.97 | 0.58 | | 3.03 | | 1.66 | | 1.89 |
| Mozambique | 1.42 | 0.79 | 0.63 | 5.90 | 22.11 | 0.44 | | 0.42 | 0.33 | 1.11 | 0.71 | 0.84 |
| Niger | 1.16 | 2.55 | 0.35 | 7.11 | 37.22 | 0.13 | | 0.36 | 0.84 | 0.73 | | |
| Nigeria | 2.44 | 2.01 | 0.66 | 9.65 | 53.62 | 0.21 | 0.31 | 0.86 | 0.13 | 0.96 | 0.52 | |
| Rwanda | 1.08 | 4.55 | 1.25 | 10.06 | 41.40 | 0.95 | 0.71 | 0.98 | | 1.40 | 0.91 | 1.02 |
| Senegal | | 1.99 | 0.62 | 2.70 | 109.37 | 0.45 | 1.05 | 0.70 | 1.06 | | | |
| Sierra Leone | | 1.36 | 1.59 | 3.42 | | 0.59 | | 0.99 | | 1.00 | 0.39 | |
| Somalia | 0.36 | 3.48 | 0.74 | 10.91 | 48.98 | 0.34 | | 0.80 | 0.28 | 0.40 | | |
| Sudan | 1.22 | 0.63 | 0.45 | 2.78 | 69.17 | 1.30 | | 0.58 | 1.54 | | | |
| Swaziland | 3.25 | 6.21 | 1.42 | | 110.42 | 0.56 | | 0.43 | 1.33 | 0.48 | | |
| Tanzania | 1.35 | 1.34 | 1.03 | 12.22 | 101.80 | 0.53 | 0.24 | 0.60 | 0.38 | 0.51 | 0.48 | 0.99 |
| Togo | | 1.04 | 1.07 | 27.85 | | 0.48 | | 0.94 | 1.22 | 0.50 | 0.21 | |
| Uganda | 2.23 | 1.29 | 1.37 | 7.87 | 12.24 | 0.73 | 1.11 | 0.82 | 0.10 | 0.26 | 0.85 | 0.77 |
| Zaire | 0.87 | 0.87 | 0.97 | 7.07 | 39.05 | 0.59 | 1.11 | 0.72 | 0.44 | 0.47 | 0.32 | 0.65 |
| Zambia | 3.57 | 1.14 | 1.71 | 3.46 | 121.91 | 0.51 | 1.48 | 0.56 | 0.72 | 1.04 | 0.93 | 1.16 |
| Zimbabwe | 5.42 | 1.41 | 0.98 | 3.98 | 110.00 | 0.72 | 1.78 | 0.28 | 1.72 | 2.13 | 1.36 | 3.13 |
| Near East/North Africa | 1.41 | 3.94 | 1.34 | | 77.26 | 0.92 | 2.26 | 1.84 | 2.22 | 0.99 | 0.51 | 1.55 |
| Afghanistan | 1.21 | 2.24 | 1.41 | | 18.92 | 1.62 | | | 1.08 | | | |
| Algeria | 0.71 | 3.11 | 0.76 | | | 0.40 | | | 0.61 | 1.07 | | |
| Cyprus | 1.39 | | 1.77 | | 0.98 | | 2.67 | 1.07 | 1.75 | | | |
| Egypt | 3.67 | 6.10 | 4.04 | | 80.86 | 2.11 | 2.59 | 1.87 | 2.70 | | | |
| Iran | 0.98 | 3.00 | 0.96 | | 75.96 | 0.70 | 2.06 | 1.89 | 1.69 | 1.07 | | 1.13 |
| Iraq | 0.91 | 2.13 | 0.95 | | 21.35 | 0.84 | 1.57 | 2.29 | 1.04 | 0.94 | | |
| Jordan | 0.86 | | 0.50 | | | 0.73 | | | | 0.65 | | |
| Lebanon | 1.23 | | 1.19 | | 24.14 | 0.96 | | 0.88 | | 1.14 | | |
| Libya | 0.70 | | 0.59 | | | 1.18 | | 1.91 | | 2.41 | | |

| | | | | | | | | | | | | |
|---|---|---|---|---|---|---|---|---|---|---|---|---|
| Morocco | 1.13 | 3.37 | 0.76 | | 87.70 | 0.68 | 1.00 | 1.33 | 2.11 | 1.61 | | |
| Saudi Arabia | 3.32 | | 0.65 | | | 1.94 | | | | | 0.40 | |
| Syria | 1.35 | 5.00 | 0.59 | | 56.25 | 0.79 | | 2.03 | 2.79 | 1.08 | | |
| Tunisia | 0.95 | | 0.65 | | | 0.69 | | | | 1.01 | | |
| Turkey | 1.83 | 4.41 | 2.02 | | | 1.00 | 2.05 | 2.30 | 2.08 | 0.96 | | 1.77 |
| Yemen AR | 0.74 | | 0.44 | | 10.00 | 0.61 | | | 0.89 | 0.87 | 0.43 | |
| Yemen PDR | 1.50 | | 1.69 | | | 0.43 | | | 1.25 | 2.59 | 1.47 | |
| Asia | 2.32 | 3.25 | 1.74 | 12.39 | 52.30 | 0.66 | 1.23 | 1.14 | 1.33 | 1.41 | 0.67 | 0.71 |
| Bangladesh | 2.19 | 2.14 | 0.81 | | 43.17 | 0.74 | | 1.12 | 0.45 | 0.95 | | 0.93 |
| Burma | 1.55 | 3.09 | 1.18 | 11.30 | 62.69 | 0.73 | 0.81 | 1.04 | 0.52 | 1.14 | 0.44 | |
| China | 2.90 | 5.28 | 3.15 | 15.56 | 57.34 | 1.30 | 1.33 | 1.94 | 2.41 | 1.85 | 1.08 | 0.35 |
| India | 1.84 | 2.22 | 0.76 | 18.07 | 56.67 | 0.53 | 0.81 | 0.85 | 0.53 | 1.13 | 0.67 | 1.58 |
| Indonesia | | 3.91 | 1.77 | 10.62 | 76.19 | 0.85 | 0.92 | 1.55 | 0.57 | 0.55 | 0.58 | 1.29 |
| Kampuchea DM | | 1.11 | 2.59 | 7.50 | 52.95 | 0.80 | 1.15 | 0.91 | 0.94 | 0.60 | 0.49 | |
| Korea DPR | 3.38 | 6.73 | 2.97 | | | 0.84 | 1.25 | | 0.80 | 1.32 | | |
| Korea Republic | 3.90 | 6.34 | 2.53 | | | 1.04 | 1.33 | 1.62 | 1.05 | 2.52 | | 0.34 |
| Lao | | 1.91 | 1.15 | 14.37 | 29.65 | 2.16 | 0.74 | 0.78 | 2.11 | 0.62 | 0.53 | 1.29 |
| Malaysia | | 2.72 | 1.53 | 10.76 | 49.36 | | 1.63 | 3.47 | | 0.63 | 0.95 | 1.34 |
| Nepal | 1.30 | 2.02 | 1.33 | | 23.36 | 0.42 | | | | 0.75 | | |
| Pakistan | 1.59 | 2.47 | 0.84 | | 36.49 | 0.51 | 0.33 | 1.19 | 1.13 | 1.73 | | |
| Philippines | | 2.55 | 1.05 | 7.51 | 47.87 | 0.79 | 0.96 | 0.85 | 2.95 | 0.93 | 0.95 | |
| Sri Lanka | | 2.99 | 0.91 | 12.35 | 39.71 | 0.66 | 0.60 | 0.56 | 2.62 | 1.10 | 1.48 | 0.86 |
| Thailand | | 2.07 | 2.34 | 15.76 | 43.69 | 0.66 | 1.38 | 1.36 | 1.22 | 0.99 | 0.89 | 0.20 |
| Vietnam | | 2.75 | 1.38 | 5.79 | 42.62 | 0.82 | 0.73 | 0.96 | 0.52 | 0.91 | 0.18 | 0.50 |
| Latin America | 1.99 | 2.24 | 2.00 | 11.14 | 61.21 | 0.55 | 1.81 | 1.47 | 1.00 | 1.31 | 0.64 | 6.17 |
| Argentina | 1.92 | 3.27 | 2.92 | 8.73 | 48.64 | 1.08 | 2.07 | 1.91 | 1.22 | 1.17 | | 4.23 |
| Bolivia | 0.70 | 1.55 | 1.25 | 9.39 | 40.02 | 1.10 | 1.49 | 1.01 | 1.10 | 1.00 | 0.85 | 2.62 |
| Brazil | 1.36 | 1.69 | 1.78 | 11.56 | 62.07 | 0.46 | 1.75 | 1.57 | 0.69 | 1.41 | 0.68 | |
| Chile | 2.05 | 4.02 | 3.54 | | | 1.00 | | | | 3.03 | | |
| Colombia | 1.59 | 4.77 | 1.73 | 8.98 | 84.22 | 0.65 | 1.95 | 1.52 | 1.75 | 1.61 | 0.77 | |
| Costa Rica | | 3.27 | 1.75 | 4.06 | 59.89 | 0.53 | 1.26 | | 2.60 | 1.34 | 1.51 | |
| Cuba | | 3.41 | 1.23 | 6.52 | 55.03 | 0.77 | | 1.00 | 0.75 | 0.66 | 0.43 | |
| Dominican Republic | | 4.32 | 1.97 | 6.00 | 55.77 | 0.80 | | 1.19 | 0.95 | 1.18 | 0.43 | |

**Table A.8** *(cont.)*

| | Wheat | Rice (paddy) | Coarse grains | Cassava | Sugar cane | Pulses | Soy-beans | Ground-nuts | Seed-cotton | Tobacco | Coffee | Tea |
|---|---|---|---|---|---|---|---|---|---|---|---|---|
| Ecuador | 1.03 | 2.89 | 1.33 | 10.00 | 63.73 | 0.60 | 1.70 | 0.87 | 0.84 | 1.65 | 0.27 | 1.99 |
| El Salvador | | 3.88 | 1.72 | 14.10 | 88.75 | 0.73 | 1.52 | 1.01 | 2.17 | 1.82 | 0.85 | |
| Guatemala | 1.47 | 3.06 | 1.65 | 3.71 | 79.55 | 0.63 | 1.11 | 1.95 | 2.69 | 1.83 | 0.57 | |
| Guyana | | 3.29 | 0.90 | | 72.14 | 0.53 | 0.71 | 0.73 | | 1.00 | 0.78 | |
| Haiti | | 2.29 | 0.83 | 4.10 | 37.35 | 0.50 | | 0.88 | 0.46 | 1.19 | 1.10 | |
| Honduras | 0.67 | 2.29 | 1.39 | 17.84 | 34.19 | 0.61 | | 1.52 | 2.02 | 1.14 | 0.61 | |
| Jamaica | | 3.39 | 1.29 | 11.13 | 56.34 | 0.91 | | 1.14 | | 1.58 | 0.31 | |
| Mexico | 4.10 | 2.94 | 1.90 | 17.55 | 68.59 | 0.62 | 1.69 | 1.27 | 2.69 | 1.46 | 0.55 | |
| Nicaragua | | 3.88 | 1.54 | 4.03 | 59.88 | 0.66 | 1.67 | 1.67 | 1.84 | 1.73 | 0.52 | |
| Panama | | 1.89 | 1.10 | 7.07 | 53.99 | 0.42 | | | | 1.70 | 0.41 | |
| Paraguay | 1.37 | 2.33 | 1.51 | 14.98 | 42.50 | 0.83 | 1.62 | 1.04 | 0.90 | 1.47 | 0.81 | |
| Peru | 1.04 | 4.41 | 1.72 | 10.76 | 136.65 | 0.85 | 1.61 | 1.89 | 1.90 | 1.24 | 0.64 | 0.77 |
| Suriname | | 3.95 | 1.64 | 6.49 | 50.27 | 0.88 | 1.00 | 1.02 | | | 0.21 | |
| Trinidad and Tobago | | 3.36 | 2.84 | 12.37 | 39.19 | 1.68 | | | | 0.93 | 0.13 | |
| Uruguay | 1.47 | 4.64 | 1.45 | | 54.87 | 0.96 | 1.41 | 0.70 | 0.90 | 1.73 | | |
| Venezuela | 0.42 | 2.87 | 1.88 | 7.90 | 61.33 | 0.49 | | 1.92 | 1.59 | 1.58 | 0.25 | |
| Developing, low income | 2.26 | 3.20 | 1.44 | 8.01 | 52.49 | 0.63 | 1.25 | 1.00 | 1.25 | 1.46 | 0.48 | 0.74 |
| Low inc. excl. China | 1.73 | 2.25 | 0.79 | 7.71 | 51.79 | 0.54 | 0.81 | 0.80 | 0.68 | 1.04 | 0.47 | 1.25 |
| Low inc. excl. China/India | 1.50 | 2.29 | 0.83 | 7.16 | 42.95 | 0.56 | 0.82 | 0.74 | 0.89 | 0.94 | 0.45 | 0.99 |
| Developing, middle income | 1.62 | 2.98 | 1.56 | 10.69 | 60.30 | 0.55 | 1.72 | 1.11 | 1.23 | 1.14 | 0.55 | 2.33 |
| Developed countries | 2.31 | 5.61 | 3.19 | | 79.61 | 1.38 | 1.93 | 2.27 | 2.21 | 1.86 | 1.07 | 1.71 |
| European CPEs | 1.81 | 3.90 | 2.03 | | | 1.33 | 0.81 | 1.23 | 2.68 | 1.59 | | 1.85 |
| Albania | 3.05 | 3.45 | 3.04 | | | 0.40 | | | 0.91 | 0.79 | | |
| Bulgaria | 3.57 | 4.48 | 4.09 | | | 0.91 | 1.11 | 0.97 | 1.21 | 1.24 | | |

| | | | | | | | | | | | |
|---|---|---|---|---|---|---|---|---|---|---|---|
| Czechoslovakia | 5.00 | | 4.28 | | 2.21 | | | | 1.49 | | |
| German DR | 5.07 | | 4.06 | | 1.72 | | | | 1.41 | | |
| Hungary | 4.90 | 3.18 | 5.29 | | 2.19 | 1.74 | | | 1.58 | | |
| Poland | 3.44 | | 2.72 | | 1.47 | | | | 2.00 | | |
| Romania | 2.65 | 3.36 | 4.10 | | 0.41 | 1.11 | | 0.38 | 0.86 | | |
| USSR | 1.47 | 3.93 | 1.60 | | 1.41 | 0.63 | 2.39 | 2.70 | 1.91 | | 1.85 |
| Developed market economies | 2.71 | 5.94 | 4.24 | 79.61 | 1.51 | 1.98 | 2.28 | 1.84 | 2.01 | 1.07 | 1.54 |
| Australia | 1.54 | 6.20 | 1.55 | 79.60 | 0.92 | 1.58 | 1.10 | 3.40 | 2.26 | | |
| Austria | 4.73 | | 5.17 | | 2.28 | | | | 1.81 | | |
| Belgium-Lux. | 6.09 | | 5.18 | | 3.53 | | | | 2.70 | | |
| Canada | 1.77 | | 2.82 | | 1.46 | 2.26 | | | 2.27 | | |
| Denmark | 6.55 | | 4.35 | | 4.38 | | | | | | |
| Finland | 3.19 | | 3.02 | | 3.13 | | | | | | |
| France | 5.88 | 4.90 | 5.28 | | 4.02 | 2.07 | | | 2.56 | | |
| Germany FR | 5.92 | | 4.63 | | 2.60 | | | | 2.41 | | |
| Greece | 2.25 | 6.11 | 4.52 | | 1.36 | | 3.22 | 2.31 | 1.44 | | |
| Iceland | | | | | | | | | | | |
| Ireland | 6.92 | | 5.18 | | 3.23 | | | | | | |
| Israel | 2.11 | | 2.30 | | 0.95 | | 5.05 | 4.01 | 0.75 | | |
| Italy | 2.83 | 5.75 | 5.31 | | 1.33 | 2.98 | 2.58 | 0.44 | 2.12 | | |
| Japan | 3.32 | 6.12 | 2.90 | 72.80 | 1.44 | 1.66 | 1.77 | | 2.51 | | 1.59 |
| Malta | 3.86 | | 3.81 | | 2.32 | | | | | | |
| Netherlands | 7.18 | | 5.99 | | 3.98 | | | | | | |
| New Zealand | 4.38 | | 4.74 | | 3.72 | 2.35 | | | 2.25 | | |
| Norway | 4.54 | | 3.75 | | | | | | | | |
| Portugal | 1.32 | 4.49 | 1.11 | 22.17 | 0.28 | | | | 1.01 | | 0.67 |
| South Africa | 1.04 | 2.31 | 1.22 | 77.69 | 0.82 | 0.98 | 0.52 | 0.79 | 1.13 | | 1.00 |
| Spain | 2.25 | 5.98 | 2.53 | 67.24 | 0.74 | 1.94 | 2.63 | 3.00 | 1.93 | 0.34 | |
| Sweden | 5.25 | | 3.69 | | 2.67 | | | | | | |
| Switzerland | 5.55 | | 5.74 | | 3.83 | | | | 2.54 | | |
| United Kingdom | 6.84 | | 5.04 | | 3.27 | | | | | | |
| United States | 2.59 | 5.62 | 5.33 | 82.13 | 1.59 | 1.98 | 3.03 | 1.74 | 2.31 | 1.10 | |
| Yugoslavia | 3.62 | 4.12 | 4.15 | | 1.12 | 1.90 | 1.45 | 0.71 | 1.18 | | |

## Notes to tables

### Table A.1

The population data and projections are from UN, *World Population Prospects: Estimates and Projections as Assessed in 1984*, Population Studies No. 98, New York 1986. (The projections are those of the medium variant.)

The agricultural labour force data for 1970 and 1980 are from ILO, *Economically Active Population Estimates: 1950—80 and Projections: 1985—2025*, Geneva, 1986. The projections are from FAO, *World-wide Estimates and Projections of the Agricultural and Non-Agricultural Population Segments: 1950—2025*, Rome 1986, ESS/MISC/86–2.

### Tables A.2 and A.3

Data in these two tables include information as available in January 1987. The growth rates are derived from the annual values of the primary product equivalent of total demand, production, imports and exports of the 33 crop and six livestock commodities of the study valued at international producer prices in 1979/81 dollars. Each commodity has the same price in all countries. The derivation of these prices is explained in the FAO, *Production Yearbook 1985*.

Production is gross production, that is before any deduction of quantities used as seed and feed. Demand data cover total domestic disappearance of agricultural products, i.e. both final (direct human consumption and non-food industrial uses) and intermediate uses (feed, seed) as well as an allowance for waste, but not additions to stocks. The growth rates of the historical periods are computed from all the annual data of the period by using the least squares method to estimate the equation $x = a\ e^{gt}$, where x is the variable (production, demand, etc.) whose growth rate is estimated, e is the base of natural logarithm, t is time in years and the estimated growth rate is g. Due to the commodity coverage and specification of this study there may be slight differences in the growth rates in these tables from those reported in other FAO publications.

Self-sufficiency ratios (SSR) are the ratios (in percent) of production over domestic demand for all uses as defined above. Growth rates of agricultural exports and imports are volume growth rates (from the FAO AGROSTAT databank). Data used in the calculation of the shares of agriculture in total merchandise trade are in current dollars. The 1980 share of agriculture in total GDP is the one given in the UN, *National Accounts Statistics: Analysis of Main Aggregates, 1983/1984*, New York, 1987 (Table 12, except for Indonesia data for which was taken from Table 5). For centrally planned economies this share refers to Net Material Product.

### Table A.4

Calories by major commodities and food use of cereals refer to direct human consumption of these commodities.

### Table A.5

'Tot. Dem.' is total demand as defined in Table A.2. 'Net trade' is the difference between exports and imports and is also equal to production ('Prod') minus the sum of total demand and stock changes (not shown). 'SSR' is the self-sufficiency ratio defined as in Table A.2.

### Table A.6

The column 'Other use' refers to use for industrial purposes, seed and waste.

### Table A.7

'Potential arable land' refers to potentially cultivable land as estimated in the FAO Agro-Ecological Zone Study with some adjustments for factors not taken into account in that study. Cereal yield includes rice in paddy.

### Table A.8

A blank space indicates that either the crop is not grown in that country or that the area under that crop is not known.

# References


Aganbeguian, A. 1987, *Perestroïka: Le double défi sovietique*, Economica, Paris.

Alexandratos N. 1976, 'Formal Techniques of Analysis for Agricultural Planning', *FAO Studies in Agricultural Economics and Statistics 1952–1977*, FAO, Rome, 1978 (Reprinted from *Monthly Bulletin of Agricultural Economics and Statistics*, 25 (6), June 1976).

Alexandratos N., J. Bruinsma and J. Hrabovszky 1982, 'Power Inputs from Labour, Draught Animals and Machines in the Agriculture of the Developing Countries', *European Review of Agricultural Economics* 9(2).

Bruinsma J., J. Hrabovszky, N. Alexandratos and P. Petri 1983, 'Crop Production and Input Requirements in Developing Countries', *European Review of Agricultural Economics* 10(3).

Cavallo, D. and Y. Mundlak 1982, *Agriculture and Economic Growth in an Open Economy: The case of Argentina*, IFPRI Research Report 36,

CGIAR 1981, *Second Review of the Consultative Group on International Agricultural Research*, Washington DC.

Coffman, W. R. 1983, 'Plant Research and Technology' in Rosenblum, John W. (ed.) *Agriculture in the 21st Century*, J. Wiley and Son, New York.

Cornia, G., Richard Jolly and Frances Stewart (eds) 1987, *Adjustment with a Human Face*, Oxford University Press, Oxford (a UNICEF Study).

Douw L., L. B. van der Giessen and J. H. Post 1987, *De Nederlandse Landbouw na 2000: Een Verkenning*, Landbouw-Economisch Instituut, Mededeling 379, Den Haag.

FAO 1972, *Agricultural Adjustment in Developed Countries* (Prepared in co-operation with the Economic Commission for Europe under the direction of P. Lamartine-Yates, document ERC 72/3).

FAO 1978–81, *Reports of the Agro-Ecological Zones Project*, World Soil Resources Report 48, vols. 1–4.

FAO 1979, *Agriculture: Toward 2000* (Conference Document C79/24).

FAO 1981, *Agriculture: Toward 2000* (Abbreviated version of Conference document C79/24).

FAO 1983, *Fuelwood Supplies in the Developing Countries*, FAO Forestry Paper 42.

FAO 1984, *Report of the FAO World Conference on the Management and Development of Fisheries*

FAO 1985a, *Report of the Conference of FAO, Twenty-Third Session 9–28 November 1985* (Document C85/REP).

FAO 1985b, *Forest Resources 1980*

FAO 1986a, *African Agriculture: the next 25 years*

FAO 1986b, *The Dynamics of Rural Poverty*

FAO 1986c, *World-wide Estimates and Projections of the Agricultural and non-Agricultural Population Segments: 1950–2025* (Document ESS/MISC/86–2).

FAO 1986d, *Economic Accounts for Agriculture 1976–1985*

FAO 1987a, *Fifth World Food Survey*

FAO 1987b, *Agricultural Price Policies: Issues and Proposals*
FAO 1987c, *Second Progress Report on the WCARRD Programme of Action Including the Role of Women in Rural Development* (Document C87/19).
FAO 1987d, *Forest Products, World Outlook and Projections*, FAO Forestry Paper 73.
FAO 1987e, *Feasibility Study on Expanding the Provision of Agricultural Inputs on Aid-in-Kind* (Document C87/20).
FAO/CFS 1987, *Impact on World Food Security of Agricultural Policies in Industrialized Countries* (Document CFS 87/3).
Garcia, J. G. 1981, *The Effect of Exchange Rates and Commercial Policy on Agricultural Incentives in Colombia 1953–1978*, IFPRI Research Report 24.
Herdt, R. and C. Capule 1983, *Adoption, Spread and Production Impact of Modern Rice Varieties in Asia*, International Rice Research Institute, Los Banos.
International Wheat Council 1983, *Long Term Grain Outlook*, Secretariat Paper No. 14, August 1983.
International Wheat Council 1987, *Long-term Outlook for Grain Imports by Developing Countries*, Press Release, November 1987.
Lipton 1985, *Land Assets and Rural Poverty*, World Bank Staff Working Paper No. 744.
*Narodnoe Khozyaistvo SSSR za 70 let* 1987 (National Yearbook of the USSR, Jubilee edition, 70th Anniversary of the Revolution), Moscow, USSR State Committee for Statistics.
OECD 1984, *Workshop on Critical Issues in Natural Resource Management*, 11–12 October 1984, Paris.
OECD 1987, *National Policies and Agricultural Trade*
Parikh, K., G. Fischer, K. Frohberg and O. Gulbrandsen 1988, *Toward Free Trade in Agriculture*, published for the International Institute for Applied Systems Analysis by M. Nijhoff, The Hague.
Paulino, L. 1986, *Food in the Third World: Past Trends and Projections to 2000*, IFPRI Research Report No. 52.
Perrens S. J. and N. A. Trustrum 1984, *Assessment and Evaluation of Soil Conservation Policy—Report Workshop on Policies for Soil and Water Conservation*, 25–27 January 1983, East West Center, Honolulu, Hawaii.
Pingali, P., Yves Pigot and Hans Binswanger 1987, *Agricultural Mechanization and the Evolution of Farming Systems in Sub-Saharan Africa*, Johns Hopkins University Press, Baltimore and London.
Sarma, J. and P. Yeung 1985, *Livestock Products in the Third World: Past Trends and Projections to 1990 and 2000*, IFPRI Research Report No. 49.
Schmidt, S. and W. Gardiner 1988, *Non Grain Feeds: EC Trade and Policy Issues*, USDA, FAER 234.
Semenov, V. 1987, 'Soverchenstvovanie Finansovo Mekhanizma Agropromechlenovo Kompleksa' (Improvement of the Financial Mechanism of the Agroindustrial Complex), *Ekonomika Selskovo Khozyaistva*, September 1987.
Singh, I., Lyn Squire and John Straus 1986, 'A Survey of Agricultural Household Models: Recent Findings and Policy Implications', *The World Bank Economic Review*, vol. 1, No. 1: 149–179.
Tyagi, D. 1981, 'Growth of Agricultural Output and Labour Absorption in India', *The Journal of Development Studies*, 18: 104–114.
UN/ECE 1986, *Economic Survey of Europe in 1985–1986*

UN/ECE 1987, *Economic Survey of Europe in 1986–1987*

US Congress, Office of Technology Assessment 1986, *Technology, Public Policy, and the Changing Structure of American Agriculture*

USDA 1987a, *1987 Fact Book of US Agriculture*

USDA 1987b, *National Food Review, 1987 Yearbook* (NFR 37).

Valdes A. and J. Zietz 1980, *Agricultural Protection in OECD Countries: Its Cost to Less Developed Countries*, IFPRI Research Report 21.

Vaidyanathan, A. 1983, 'Estimating Employment Potential in Animal Husbandry: Data Base and Methodology', AGDP Working Paper, FAO, Rome.

World Bank 1986a, *World Development Report 1986*

World Bank 1986b, *Price Prospects for Major Primary Commodities* (Document 814/86).

World Commission on Environment and Development 1987, *Our Common Future*, Oxford University Press, Oxford.

# Index

MONTGOMERY COLLEGE LIBRARIES
0 0000 00499296 2